INVEST
WITH
SUCCESS

Also by Dr. Charles B. Schaap

ADXcellence—Power Trend Strategies
(available at StockMarketStore.com)

INVEST WITH SUCCESS

BIG PROFITS FOR SMALL INVESTORS

DR. CHARLES B. SCHAAP

SMS

STOCKMARKETSTORE
Las Vegas, Nevada USA

INVEST WITH SUCCESS—Big Profits for Small Investors

ISBN 978-0-9777132-2-6

Printed in the United States of America.

Cover Design: Donna Tremonte

ΔΔΔ

Published by
StockMarketStore
Las Vegas, Nevada 89074

www.StockMarketStore.com

Per te, Caramella,
e la dolce vita.

CONTENTS

FOREWORD

It might seem forward of me to write the foreword for a book my husband wrote. I admit right upfront that I am an unabashed admirer. I love and admire Charles. I love his gentleness and his patience with me and kindness towards family and friends. I love his sense of humor and I laughed and cried as I read the manuscript. Charles and I are partners, in life and trading. I am the lucky one, he is a great man.

My husband, Dr. Charles B Schaap, has created directions to do exactly what the title says, *Invest with Success*. He gives a step-by-step process to know exactly how to learn everything you need to know about the care and handling and growing of your money. Think of this book as a 300-page lesson plan.

When Charles retired from medical practice, he had more time for writing and studying the stock market. We were home together many more hours. I have been a trader for many years, and Charles helped me organize our knowledge about trading. We enjoyed the process. In spite of our efforts, we found that we couldn't help anyone else until they learned to stop losing money. It seemed an impossible task to overcome the hype of the media and to make a case for money management. Charles created the 50-50 Strategy to help investors get started on the right path to success.

The strategy incorporates capital preservation. Charles says I helped him develop the 50-50 Trading Strategy, but he did all the work. I liked what he did, and it made so much sense, I started teaching it. When you have to explain something you know, you end up learning the subject more thoroughly. This book is really a work of love, a profound commitment to share and help others.

Charles has a great way with words. He explains complicated things very simply. You will learn where to find what you need to know, how to see and understand the stock market, and how to put your money to work. Money is a very personal thing, and each person must find his or her own way to meet the goals that suit their own life plan. Charles will show you what you need to learn and to how to do what you have to do to invest with success. His bedside manner works! You will take it and like it and thank him.

Each chapter has one of his quotes at the beginning. You will come to enjoy his humor and wisdom as much as I do. Don't hesitate a minute. Dig in and enjoy the story, because story it is. It is our story and your story; it is the story of how to make money.

I believe it is a moral obligation to do well, for everyone to do their very best. Do well and then do good. My husband, Dr. Charles Schaap, has written this well, and it will do you good.

Candy Schaap
April 2008

ACKNOWLEDGMENTS

First, I must thank my wife, Candy, the "Italian battalion," who deserves credit for urging (prodding) me to write *Invest with Success*. More than anyone, she recognized the need for an investment book that focused on common sense education about personal finances and investing in the stock market. Candy was the main content editor of the book. When I wandered off on tangents or became verbose, she was always there to say, "Cut!" Candy also wrote the Glossary, which I think will be of benefit to all readers.

I want to especially thank Madelyn Pegg and Laura Darnell, the "sin city syntax girls," who were the primary editors of the manuscript. Their tireless editing of the book enhanced the content and clarified the message of the book. They were committed to the mission of writing a book that everyone could read and understand. They also improved my writing, and for that I am grateful.

A writer is usually too close to his work to see it objectively, and he must upon rely on others to tell him what works and what doesn't work. I was fortunate to have several readers who reviewed the manuscript: Nick Corvi, James Hill, Curt Pegg, Carl Darnell, and Julieanne Case. They gave important feedback on content, message, and style.

I also want to thank Dr. Martin Schaffer, M.D., "the wizard," and his wife, Sharon Schaffer, M.D., for their careful and methodical technical review. They both worked on the manuscript to improve its accuracy and validity.

Finally, I must thank Donna Tremonte, from Harvard University, for her graphic artwork and the cover design of the book.

A man who has good friends is already rich. All of the individuals involved in the book project are my friends; they cared about the book because they cared about me. I know that made all the difference.

ABOUT THE AUTHOR

Dr. Charles B. Schaap transitioned from health care to wealth care in 1999. He is the author of *ADXcellence—Power Trend Strategies,* a book for advanced technical traders. Dr. Schaap is an equity strategist and active trader in stocks, futures, and commodities. He is an international speaker and a recognized authority on technical analysis of the financial markets. Dr. Schaap is a widely published author and a former Director of the Hedge Fund Association.

PREFACE

Invest with Success began on a ferry boat ride to the Mediterranean island of Elba in Italy. For the previous two weeks, my wife, Candy, and I had invested our way across Italy. In Rome, Florence, and other cities, we had stopped at internet cafés to check and manage our portfolio of stocks. Now, with a week left to travel, we decided to spend a few days of complete relaxation on Elba, a place off the beaten path of the tourist crowd.

We sat together on the top deck of the ferry. The sun warmed our skin, and the ferry rocked gently in the azure sea. The breeze was scented with the fresh smell of the sea. The passengers around us talked in Italian, mostly by waving their hands. We shared a delicious bar of dark chocolate, Candy's favorite. I opened up my Italian guidebook to the section on Elba and studied the map of recommended sites.

"Let's make a plan for what we want to see," I said. "We want to make good use of our time."

"Just locate a sandy beach, and I'll be happy," said Candy.

"It says here that Elba's most famous resident was Napoleon. He lived here in exile after the fall of Paris in 1814. The guidebook says we should rent a car at Portoferraio. It shows a travel route with stops to make. We'll drive to Napoleon's residence first; then we'll travel to the medieval town of Marciana Alta and take the cable car up to the top of 3,300-foot Monte Capanne."

"That sounds rather far from the beach."

"Then we'll drive back to Marciana Marina to spend the night." I turned the pages of the guidebook. "I see a list of good hotels here. The book names a local restaurant which is known for linguine with truffles and mushrooms. They even recommend the local wine—*Santa Cristina*."

"Fine, as long as I wake up to sunshine and a sandy beach."

"Oh, cool. There's a 17th century fortress to hike around on."

"You told me we came here to relax on the beach."

We finished off the chocolate and settled back in our bench seat. I put down the guide book and we talked about our favorite topic: investing. Candy and I are trading partners, and we enjoy bouncing ideas off each other.

"Learning to invest in the stock market is a lot like traveling to a new country," I said. "You take a journey to some place you've never been before, try to navigate your way around a new landscape, and you don't even speak the language. No wonder it's so hard for people to learn how to invest."

"The problem is most people can't overcome the bad information they've heard all their lives," said Candy. "People just don't know where to go to learn. Most of the information out there is from salesmen trying to get them to buy stuff. How can they possibly figure anything out?"

"Too bad there isn't a guidebook for investing in the stock market!"

"Why don't you write one?"

"I wouldn't know where to start. Most small investors don't really know how the market works. The big institutions rule the market."

During the next four days on Elba, I thought about the challenge of writing a book that beginners could use like a guidebook, a book anyone could read to find directions on how to invest with success. Candy suggested I keep it simple by using the 50-50 Strategy which I had created for building wealth with stocks.

We followed the sightseeing plan laid out in the guidebook for touring the island, while I started to plan out the investing guidebook. Candy got plenty of time to lie on a sandy beach and enjoy the sun. We spent the next four days exchanging ideas about the book. Mainly, we discussed how to keep it simple and easy to understand. I jotted down our ideas in a small notepad which I also used to kept track of our daily travel expenses.

For beginners, I knew that learning investment terminology would be much like learning a foreign language. I also knew you don't need to speak Italian to travel around the country and have a successful trip; you can get by with a few survival phrases and a small dictionary. With basic terminology, any investor could travel to Wall Street and learn to say *grazie* for his profits.

Guidebooks tell you the essentials; they don't try to cover every city and town in the country. They explain the main sites of interest and highlight the things you can't afford to miss. They give recommendations for places to eat and sleep, so you don't have to spend valuable vacation time hunting for places. At the end of our four days on Elba, I decided to write the book.

On the ferry ride back to the mainland, Candy and I sipped a cup of espresso and savored a few biscotti cookies. I studied my Italy guidebook to find our next internet café where we could check our stocks. As we planned the rest of our days in Italy, we also planned our next journey back to Italy—traveling there brings richness to our lives.

"On our next trip," I said, how about going to the Chianti region in Tuscany and the hill towns in Umbria? They have castles and fortresses there."

"Are there any beaches?" said Candy.

"They won't be the Mediterranean, but there's Lake Trasimeno. Hannibal defeated Flaminius and the Roman army there in 217 B.C. The lake is near the city of Perugia which is famous for its chocolate factory."

"Did you say, 'Chocolate'?"

Part ONE

Wealth is not the key to success;
success is the key to wealth.

1 Trilogy of Success

Anyone can invest with success. Investing is a skill you can learn, the same way you learned to drive a car or use a computer. No prior investing experience is needed. It is not necessary to be an economist or financial wizard, and you won't need a degree in accounting or finance. You *can* learn the basic skills necessary to build wealth in the stock market.

If you want to get rich quick, this is not the book for you. There are plenty of salespeople out there who are anxious to sell you a magic system and will promise to make you richer than you ever imagined. If you have common sense, you'll wonder why these salespeople aren't at home making themselves obscenely rich instead of trying to sell the system to you. Sellers sell magic; investors use skill. Skill is not magic.

You cannot buy success. Learning to become a successful investor will require your eyes, your brain, and a desire to improve yourself and your financial condition. Each person must learn in his own way, using his own unique abilities and strengths. The process is much easier if you follow a proven and successful plan for building wealth—a plan built on solid investment principles.

If you don't have a plan, you will end up learning by the trial and error method—a slow and costly way to learn. It helps if you are guided by someone who can teach you the right way to process the information and distinguish between what is important and what is not important. To invest with success, you don't need a magic plan. You just need a successful plan!

If you are new to investing, rest easy. I will start at the beginning and take you through the whole process. If you are an experienced investor, you can improve your investment results by stepping back and taking a *new* look at important principles. Like many things in life, the difference between failure and success is often just a small piece of information or a slightly different way of thinking.

Learning to invest is a journey that begins with the desire to be somewhere different than you are now. A journey is a process of change that requires effort; you begin by putting one new thought in front of the other.

FOLLOW THE BIG MONEY

There are two types of investors in the stock market—big money and small money. Understanding the difference is important for a successful investment plan. Big money is represented by large investment banks, mutual funds, endowment funds, and insurance company funds. Unless you have about $10 million in cash to invest, you are small money.

Big money rules the stock market; small money only rules a portfolio. Big money invests with other people's money; small money invests with its own precious money. Big money can survive big losses; small money cannot. Small money profits when it recognizes what the big money is doing.

The big challenge of investing is to capture profits in the market without getting in the way of the big money. Big money invests with millions, sometimes billions of dollars, and can't hide its actions. Once you can spot the big money buying a stock, you will always have a chance to make big profits.

INVESTING SKILL

To make big profits in the stock market, you must buy when the big money is buying. But first you must develop investment skill. To do anything well, you need knowledge and the ability to apply it effectively.

Investment skill develops from knowing how the stock market works, using a plan to exploit opportunities, and having the mindset to make big profits.

It takes time to learn any new skill. Any new investor who tells you they made easy money in the market most likely got lucky. Luck, unfortunately, rarely lasts. Some people boast about their big wins because they're in the market for thrills. They like to feel big, but they usually fail to mention their big losses. I can't promise you fast money, but I can promise you some fast knowledge. Be a skill seeker, not a thrill seeker. Learn to invest properly.

If you don't understand how the game is played, you'll be at a great disadvantage. Few people ever learn the rules on how to invest successfully. It is not taught in school. Fortunately, the rules can be learned. Investing skill gets better with experience, provided the experience is based on solid investment principles.

Skill is not magic. Some people don't want to accept the fact that they must apply themselves to make money in the stock market. Acknowledging this truth would deny them the dream of getting rich quickly, with little training or effort. Successful investors are committed to learning the skills that will last them a lifetime. If you have the will, you will find the skill.

TRILOGY OF SUCCESS

There are three main disciplines of investment success. First, you must have a proper mindset, an attitude conducive to making big profits with small risk. Second, you must have the requisite knowledge of how the market works and why stocks change in value. Third, you must have a plan that spells out the specific steps for you to implement.

These three disciplines of success can be visualized as different sides of a triangle. Each discipline is interdependent on the other two, and all three work together to create investment success (Figure 1.1).

You may be knowledgeable, but lack a good plan. You may have a great plan, but not have the knowledge to use it properly. And you may have both knowledge and a plan, but lack the mindset to capitalize on them. Mindset, knowledge, and plan are all necessary to invest with success.

Figure 1.1 *The Trilogy of Success.*

MINDSET

Mindset reflects one's values, attitudes, beliefs, and feelings. It is the filter through which you will interpret and react to market information. More than anything else, your mindset determines how successful you will be at gaining new knowledge and executing an effective investment plan.

Mindset is also having the right attitude about money. It is knowing you worked too hard for your money to be frivolous with it. Mindset is knowing the stock market is a place to put your dollars to work. You've already worked hard for your money; now let your money work hard for you.

Part of learning to invest with success is seeing things as they are and not how we want them to be. I have talked to many intelligent investors over the years, and some always seem to struggle. It's not that they don't understand the market or don't have a plan. Most of them simply let their emotions override good decision making. We cannot eliminate our emotions, but we can learn to prevent most of our emotional mistakes with the right mindset.

The most important aspect of mindset is your desire to find the truth; it requires independent thinking. It is hard to find the truth about investing because there is so little financial education in schools and so much misinformation in the media. As long as you look to others for answers, you will be a dependent thinker rather than an independent thinker.

The best investors search for truth and accept it. They don't try to qualify it, resist it, or change it. They quickly adopt ideas that produce results and move on. They do not get mentally stuck. It is only through independent thinking that we step away from the crowd and learn to be successful.

KNOWLEDGE

One of the biggest problems facing investors is not a lack of information, but *too much* information. Sorting through the myriad of investment resources to find useful information is a daunting task. It keeps many would-be investors from making the proper effort to prosper.

It's hard to know where to start, because the average person doesn't know what he needs to know. Investors who search for the right information are often led astray. It is common for investors to go from one investment guru to the next, searching for a winning system. They may spend as much as $20,000 on software, subscriptions, and other services. This is unnecessary, and it only delays them on their journey to real knowledge.

Some investors work hard at doing all the wrong things, and then wonder why they aren't making money. They work hard because they are using the wrong information. Information can make sense, yet not be true. Knowledge is information which is true. Knowledge will move you farther along your path to success.

Forget about watching financial programs on TV or listening to the so-called "experts." You should wonder why these "experts" are selling advice instead of buying stocks. Most knowledge is free, but you will pay for it with your time and effort. You won't need magic trading systems, software, or other gimmicks which are guaranteed to make you rich. These things will only distract you and cost precious money and time. Save your money for investing. Save your time for your family.

PLAN

Many investors confuse knowledge with the ability to make money. There is no point to having knowledge if you don't have a way to use it. You must have an investment **plan*** that spells out everything in advance—before you risk your capital. The plan determines what to buy (stocks, mutual funds, etc.), how many shares to buy, and how much risk you will take. The plan should be easy to follow and must include a trading **strategy** which has been tested and proven.

Investing is a matter of knowing what to buy, when to buy, and when to sell. Successful investors use a strategy to make these decisions; the strategy tells you when to buy and sell. Your job is to execute the strategy and take your emotions out of the process as much as possible. You will learn a single strategy called the **50-50 Strategy**.

Why not learn several strategies? Because you only need one—one that works and works well. You don't need to be an investment expert with a different strategy for every market condition. By using the same strategy over and over, it will soon become second nature. Repetition accelerates your learning and builds confidence.

A trading plan should address each investor's financial needs and objectives. A person just entering the work force has different needs than a person who is already retired or nearing retirement. Investment decisions are predetermined by your plan; they should not be a source of stress each time you invest. All you need to do is execute your plan.

Don't fail to have a plan, unless you're planning to fail.

STOCK INTERVIEW

It is normal to wonder how a beginner, with little or no stock market knowledge, could learn to invest with success. The answer is to keep it just as simple as the pros do. A common misperception is that investment strategies must be highly sophisticated and complex. The reverse is true. The hardest part of investing is keeping the strategy simple. Beginning investors often want to make it complicated while pros want to make it easier.

When you get in your car to drive somewhere, you need to know how to turn on the ignition, shift the car in gear, step on the gas and brake pedals, and turn the steering wheel. You don't need to know all the parts of an internal combustion engine, gear ratios for the transmission,

*** Note: All bold-faced words are in the Glossary.**

or specifications for the electronic ignition. You might not know how the hydraulic braking system works, but you can still tell if the car stops when you step on the brake.

Right now, I want to give you an overall look at how you will make money buying stocks. Don't worry about unfamiliar words or other details. I just want you to settle into the driver's seat, adjust your mirrors, and get familiar with the instrument panel. Don't concern yourself with what kind of engine is under the hood, because it won't matter. What matters is how you learn to drive safely to the bank with your profits.

It's your money's job to go to work for you. It's your job to hire the right workers. The first step in hiring a good worker is the job interview. You want to see what the applicant has done in the past because it will reflect strongly on what he is capable of doing for you in the future. Every potential employee has a track record.

The track record for stocks is a stock chart. It records what the stock's price was able to accomplish in the last few years, as well as what price is doing now (Figure 1.2). Charts such as these are found free online (www. stockcharts.com) or through an online brokerage account such as TDAmeritrade (www.tdameritrade.com)

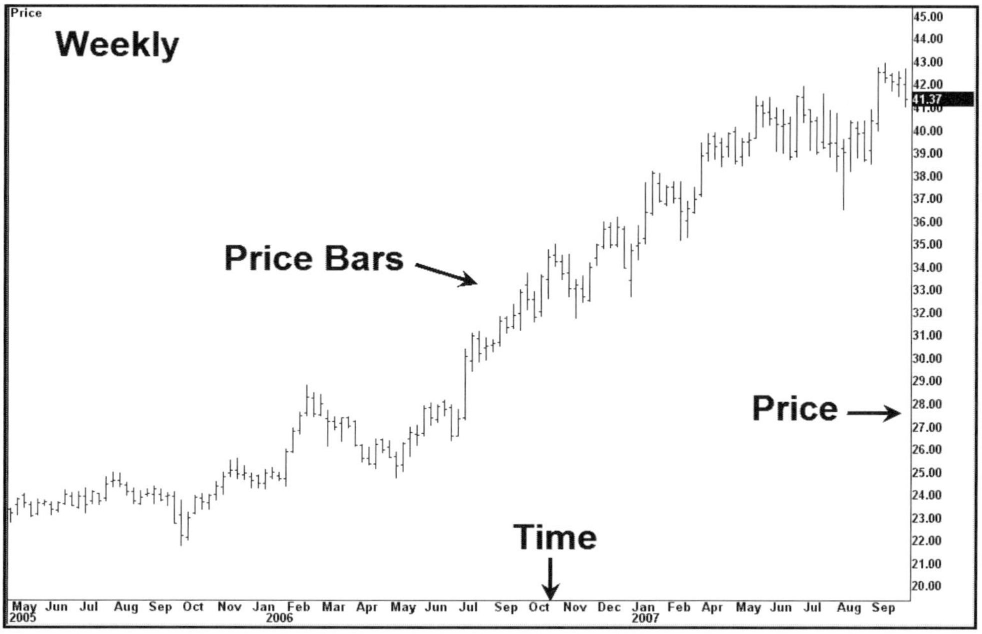

Figure 1.2 *A chart window has price bars which show the stock's trading history. Each bar represents one week. Price is on the vertical axis (right) and time is on the horizontal axis (bottom).* (Chart: TDAmeritrade)

Each small vertical line on the chart is a **price bar**, and each bar represents the **range** of prices for one week of stock market activity. A price scale is on the right side of the chart (vertical axis) and time is along the bottom of the chart (horizontal axis). Moving from the left side of the chart to the right shows the history of price movement. At the far right edge of the chart is what price has done most recently.

The most important thing to see on a chart is the direction of price. If price rises from left to right, it is an **uptrend**. If price falls from left to right, it is a **downtrend**. Do you see the stock in Figure 1.2 trending up or down? Keep it simple; you want the overall direction.

What does keeping it simple really mean? It means don't take something easy to understand and complicate it. Stock prices only move in three possible directions—up, down, and sideways. If you can tell up from down, you can invest.

The stock in Figure 1.2 is going up. Did you see it correctly? You've completed the stock interview, and the stock is in an uptrend. This "employee" has worked hard in the past, and probably has his best years in front of him. Up is the only direction in which you will invest.

DIAGNOSING STOCKS

I will tell you something that might be hard to believe; about 80% of your success will be due to the information I present next. The rest of the book will fill in the details, but the next few charts show the main things you need to know. (I said this was simple.) First, let me tell you a short story.

When I did my ER clerkship in medical school, I studied books on emergency medicine, learning how to diagnose all sorts of conditions which might require immediate treatment. It was stressful trying to remember everything. I wondered what would happen if I didn't make the correct diagnosis. What if I chose the wrong treatment?

The Chief of the ER department took me aside one day and said, "Emergency medicine is basically simple—breathing or not breathing, bleeding or not bleeding, conscious or unconscious. Start there and everything gets easier."

There are only two things you will have to look for on a chart—rising or not rising; strong or not strong. You'll remember both of these conditions by two numbers: *50-50*.

HOUSE OF THE RISING SUM

The first "50" is to see if the price bars are above a rising 50-week moving average. A **moving average** line represents the **average price** of the stock over time; it is placed in the same chart window as the price bars. A moving average line makes it easier to see direction. Price bars fluctuate up and down, but the moving average follows a straighter path. Look at Figure 1.3 and decide if the moving average is rising or not rising.

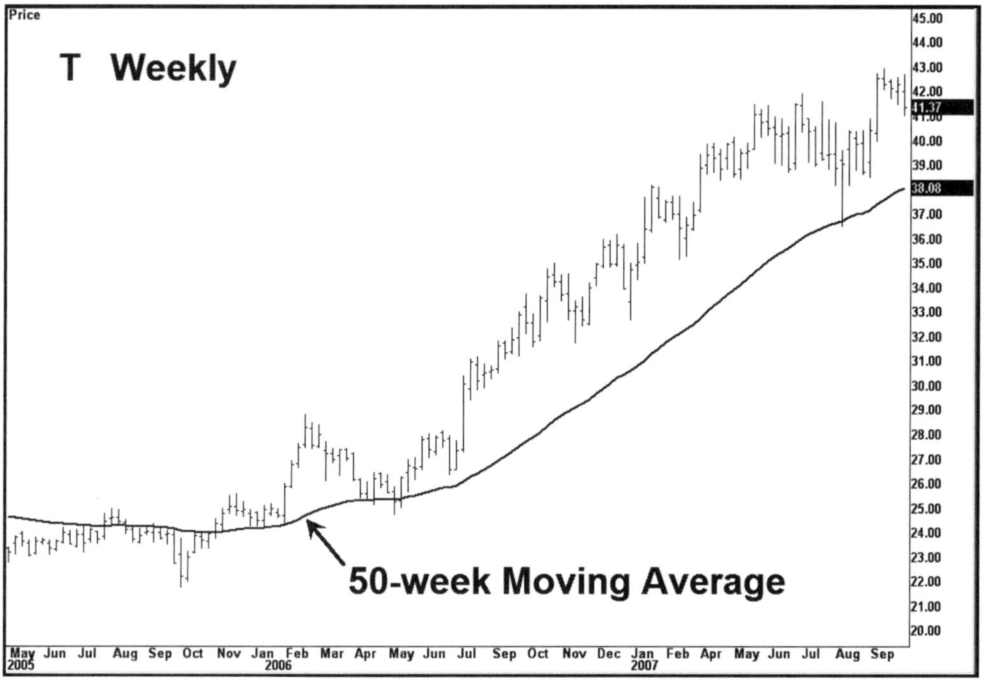

Figure 1.3 *This is a weekly chart. The moving average line shows the direction of the stock by smoothing out price bars. A 50-week moving average represents the average price of the stock over a period of 50 weeks (50 price bars).* (Chart: TDAmeritrade)

Figure 1.3 is the same stock as Figure 1.2 but with a moving average line. Compare both charts and see if the 50-week moving average makes the direction easier for you to see.

Moving averages lag actual price movement, so we also want to be certain that price is above the moving average when we are considering the investment. If price is below the moving average, then we must wait for it to get back above the moving average before we can declare the uptrend intact. You can earn rising sums of money for your household, but only when stocks are trending up.

The second "50" involves how strongly price is rising. One way to tell is by adding an **indicator** to the chart. An indicator is like the speedometer in your car; you don't need it to tell you're speeding, but it shows you how fast you're actually going.

The chart indicator we'll use is the **Relative Strength Index (RSI),** and it is placed in a separate chart window below price. RSI is a line which gives us a measure of how strongly price is rising, or how weakly it is falling. The values for RSI range from 0-100 and 50 is the midpoint which divides weak (0-50) from strong (51-100).

Figure 1.4 shows the same stock from Figures 1.2 and 1.3, but RSI has been added.

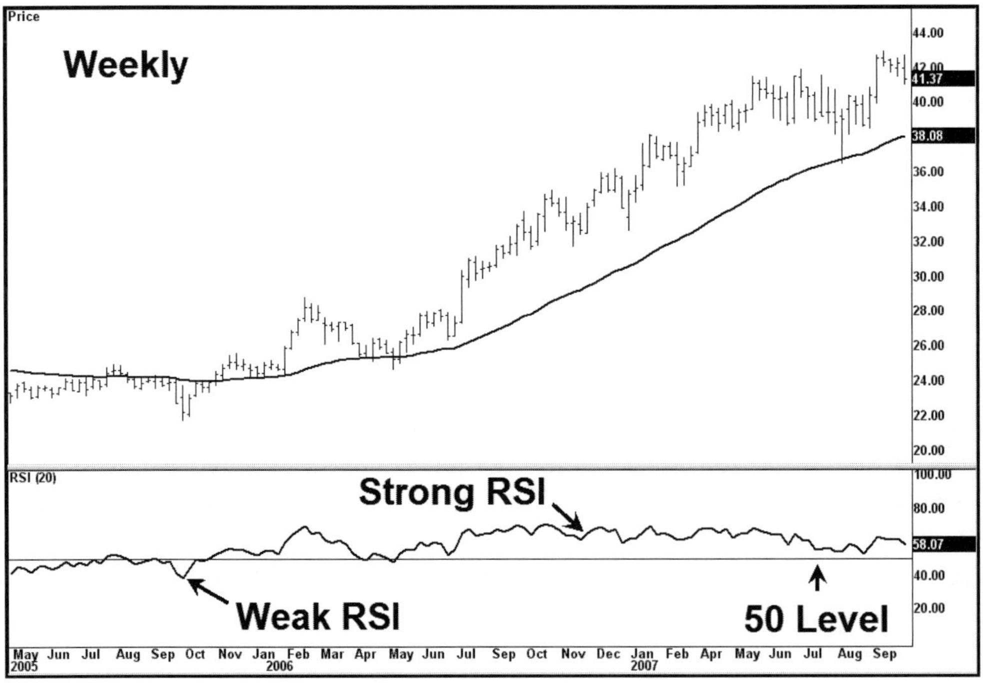

Figure 1.4 *The Relative Strength Index (RSI) shows the strength of the uptrend. Values range from 0-100. Above 50 is considered strong. RSI 20 measures the strength over a period of 20 weeks (20 price bars).* (Chart: TDAmeritrade)

The "50" level for RSI is key. When the RSI line crosses above 50, price goes from weak to strong; when the line crosses below 50, price goes from strong to weak. A stock with an RSI below 50 will have difficulty trending up until the RSI is back above 50. Investors should only buy when RSI is above 50.

Both of the lessons you just learned are part of the **50-50 Strategy**. The 50-50 Strategy is the method you will use to know when to buy a stock. I will go over the strategy in more detail in Chapter 15, but the basic strategy will be the same from here on out. Throughout the rest of the book, the charts will be similar to the ones you just studied. I won't make them any more complicated.

You have a signal to buy when a stock meets the 50-50 Strategy criteria:

1. **Price is above a rising 50 MA.**
2. **RSI 20 is above the 50 level.**

In the next chart (Figure 1.5), use the 50-50 Strategy to decide if the stock is a "buy" at the price area shown by the arrow. Then move on to the next chart (Figure 1.6). A word of advice: don't think. Thinking will make it too complicated.

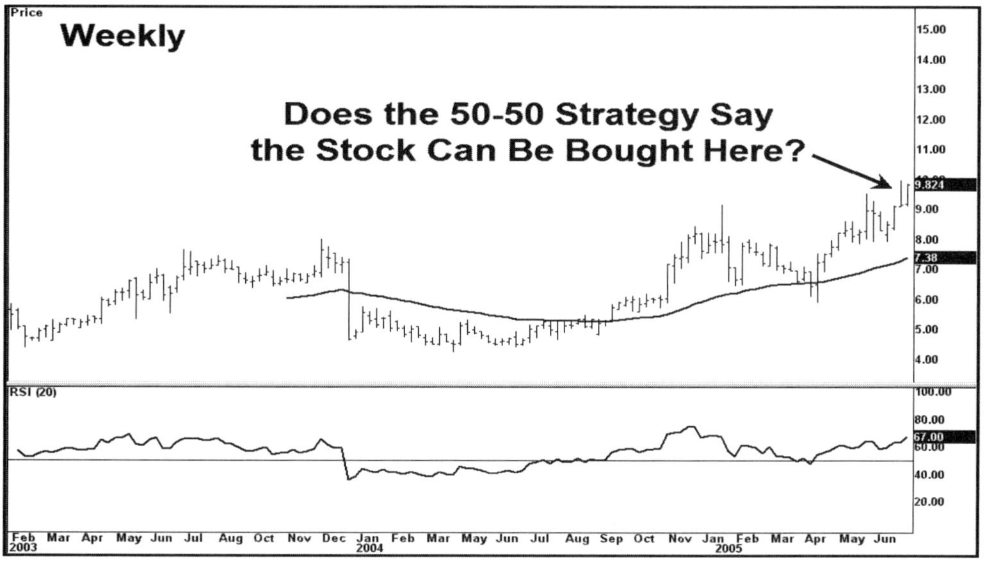

Figure 1.5 *Is this stock a buy at the arrow? Apply the 50-50 Strategy and see.* (Chart: TDAmeritrade)

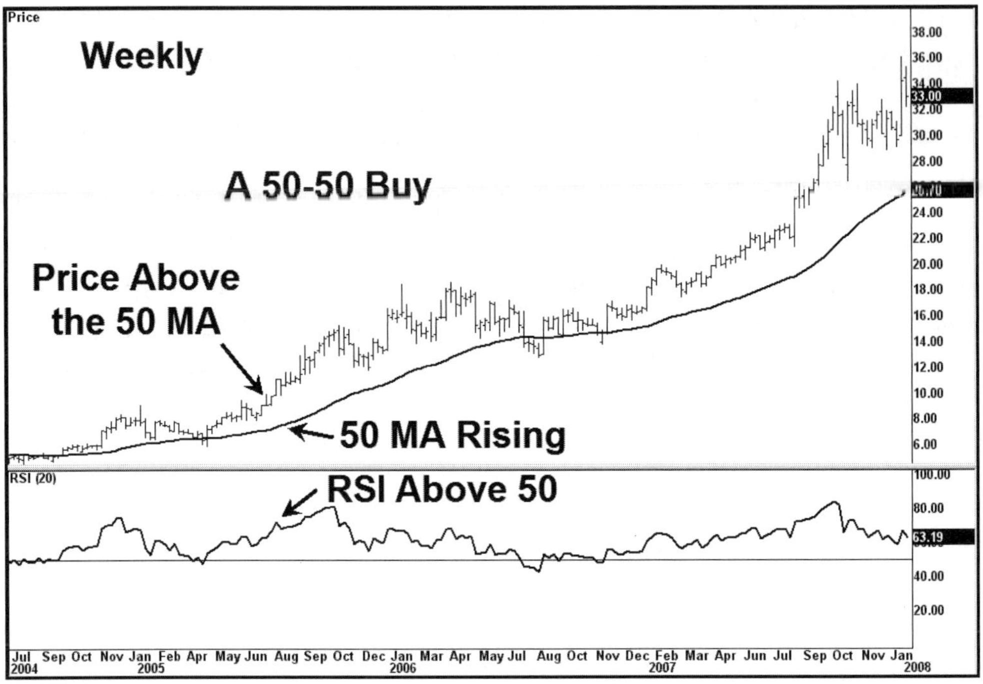

Figure 1.6 *This is the same stock as in Figure 1.5, two and one half years later. It shows what would have happened if you had bought the stock at the point of the arrow in Figure 1.5. The price of this stock rose about 200%.* (Chart: TDAmeritrade)

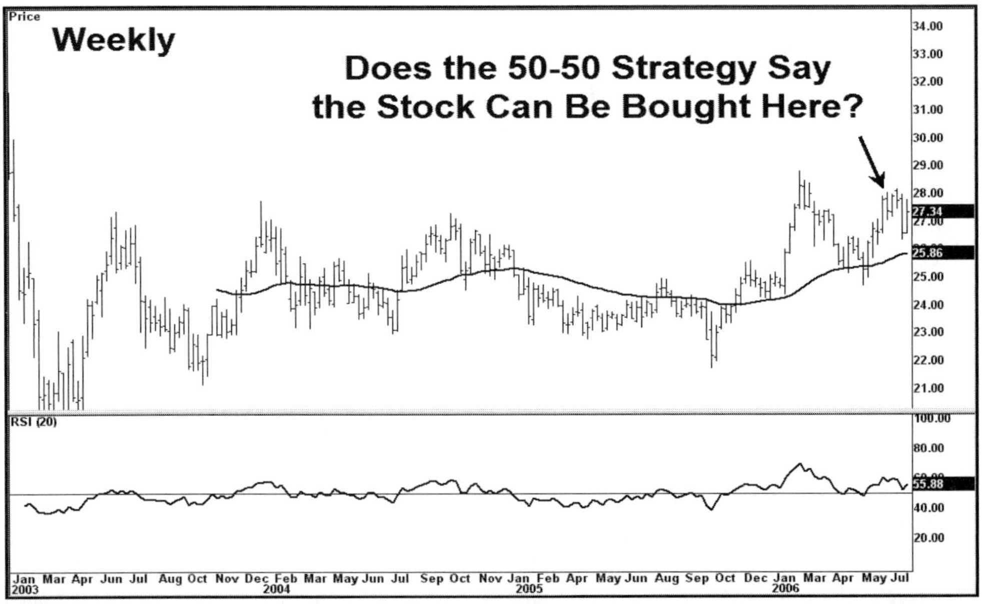

Figure 1.7 *Is this stock a buy?* (Chart: TDAmeritrade)

Let's do one more example. Look at Figure 1.7 and apply the 50-50 Strategy. Is the stock a buy?

Figure 1.7 meets both criteria for the 50-50 Strategy. Price is above a rising 50 MA and RSI is above 50. Don't think too hard, and you'll have a chance to make big profits. Many investors let what they think affect their investment decisions. If you must think, think about what you're going to do with your profits. Now look at Figure 1.8.

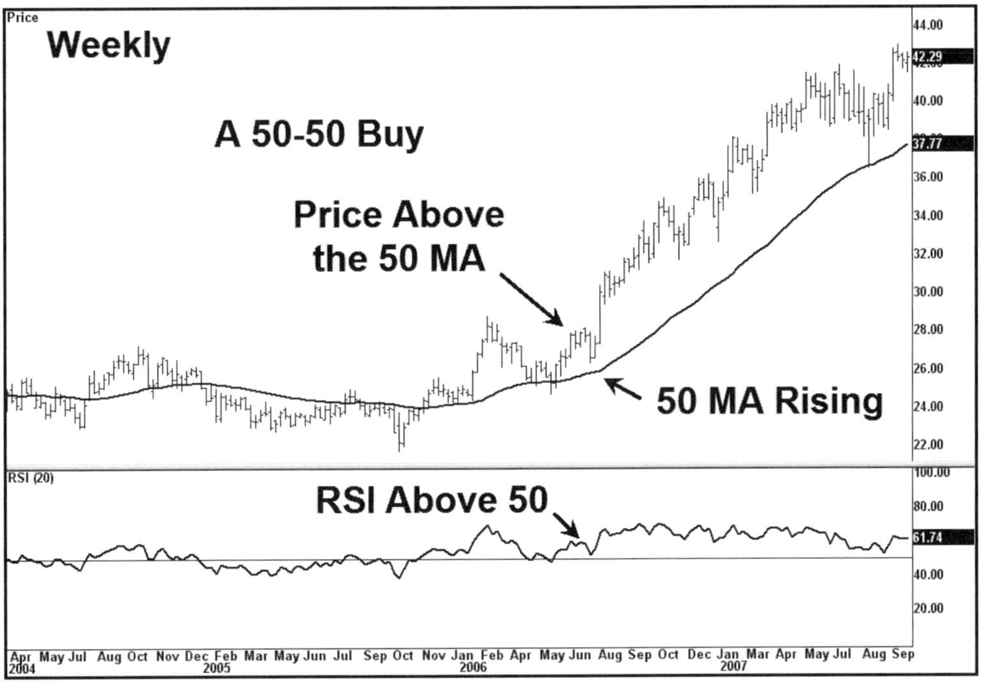

Figure 1.8 *This is the same stock as in Figure 1.7, one year later. It shows what would have happened if you had bought the stock at the arrow in Figure 1.7. The stock rose 100% in just over a year.* (Chart: TDAmeritrade)

Have you noticed anything missing in the stock charts up to this point? None of the charts to this point have shown the names of the stocks. I did this purposely to teach an important lesson: *always look at price* separately from any other information. Often, the name of a stock can influence our decision to buy it before we have studied the chart. For instance, if you dislike financial companies, you're not going to care how good price looks on a chart of a bank. Likewise, if you prefer healthcare stocks, you may be inclined to buy a stock without a thorough study of price. People will often see their "opinion" on a chart easier than they will see price.

From this point forward, I will show the names of stocks on the charts. They will be represented by a **stock symbol**. Stock symbols are just a short-hand method to list stocks. For instance, Starbucks symbol is "SBUX."

At one lecture I gave at a trading conference, I showed a few charts like the ones above, and I asked the audience to raise their hands if they thought a stock was a *buy*. At the end of the exercise, a man stood up, and his face muscles tightened. "You're not being fair," he said. "You're only showing us good-looking charts."

I replied, "I always try to invest in good-looking charts. What do you do?"

The eyes cannot see what the mind does not already know. Now you know the 50-50 Strategy. Practice with each chart as you go through the book. You'll find good-looking charts too.

50-50 STRATEGY CRITERIA

I will cover a great deal of material in the next 20 chapters. You will learn everything you need to know about how to invest with success. Whenever it seems like too much information, just relax and remember the few basic things you *need* to know. Fill in the blanks below, then write a note with the two 50-50 Strategy criteria. Stick the note on your bathroom mirror. Memorize it. No matter what you learn about the stock market or investing, you can be successful if you can remember to buy stocks which meet the following two criteria:

1 **Price is ________ a ______________ 50 MA.**
2. **RSI 20 is _____________ the ________ level.**

INVEST WITH SUCCESS

Successful investing is not about beating Wall Street. It's about not beating yourself. It is doing things the right way, with confidence and determination. Successful investors search for the truth, think for themselves, and make informed decisions to the best of their ability. They follow their plan rather than following the crowd.

I will give you the best of my knowledge about how to invest with success. You will gain relevant knowledge, develop a proper mindset, and master a trading strategy which makes the most amount of money with the least amount of risk. I have assembled all the information in this book.

If you are new to investing, you will start your journey on the right path to success. If you are already an experienced investor, you will find useful information to make you a better investor. You will also be able to monitor anyone who manages your money. Know when your investments are working and when they are not, and gain greater control over your financial destiny.

I can't teach you all there is to know about the stock market, but I will teach you what you need to know to make money. I promise to keep it simple and straightforward. I cannot guarantee you will build wealth, but I can guarantee you will know how.

SIGNPOST

Investing is a journey. I have just shown you an overview map of the 50-50 Strategy, and you now know what you will learn on your journey—mindset, knowledge, and plan. I will be your guide, so you will not get lost on your way to financial freedom. It is not the easiest path, but it is the most direct.

You will see a signpost which marks the trail head of your path to success. The sign reads, *Head Trail—Closed Minds Should Take an Alternate Route.*

Now, let's be on our way!

ΔΔΔ

The greatest wealth is a rich life.

2 The Investor

The first step toward investment success is making the decision to take control of your financial destiny. Successful investing is a philosophy of fiscal responsibility and financial independence. Whether you have a little money or a lot, the principles are the same. One does not achieve wealth by wishing and hoping. Wealth results from choices we make about how to put our hard-earned money to work.

While there is a lot to learn about investing, there is much more that you *don't* need to learn. Many investors begin by filling their minds with as much information as possible. Then they try to make sense of it, not having the experience to know what is and is not important. It is better to start by learning a few essential principles. Build a solid mental framework, and then add knowledge as you travel on your journey. Focus on the process of investing, rather than the financial outcome.

The better you understand yourself, the better you will understand your investing. Know the investor that lives inside you now. How do you value money? What is your attitude toward risk? What is your motivation for investing? How honest are you with yourself? I cannot make you a successful investor, but I can bring out the successful investor in you.

Most importantly, you must know what makes your life worth living. While everyone may want to be rich, not everyone has the desire to pursue wealth. Any new endeavor in life can create some stress. There is no amount of money worth sacrificing happiness or peace of mind. You should not try to fit your life into investing; investing should fit into your life.

ROMANCING THE STONE

My wife and I love to travel to Italy. We rent a car and get lost in the hill towns of Tuscany and Umbria. There we walk along winding, cobblestone streets of medieval towns and pause at an ancient fountain. We submerge our hands in water that still flows from a Roman aqueduct. I try to imagine how the people of the ancient town congregated at this fountain to gather water and talk about their day. I sense their concerns were not so different from mine.

We amble along the Via Flaminia, part of a 1,000-mile stone road built in the third century. We pass under a stone arch where centurions marched off to war. We run our hands along grooves in the stone roadway made centuries ago by chariot wheels. I hold my wife in my arms and ask, "What's better than this?"

We walk and find a local café where we sit outside in the warm sun. We eat handmade rigatoni pasta, fresh pecorino cheese, and drink Brunello wine. Spending the day together is a way my wife and I invest in each other.

By early evening, it is time to head back to our room at the villa and start up our laptops. The U.S. markets will be open soon. Trading is another love we share.

I open up my trading platform to look at my portfolio. I see a rainbow of colors, numbers flashing, streaming quotes, and the stock ticker sliding across the bottom. With a click of my mouse, my buy and sell orders travel across the ocean and are filled in America. A few hours later, we finish trading, and it is still early enough for *passegiatta* (the evening stroll) where we stop for some tasty gelato.

What you do in life, is what you value. Financial wealth is only one part of living a rich life. Not everything of worth has a monetary value. Making big profits is not just about the money. It's about what the money can *do* for you. Some of our best experiences in Italy are free, but we could not travel there without money.

I'll appreciate any money I make during my evening of trading, but what value will I place on the experiences of my day? Some things are priceless, like visiting ancient ruins with my wife (Figure 2.1). In a few weeks, I may forget which stocks made money. But in a lifetime, I won't forget running my hand over the chariot grooves in the ancient stone.

Figure 2.1 *Arco di Traiano* (220 B.C.)

A RICH LIFE

Many people think being rich means possessing excessive material and monetary wealth. While the pursuit of big profits is the main theme of this book, it is best to think of investing as simply one part of an integrated life. It is necessary to attend to the financial needs of yourself and your family. Big profits will lead to your financial security and independence.

Financial security is confidence in your ability to sustain your quality of life based on your investment plan. Just as you plan a vacation, you must plan for the costs of college tuition, housing, starting a business, or retirement.

You may be disciplined enough to go to the gym three times a week, but how much time will you devote to building investment "muscle"? You need to attend to your wealth needs just as you do your health needs. Make a plan and take control of your finances. Living a rich life is about having power over money, rather than letting money have power over you.

Financial independence is the reliance upon one's own will and judgment for financial decisions. You don't need to rely upon others, although you may seek out the advice of investment professionals. You may choose to let others manage a portion of your money, but you must take responsibility for having given it to them, and you should watch over their management.

Wealth is a choice. You will not get rich by accident, but by a concerted effort to reach your investment goals. Successful investing makes it a priority to learn what is necessary and to put that knowledge to use. Investing with success is a lifelong process, not a way to get rich quick.

WHY YOU ARE INVESTING?

There is no point in learning how to invest if you are not clear *why* you want to invest. I ask new investors why they want to invest. They often respond by describing some life problem—they hate their job, need to pay off bills, or want to work from home. People never admit they are in it for the thrill of making some fast money, and few ever say they want to learn investing in order to build wealth and improve their life.

An important reason for investing is to accumulate money for retirement. Many people have retirement plans through work but may want to supplement their retirement by investing personally. As better healthcare is letting us live longer, we may need to accumulate more money to last throughout our golden years. The sooner in life we start investing for retirement, the better we will meet our financial needs. It's never too late to start.

Time is your best investment partner because of **compounding interest.** Compounding interest is interest earned on the deposit amount plus any interest gained on the deposit each year. If you invest $5,000 at 10% per year, the first year you will make $500 interest (.10 x $5,000 = $500). You now have $5,500 ($5,000 initial investment + $500 interest = $5,500). The second year you earn $550 (.10 x $5,500), $50 of which is 10% interest on the $500 made on interest in the first year. After the second year, you will have $6,050 ($5,000 initial investment + $500 first year interest + $550 second year interest = $6050). In the third year, you will have $6,655 ($5,000 initial investment + $500 first year interest + $550 second year interest + $605 third year interest = $6,655). Each year, the interest compounds.

Now let's do an example where you start with $5,000, and you add an additional $5,000 each year in your tax free **Individual Retirement Account (IRA)** at an interest rate of 10%. In 10 years, you will have over $100,000! Compounding interest effectively doubled your money. See Figure 2.2 for more examples of compounding interest.

Amount Invested per Year	10 Years at 10% Interest	20 Years at 10% Interest
$5,000	$100,625	$348,650
$10,000	$201,249	$697,300
$15,000	$301,874	$1,045,950
$20,000	$402,498	$1,394,600
$25,000	$503,123	$1,743,250

Figure 2.2 *Examples of the growth of money over 10-year and 20-year periods at an interest rate of 10% compounded.*

Investing is also important for creating supplemental income. Some people are still working and have income, but they want to supplement their income to improve the quality of their life. Some people are retired, and this is a way to maintain a higher standard of living and an active lifestyle. Another reason to invest is to save money for a special purpose such as a down payment on a home, college tuition, an RV, or a special vacation. Whatever the purpose, money can be set aside in an investment account for the money to grow. The money management rules you learn can take an ordinary savings account and turn it into a wealth building account.

The investor profits when a stock sells at a higher price than it was bought. The amount of money received from selling the stock, less the initial investment, is the **capital gain** (See Appendix A, How to Calculate Captial Gains**).** Figure 2.3 is a weekly chart of BMC Software (BMC) showing about a 65% return in one year. The investor sold the stock at $35 per share and paid $21 per share, for a gain of $14 per share ($35 - $21 = $14).

Stocks also make money if they pay a **dividend**. Dividends are company profits periodically distributed (usually quarterly) to shareholders. Dividend-paying stocks are **income** stocks because they provide regular income to the investor. About 50% of stocks will pay a dividend.

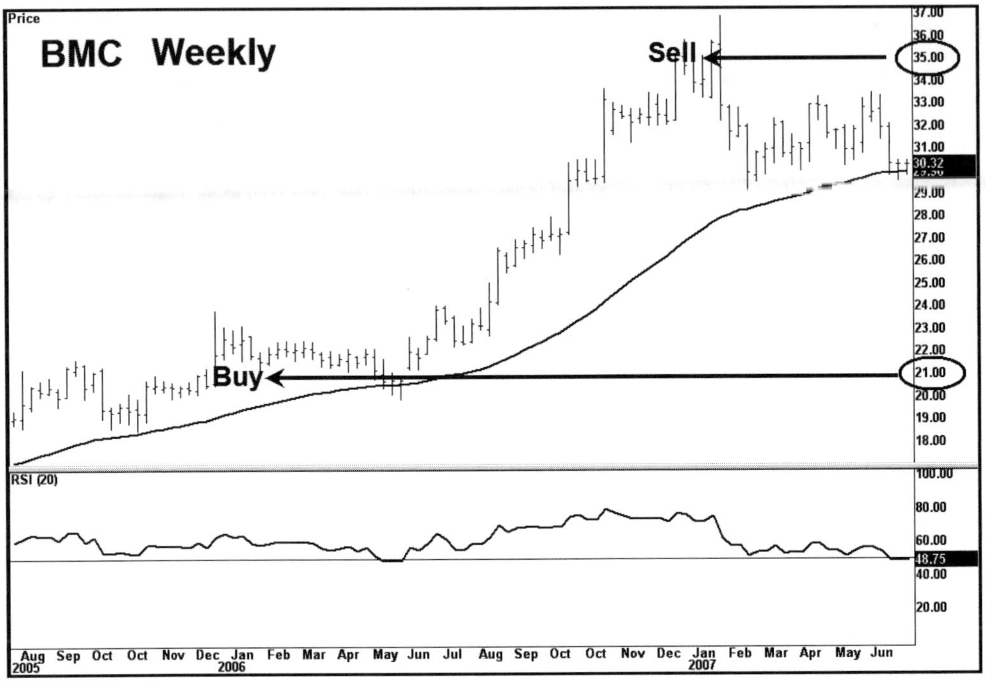

Figure 2.3 *Between January 2006 and January 2007, BMC went from $21.00 to $35.00, a 65% capital gain.* (Chart: TDAmeritrade)

Figure 2.4 is an example of Chesapeake Utilities (CPK) which pays a 4% dividend (See Appendix A, How to Calculate Dividend Yield). The dividend payments appear in the lower window of the chart (in place of RSI). Notice that the price of the stock went sideways for over two years, so there was no capital gain. Dividend stocks are purchased mainly for the dividend income.

In general, the returns from capital gains will be higher than the returns of a dividend-paying stock. However, dividend payments are a consistent form of income, whereas capital gains can vary greatly depending on whether or not the stock rises (capital gain) or falls (capital loss).

Be clear and honest with yourself about your purpose for investing. Do you want to grow wealth? Do you need income now? Do you need both? Your purpose directs the type of investment plan for you to pursue. Investing is not a quick fix for life's problems. Rather, it is a skill which requires time and commitment to master.

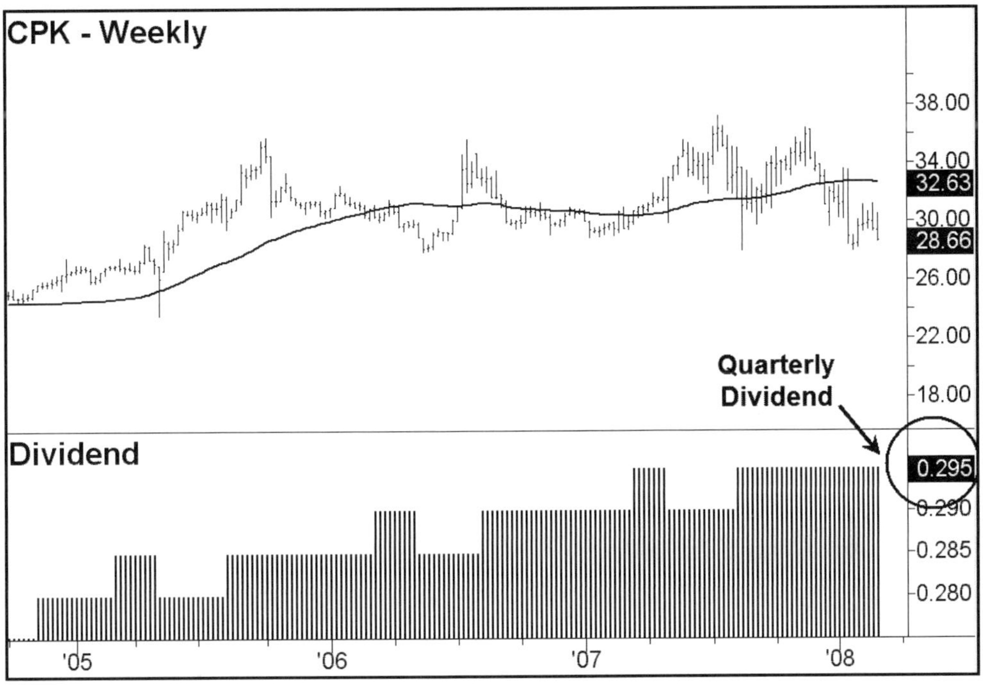

Figure 2.4 *CPK went sideways for over two years and paid a 4% dividend.* (Chart: TradeStation)

WHO ARE YOU?

You meet all kinds of people involved in the stock market. Some people consider themselves investors; others say they are traders. Do not get bogged down by labeling yourself. The main purpose of investing is to make big profits and build wealth.

You cannot invest without making a **trade**, and you cannot trade without making an investment. Whether a trade lasts two weeks or two years doesn't matter, so long as we remain focused on profit. When I refer to trading, I mean the act of making the trade in your **brokerage account.** A brokerage account is an account that allows you to buy stocks, bonds, and mutual funds.

Some investors limit their opportunities by letting their investment style override good judgment. The staunch **buy and hold** investors lost a great deal of money during the 2000-2003 bear market. Buy and hold investing is essentially buying a stock and holding it long-term (10 years or more), staying fully invested during major market declines. It makes no sense to hold onto a stock when it is losing money for two or three years of a market decline. Accepting this principle is part of using common sense, and it is part of how one develops the mindset necessary to prosper in the stock market.

Try not to think in terms of how long you plan to hold a stock. Think in terms of how long the stock is profitable. You will hold on to your investments for as long as they make you money.

Avoid personalizing terms. Any time you begin a sentence with "I am," you have personalized whatever comes after it. Traders in particular like to tell others they are **day traders** or **swing traders** because they think it sounds cool and impresses others. Day traders enter and exit trades on the same day; swing traders hold trades for a few days to a few weeks. Some people just want to trade, and some people just want to profit.

Investing is what you do, not who you are. If anyone asks, simply say you are a **profit investor**.

ANIMAL FARM

You will frequently hear the terms **bull** and **bear** when referring to market conditions. A bull market has long-term rising prices; a bear market has long-term falling prices.

People also describe themselves as bulls or bears, meaning they believe prices will rise or fall, respectively. These terms tend to personalize one's attitude toward market conditions, something which makes it more difficult to be objective when making trading decisions.

I cringe when the TV announcers start shouting that "the bulls were in control of the market today," or "there was a bear raid on the market." This is an animal farm mindset, and you should drive it out of your head as soon as possible. Prices fluctuate— that is a fact of the stock market. While some stocks are falling, others are rising. There is always an opportunity to profit in the stock market, and that is all humans need to think about.

THE GAMBLER

Investing is not gambling, although there are similarities. Gambling is when you bet on an uncertain outcome, and where you assume a high degree of risk without a reasonable expectation of a return. Gamblers put money at risk primarily for the entertainment value—they like the thrill.

The profit investor must not have a gambling mindset. If you have a gambling mindset, you should not be in control of your family's investments. Gamblers use terms such as, "take a shot," "let it ride," and "go for broke." Do not gamble with the money that provides security for you and your family.

Speculation is when investors assume risk in order to obtain a higher return than what they can get in a risk-free bank account. Keep in mind that successful investors do not speculate in all of their investments. They divide up their money and invest into different assets with different degrees of risk. This is part of **money management**.

Money management is mostly **risk management.** Risk management is when an investor assesses the risk of an investment and then addresses that risk in order to achieve the best return. Risk management is usually the difference between loss and profit.

Successful investors give ample consideration to risk before they commit their capital. Gamblers think first about how much money they can win, while investors think first about how much money they can lose. Figure 2.5 is a chart of an Exchange Traded Fund (ETF) where a loss could have been avoided by selling the stock when it crossed under the 50-week moving average.

CHANGES IN ATTITUDES

If you want insight into what kind of investor you will be, you need only look at other areas of your life. Our attitudes and values about money play out in everything we do, and investing will be no different. That does not mean you cannot change your habits once you understand your personal tendencies.

Some people just hate to sell anything. They like to gather and accumulate material things and seldom want to throw anything out. Their garages become packed with boxes. When there is no room left, they buy shelving so they have more space to collect things on the walls and ceiling of the garage. Why would stocks be any different? These investors are usually resistant to selling a stock once they have collected it.

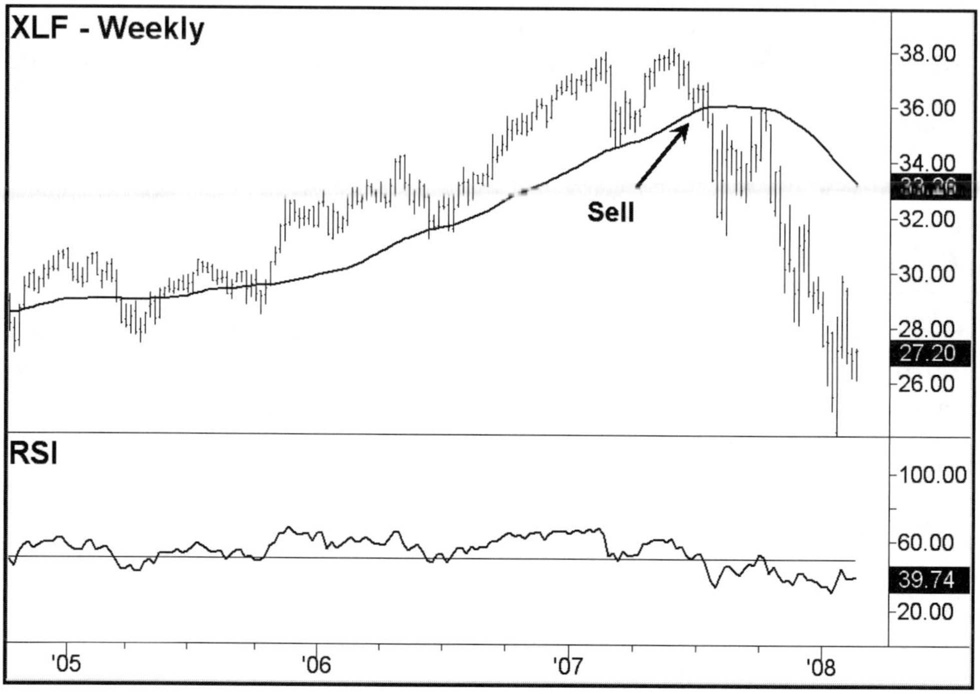

Figure 2.5 *A big loss was avoided in XLF (SPDR Select Financial Sector ETF) by controlling the risk and selling when price dropped under the 50-week moving average (arrow).* (Chart: TradeStation)

Some people love to go shopping and spend money. When they walk into a store, they automatically grab a shopping cart because they know they'll need it. They are not very concerned with price. They are more stimulated by the all the different colors and models from which to choose. If they had enough money, they would buy one of everything. Why should stocks be any different? These investors will be more prone to buying every stock that looks good, and they will give little consideration to the cost or risk involved.

Knowing yourself is an important insight into your investment mindset. There is no right way to be, but you must be cognizant of your own tendencies, so you can use them to your advantage rather than to your detriment. To manage your investments well, you must manage yourself well.

LEARNING A NEW SKILL

Many people who start investing approach it in the same way they approached other endeavors in their lives. I became a doctor by applying myself to textbooks, listening to my professors, and learning all I could about anatomy and physiology. I naturally believed I could conquer the investment world the same way, by using my brain and studying hard. I read all kinds of investment books, studied all aspects of technical analysis, and analyzed all types of trading methods.

What I discovered is that the qualities which make you a success in one area of life often have limited value in another area of life. To invest with success, I needed to learn a new set of skills and apply them with a new mindset. Past successes in your life can lead you to a false sense of confidence in your investing ability. For instance, if you did well in real estate, you may think you'll do just as well with stocks. Think again.

Often, people with a lot of money think they will naturally be great investors. Money doesn't make you smart or suddenly knowledgeable about everything. Money doesn't help you understand how the market works, or how to find profit opportunities. No matter how much money you have, you should start investing with small amounts until you learn how to invest with success.

Confidence is important, but do not overestimate your investment skill.

THE YIN AND YANG OF INVESTING

In the last several years of my medical practice, I specialized in the treatment of musculoskeletal pain. To expand my ability to treat pain, I became a medical acupuncturist. One of the acupuncture principles I studied was *Yin* and *Yang*. These are two opposing, yet complementary forces that help to explain the world around us. Yin and Yang sheds light on our character traits.

Our best qualities are often mirrored by our worst qualities. Neither is absolute; they are ever present and changing within us. For instance, you might be attracted to someone because they are adventurous and spontaneous. But if you marry that person, you may not like that they may suddenly be off on a new adventure instead of holding down a steady, mundane, job. It is not fair to love one part of someone and yet criticize them for the same thing in a different context.

Our traits play a big role in success. If you are a rigid, routine-oriented person, forming a trading plan will probably be your strength. In contrast, you may get lost in the details of the plan and lose sight of the greater purpose. If you are more intuitive and flexible, you may have difficulty following a plan, but you may be better able to adapt when the plan is not working as expected. Neither person is right or wrong.

Yin and Yang tell us that our best and worst traits are relative; they are ever present and ever changing inside us. Each trait has an opposite side of which we must be aware. Do not be judgmental about who you are; instead, understand the whole of who you are, and use your insight to bring out the best investor in you.

YOU ARE WHAT MATTERS

There is nothing I can tell you that will be more powerful than your willingness to learn. Investing is not just a financial journey; it is also a personal journey toward understanding yourself. Investing has the power to change you, not just increase the size of your savings account. I have learned more about myself through investing than I have from any other life pursuit.

Knowledge of investing will give you the power to make money. But ignorance of oneself will diminish your ability to use your knowledge effectively.

Learn the basic investment skills, and use them in a manner that best fits your personality. Let your knowledge and confidence grow naturally from the lessons of your journey. Don't try to force your will on the market. The market doesn't care who you are, or what you think or feel.

No one cares more about your money than you. You are the person ultimately responsible for building your wealth. You must either manage your money, or manage the person who manages your money. Either way, you will be empowered by a greater understanding of yourself and how you can best achieve your investment goals.

ΔΔΔ

Investing is simple;
we are complicated.

3 Profit Mindset

When I lecture to large groups, I often start by saying, "Pretend you aren't a great investor, pretend you don't know what the market is going to do, and pretend you have a lot more to learn about investing."

I usually get a few laughs from the audience. By asking them to *pretend,* I put the audience at ease and give them permission to let down their guard and to not have to know everything. By far the hardest thing about teaching small investors is getting their minds to open up to new information or to a new way of thinking.

There are three types of aspiring investors: those who know nothing, those who know something, and those who think they know everything. Most people already have preconceived ideas about the stock market. Some are slow to change their beliefs, often because their ego is too invested in the payoff of being right. Unfortunately, the account balance of a losing investor will usually drop faster than they can drop old beliefs. You can be right, or you can be profitable.

Learning how to invest is not easy, but unlearning bad habits is even harder. Many investors lose money in the stock market simply because they are mentally stuck, unable to change what isn't working. Prepare to wipe your mental slate clean of everything you think you know, and stand ready to take a different path on your journey to success.

It will not be the highly accessible, well-worn path of the crowd. It will be the poorly-marked, narrow path of the independent thinker.

PROFIT MINDSET

Most of our problems in life come from a failure to face the truth. The investor's journey is no different. The speed of your success will come from how committed you are to accepting the truth. The more lies and nonsense you are willing to believe, the more you will become disoriented and lose your way. A successful investor has a belief system built on truth.

It is normal to resist change. As humans, why go through all the trouble of forming opinions if we're not going to stick by them? We are proud of our beliefs, and our egos will defend them to the detriment of our portfolio. If your ego has to choose between making money and being right, it will usually choose being right.

In order to change our thinking, we have to give up something, and it is usually a long-held belief in which we are personally invested. The sooner we adapt our thinking to how the market works, and not to how we *want* it to work, the sooner we will have investment success.

Beliefs are the filter through which we see and interpret information. Our beliefs allow us to be more efficient because we don't have to analyze the same information over and over. If our belief is to obey traffic laws, we will habitually stop at every traffic light rather than having to decide whether or not to stop each time.

By their very nature, beliefs can also stop us from thinking. False beliefs create huge obstacles on the path to success. Successful investors must remain vigilant to the possibility of mental stagnation, and reassess beliefs when they fail to result in profits. Your understanding of the stock market will evolve and the truth will become evident. Try to remain a student rather than acting like a professor.

Let me warn you in advance that the truth may not make sense to you. To learn to invest with success, shift your mind from what makes *sense* to what makes *money*. This is the profit mindset.

PROFIT ABILITY

A successful mindset is a profit mindset. It focuses on finding opportunities to profit and managing risk to keep losses small. It ignores opinion, hype, and other distractions. A profit mindset follows a plan; it does not follow an investor's impulses or his need to be smart, to be proved right, or to boast.

As you sort though information about the market, I challenge you to repeatedly ask one question: how will this information help me profit? In the stock market, there is no right or wrong; there is only profitable and unprofitable. If something I believe helps me profit, then it is worth believing. You will probably not agree with everything I say, but if we use profits as the judge of what information is useful, then we are likely to agree on many things because profits are objective.

Investors like to theorize and invent esoteric new approaches to investing. They sometimes get lost in extensive research in **fundamental** (see Glossary) and **technical analysis** (see Glossary), as if their prowess in these areas will make them successful. They sometimes forget that profits are the only true measure of success. When you have profit *ability*, you will have profitability. Profits lead you in the right direction on your journey.

One investor told me he was buying all the Sepracor (SEPR) stock he could afford. His whole plan for retirement was to keep buying the stock and accumulate all the shares he could afford. He started buying it when it was $105 and he said the stock would rise over $500 because of a new wonder drug the company was making. I told him the stock was going down and it was not the time to buy. He kept buying more stock. When the stock fell further in price, I suggested he sell, but he said he was buying even more since the stock was even a better bargain (Figure 3.1).

You should not buy a stock just because it feels right. You should base investment decisions on *objective* information. For instance, a stock is either above the 50-week MA or below it. **Uptrends** occur when a stock is above the 50-week MA, while **downtrend**s occur when a stock is below the 50-week MA. I was able to tell the investor he shouldn't buy SEPR (Figure 3.1) because it had crossed under the 50-week MA and was trending down. I used trend analysis and objective price evidence. The investor believed the stock would go up despite the lack of evidence.

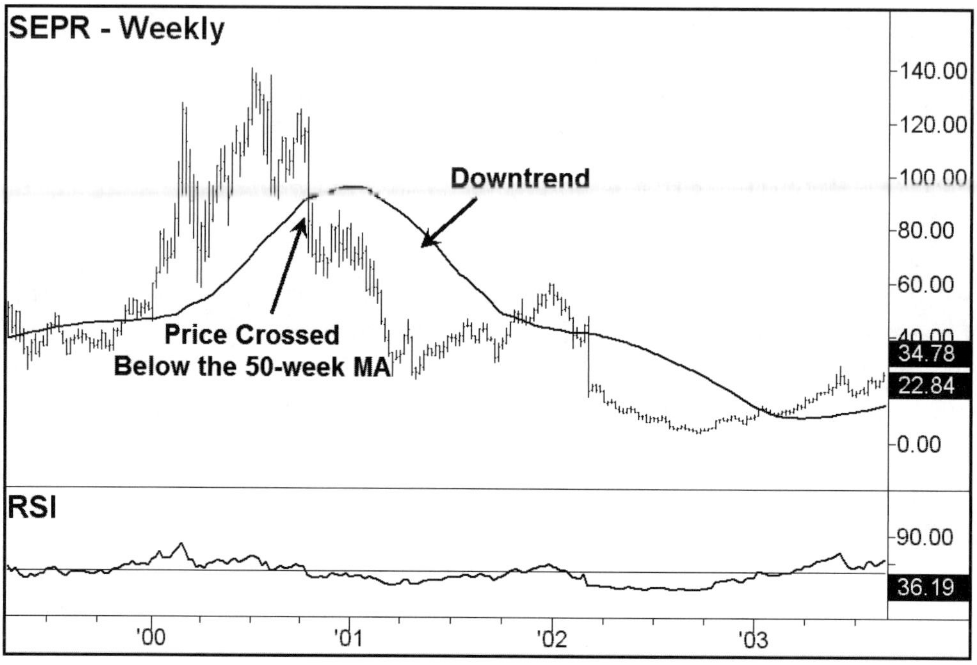

Figure 3.1 *Sepracor (SEPR) was in a downtrend for three years, but the investor continued to buy more shares. No matter how much you like a stock, don't buy it when it is going down.* (Chart: TradeStation)

THE TRUTH SLAYER

Ego has a powerful influence on how you think and can be destructive to your mindset. Egos will often prevent people from learning. They get stuck in what they want to believe rather than what they should believe. A person's ego doesn't care about the truth. Some people would rather lose money than admit being wrong.

When I meet investors, some are compelled to tell me they are *good* investors and make a lot of money. When I am asked about a stock, it is only so the investor can brag that he bought it when it was much cheaper. This is his ego talking, and he is not ready to learn. The investor is trying to convince himself he is successful in order to continue doing whatever he pleases.

Ego likes to have fun at our expense. Taking the ego out of investing may lessen the fun for some people because ego investors are in the game for kicks and not for money.

They like to talk the talk, boast about their latest score, and boldly predict the future direction of the market. They fail to see the truth.

The ego cannot hear the truth and will lie to save face. If you cannot be truthful with yourself, you'll always struggle to learn new information. Your ego will take control of you, and then you will no longer be in control of your portfolio. Your ego will sabotage your efforts to receive help and advice from others. And it will laugh all the way *from* the bank. Your ego loves what you think, but nobody else cares. Investing is not about you; it's about your portfolio.

Investing is a journey. I'll help those who struggle to find their way, but they must first admit they are lost.

"WHY" DOESN'T MATTER

We are generally comfortable in our lives to the extent to which we feel we have control. We lose a sense of control when we don't understand why something happened. It is normal to question why, but *why* seldom matters. Investors spend endless hours trying to figure out why something happened when they should be figuring out what to do about it.

Looking for or accepting explanations for what happens in the market will inhibit your analysis, and you will be slow to acknowledge events that contradict the explanation. This is especially true if you are counting on the explanation being true. It is easier to believe a lie about something you want to happen than the truth about something you don't want to happen.

Buy into stocks; don't buy into false tales to explain the market. The less nonsense you have in your head to think about, the clearer you will see what is really happening. It is mentally liberating to stop trying to make sense of everything that happens in the stock market, and to start making sense of your investment plan.

Too much information and too much thinking usually get in the way of making big profits. You'll outsmart yourself if you think too much. You only need to think about one thing, and that is how to follow your plan.

Don't attempt to understand what cannot be fully understood. Why doesn't matter.

NO TIME TO OPINE

Investment media is obsessed with opinions and predictions. On TV and in print, the experts boldly predict the hot stocks for the year. Commentators constantly ask their guests for an opinion about where investors should put their money. Investment magazines focus on stocks and mutual funds and predict which ones will be outperformers. The job of the media is to sell advertising. They'll do anything to get your attention, and one way is by having experts give their opinions. In the stock market, opinions are useless. The "experts" are wrong as much as they are right.

Whether someone is an expert or not, any given trade has about a 50% chance of making a gain versus a loss. You might as well toss a coin. Big money is not made by picking great stocks to trade. It is made by great management of the trades you pick.

Many people become too invested in their own opinion about a stock. You will advance your investing mindset significantly by looking in the mirror each week and saying, "My opinion doesn't matter; price is what matters." Your ego may not like it, but your portfolio will. If price is going up, you can make money. If it is not going up, you can't make money, no matter how many experts pick the stock or how much you believe in the stock.

When people ask my opinion of what the market or a stock is going to do, I can say with complete confidence, "It's either going to go up, down, or sideways."

THE WIZARD OF ODDS

Some investment gurus are referred to as "market wizards." Market wizards appear to possess a magical ability to outsmart Wall Street. The crowd calls them wizards because they always seem to beat the markets, while so many other investors struggle. The crowd is dazzled by wizards and will try to emulate them. The crowd likes to believe the market wizards always make money, so they attend their lectures and seminars, hoping to take home the wizards' magic potions.

In my hometown of Las Vegas, there are many magic acts. They enchant and mystify the audience with their skill at sleight of hand. They have a hypnotic effect on the audience because it's fun to be charmed. We want to experience something greater than ourselves and the mundane trials of life. For one show, we are lost in a world where reality is forgotten and anything is possible.

Mysticism and magic appeal to the universal dream that anyone can turn rags into riches with just a little luck. Years of practice go into magic acts. Magicians cannot make their bills disappear, nor make money suddenly appear. They cannot foretell the future; if they could, they would always make perfect bets and own the world. Still, it is fun to believe in magic.

Magicians perform magic, but do not possess it. It is the same with investors. The magic of investor success is based on study and practice. But once you learn the tricks, you can perform your own magic show, even if knowing how a trick is performed spoils your sense of whimsy. You'll just have to get your thrills from putting money in the bank.

DE PLAN! DE PLAN!

Many small investors have no plan for how they will make investment decisions. They "kinda," "sorta" know what they want to do, but have no clear or consistent methodology. When asked, they are unable to articulate their plan. This type of investor will always be a reactive investor, reacting to what the market does. They will listen to the news and become overly optimistic when the news is good and overly pessimistic when the news is bad. Reactive investors are usually a step behind profit opportunities.

A good **plan** is necessary to invest with success. When you take control of your finances, your plan is a call to action, not reaction. A plan is a **P**reset **L**ist of **A**ctions **N**ecessary to be taken.

The big money is made by investors who are able to step outside of themselves to follow the plan. For example, when you want directions to a new restaurant, it's easy to go to *www.mapquest.com* and print out specific directions for how to get from your house to the restaurant. You know you'll arrive at your destination if you follow the directions. Now imagine going to a website named *www.50-50strategy.com*. You print out the directions and agree to follow them until you reach your financial destination. This is how to think about the plan—as directions to follow.

Your plan does not have an ego, and it doesn't get stressed over decisions. The plan doesn't feel bad if a trade lost money, and it doesn't celebrate when a trade makes big money. Judge yourself by how well you follow your plan; do not judge yourself on the results of every trade. The plan will work if *you* work.

Stocks don't know you have a plan for them. If a stock ends up a loser, simply accept that the stock failed to go up. You did not fail, and you are not a loser. Do not beat yourself up. If the stock ends up making big profits, the reverse is also true; you were not a winner, your stock simply went up. The only time to get upset is when you don't follow your plan.

FINDING YOUR WAY

The greatest barrier to investment success is the acceptance of truth. One must seek out the truth about the markets, investments strategies, and the skills necessary to be successful. But most importantly, an investor must center on the truth about oneself. It is the most difficult obstacle you will encounter on your journey.

If you consider yourself clueless about the stock market, you will have a big advantage. Most long-time investors think they know more than they do about the stock market. They fall in love with what they think, and it is their downfall. The path to success is narrow. For you to go forward, your ego must stand aside.

I will show you the path to becoming a successful investor, and I will give you a plan to follow. Ultimately, you will decide what resonates as truth and what you will adopt as a belief system. Only you can determine what to do with the knowledge you receive. If the plan is wrong, you can fix it. If you are wrong, the plan *cannot* fix it.

Sometimes you will follow the plan and lose money. Sometimes you will ignore the plan and make money. You will make mistakes and learn from them. Every journey has setbacks. You will know you have arrived at your destination when you can follow your trading plan to big profits.

ΔΔΔ

The greatest risk is the one you're not prepared for.

4 Risk and Reward

One's attitude toward risk is a major part of mindset. You should know your risk tolerance, so you can match your investments to your comfort level. The central question of risk tolerance is whether or not the expected return on the investment makes it worth taking the perceived risk? Every invdividual must answer for himself.

My attitude toward investment risk changed one day while my wife and I were driving across America in our minivan. When we travel, we enjoy talking about investment ideas. I said to my wife, "Most people aren't aware of how much risk there is when they make a trade."

The three-lane interstate was jammed with cars racing along at 75 miles per hour. I had cars on each side of me, just a couple of feet away. It was starting to turn dark, and a light mist had decreased visibility. An 18-wheeler came up on my right side and my windshield was covered in a spray of water that splashed off the wheels of the truck.

I fumbled to quickly turn on my windshield wipers. Suddenly, the car on my left decided to cut in front of me. At the same time, the driver in the car up ahead jammed on the brakes. I was trapped and couldn't maneuver. I hit my brakes, skidded, and barely kept from rear-ending the car ahead of me. Fortunately, I was able to avoid an accident.

When the danger was over, my wife calmly said, "Yeah, that trading is risky all right."

RISK PRECEDES REWARD

No matter what you do in life, there is seldom a reward without risk. **Risk** can be described as the chance of something happening which is different from what you expect to happen. When someone gets in his car to drive to the grocery store, his expectation is that he will get there and back safely. There is always the risk he will get into an accident and be injured.

To protect against the risk of injury, he wears a seatbelt, obeys traffic signs, and drives with caution. These are all steps to minimize the risk of an accident and injury. The driver has lessened his fear of getting into an accident because he has taken steps to protect himself from serious injury.

When you buy a stock, you have the expectation that it will rise in price, and you will make money. However, there is a risk you will lose money instead. That shouldn't stop you from investing. Instead, you will learn to fasten the seat belt on your investments to reduce the risk of injury to your capital.

No matter how many safety measures we take in a car, we cannot always prevent an accident. We accept the risk, and do all we can to prevent serious injury. Similarly, you cannot prevent losses in your stock investments. Instead, you learn how to reduce the risk of serious injury to your capital, and accept a fender-bender loss as part of investing.

LIFE IS RISKY

There is risk in any investment. We invest time into our career, love into our marriage, and money into our portfolio. Life is risky; investing is part of life.

What is the emotional and financial risk of a failed marriage? What is the risk of going to college to earn a degree and then not getting a job? What is the risk of not having enough investments for retirement? The risk does not stop us from moving forward in life.

We tend to get immune to risks to which we are constantly exposed.

Think about driving down the freeway at 75 miles per hour. There are cars all around us, just a few feet away. Drivers are changing lanes without using their turn signals. They are talking on their cell phones, drinking coffee, and looking at their navigation systems. Maybe someone is drunk or starting to fall asleep at the wheel. If you constantly thought about all the possible risks, you might be afraid to drive.

Just as you learn to accept the risks of daily life, you will learn to make risk management a routine part of your investment strategy; you will also become immune to small losses. Losses become part of making money. They are something you anticipate to happen, just as you anticipate a car might suddenly swerve in front of you on the freeway.

The better you understand risk, the more you can invest with confidence. The acceptance of risk is an important component of your investing mindset. If you accept and properly manage risk, you'll be surprised how the profits add up.

TYPES OF RISK

Company risk is the risk that some event involving a company will negatively affect the stock price. If the company is under investigation for accounting issues, it could cause investors to sell their stock and drive down the price. The collapse of Enron was an extreme example of company risk.

In order to reduce the amount of company risk, investors build a **portfolio,** or collection of assets, using several different stocks. If one stock takes a big drop, it will have a smaller impact on the overall portfolio. When investors buy a diverse group of stocks to reduce company risk, it is portfolio **diversification**.

Market risk is the risk that the general stock market will fall in price. Most stocks follow the direction of the overall market, so a stock is at higher risk of falling in price when the market declines, even though the company is still healthy and profitable.

Market risk is always present and cannot be diversified away. You will learn to see when the market is going down, so you can manage your risk by taking profits and reducing the number of stocks in your portfolio.

A major market decline will give an objective signal that it is entering a downtrend, giving the investor time to sell stocks and take profits, thereby missing the major decline. An example of the overall market is

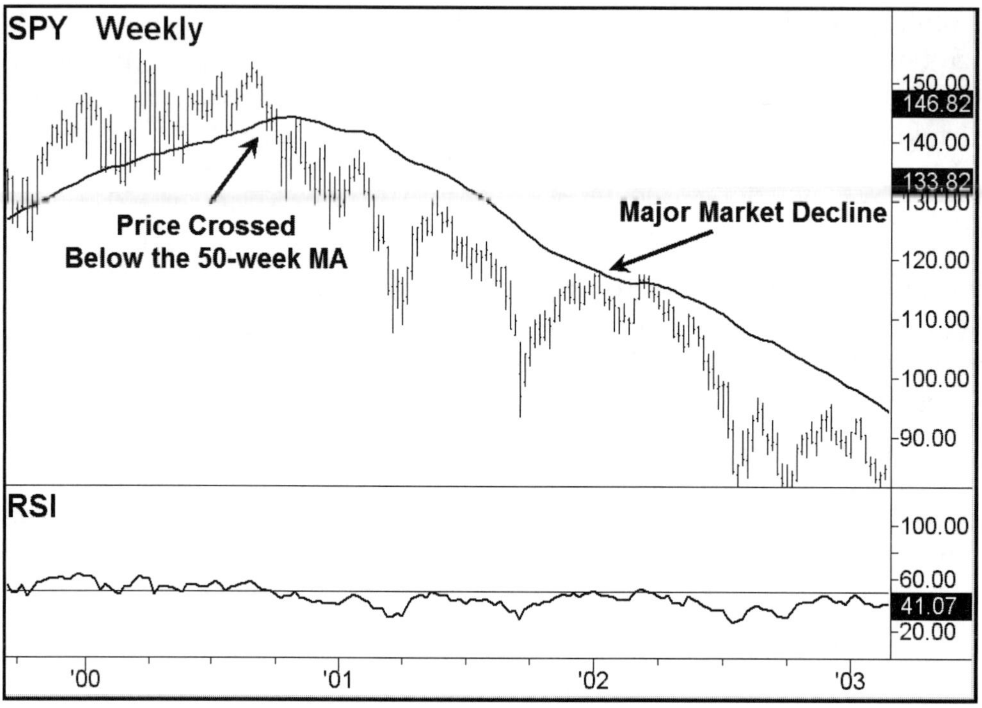

Figure 4.1 *The chart shows the SPY ETF which represents the overall stock market. It dropped below the 50-week moving average in September of 2000 giving objective evidence of a downtrend.* (Chart: TradeStation)

As you learned in Chapter 3, price enters a downtrend when it crosses *below* the 50-week MA. The SPY (Figure 4.1) crossed below the 50-week MA in September 2000, after which the market declined for the next two years and price of the stock dropped 40%.

WHY TAKE RISK?

Understand why you take risk in the stock market. When you invest, you expect to receive a profit; otherwise, why take the risk? Your risk is the chance that your return will be different than what you expect. The profit you make is your **return**, which represents your reward for having taken the risk.

There is a tradeoff between risk and return. One of the basic principles of investing is that the amount of risk associated with any investment is directly related to the amount of the expected return. If you want low risk, you can expect a low return. If you assume a higher risk, you will expect to receive a higher return.

You can accept no risk if you choose. **Money market** funds, **Certificates of Deposit (CD)**, and savings accounts are considered risk-free investments. They will pay a relatively low return. Risk-free investments take much longer to grow wealth compared to the higher returns obtained with stocks.

It is generally recommended that a significant portion of a person's assets be in stocks. The percentage of stocks generally decreases as the investor approaches retirement, when there is more concern with preserving assets and receiving investment income.

FROM HERE TO RETURNITY

I was lecturing at a major trading exposition when a man came up to me after my lecture. He said he liked my presentation but was a little skeptical. He wanted proof that the 50-50 Strategy would make him high enough returns.

I said to the man, "Well, it won't make you rich overnight. Some people don't have the experience, but they still expect to go out and make a 300% a year."

His eyes opened widely. "I'm not like that," he said, "I'd be happy with just 200%!"

Expectations are an important component of mindset. If you expect to make a 200% return, you will probably be disappointed most of the time. You can make 100% on some stocks, but it doesn't happen all the time. You will have some small gains and small losses. There are also commission costs. All of these factors will affect your average return.

It is helpful to be aware of the historical returns of stocks. Let's assume you bought every stock in the market. This assumes you don't make any stock choices. Some stocks in the market will have positive returns, and some will have negative returns. It will all average out to about a 12% per year return. To improve your returns above 12% in stocks, you have to invest in the stocks going up and avoid the stocks going down. The 50-50 Strategy gives investors a chance to make big profits because it selects stocks with higher profit potential.

Stock returns are reduced by the effect of **inflation**. Inflation is the rate at which the cost of products and services in the U.S. rise over time. It can significantly reduce investment returns. The long-term rate of inflation is 3%. This means your money is worth 3% less each year, reducing your purchasing power. If you have a 12% return in the stock market, your real return (adjusted for inflation) is 9% (12% return - 3% inflation = 9%). If you decided to put your money in a bank savings account earning 2%, your average return (adjusted for inflation) is -1% (2% savings return – 3% inflation = -1%).

RISK CONTROL

When you buy a stock, there is a risk it will drop in value. If it does, your account statement will show a negative gain (loss) for the investment. The total value of your account will be decreased by the amount of the loss, even though you have not sold the stock. How much of an investment loss are you willing to accept? If you will accept an unlimited amount of loss (even down to a zero value), then you have the mindset of a buy and hold investor.

The only thing you can control in a trade is your risk. The successful investor does not accept unlimited risk in return for a chance at limited returns. The risk must be controlled, and the profits must be allowed to grow. The primary method used to limit risk is a **stop-loss order**.

A stop-loss order is a standing order to sell your stock at a predetermined price if the stock falls to that price. The order is entered into the trading account and is executed automatically, allowing the investor to avoid worrying about the day-to-day fluctuations in a stock's price. The order remains in effect until you cancel it, so you are always protected.

You will enter a stop-loss order for every stock position. With a stop-loss, you get to decide when to sell the stock. Your mind is at ease, and you will sleep well at night knowing you are protected (Figure 4.2).

Without a stop-loss in place, a stock can drop fast, creating a big loss. You will be forced to sell when the stress of the loss becomes too great to bear. If you don't use a stop-loss order, you can lose money in two ways. First, you lose money from the drop in the stock's price. Second, you lose the use of your investment capital while you sit in a losing trade; this is capital that could have been used to make positive gains in a different investment.

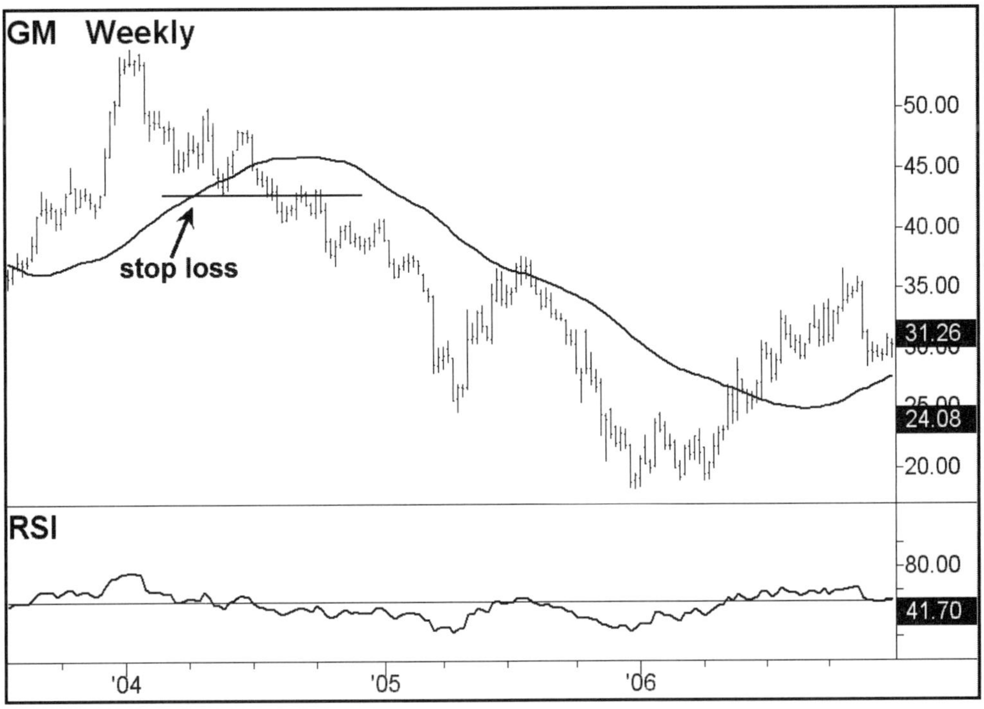

Figure 4.2 *A stop-loss order (placed at the level of the horizontal line) prevents capital losses by automatically selling the stock when price falls to the stop-loss price. The stop loss also prevents the "lost use of money" by holding on to a loser. General Motors (GM) fell in price for two years after price dropped below the stop-loss.* (Chart: TradeStation)

No trade is ever perfect, and you'll make mistakes; it's part of the process. You can make mistakes and still make money as long as you properly manage your risk. You can also do everything right and lose money if you fail to manage your risk.

OH STOP!

In order to keep losses small, the maximum amount of loss allowed will be limited to 15% of the purchase price. That is the basic rule you follow with the 50-50 Strategy. However, investors must make up their own minds about how much loss they are willing to take. When I teach investors, I always ask one question: "How much money are you willing to lose in order to see if the stock's price can go higher?"

Notice I used the word *lose,* and not risk. In our minds, risk is not always perceived as real. When someone goes hang gliding, they're not expecting to crash. The only way to face the real risk of an investment is to assume you have already lost it. Consider it the amount you agree to pay in order to get the chance for greater profits. If the amount is too much for you, then you must reconsider if the investment is appropriate.

Part of the 50-50 Strategy is finding stocks that are trending higher, not lower. To make big profits, you will learn to find stocks with the potential for gains which are several times greater than the amount of the potential loss. In general, stocks with earnings growth are less likely to fall in value compared to stocks without earnings.

The stop-loss will not prevent a loss, but it will prevent a big loss. Big losses are severely damaging to a portfolio because they erase the hard-earned profits made on profitable trades. Big losses destroy precious capital, and if too much capital is lost, investors irreparably damage their chances of building wealth and meeting their financial goals.

MIND YOUR STOP, STOP YOUR MIND

Suppose you buy stock ABYZ because you believe it is going to go up. It's a great company, has earnings, and everybody is talking about it. You even see the CEO on TV saying how great the outlook is for the company and how they're expanding to new markets every year. Earnings just came out and they are good, so you decide to buy the stock today at $50.

You spend $50,000 to buy 1000 shares, aware that if the stock goes up to $80 next year, as everyone predicts, you'll make a quick $30,000.

You're so sure this stock is a winner; you decide not to use a stop-loss. Last time you used one, you were **stopped out**, and then that stock took off and you missed some really big profits. You think: that's not going to happen this time. You're smarter now, so you won't place a stop-loss order.

Tomorrow the stock gaps down to $45, and the TV news has the reason: the earnings were good, but not as good as the analysts expected. You are down $5,000, but only on paper. Now you're really glad you didn't use a stop-loss, because you would have been stopped out, just as you thought. You're sure the drop is just market manipulation, and you're not going to fall for it.

Next week you're happy when the stock rebounds $3. By the end of the week, the stock falls to $42, and now you're down $8,000. You're starting to think you should have used a stop-loss. What if the stock falls further? Do you sell?

No way. You really believe in this stock. It's one of your favorite companies. It seems like everyone uses the company's product, so it must be a good company. You're tough, so you decide to hang in there.

Two months later, the stock is at $35, a $15,000 loss. You start thinking: *there's no way I'm taking a $15,000 loss, that's too much*. You ask yourself how you could have let this happen. It doesn't make any sense. You remember the last time you sold a stock for a big loss, and that stock eventually turned around and went back *up*. You decide to hold on. You'll just tell your wife you intended for the stock to be a buy and hold.

A month later stock ABYZ is now at $32. Do you sell? What if it drops to $30? You make an appointment with your doctor because you want to get a prescription for some sleeping pills. While you're there, you'll also ask for a medication for your upset stomach.

Pretty soon the stock is at $25, and you have a $25,000 loss! You decide to not look at your brokerage statements anymore. You're not happy. You want to quit investing, and you blame the market for taking advantage of the small investor. You decide the market is just not fair. You give the account to your wife and let her manage it from now on.

As you read this story, you probably noticed that the decision to sell a stock gets harder as the loss becomes greater and greater. Losses are painful, so we try to avoid them. Trying to avoid a loss usually leads to a bigger loss. Could you have prevented this whole debacle? Yes, by using a stop-loss order.

If you don't use a stop-loss order, eventually, a story like this will happen to you. It has happened to nearly every investor at one time or another. It happened to many investors after the internet bubble burst in 2000. For example, Cisco Systems (CSCO) was a widely held stock at the market top of 2000. By 2003, approximately 90% of investors who bought near the high price of $80 were still holding their stock in 2003, after the price had dropped to $20.

A successful investor determines the amount of loss he is willing to take on a trade and enters a stop-loss order. By doing so, he no longer has to be stressed over the potential decision of when to bail out and sell his stock. He can sleep well at night, knowing he is protected. He saves money on doctor bills, too.

FREE COINS IN THE FOUNTAIN

In my experience, the greatest risk to a portfolio is not a stock that falls in price or a market that enters a major downtrend. The greatest risk is the investor who does not have the proper mindset, knowledge, or skill to be investing. You will be different.

Money is easier to manage than managing ourselves. Some people throw money at the market without a proven plan for how to be successful. They throw money like they were tossing coins into a fountain, hoping for something good to happen. Or they throw money because they just want to be right; the risk of not being right scares them more than the risk of losing money.

The essential thing to understand about risk is how to manage it. Big profits are not dependent upon taking big risks. On the contrary, big profits are the result of taking small risks when the potential for rewards is high.

ΔΔΔ

The market is not supposed to make sense; it's supposed to make money.

5 Market Myths

Every major endeavor in life begins with a philosophy. Philosophy involves a system of beliefs or principles by which we live. Investing is no different. What you believe about the stock market and which principles you follow will guide everything you do with your investments.

When I lecture to investors, there's always one man in the crowd who asks a question based on a false belief about the stock market. Before he can finish asking the question, I already know his viewpoint, and I also know he will be difficult to teach

As soon as I point out a different way to view the market, the man wants to debate. I have heard the same argument many times. I state my case for the truth. He can accept it or not; it will not affect my investing. He cannot let it go. Instead, he doubles his effort to convince me of his belief.

I say, "If you're making a profit with your approach, there is no need to change anything." I know he is not profitable, or he wouldn't be defending his position so strongly. If he is right, then he can blame his losses on the market. If he is wrong, he must take responsibility. By arguing, he is trying to get me to tell him he is right, but I cannot. He will struggle to understand how to make big profits because his mind is ingrained with a false belief, and he cannot let it go. He cannot see things in a different way.

Your success will depend on developing a winning philosophy for building wealth. That is why mindset is so important. Sometimes you must let go of old beliefs in order to adopt new ones. If your mind is weighted down with false beliefs, and your ego is determined to carry them along, you will have difficulty moving forward on your path.

MARKET MYTHS

Market myths are beliefs or perceptions about the stock market that have no real basis in fact. Myths represent a collective belief that is pervasive among the crowd. Myths are dangerous because they are used to explain and justify bad trading decisions.

Myths are promoted and reinforced by the media, as well as those who want to tell you how the market works. Myths create mental blocks to learning. Unfortunately, they are often accepted as fact because they can sound plausible and are not easily proven right or wrong.

Investors cling to myths in order to understand the market and make sense of what happens with their stocks. Until you are more experienced, you will have to accept certain truths to move forward, even if they don't make sense to you. One should place emphasis on whether or not a belief helps you make money, rather than whether or not it is an absolute truth. Let me give you an analogy.

Suppose you are from the USA and you rent a car in the UK. You'll have to adjust to driving on the left side of the road no matter how odd and wrong it might seem. You can debate whether it is better or more natural to drive on the right side of the road, but it won't do you any good. In the UK, you either drive on the left side of the road or risk being injured in a head-on collision.

Part of a healthy mindset is the ability to let go of how you want to think. Instead, you should focus on the type of thinking that will help you profit on your journey to success.

MYTH: THE NEWS MOVES PRICE

This is the myth that is most difficult for people to discard. I admit it seems sensible that news should affect stock prices, but I have yet to find any investor who can tell me his strategy for investing with the news. If anything, news is just an excuse for why prices go up or down. The small investor never sees the real forces that move stock prices.

If news comes out and it's good, do you automatically buy? If the news is bad, do you automatically sell? Most people will answer *no* to both these questions, which proves my point. If you have watched how stocks behave, then you've seen that price is poorly correlated to the news. The best news about companies sometimes comes out just before the stocks begin a significant decline in value.

In January of 2008, Apple beat Wall Street expectations for earnings, but the stock began a seven week decline (Figure 5.1).

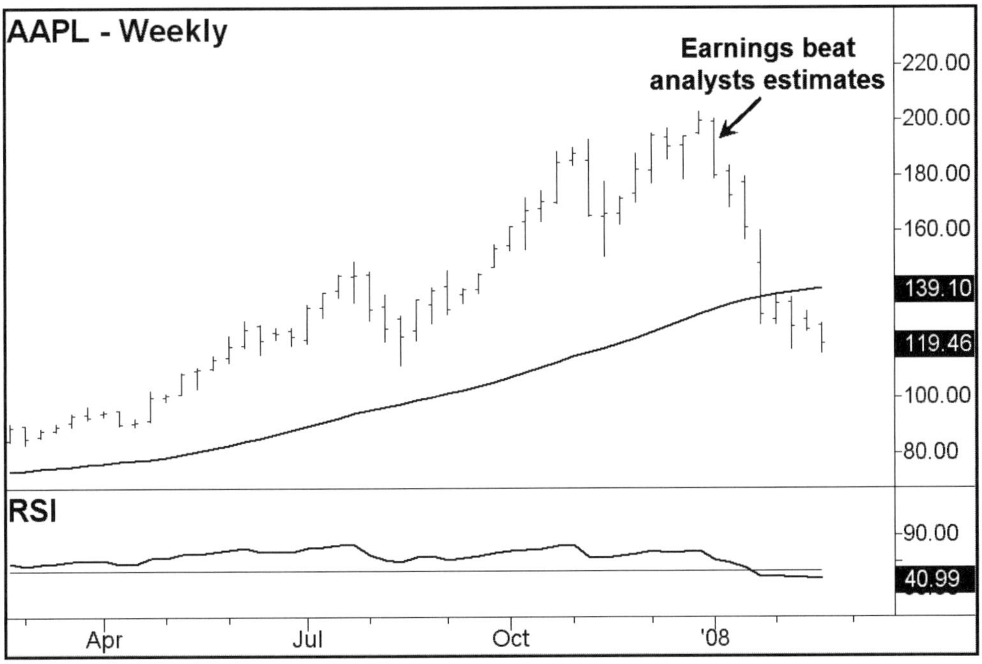

Figure 5.1 *Apple (AAPL) reported earnings (at arrow) which beat analysts' estimates, but the stock immediately fell in price, dropping over 30% in seven weeks.* (Chart: Tradestation)

People often point to company earnings as the source of price movement. That is true, except professional investors who work for mutual funds or large banking institutions do not buy on the news of today's earnings. They buy stocks from one to several years out. They study projected earnings of companies and do intensive research on the business of companies in which they invest. By the time the good news comes out, they sell the stock to the small investor who thinks the good news is suddenly a reason to buy.

There is very little real news for the small investor. By the time you hear news about a company, it's no longer news. The big money has already known the news for quite some time, and they've invested accordingly. The small investor is an outsider and must use other signals for finding the best time to buy or sell.

News is often released to the public in order to create a reaction. News is seldom for your benefit. It is for the benefit of those releasing the news. When a grocery store wants to get rid of an oversupply of a product, they run a two-for-one sale. Those who want to dump their stock will do the same thing. Beware of CEOs who appear on TV and tell you their company is in great shape.

Don't listen to news. It will clutter up your mind and distract you from your investment plan.

MYTH: YOU CAN'T TIME THE MARKET

Some people believe you can't time the market and suggest you shouldn't even try. This is nonsense. Everyone times the market in one way or another. How would you like your investment advisor to say, "I plan to put you into several stocks, but I have no idea if this is a good time to buy or not. In fact, it could be a really bad time to buy; I just don't know."

We expect the experts to have some idea of market conditions. **Market timing** means reading the overall trend of the market and assessing the state of the economy in order to determine if conditions are favorable for investing in stocks. The investor hopes to avoid committing capital to a weak market, but wants to take advantage of strongly trending conditions.

One of the major principles of investing is that you want to be invested as early as possible at the beginning of a new **bull market**, and you want to exit your positions near the end of the bull market (or as soon as you recognize it's a bear market). By doing this, you improve overall returns. It is not necessary to pick the exact bottom of a bear market, but it is important to recognize the change to a new bull market.

Some people confuse market timing, thinking it is used to predict when the market will turn directions. The market goes up when the economy expands, and the market goes down when the economy contracts. As I have said before, no one can predict the future. The important thing to recognize is when the market has changed direction, so you can adjust your portfolio to reduce potential risk to capital.

In later chapters, you'll learn one simple rule to determine if the market is in an uptrend and conditions are favorable for investing. It's not a mystery. If you were invested in the 2000 dot-com bubble, you may kick yourself for not knowing the rule back then. It will seem obvious when you look back at the signals.

During the **bear market** which occurred in 2000-2003, five trillion dollars of market value was lost in technology companies alone. Many U.S. investors had their retirement accounts wiped out when they remained fully invested in stocks while the overall market declined. Small investors can make big profits, but not if they remain passive and accept big losses in a bear market.

MYTH: YOU CAN'T MAKE MONEY IN A BEAR MARKET

One of the biggest misconceptions about investing is the idea you can't make money in a bear market by buying stocks. Bear markets are associated with economic recessions, where the vast majority of the stocks will decline in value. As stock prices decline, the media constantly remind us of how many stocks are making new yearly lows, and they express a "gloom and doom" attitude.

Let me say it plainly: there are always opportunities to invest in stocks.

Most stock mutual funds can only buy stocks, and the majority of capital must be invested at all times. What do they do in a bear market? Do they sell all their stocks? No, they must stay invested in something. They shift the money into other stocks less affected by a bear market. They also hunt for stocks considered to have upside potential—new growth stocks expected to be leaders in the *next* bull market.

For instance, during bear markets, companies that supply personal products and consumer staples usually rise. People are not going to give up the basic necessities of everyday life like soap or toothpaste; nor will they give up food, tobacco, or alcohol. A minority of growth stocks will also emerge, and savvy investors can find some gems. Stocks that meet 50-50 Strategy criteria are still valid considerations. There is always a stock somewhere that is in an uptrend.

Let me prove the point. During the bear market of 2000 to 2003, many investors didn't protect their profits. Instead, they complained about how bad things were. The media made it seem like everybody was in the same sinking boat, helpless to do anything about it. That was a mistake. Below is a table showing a few of the stocks that performed well during the bear market of 2000-2003 (Figure 5.2).

Stock	Percent Gain From 9/00 to 3/03
Alliance Gaming (AGI)	2145%
Bradley Pharmaceuticals (BDY)	834%
Novagold Resources (NG)	734%
Immucor (BLUD)	716%
FTI Consulting (FCN)	601%
Flir Systems (FLIR)	535%
Multimedia Games (MGAM)	526%
Par Pharmaceuticals (PRX)	464%
Jos A Bank Clothiers (JOSB)	409%
Usana Health Science (USNA)	406%

Figure 5.2 *High stock returns during a bear market are possible using the 50-50 Strategy and avoiding the pessimistic news about market conditions.*

The worst performer in Figure 5.2 had an average annual gain of over 400%! Could you accept that gain in a bear market? During bear markets, you may want to cut back on the number of stocks in which you invest, but you only need a couple of these big winners to have fantastic returns. Big profits come from trading individual stocks with a strategy, not from passively taking what the market gives.

MYTH: MONEY IS MADE BY PREDICTIONS

Small investors are drawn to market experts who make predictions about how the market or individual stocks will perform. On financial TV programs, commentators congratulate the "hot hand" of the expert and spew out accolades like, a "gutsy call." It creates drama, especially when there is a contest to see which expert can best predict the future.

The reason behind predictions is simple—entertainment. What kind of TV show would it be if an expert said, "I don't know what the market is going to do, and I have no idea which stocks you should buy."

No one can predict the future. If you buy into the myth that you can, it will negatively impact your mindset. Worse, you may be caught up in the prediction business yourself. Some investors love to spout their opinions. There is something in us which makes us want to declare ourselves. Predictions are bold and exciting, but they are the soapbox of the ego.

You do not need to know what the market is going to do. You need to know what *you're* going to do when the market does what it does. Predictions are not the way to make big money in the market. Big money decisions are based on probability and signal recognition, both of which will be explained later in the 50-50 strategy.

Novices predict; pros prepare.

MYTH: YOU CAN GET RICH OVERNIGHT

It is tempting to hear the infomercials on TV: "I've more than doubled my account in just one month"..."I made $20,000 in two weeks"..."I only started with $10,000 of capital"..., and "I made $9,000 in one day!"

The companies that promote this hype do a disservice to the small investor. It's hard to be disciplined about investing when you're told you don't need to learn how to invest in order to make big profits. You just need to buy software that tells you when to buy and sell. Ultimately, investors are to blame if they don't use common sense. If there was a magic system you could buy to get rich, then we would all be millionaires.

If you approach investing with the idea of getting rich overnight, then you will be disappointed. You should make money doing what you know how to do, and then put your money to work with a sensible investment plan.

Preserve and grow your capital for the future; it's the best advice I can give you.

SIGNPOST

Whether you believe them or not, market myths won't help you make money. If your common sense is stronger than your need to believe in myths, you will overcome the allure and move confidently in the direction of your investment goals.

You have now reached the second signpost on your journey—the end of Part One covering mindset. We will now move on to the next discipline in the Trilogy of Success— knowledge.

Understand that each discipline is not separate from the other. Each is presented separately to better organize the material under discussion. You may have found knowledge in your study of mindset, and you will continue to develop your mindset as you gain more knowledge.

Congratulations for making it to the second signpost on your journey down the path of success. The message on the signpost should be clear: *Only Independent Thinkers Beyond this Point.*

ΔΔΔ

Part TWO

Knowledge

Knowledge isn't just a matter of learning facts; it's learning the facts which matter.

6 The Market

In Part Two, the focus is on essential knowledge of the stock market. The first thing to know is that *you can do this*. The basic steps of investing are fairly simple. You don't have to be a financial expert to have success. All you need is the commitment and patience to learn.

Over the years, I have spoken to numerous individuals who asked me how they might get involved in the stock market. I frequently heard the same comment; they knew nothing about the stock market and didn't know where to start. If you're one of these individuals, consider yourself lucky. You can begin without any preconceived notions of how the market works.

When I decided to write this book, I wanted to be sure I didn't leave anyone out, so I aimed my message at the reader who knows "nothing" about the stock market. Consequently, this chapter will cover some basic terms and principles. Some general knowledge of the market is necessary before I go into specific investment topics. I will not tell you everything there is to know, but I will tell you everything you *need* to know. Part of keeping investing simple is excluding complicated concepts which do not directly lead to profits.

MARKETS IN SOCIETY

The United States is a capitalist country, and capitalism serves to meet our daily needs. This is made possible by an open **market** system. A market is simply a place where buyers and sellers of a particular product or service come together to do business. Your local farmers' market is a perfect example.

The farmers bring their supply of produce to the market where the public comes to buy what they need for their household. When products or services are traded between two individuals, the basis of the trade is that each person values the product differently. The farmer has a greater **supply** of produce than money and is willing to sell produce for money. The public has more money than produce and is willing to pay cash to meet their **demand** for food. Markets are driven by a balance between supply and demand.

Markets benefit society because of their efficiency. Rather than growing your own string beans, tomatoes, and corn, you can work at your job and make money to buy produce cheaper than you could grow it yourself. Likewise, the farmer takes money from selling produce and pays for his children's medical checkups. Paying the doctor is more efficient for the farmer than going to medical school in order to take care of his family's health care.

Each person has a role in society, and each of us benefits from everyone else's efforts through the efficiency of a market-driven economy. A market economy allows a higher standard of living and greater ease of survival by the division of labor, invention, and innovation.

The **"stock" market** is where investors go to buy stock in a company. Rather than starting their own company, investors use money to buy part ownership in a company and share in a portion of that company's profits. This allows the investor to generate a second source of income which is more efficient than going back to school to learn a second career, especially since there are only so many hours in the work day. Investors enter the job market to make money; they enter the stock market to have their money work a "second" job.

STOCK EXCHANGES

The stock market is composed of over 10,000 stocks which trade on three main **stock exchanges**. A stock exchange is an organization which matches stock buyers with stock sellers. The oldest and largest exchange is the **New York Stock Exchange (NYSE).** The **American Stock Exchange (Amex)** generally lists smaller or newer companies and features Exchange Traded Funds (ETFs) (discussed later). The **National Association of Securities Dealers Automated Quotation System (NASDAQ)** is a computerized exchange which lists a large number of technology stocks. You will hear these terms used frequently, but it is not important for you to know much about them in order to buy a stock.

The U.S. stock market has regular session hours Monday through Friday from 9:30 a.m. to 4:00 p.m. EST. A trading *week* is five work days, not seven calendar days. There are *pre-market* and *after hours* trading sessions for NASDAQ stocks, but investors should not bother with these sessions. **Long-term** investors are only concerned with stock prices from one week to the next. Wealth-building investments are based on long-term **uptrends** in stock prices. Long-term uptrends last from a few months to a few years, and they are best seen on a weekly stock chart.

SECURITY CHECKPOINT

Stocks are a type of **security**. A security is simply an **investment vehicle** which involves risk and can be exchanged for something of value. The two most common types of securities are **stocks** and **bonds**. Two other common securities are **mutual funds** and **exchange traded funds (ETFs).** The principles you learn about price **trends** apply to all types of securities.

Companies issue stock **shares** in order to raise business capital; this point is of no concern to us. The idea of ownership is detrimental to our mindset because we don't want to personalize stocks. The goal is not to own companies, but to own stocks with *profit opportunity*.

Never buy a stock solely because you think it is a *good company*. Lots of investors buy what they "believe" are good companies and end up losing money. They are left wondering how such a good company could give such bad returns. Stock prices often do not represent an investor's perception of a company's value.

A good example is Dell computers (DELL) (Figure 6.1). Dell is one of the best known companies in America and sells computers all over the world. The stock dropped from $40 to $20 in a one-year period from 2005 to 2006, losing half of its value. By 2008, the price was still unchanged at $20. Does the price trend of DELL mean it is a "bad" company?

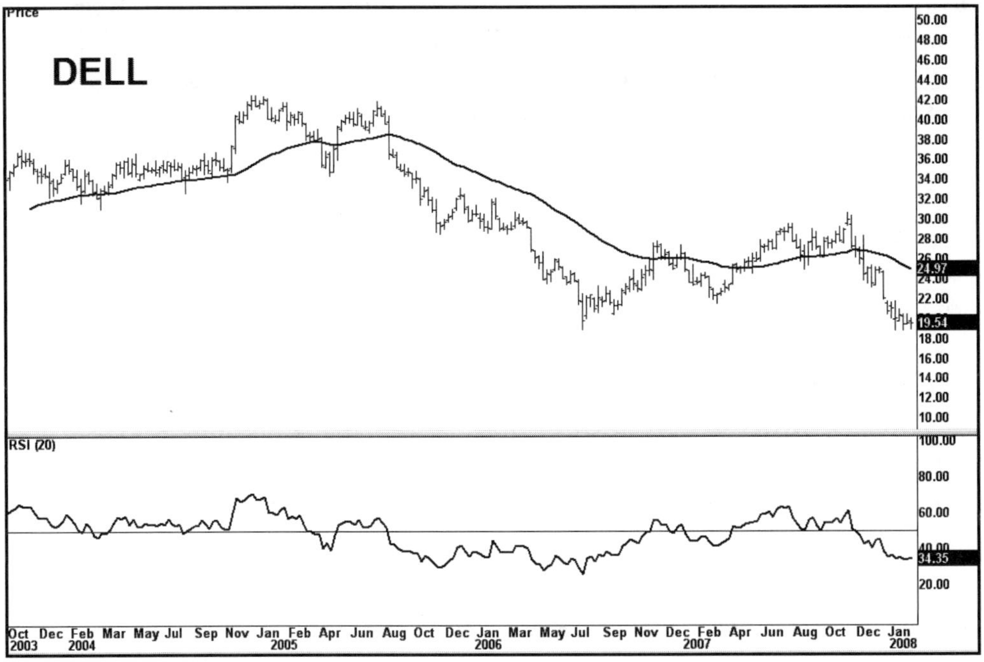

Figure 6.1 *Many people own Dell computers, but the stock performed poorly during 2005-2008. A company's stock price can be much different than the perception of the company's value.* (Chart: TDAmeritrade)

Stock brokers like to sell clients stocks of "good companies" because the brokers will be less open to criticism if the stock loses money. You'll think it's not my broker's fault, it was a good company. If your broker puts you in an unknown stock and you lose money, you'll wonder why he recommended a company that no one has ever heard of.

Stocks, mutual funds, and ETFs all have **ticker symbols** for identification. For instance, the four-letter symbol for Microsoft is MSFT. The ticker symbol is what you'll see on the **ticker** moving sideways along the bottom of your TV screen or computer.

Stocks can have symbols from one to four letters long. ETFs usually have three-letter symbols. Stocks and ETFs both trade on stock exchanges, but mutual funds do not. Mutual funds have symbols with five letters; they are not listed on the ticker because they are not traded on a stock exchange. Mutual funds are purchased directly from a mutual fund company or through a stock broker.

THE LONG TERM

Like most professions, investing has its own terminology. When you buy a stock, it is called going **long**. The price of a stock and the number of shares you buy is called your stock **position**. For example, if you buy 200 shares of Office Depot (ODP) stock for $20 a share, you would say, "My position is long 200 shares of Office Depot at $20." Long positions are closed out by selling the stock at a higher price when there is a profit, or at a lower price if there is a loss. When you "go long," you are buyng, or entering a long position (Figure 6.2).

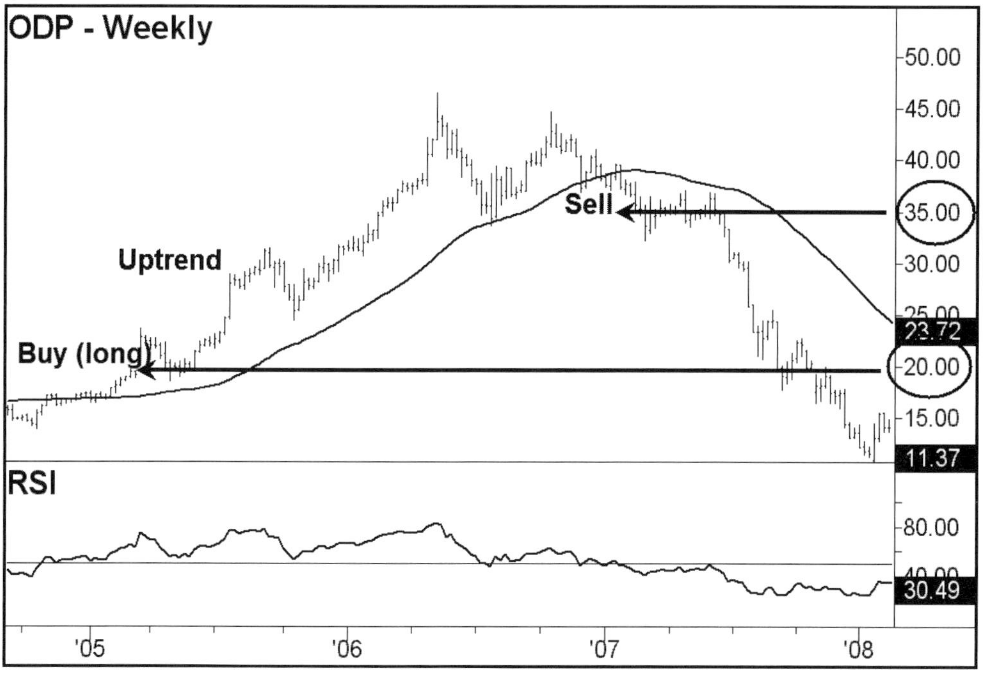

Figure 6.2 *Office Depot (ODP) provides an example of a typical long position. ODP was bought at $20 and sold at $35, netting $15 per share.*
(Chart: TradeStation)

You have already learned that investors use the 50-50 Strategy criteria to go long when price is above a rising 50-week MA and RSI is above the 50 level. Downtrend conditions exist when price bars cross below the 50-week MA and RSI crosses below the 50 level. Investors must exit a long position (if they have one) as soon as price enters a downtrend. They should not buy a stock in a downtrend until price reverses to an uptrend, when price is back above the 50-week MA and RSI is above 50.

The two signals for exiting a trade are shown in Figure 6.3. For a downtrend to begin, price must cross below the 50-week MA and RSI must cross below 50.

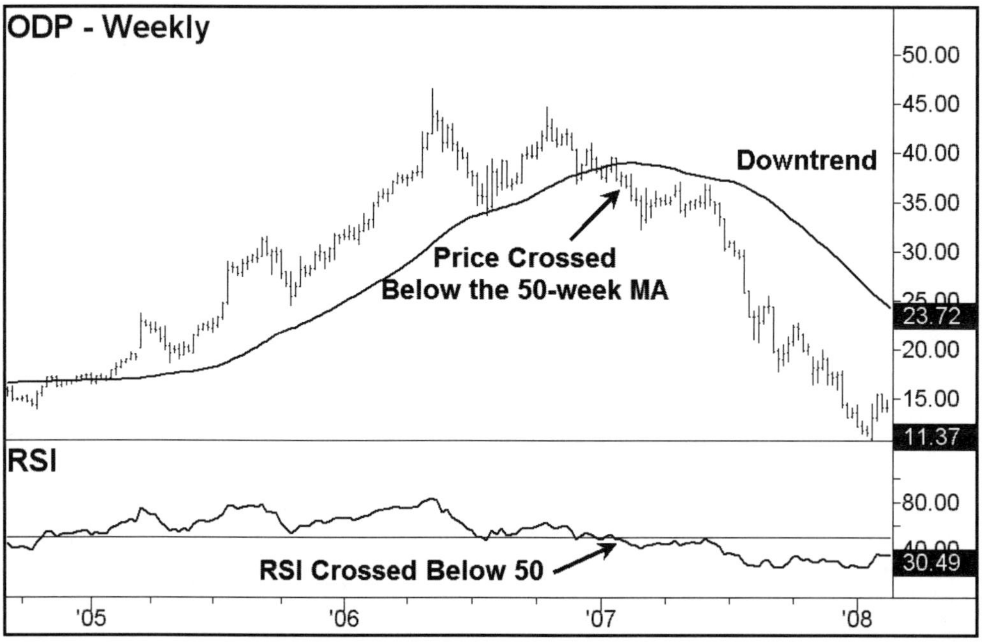

Figure 6.3 *For investors, the beginning of a downtrend is a signal to exit a long position. Here is ODP with the two signals for a downtrend (arrows).* (Chart: TradeStation)

SUPPLY AND DEMAND

Stock markets function due to varying levels of supply and demand. Supply is created by investors or traders wanting to sell stock, and demand is created by those wanting to buy stock. Markets exist because participants value stocks differently; one investor believes a stock is a buy, another sees it as a sell. It is vital to understand that without stock sellers there would be no supply of stock to meet buyer demand.

The price of a stock is determined by supply and demand and not by analysts and experts. When there are more buyers than sellers, the price will go up. When there are more sellers than buyers, the price will go down. No matter what you might think a stock is worth, the stock is only worth what someone is willing to pay for it.

Supply and demand are in a constant flux, adjusting to the multitude of different interests of market participants. Someone who is selling stock may not dislike the stock, but is simply taking profit. Likewise, a mutual fund may be selling stock simply due to redemptions by investors.

We cannot know what every market participant is doing, or why they are doing it; it is futile to even wonder. Your job is to focus on your plan—what stock you want to buy, at what price, and how you will manage risk. Don't get drawn into the media hype about *why* stocks are going up or down. No one really knows, and wondering about it will only distract you from making big profits.

VALUE JUDGMENTS

There are two basic methods of price analysis which have been historically used to gauge the "fair" price of stocks: **fundamental analysis** and **technical analysis**. The discussion which follows will explain the two methods. You will not need to determine the fair price of a stock. You only need to determine when a stock's price is trending up and whether or not there is a signal to buy.

Fundamental analysis reviews the company's financial information to arrive at a fair value for a stock. When a stock's price is higher than its fair value, the stock is considered **overvalued** and unlikely to attract buyers. When the stock's price is lower than its fair value, the stock is called **undervalued** and investors are attracted. Investors buy undervalued stocks when they believe the stock will rise in price to equal its real value. Fundamental analysis is not an exact science, and experts often disagree.

When you first look at fundamental information, it can be overwhelming, and you might wonder how you will ever figure it out. If you have ever received a stock **prospectus** in the mail and tried to make sense of it, you know what I mean. Fortunately, you don't have to be an accountant or financial expert to use fundamental analysis effectively.

Fundamental analysis is calculated by computers and reported in an easy-to-read format.

You don't have to pay an expert for stock analysis; you'll have the same information they have. You will learn to interpret the essential information using the **SCORE** method of rapid fundamental analysis. I created the SCORE method to make fundamental analysis effective and fast. If your fundamental analysis takes longer than thirty seconds, you are working too hard. Think of it like reading a report card; it doesn't take long to distinguish students who are passing from those that are failing. You simply look at the pass/fail grades for each of the class subjects. Investors want to find the stocks which have passing grades in all of their fundamental "subjects." Figure 6.4 shows a webpage from Yahoo (www.finance.yahoo.com) where you'll find everything you need to know for free. The five "class subjects" are circled. I'll explain how to interpret stocks using SCORE in Chapter 10.

TECHNICALLY SPEAKING

Another method to determine a stock's fair price is technical analysis which studies the past and present behavior of price. Technical analysis assumes that all fundamental information known about a stock is already reflected in the price, and that the forces of supply and demand continuously adjust the stock's price to a fair value.

Technical analysis is often defined as a method to predict the future direction of price. This is the *wrong* way to think about technical analysis. Predictions are a waste of time because there is no way to determine what price will do in the future, and it is not necessary to know what price will do—it is necessary to know *when* it is doing it. You will learn technical analysis a different way, a way that focuses on what price is doing now and what you can do now to make big profits.

Technical analysis is used in three ways: 1) to determine the price trend, 2) to assess risk, and (3) to provide timing **signals** for entry. The main tool of technical analysis is the price chart, and its primary use is to analyze trend. **Trend** is the prevailing direction of price. A stock's price is in an **uptrend** if the 50-week MA is rising (Figure 6.5). Only buy stocks in an uptrend. A stock's price is in a **downtrend** if the 50-week MA is falling. When the 50-week MA is relatively flat, it is a **sideways trend**. The investor should not buy a stock in a downtrend or sideways trend, although the trend could change in the future.

Management Effectiveness	
Return on Assets (ttm):	3.66%
Return on Equity (ttm):	7.06%
Income Statement	
Revenue (ttm):	6.97B
Revenue Per Share (ttm):	4.962
Qtrly Revenue Growth (yoy):	7.60%
Gross Profit (ttm):	3.75B
EBITDA (ttm):	1.35B
Net Income Avl to Common (ttm):	660.00M
Diluted EPS (ttm):	0.47
Qtrly Earnings Growth (yoy):	-23.40%
Balance Sheet	
Total Cash (mrq):	2.00B
Total Cash Per Share (mrq):	1.435
Total Debt (mrq):	749.63M
Total Debt/Equity (mrq):	0.079
Current Ratio (mrq):	1.407
Book Value Per Share (mrq):	6.835
Cash Flow Statement	
Operating Cash Flow (ttm):	1.95B
Levered Free Cash Flow (ttm):	370.50M
View Financials (provided by EDGAR Online):	

day)[3]:	
Shares Outstanding[5]:	1.39B
Float:	1.25B
% Held by Insiders[1]:	10.00%
% Held by Institutions[1]:	74.20%
Shares Short (as of 26-Dec-07)[3]:	39.10M
Short Ratio (as of 26-Dec-07)[3]:	1.9
Short % of Float (as of 26-Dec-07)[3]:	3.30%
Shares Short (prior month)[3]:	55.53M
Dividends & Splits	
Forward Annual Dividend Rate[4]:	N/A
Forward Annual Dividend Yield[4]:	N/A
Trailing Annual Dividend Rate[3]:	N/A
Trailing Annual Dividend Yield[3]:	NaN%
5 Year Average Dividend Yield[4]:	N/A
Payout Ratio[4]:	N/A
Dividend Date[3]:	N/A
Ex-Dividend Date[4]:	N/A
Last Split Factor (new per old)[2]:	2:1
Last Split Date[3]:	12-May-04

Figure 6.4 *The report card showing the five key fundamentals of the SCORE method of rapid fundamental analysis.*
(Source: Yahoo Finance)

Figures 6.6-6.8 are examples of an uptrend, downtrend, and sideways trend, respectively. Study the 50 MA in each of the three charts. The 50 MA will be rising in an uptrend, falling in a downtrend, and moving sideways in a sideways trend. In sideways trends, the 50 MA often looks "wavy," moving up and down, but overall moving sideways.

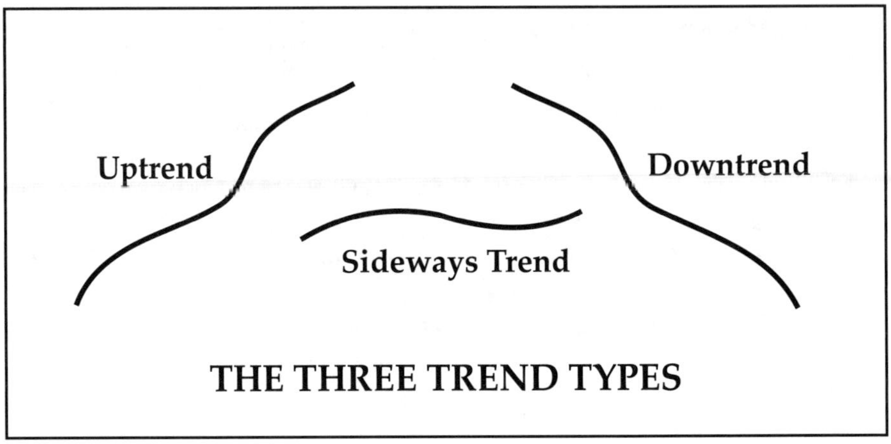

Figure 6.5 *The three types of trends are represented by moving average lines.*

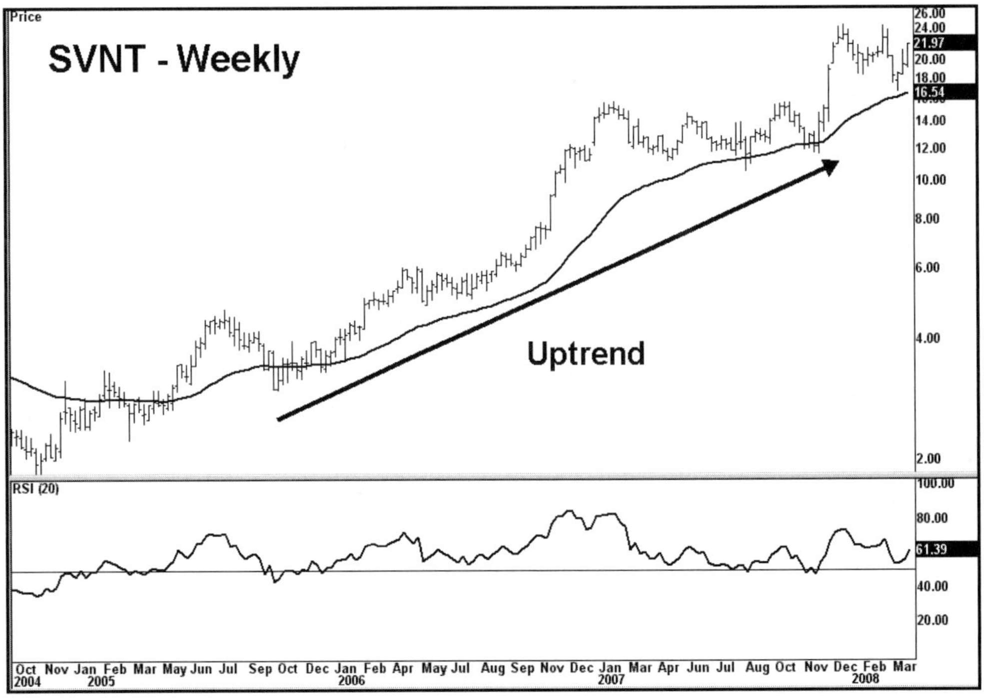

Figure 6.6 Savient *Pharmaceuticals (SVNT) has a rising 50 MA. It is in an uptrend.* (Chart: TDAmeritrade)

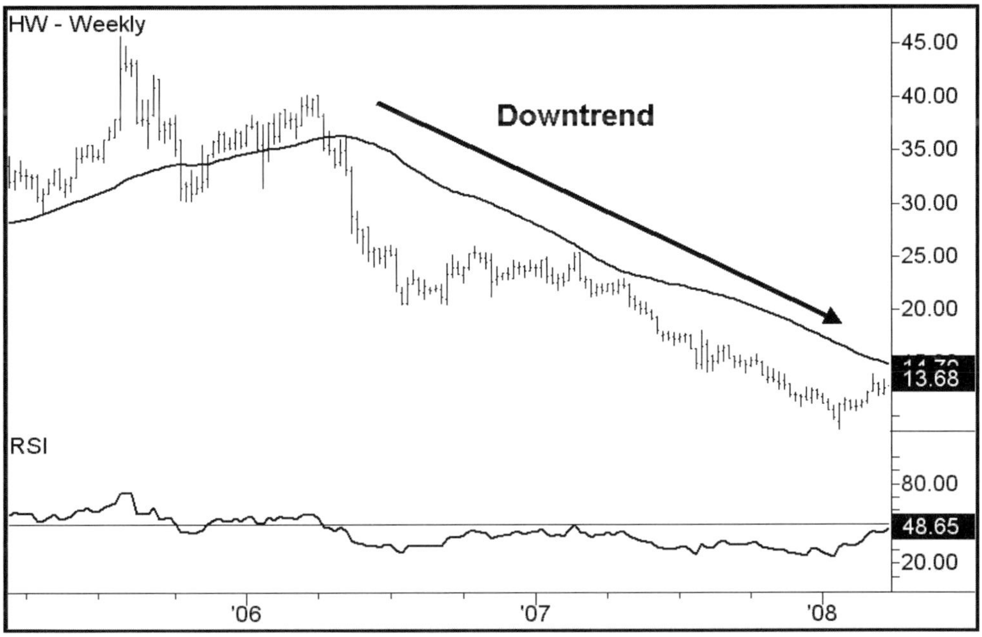

Figure 6.7 *Headwaters (HW) has a falling 50 MA and is in a downtrend.* (Chart: TradeStation)

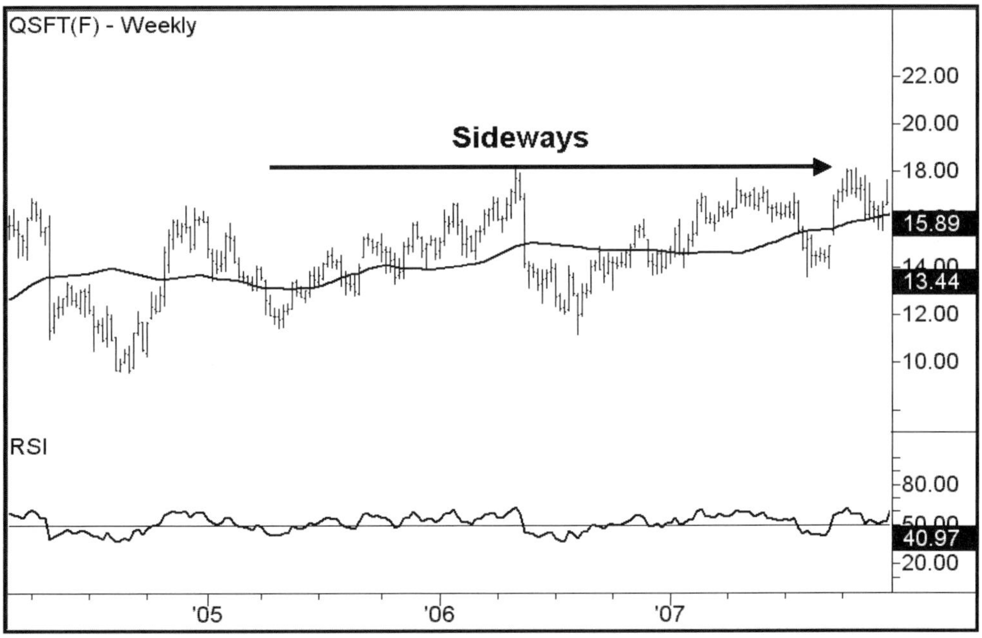

Figure 6.8 *Quest Software (QSFT) is in a sideways trend. The 50 MA is wavy and moving sideways overall.* (Chart: TradeStation)

In theory, fundamental and technical analysis are separate approaches. Many investors tend to gravitate to one method or the other based on what makes the most sense to them. People with a finance background might be drawn to fundamentals. Investors with visual skills tend to prefer charts. The successful investor is not stuck in one way of thinking, but uses both methods to find the best profit opportunities. For best results, one method should confirm the other. For instance, a stock in a technical uptrend should receive stronger consideration when the company has a fundamental "report card" with straight As.

Technical analysis is an extremely powerful tool for determining whether or not to buy a stock. With a quick glance at a stock chart, the successful investor can quickly tell whether or not a stock is a buy. This puts the small investor on an even level with so-called "experts."

THE BIGS

The big money in the stock market comes from **institutional** investors with large pools of assets valued at billions of dollars. Institutional investors are large banks, insurance companies, pension funds, mutual funds, and endowment funds. I call these "**B**ig **I**nstitutional **G**uns" the **BIGs**.

The small investor goes to the market and buys a few hundred shares of stock; BIGs may buy tens of thousands of shares at a time. As a result, the BIGs push stock prices up when they buy and drive prices down when they sell. The BIGs have many advantages over the small investor. The BIGs are highly sophisticated and knowledgeable about the investment world and have greater access to inside information about companies. The BIGs hire a staff of financial whizzes who work full-time to make investment decisions. They have better contacts and better methods of executing trades.

The BIGs represent Wall Street. Don't subscribe to the myth that you can beat Wall Street at their game. It sounds triumphant, but it's nonsense. The BIGs are the primary force that drives stock prices. Your job is to recognize when the BIGs are actively buying stock shares, and then to buy along with them. I tell investors, "Your stock ain't flyin' if the BIGs ain't buyin'."

You will never outsmart the BIGs, and you should never go against them. When several of the BIGs decide to sell a stock at the same time, the price can drop precipitously. It doesn't always mean the stock is no longer a good investment. The BIGs periodically adjust their portfolios by increasing or decreasing the percentage of certain stocks they own.

No matter what you might hear on TV ads about how the small investor can use his computer to become master of his domain, the truth is the BIGs rule the market. You will always be at a disadvantage. The BIGs move the market—not news hype, analyst's predictions, or economic reports.

ENERGY EFFICIENT VEHICLES

Wealth is created by the accumulation of **assets** which grow in value. An asset is an item having value that can be owned and exchanged for something else of value. Building wealth is a process whereby the investor chooses different types of assets, or investment vehicles, with the expectation that they will grow in value or produce income. Stocks are commonly chosen as investment vehicles because they are time efficient and don't require much energy to manage after they are purchased.

There are two major types of assets—**securities** and property. Securities are investment vehicles that represent ownership or debt. For example, s**tock** shares are units of ownership in a company and **bonds** are a debt obligation which must be paid back to the owner, or holder, of the bond. Property is another type of asset which can be bought and sold for investment purposes. Examples of property are real estate, gold, art, antiques, and other collectibles.

The successful investor may use several types of investment vehicles to meet his financial goals. The total collection of an investor's assets is referred to as a **portfolio**. Realize that your stock investments are only one part of your total portfolio. How to divide your money into various assets will be discussed later.

UNDERVALUED

Investors sometimes tell me they don't have a portfolio. I tell them they have the wrong mindset. Your portfolio is whatever you invest in, whether it is a car, DVD, cell phone, or a leather jacket. If you buy assets that decrease your wealth, they are still part of your portfolio.

How you spend your money tells you what you value. There is always a balance between spending money to enjoy life now and investing money to enjoy life later. Each individual decides what is best for him or her. The main thing is to have a plan.

Investing is a measure of how we value our time and effort. Some people undervalue the hard work it takes to earn money. By investing, our hard work continues to pay off. Money can work harder than we can, because it works twenty-four hours a day and doesn't take any vacations. If we invest well, we get to take many vacations.

ΔΔΔ

Before you invest in stocks,
invest in yourself.

7 Stocks

The company selling stock is trading stock to get cash to grow the business. The investor is trading cash for stock, giving him an opportunity to share in a portion of company profits. The U.S. stock market has over 10,000 stocks from which investors can choose. Stocks are classified into different groups so investors can more easily target the type of stocks that meets their investment plan. The two main types are **growth stocks** and **income stocks**.

Choose the type of stocks you want to serve your purpose. To build wealth, look for growth stocks. If you want regular income, look for income stocks. You can also buy a combination of growth and income stocks. Another option is to buy a mutual fund or ETF comprised of the type of stocks you want. Mutual funds and ETFs are usually classified and named for the type of stocks they own. For instance, a *growth fund* will have mostly growth stocks. An *income fund* will have income stocks. A *balanced* fund will have a mixture of growth and income stocks.

For big profits, use the 50-50 Strategy to invest in growth stocks. Growth stocks can easily earn 20-40% per year, and some will provide returns in excess of 100% over one or more years. Most of the growth stocks are small companies which have yet to reach their full potential; they create profit opportunities for the small investor. To build wealth, only buy stocks in uptrends, those with the potential to continue rising in price. If your stocks do not trend up, neither will your account balance.

EVOLUTION OF A COMPANY

Most individuals who decide to start a small business don't have enough money to finance all the startup expenses: office lease, equipment, salaries. They usually go to a bank and take out a business loan to cover expenses until they are profitable. Each business member of the corporation owns private shares of the company stock. Other individuals cannot invest in the company except by invitation.

If the business grows to considerable size, it may expand its offices (or franchises) as well as its product and service lines. However, expansions are costly. Now the company needs to raise money in much larger amounts. One alternative is to offer shares of stock to the public through an **Initial Public Offering (IPO)**. The company, with the help of investment bankers, gets the stock listed on one of the stock exchanges and stock shares are sold to the public.

I generally do not recommend investing in IPOs. Buying IPO stocks is like hiring an employee right out of college—they have no work history. IPO stocks have no track record in the stock market and are generally not owned by the BIGS until they can establish an earnings record. It may take several years for a company to establish enough public awareness and product demand to achieve strong earnings growth.

IPO stocks will often show a rapid rise in price after their initial release to the public; this can be a trap. If the media hypes the stock, it attracts public interest regardless of the company's earnings record. What isn't known is that shares of stock are getting ready to be dumped on the unsuspecting public. The investment bank which launched the company wants to sell its stock shares and take profit. Consequently, new issue stocks can fall dramatically in price, and many fail to recover for several years, if at all.

Figure 7.1 is an example of an IPO stock released to the public in late 2006 at $19 per share. In less than a year it rose to $34 per share. By June of 2007 it began a sell-off which saw prices decline to $10 a share, a 70% loss in value.

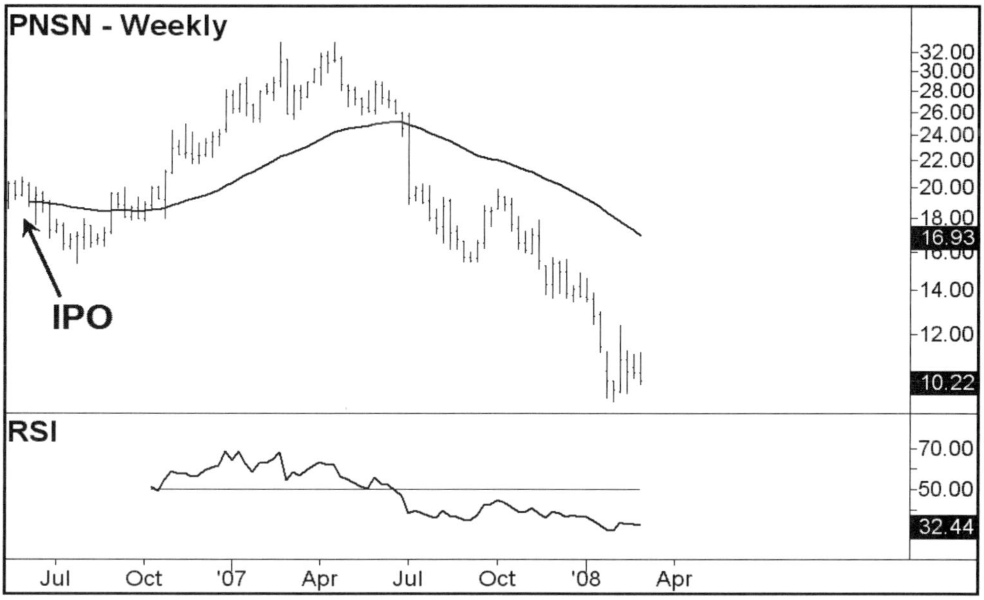

Figure 7.1 *Penson Worldwide (PNSN) was an IPO released in late 2006. It initially rose in price, but then dropped well below the IPO price.*
(Chart: TradeStation)

Figure 7.2 is a chart of a company associated with a name known for great wealth and financial expertise. However, Trump (TRMP) was just another poorly performing IPO after it was released in late 2005.

CLASSIFIED INFORMATION

Stocks can be classified in a few different ways. For example, stocks may be classified according to the *type of return* they produce: income, growth, and value. When classified according to *company size* the types are small-cap (capitalization), mid-cap, and large-cap stocks. Classifying stocks makes them more manageable for investors, especially when constructing a balanced portfolio.

Growth stocks are less likely to pay a dividend (income) because they reinvest their profits in company growth. Income stocks pay a dividend and provide a source of regular income. However, stocks don't know they've been classified, so the type of stock is not as important as whether or not there is an opportunity to profit. Some income stocks can have growth spurts and some growth stocks pay a dividend.

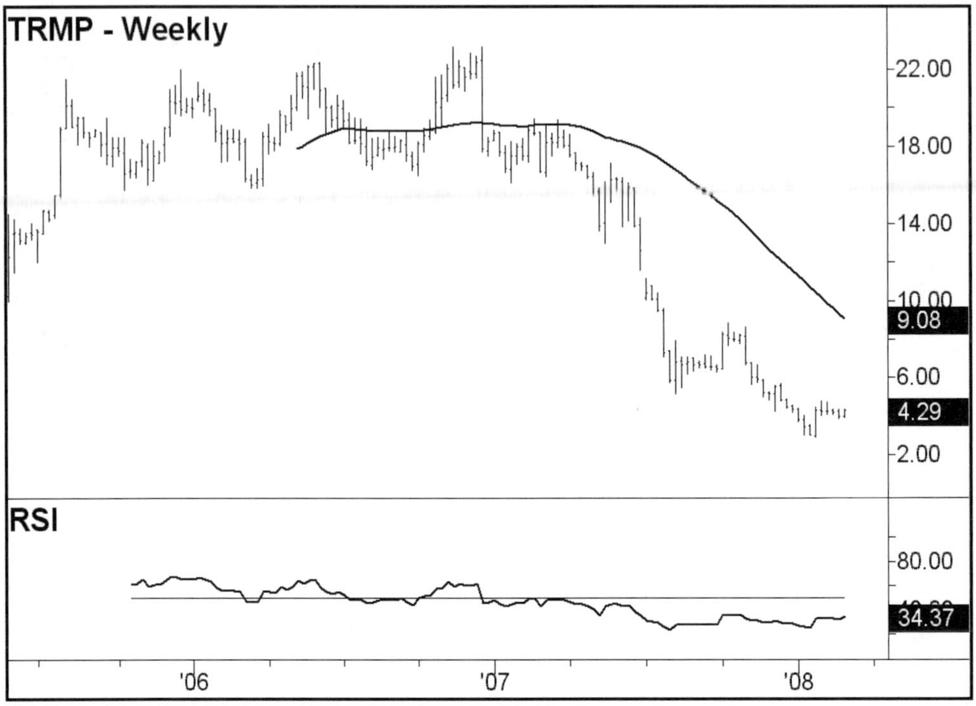

Figure 7.2 *The fate of an IPO. Trump Entertainment Resorts (TRMP) was released in 2005 and attracted buyers at $16 to $18 for over a year before falling to $4.* (Chart: TradeStation)

A mutual fund comprised of growth stocks often contains the term "growth" in its name. For example, if you buy the Vanguard Growth Equity Fund (VGEQX), you can expect the majority of the stocks in the fund to be growth stocks (Figure 7.3)

Beginning investors who want a growth investment vehicle can consider mutual funds. Rather than having to choose several stocks, the investor only has to choose one mutual fund. Mutual funds are usually advertised to the public based on their performance, but past returns do not predict future returns. Make sure any mutual fund you buy meets the 50-50 Strategy criteria for an uptrend. You'll only make money when price is rising. ETFs are especially good for beginners; they have lower expense fees than a mutual fund and trade just like a stock. Use the 50-50 Strategy to buy ETFs, too. Figure 7.4 shows how an ETF's chart looks the same as a stock chart.

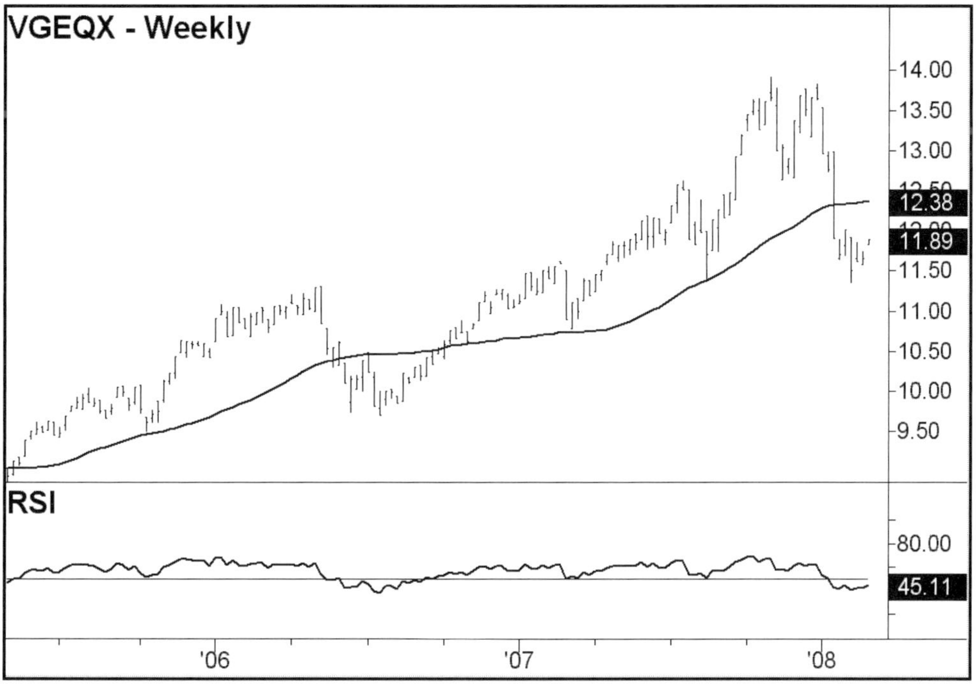

Figure 7.3 *This chart looks just like a stock chart, but it is the Vanguard Growth Equity Fund (VGEQX).* (Chart: TradeStation)

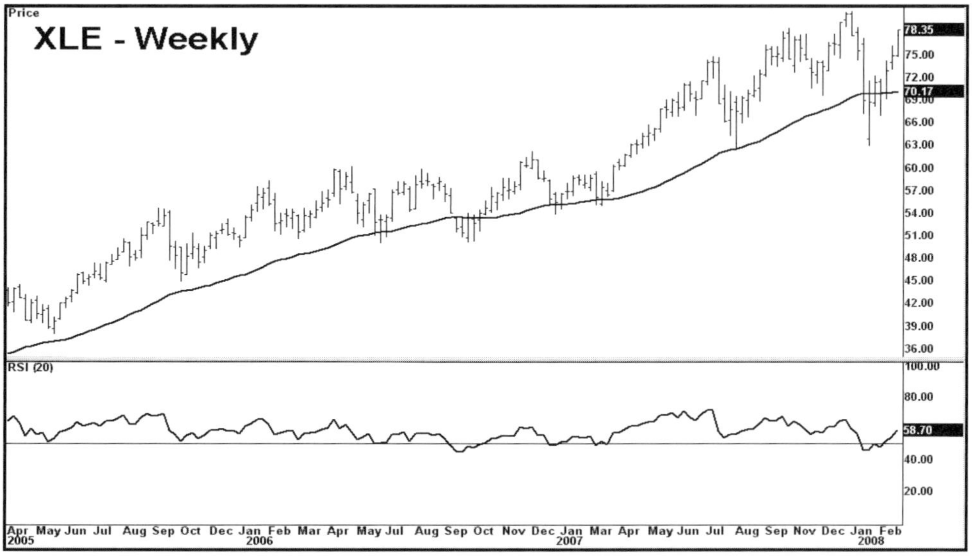

Figure 7.4 *XLE is the Select Sector SPDR Energy ETF. The ETF chart looks just like a stock or mutual fund chart. Use the 50-50 Strategy criteria to buy ETFs. (Chart: TDAmeritrade)*

BEWARE OF BEHEMOTHS

The stocks of **behemoth** companies are generally not good growth stocks. Behemoths are the big companies that everyone has heard of, such as General Electric (GE), Wal-Mart (WM), Exxon Mobil (XOM), and Microsoft (MSFT). They are classified as large-cap stocks. Behemoth's represent only 5% of the stocks in the U.S. market, but they account for about 75% of the total value of the stock market.

In the stock market, bigger is not better. While behemoths are well-known, they generally do not make good investments if you are looking for big profits from growth. Behemoth stocks are older, well-established companies that have already gone through their main growth cycle. At one time, they were small start-up companies, providing opportunities to build wealth. Now, those opportunities have been lost.

These big companies are fat and happy. The crowd flocks to behemoth stocks because there is a comfort level with them; they are in our psyche. Who doesn't shop at Wal-Mart or own a Microsoft product? While these big companies dominate the market and are unlikely to go out of business any time soon, the successful investor should look for stocks that are *thin and hungry* for growth.

Most behemoths rise in price when the economy does well, but they drop in price when the economy does poorly. They seldom have periods of rapid growth. Figure 7.5 is a chart of Wal-Mart, showing its lackluster performance during a period when the stock market rose over 70% percent. Wal-Mart is the largest retailer in the world with annual sales which exceed the second, third, and fourth largest retailers combined. One might think this stock should perform well, but when investing, we shouldn't think. Follow price.

GROW ME THE MONEY!

The stocks of small companies (small-caps) have the greatest potential for growth and historically produce the highest returns. They provide many opportunities for the small investor to build wealth using the 50-50 Strategy. Some of these stocks have the potential to double or triple in value. Illumina (ILMN) is typical of a small company which went through a period of growth from 2005 to 2008 (Figure 7.6).

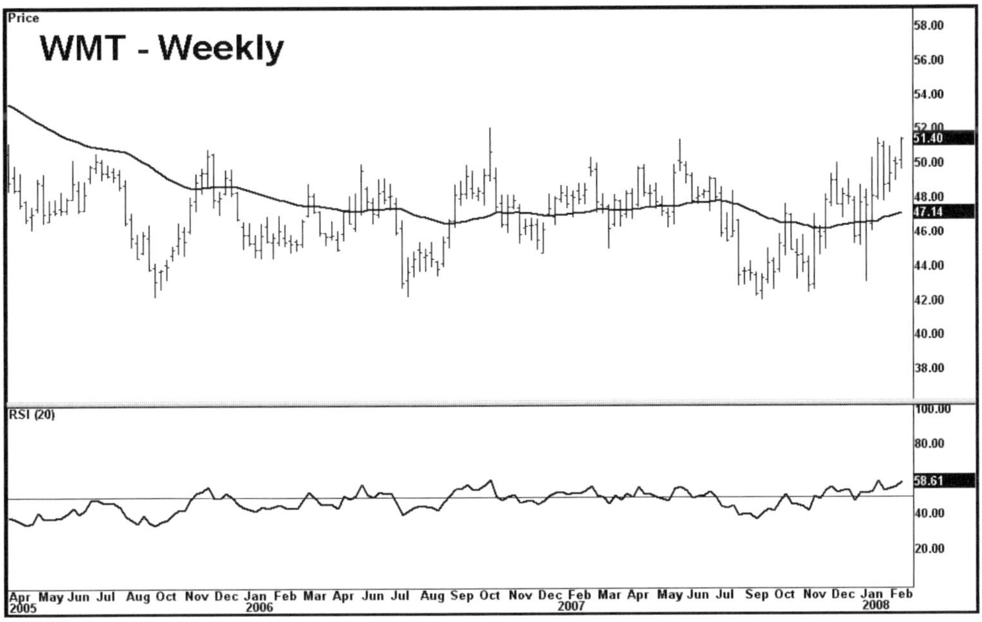

Figure 7.5 *Wal-Mart remained in a $42 to $52 range for four years during a strong bull market from 2003-2007. This is a sideways trend.* (Chart: TDAmeritrade)

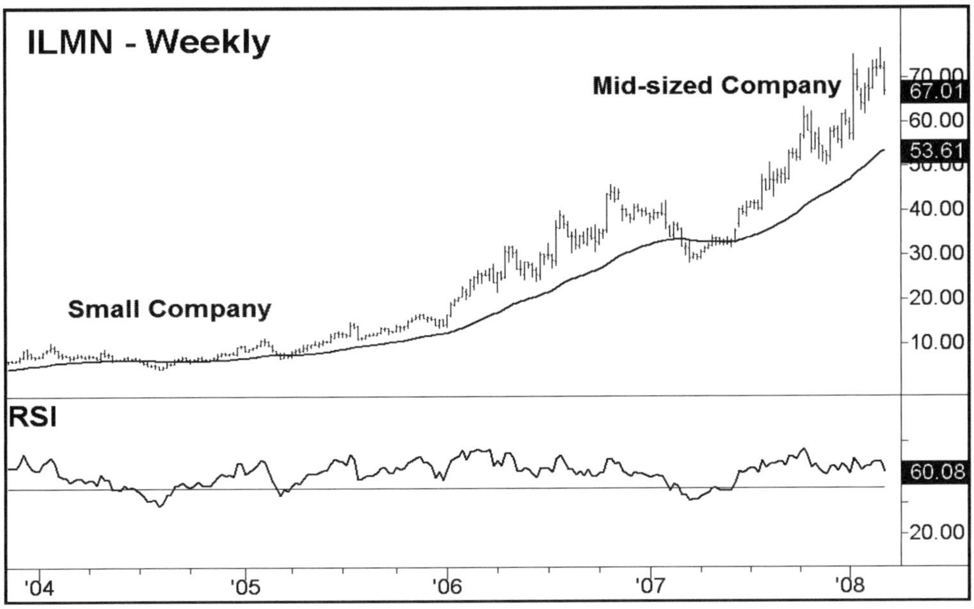

Figure 7.6 Illumina (ILMN) is a small-cap stock that rose from $10 to $70 in three years, a 600% gain! Those are big profits! (Chart: TradeStation)

There is big upside potential for small companies early in their growth cycle. You only need a couple of big winners to give your portfolio some sizzling returns.

You might not have heard the names of many small stocks, so they probably won't have the same comfort level as a well-known behemoth stock.

At one presentation I did for a group of investors, I put up charts on the projector screen and asked the audience, "Would you buy or sell?" I went through several small stocks which had performed well.

After viewing a few stocks, a man from the audience shouted out, "You're showing us stocks we've never heard of before. How do you expect us to decide?"

He missed the point of the exercise which was purely technical. Stock names don't matter, but stock prices do. Don't ignore a profit opportunity because you've never heard of the stock.

GROWING OPPORTUNITIES

Growth stocks are usually newer, smaller companies that are increasing their presence in the American economy. The term "growth stock" means the stock is growing in value faster than the majority of stocks in the economy. They have new products or services that are entering the marketplace and experiencing increased demand.

Growth stocks have a rapid growth in revenues and earnings. A classic growth company was Starbucks (SBUX) during the 1990s. If you are older, you probably remember when the first Starbucks came to your city; now it seems like there's a Starbucks on every corner. If you had bought Starbucks in 1995, you would have amassed considerable wealth from the rise in value.

Growth stocks have a rising 50 MA which signifies an uptrend. Starbucks was an example of a growth stock which began rising in 2003 when the bull market of 2003-2007 was just underway (Figure 7.7). The stock market grew over 50% from 2003-2006, but Starbucks grew faster, rising over 170% during the same period.

To grow wealth over time, a major portion of your investment capital should be in growth stocks. Growth stocks are bought with the expectation they will increase significantly in value. Small investors can make big profits in growth stocks by buying them early in their growth cycle and selling them at a much higher price.

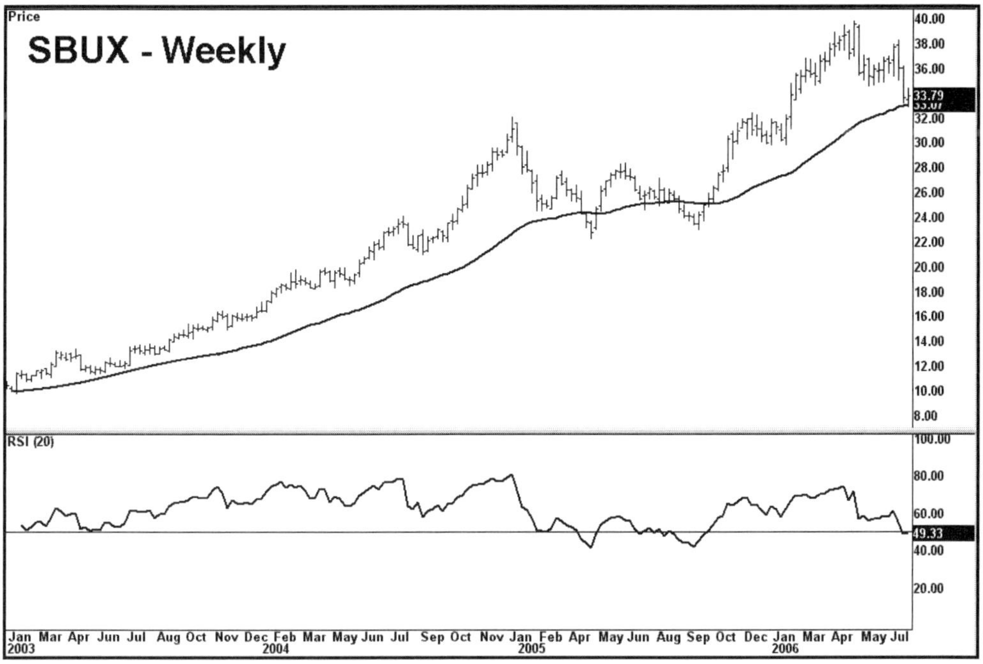

Figure 7.7 *Growth stocks outperform the market. Starbucks (SBUX) began an uptrend in 2003 and grew over 170% by 2006.* (Chart: TDAmeritrade)

Do not expect growth stocks to pay dividends. These companies are expanding, and the earnings are put back into the company to finance more product lines and business locations.

STEADY WORKERS

Income stocks pay a dividend but are less likely to be growth stocks. They are a good choice for the investor who needs income or has a low risk tolerance. Income stocks are generally considered lower risk than growth stocks. However, I consider any stock a high risk when a **stop-loss** is not used to prevent a big loss.

Income stocks are associated with well-established, older companies; investors own them mainly for the stable income they produce. The company makes money and distributes a portion of the profits (after expenses) to its shareholders in the form of a **dividend**. Even if the stock price falls, the investor is still being paid to own the stock.

Income stocks are not expected to rise dramatically in price. In contrast, they are steady workers for your portfolio, bringing in a regular quarterly paycheck. Income stocks tend to rise and fall with the economic conditions. The 50-50 Strategy is still used to buy income stocks in an uptrend. If you buy a stock that rises in price, *and* it pays a dividend, you get paid twice (Figure 7.8)!

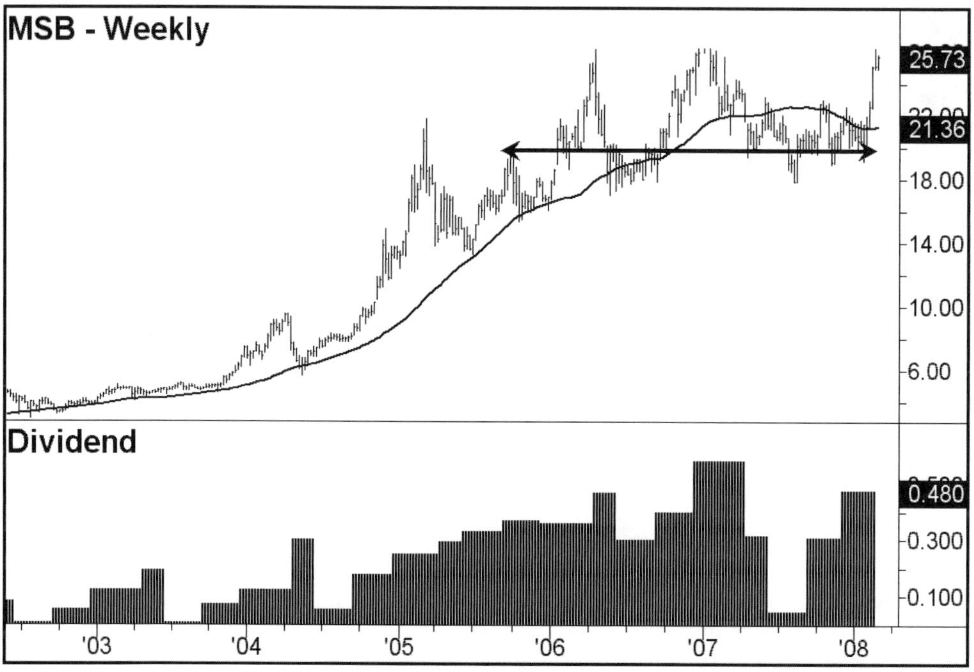

Figure 7.8 *Mesabi Trust (MSB) paid an 8% dividend and had a growth phase from 2004-2006, rising over 200%.* (Chart: TradeStation)

MSB (Figure 7.8) moved sideways (area of double arrow) following the growth spurt from 2004-2006. (Note: In the lower window of the chart, the RSI indicator has been removed and a dividend indicator is shown.). It is all right to hold a dividend-paying stock in a sideways trend because you are still receiving the dividend income. However, the crowd often makes the mistake of buying an income stock solely for the dividend; they do not consider the stock's trend or the potential risk of the stock falling in price. Buy income stocks in uptrends using the 50-50 Strategy. Do not buy income stocks in a downtrend; you can easily lose money on income stocks if the capital loss from the downtrend is greater than the dividends you receive (Figure 7.9).

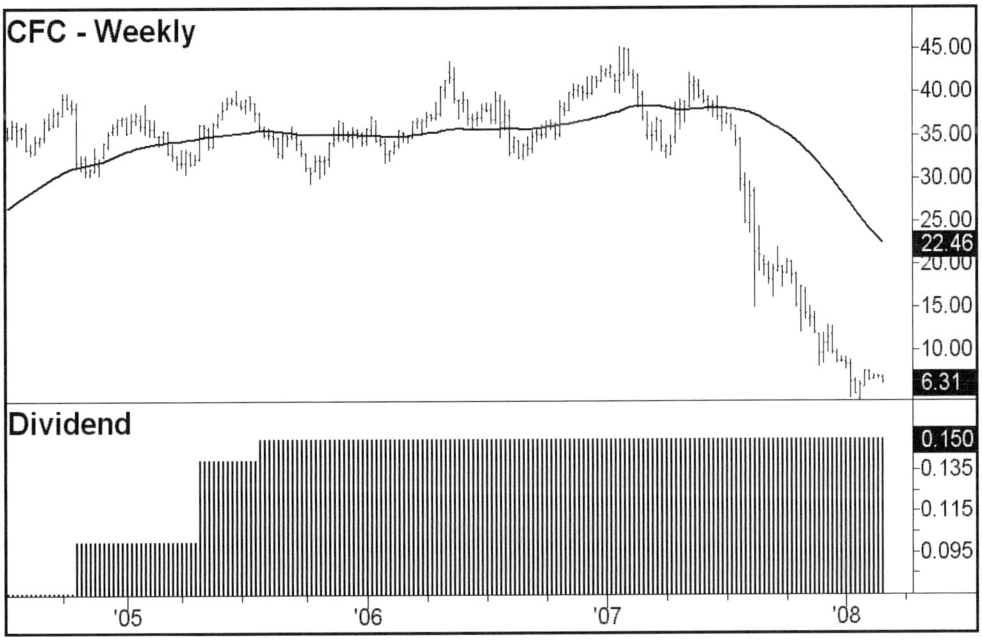

Figure 7.9 *Countrywide Financial (CFC) is an example of an income stock paying about 9%. It had a sideways trend for two years before it entered a steep downtrend resulting in a loss of over 80%.* (Chart: TradeStation)

OVERWEIGHT STOCKS AND SLIM PROFITS

Many of the large brokerage firms put out analyst recommendations, or ratings, on stocks—ignore them all. There is no standardized rating system, and firms make up their own rating terms which are often confusing. They use words such as: overweight, market perform, neutral, and peer perform. I have no idea what these terms mean, and I doubt most small investors do either. Analyst ratings are general opinions and can't be used for timing the purchase of a stock. There are only two rankings you need to understand— buy or sell.

Stock rating firms are often too late in their recommendations. Just before the major market decline that began in 2000, the majority of stocks were still listed as "buys" by many investment firms (Figure 7.10). When the market entered a downtrend, many analysts were still overly optimistic with their stock ratings. Some stocks had dropped over 80% in price, yet they were still recommended as buys.

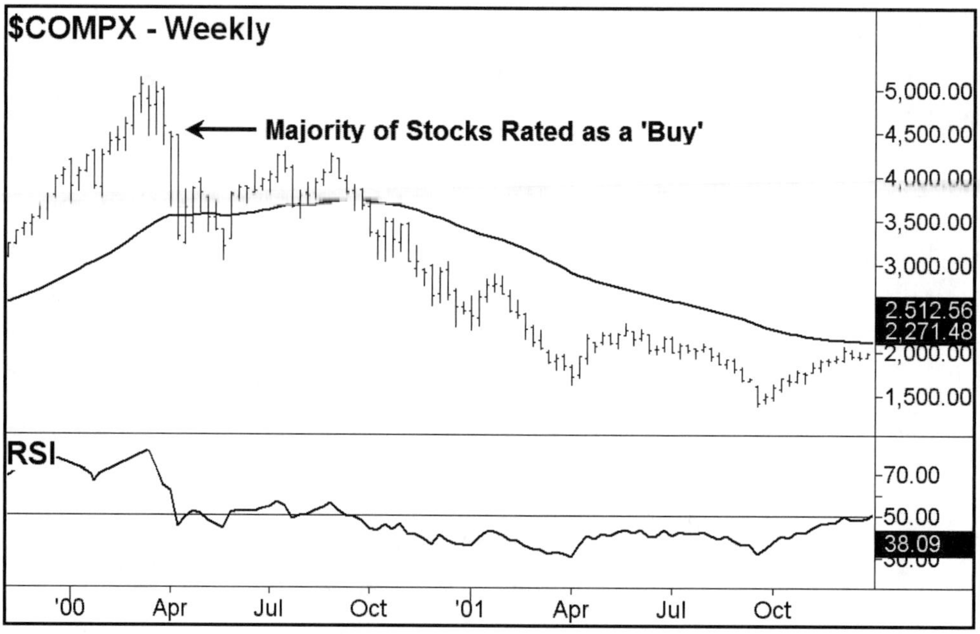

Figure 7.10 *The majority of stocks were still listed as "buys" just before the major market decline of 2000-2002. Only a small fraction of stocks were listed as "sells."* (Chart: TradeStation)

Scandals resulted after buy recommendations were issued on stocks that subsequently went bankrupt. In 1999, a major firm rated Enron as a buy. Over the next 18 months, Enron declined from $80 to $1 and eventually went bankrupt. The scandal resulted in new legislation which reformed corporate accounting practices.

The lesson is simple—stock ratings are unreliable. Never get buy and sell decisions from a rating service; do your own analysis. There are too many conflicts of interest. It's not surprising the **Securities and Exchange Commission (SEC)** enacted rules for fair disclosure, requiring all company information be released to the public rather than diverted privately to analysts. Still, the average investor is, and always will be, at a disadvantage with company information.

Wall Street is biased; their business is to get people to buy stocks, not sell them. When a big brokerage firm owns too much of a certain stock, they have to sell shares. They may do this by recommending it as a buy to their customers, so the unsuspecting public will take it off their hands. Don't let it be you. Always do your own research and make your own decisions about which stocks to buy.

BUY OPPORTUNITIES, NOT HYPE

Build wealth by finding opportunities to profit. It doesn't matter whether or not you like the company, own its products, or use its services. What you think about the company doesn't matter. There are no good and bad companies, just good and bad opportunities to profit.

You may remember the Krispy Kreme Doughnuts (KKD) craze of 2001. People stood in long lines at locations around the country just to buy doughnuts. The media hyped the situation by making the huge doughnut demand a news story. Some investors bought the stock as fast as they bought the doughnuts. The stock reached a high of $48 by 2003. In 2004, the stock started a downtrend and dropped to $5 by 2005. The doughnut they served in 2003 was the same doughnut they served in 2005, but look at the stock price (Figure 7.11). Krispy Kreme's dough may have been rising, but the stock's price sure wasn't!

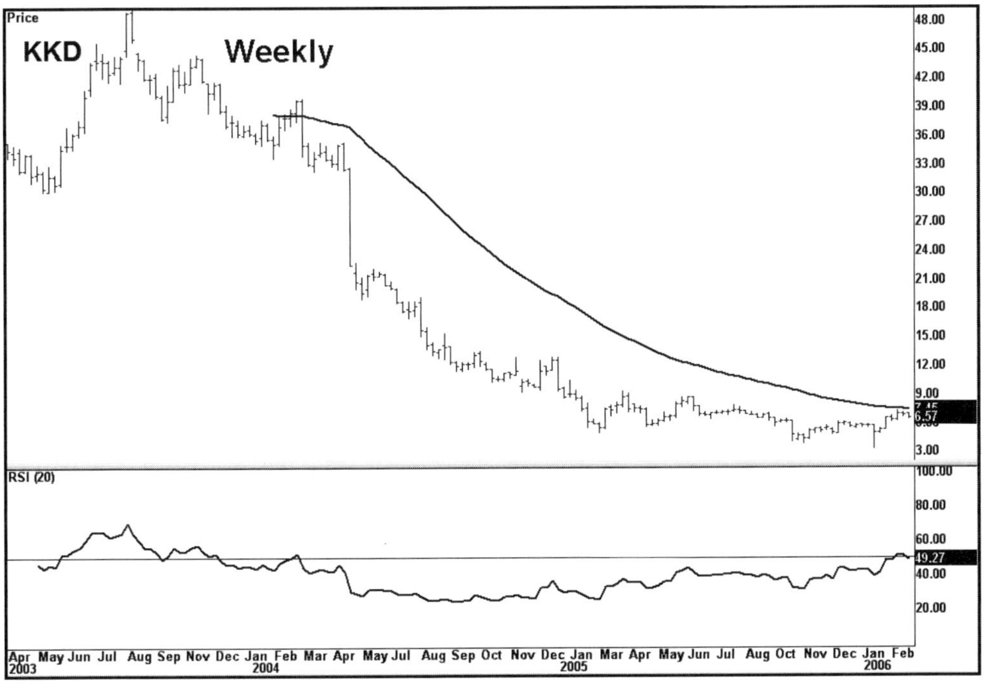

Figure 7.11 *Krispy Kreme (KKD) doughnuts did not change between 2003 and 2005, but the stock price may have left an unpleasant taste in the mouth of investors.* (Chart: TDAmeritrade)

Don't buy a stock just because you like the product or get the bright idea that the company just *has* to be a good buy. This is how the crowd likes to think, as if what they think matters. The market is what determines the price of a stock, not how good the doughnuts taste, or how many people want to stand in line to pay for them.

Products are not stocks, and stocks are not products. No matter how great a product is perceived to be, money is made by trading price and price alone. There is often no rational explanation as to why some stocks go up and others don't. At times, you will see highly-rated stocks plummet and poorly-rated stocks skyrocket— it won't make sense. That's why you shouldn't try to make sense of the market. You should only care about finding profit opportunities and managing your risk.

POOL PARTY

Many **mutual funds** and **exchange traded funds (ETFs)** are comprised of stocks. Mutual funds are a common type of investment, and at least half of all American households own them. Mutual funds are financial companies that pool money from a large number of investors, and then invest that money in a variety of stocks and other assets to create a single fund. Small investors can buy shares of a mutual fund rather than investing in individual stocks. While the small investor has little effect on the price of stocks, the pooled money from millions of investors has a major effect.

Mutual funds have two main benefits. First, they are managed by investment professionals who make the stock selections for the fund. This is a benefit for the individual who lacks investment experience or knowledge. Second, mutual funds are lower risk investments because they are collections of stocks; owning many stocks reduces the risk that one poorly performing stock will negatively affect the overall returns of a portfolio.

Exchange traded funds (ETFs) are the latest type of fund to make a big splash in the stock market. They are different than mutual funds because they are not pooled assets. ETFs are composed of a fixed composition of stocks, so it's more like taking a pool of assets and packaging them in small units (shares) for sale to the public. ETFs are lower risk than buying individual stocks. Investors can set a stop-loss order on ETFs, something you can't do with mutual funds.

Both ETFs and mutual funds make good long-term investments. While both can provide decent returns, they are unlikely to produce the big profits which can be realized by investing in individual stocks. Because ETFs are less risky, they are good choices for the beginning investor until he has enough practice with buying individual stocks. Mutual funds and ETFs will be covered in more detail in Part Three, Chapter 19.

LIKE A BOX OF CHOCOLATES

The stock market has thousands of stocks, and it's sometimes hard to see the "Forrest" for the trees. If you wanted to know how the overall drug industry was performing, you would have to study the performance of about 80 drug companies. That's way too much work! So market **indices** were invented as a way to gauge a large portion of stocks in the market. An index is a collection of related stocks, much like a sample box of chocolates. When you go into a candy store like Ethel M Chocolates in Las Vegas, you may want to buy one of each type of chocolate candy they make, but that's a lot of chocolate. The store provides a sampler box containing a representative sample of all their chocolates.

A stock index can include the entire collection of stocks or it can be composed of a representative sample of the collection. For example, the NYSE Composite is an index of all of the stocks that trade on the **New York Stock Exchange (NYSE)**; there are about 2,000 stocks in the index. Many ETFs are based on market indices. The iShares NYSE Composite Index Fund is an ETF based on the NYSE Composite.

An index can also be a representative sample of stocks. The NASDAQ Composite index contains over 3,000 stocks which trade on the NASDAQ. The NASDAQ-100 is a representative sample of the NASDAQ Composite and contains only 100 stocks. The ETF which tracks the NASDAQ-100 is the QQQQ ("Cubes") ETF which was created by Powershares (www.powershares.com). Powershares is an ETF company that offers over 100 other ETFs.

Investing in stocks is like a box of chocolates. You never know what return you're going to get until you look inside your account statement.

TAKE STOCK IN YOURSELF

Before you invest in stocks, invest in yourself. Get the knowledge you need to be successful. Learn how to recognize uptrends and to find stocks with profit opportunities. Avoid being "personally" invested in your stock positions. Don't rely on tips, hype, or other opinions. Do your own research instead.

Buy stocks for long-term accumulation of wealth. Growth stocks are best for building wealth because they are more likely to experience a major rise in price. Buy income stocks if you need dividends to provide a regular source of income. It may be reasonable for investors to buy both income stocks and growth stocks to meet their financial goals.

Ignore ratings and the opinions of experts. You will become a successful investor once you learn to rely on your eyes and brain to show you the way on your journey to success.

ΔΔΔ

The tool most underused by investors is their eyes.

8 THE CHART

Stock **charts** are the basic tool of technical analysis; they are a graphical representation of price movement over time. The main use of charts is to identify stocks trending up and to provide objective signals for timing a stock purchase. Chart reading is the same for stocks, mutual funds, and ETFs. Whenever you look at a chart, the first thing to study is the price trend.

One of the important principles of technical analysis is that a trend is more likely to continue than reverse. If a stock is trending up, there is reason to expect it to continue rising in price. If a stock is trending down, the odds favor it continuing to fall in price. This is a simple principle, but some investors ignore its implications. They want to impose their hopes and dreams onto the chart and see things that are not there. The proper mindset for chart reading is one of *objectivity*. The stock is either in an uptrend or it isn't. RSI is above the 50 level or it isn't. There is no room for "what ifs" or "maybes."

As you have already seen, the 50-50 Strategy has specific criteria for entry. Following objective criteria reduces the stress associated with decision making. Some investors want to predict which stock will go up, and they will buy a stock to prove they are right. You do not need to prove yourself—the stock does—and you are not required to predict.

Watch for objective 50-50 Strategy signals to tell you when to buy a stock. Remain as objective and unemotional as possible.

WINDOW TO WIN DOUGH

A chart is a window into which we see the history of a stock's price. The basic unit of a chart is the **price bar**. Each day when the opening bell rings on Wall Street, a stock records an **opening price,** or the first price of the day. Throughout the next six and one-half hours the market is open, price fluctuates up and down due to buying and selling pressure (demand and supply). At the end of the day, the last price recorded is the **closing price.**

A price bar is a vertical line which represents the range of prices for the day (Figure 8.1).

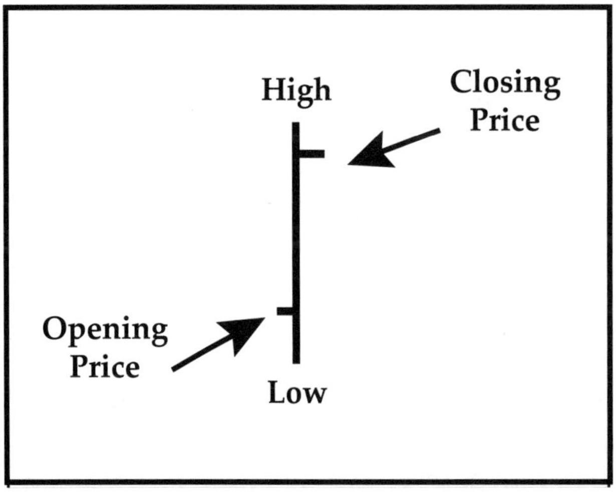

Figure 8.1 *A daily price bar represents the price action for a day. Each bar has four price points—the open, high, low, and close. Only the closing price is used with the 50-50 Strategy.*

The high price for the day is the point where sellers turned back the buyers. The low price for the day is where the buyers turned back the sellers. A small horizontal line on the left of the vertical line is the opening price. Another small horizontal line on the right side of the bar represents the closing price of the day. For our purposes, we are only concerned about the closing price. The closing price represents the final opinion of the market about a stock's value. Figure 8.2 is a daily chart of J. C. Penny Company (JCP) over a two-month period; the open, high, low, and close are marked for one of the price bars.

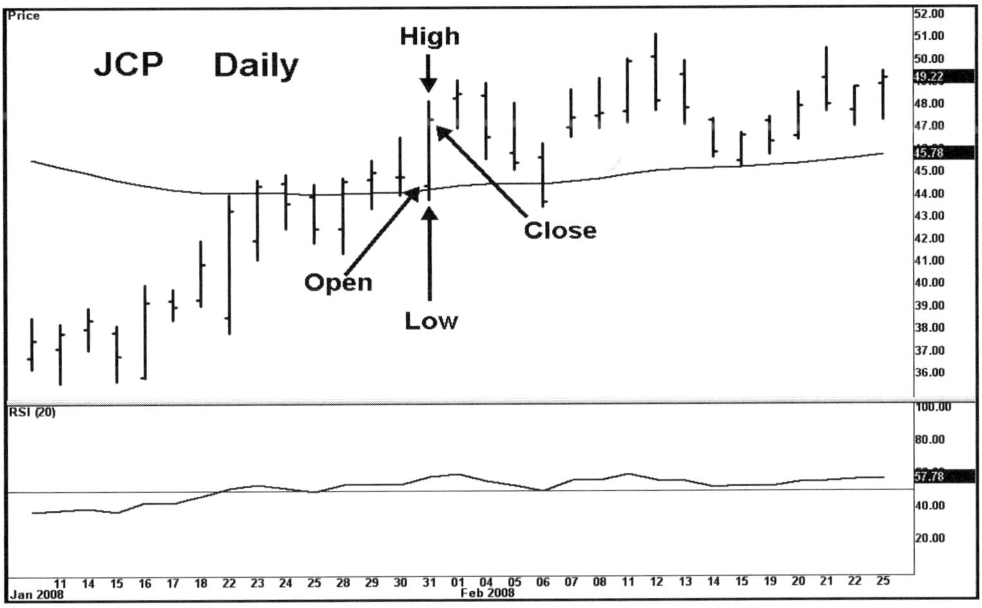

Figure 8.2 *This is a daily chart of JCP over a period of about two months.The open, high, low, and close are shown for one of the price bars.*
(Chart: TDAmeritrade)

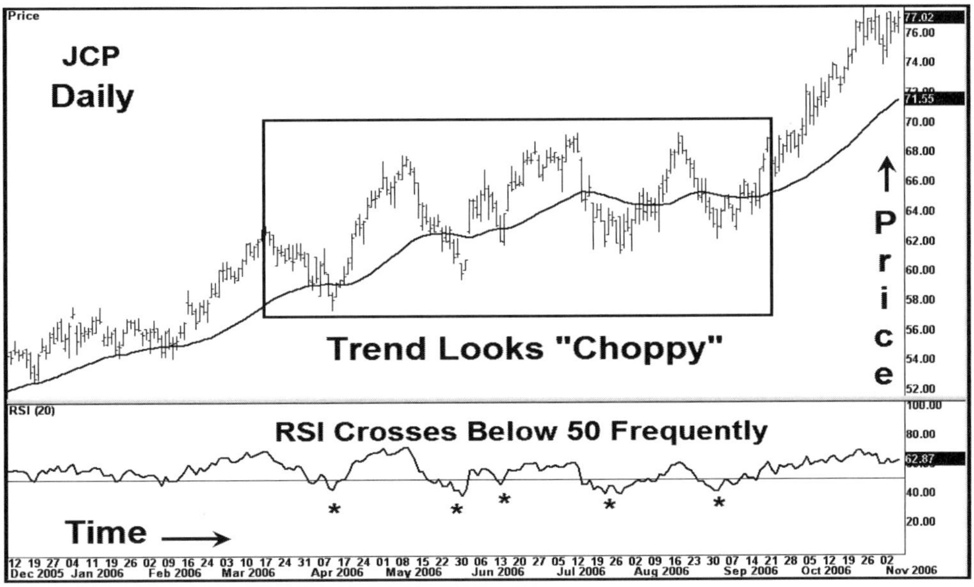

Figure 8.3 *This is a daily chart of J.C. Penny Company showing daily price bars, price on the vertical axis, and time on the horizontal axis. Notice the period of choppy price (rectangle) where there are frequent crosses of RSI below 50.* (Chart: TDAmeritrade)

Charts have a price scale on the vertical axis (right side of the chart) and time is represented by the horizontal axis (the bottom of the chart). Charts can record several months or years of price action. A **daily chart** is composed of daily price bars, where each bar represents one day's price action. Daily charts can sometimes appear "choppy", where price swings widely up and down (Figure 8.3).

One day of price movement is just a small blip. If you try to make sense of daily price fluctuations, you will soon get frustrated. It is analogous to reading one sentence from a paragraph and hoping to understand the whole story. It is better to use a **weekly chart**. A weekly chart has weekly bars, where one price bar represents the entire week's price movement, from the open on Monday to the close on Friday (Figure 8.4).

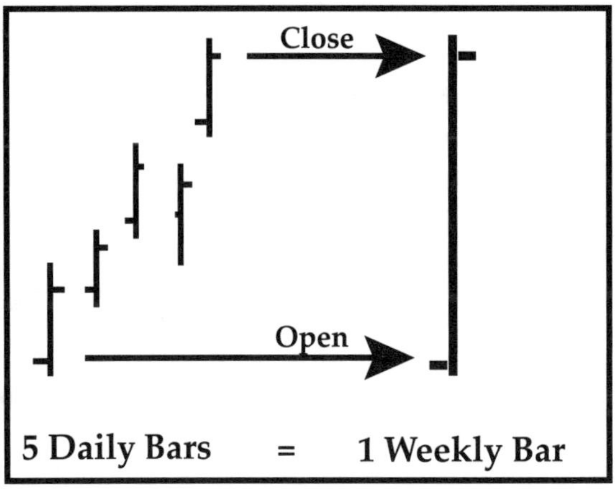

Figure 8.4 Each weekly price bar represents five daily price bars.

The long-term trend is seen more easily on a weekly chart. The price movements usually appear smoother and more consistent. Weekly charts benefit the small investor by giving more reliable signals for buying and selling. Weekly trends last longer than daily trends, so the investor can remain in a weekly trend longer and let more profits accumulate. Figure 8.5 is a weekly chart of J.C. Penny Company (JCP).

The 50-50 Strategy uses weekly charts to find longer-term investments that can trend for several months to a few years, allowing big profits to accumulate. In Figure 8.5, the weekly trend of JCP lasted for three years, and price went from $20 to $80, a 300% gain.

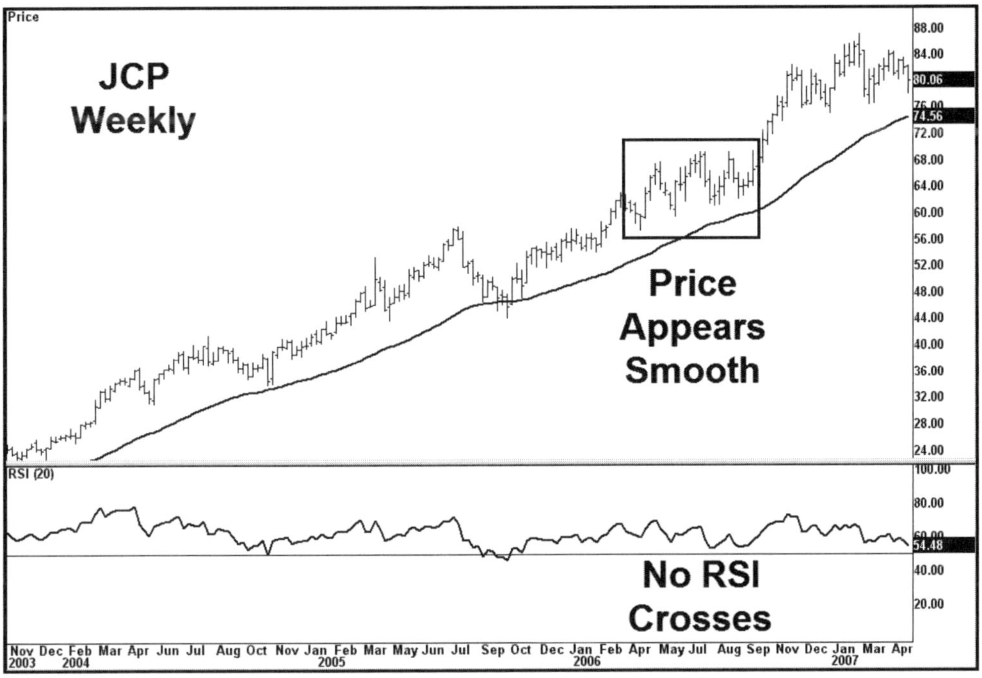

Figure 8.5 *This is a weekly chart of J.C. Penny Company (JCP). Each bar represents a week of price action. The small rectangle corresponds to the rectangular area seen on the daily chart in Figure 8.3. Notice how the price fluctuations on the daily chart appear smoother on the weekly chart, and there were no weekly RSI crosses during the same time period.*
(Chart: TDAmeritrade)

A weekly chart can show about three to five years of price history. The best profit opportunities take time to develop, and the more information you have about a stock, the more confident you will be when it's time to buy. A big reason to use weekly charts is they are the best for seeing the buying activity of the BIGs. Remember, we are not trying to outsmart the market. We simply want to observe when there is strong, sustained buying by the BIGs, and then we can buy and go along for the ride.

I'M READY FOR MY CLOSEUP

Make sure your chart shows a minimum of three years price history; a weekly chart normally shows about three to five years. Most charting programs allow you to adjust the number of years shown on the chart.

When you add more years to a chart, the price bars will get closer together. This is *zooming out,* and makes price look farther away. Zooming out helps you see the big picture of a trend. When you remove years from a chart, the bars get wider apart. This is *zooming in,* like taking a close-up photograph. Zooming in helps you see more detail in a particular area, especially when looking for price crossing the 50 MA or RSI crossing the 50 level.

Figure 8.6 is a chart of Almost Family (AFAM) covering a one year period. Compare it to Figure 8.7 which has three years of price history.

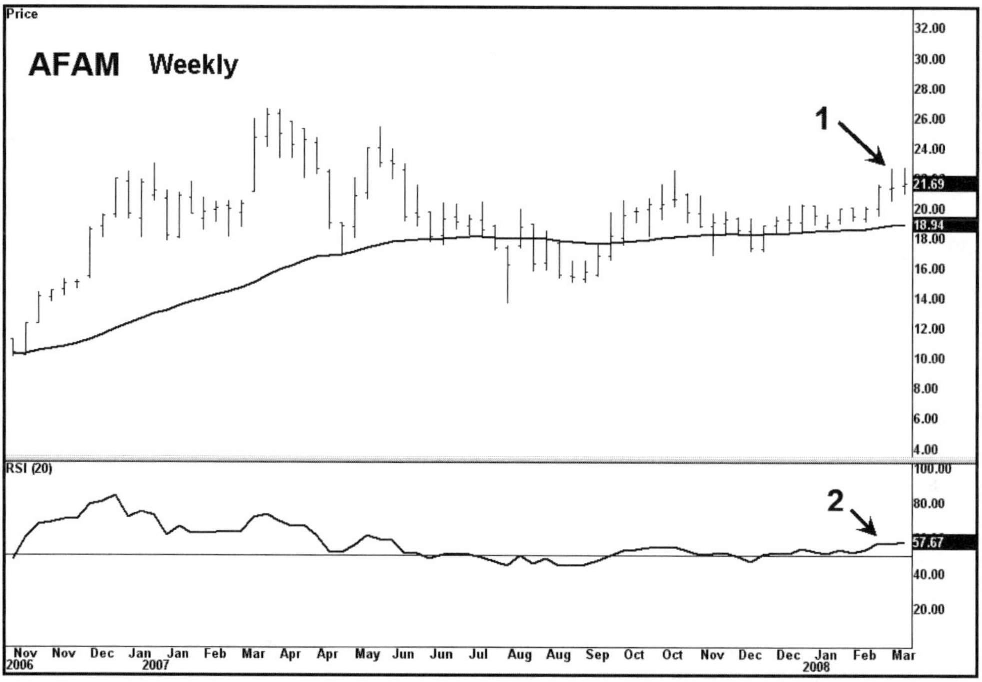

Figure 8.6 *Almost Family (AFAM) shows the two 50-50 Strategy criteria: price above the 50 MA (1) and RSI above the 50 level (2). However, price appears to be moving in a sideways trend rather than an uptrend.*
(Chart: TDAmeritrade)

IT'S NOT MY DEFAULT

A chart indicator helps us read price and is a common tool used in technical analysis. Indicators are a graphical representation of a mathematical formula. They take price data and rearrange it in a way

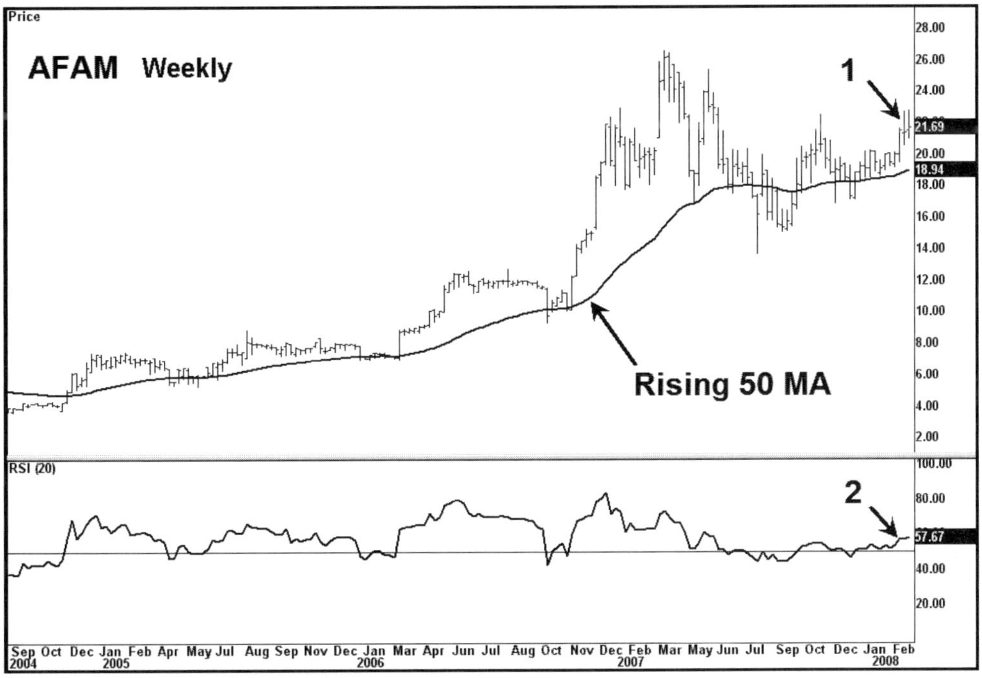

Figure 8.7 *A chart of Almost Family (AFAM) is shown after zooming out to see at least three years of price history. The last year of sideways price is now seen within the larger context. There was a strong two year uptrend, making the stock more likely to continue trending up.* (Chart: TDAmeritrade)

that makes it easier to interpret. As a result, the investor can gain information that is not easily seen by price alone. But make no mistake; price is paramount, and indicators are ancillary information. Price crossing above or below the 50-week moving average is more significant than RSI crossing above or below 50.

Hundreds of indicators have been created; most are redundant, giving the same information in a slightly different way.

Some investors fall into the trap of searching endlessly for the perfect indicator—there isn't one. Indicators indicate; only *you* can make investment decisions. Some investors think *more is better*, so they clutter up their charts with four or five indicators, thinking more indicators give them more information. They do not. In my experience, two different types of indicators are all that are necessary; using more just creates indecision or confusion.

Indicators have **settings**, or parameters, which are used to program the indicator. Most indicators have **default**, or standard, settings. The default settings are usually preprogrammed into the charting program. You will use the same indicator settings for everything you chart, but you may need to initially change settings on your charting program to use the 50-50 Strategy. Some indicators are placed in the same chart window as price, and some are placed in a window below price.

You will only use two indicators for the 50-50 Strategy—the **50-week moving average** and the **Relative Strength Index (RSI)**. The setting for the 50-50 "moving average" is 50. A 50-week moving average is common and may be a default setting on many charting programs. Charting programs may ask you to choose between **simple** or **exponential moving averages**. Chose exponential and don't give it another thought. From this point forward, I will simply refer to the 50-week moving average as the **50 MA.**

The default setting for RSI on most charting programs is 14, but use an RSI setting of 20 instead; it represents a 20-week average of RSI values. It is helpful if the RSI window has a horizontal line at the 50 level to easily see when RSI is above or below 50. Not all charting programs have one, but they should at least give you the value for RSI. From this point forward, I will simply refer to the weekly RSI 20 as **RSI**.

Some websites have a basic chart with fixed parameters for the indicators, as well as an advanced, or interactive, chart which allows you to change indicator settings. If you see this, always choose interactive. The Yahoo Finance website has two choices, and here is how to set up the interactive chart for the 50-50 Strategy:

Setting a Yahoo Finance Interactive Chart with the 50-50 Strategy Indicator Settings

1. Go to the main page of Yahoo Finance (www.finance.yahoo.com) and place your mouse over the *Investing* tab. Find *Stocks* on the pull down menu and click on it.

2. On the next page, find the *Research Tools* (right side) and click on *Historical Quotes*.

3. When the next page comes up, enter the symbol of a stock (top left box), and click on *Get Quotes*.

4. On the next page, in the left column under the category of *Charts*, click on *Interactive*. The next page will show an interactive chart (which means you can interact with it to change the chart settings) (Figure 8.9).

5. At the top of the chart, click on the small arrow to the right of *Technical Indicators*. This brings up a drop down menu. Click on *Relative Strength Index (RSI)*. A window will pop up to show the default setting of 14. Change it to 20 as shown in Figure 8.8. Then click *Draw*.

6. Go back and click on the arrow next to *Technical Indicators*. This time click on *Exponential Moving Average*. A window will pop showing the Line 1 Period which is 50 by default (if not, change it to 50). Click on *Draw*.

7. Go back to the top of the chart and click on the arrow to the right of Chart *Settings*. Run your mouse over *Line Type* and click on *OHLC*.

8. At the bottom of the chart, click on *5Y* to show five years of history.

9. To make the chart larger, click on *Full Screen* at the upper right of the chart. (Note: don't close the chart window; just keep putting in new symbols of stocks you want to study.

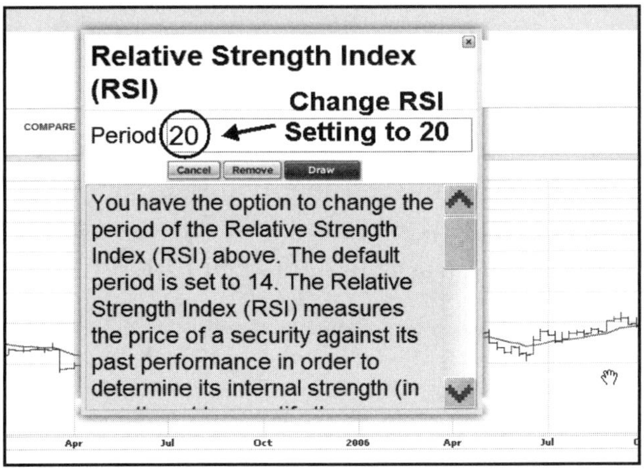

Figure 8.8 *Change the RSI default setting of "14" to "20."* (Source: Yahoo Finance)

Figure 8.9 *An interactive chart showing the 50 MA and RSI 20.* (Chart: Yahoo Finance)

THE DYNAMIC DUO

The 50 MA and RSI 20 are the only two indictors used with the 50-50 Strategy. They are a powerful combination, and each has a specific purpose. The 50 MA is used to read the direction of the trend. Buying a stock near the 50 MA is low risk because the 50 MA represents the average price of the stock. When price falls to the 50 MA, it attracts buyers. The 50 MA is a zone of potential price **support**, an area where buying demand overcomes selling, stopping prices from falling further. As long as the 50 MA is rising, a stock is a potential investment candidate using the 50-50 Strategy criteria. An example of support is seen in Figure 8.10.

You might have noticed that the 50 MA does not travel in a straight line. It curves up and down, and sometimes it moves sideways. When the 50 MA rises and then turns downward, it is called a peak, or **high**. When the 50 MA falls and turns upward, it is called a trough, or **low** (Figure 8.11). Highs and lows become important later when you learn how to tell when conditions are right to apply the 50-50 Strategy criteria (Chapter 9).

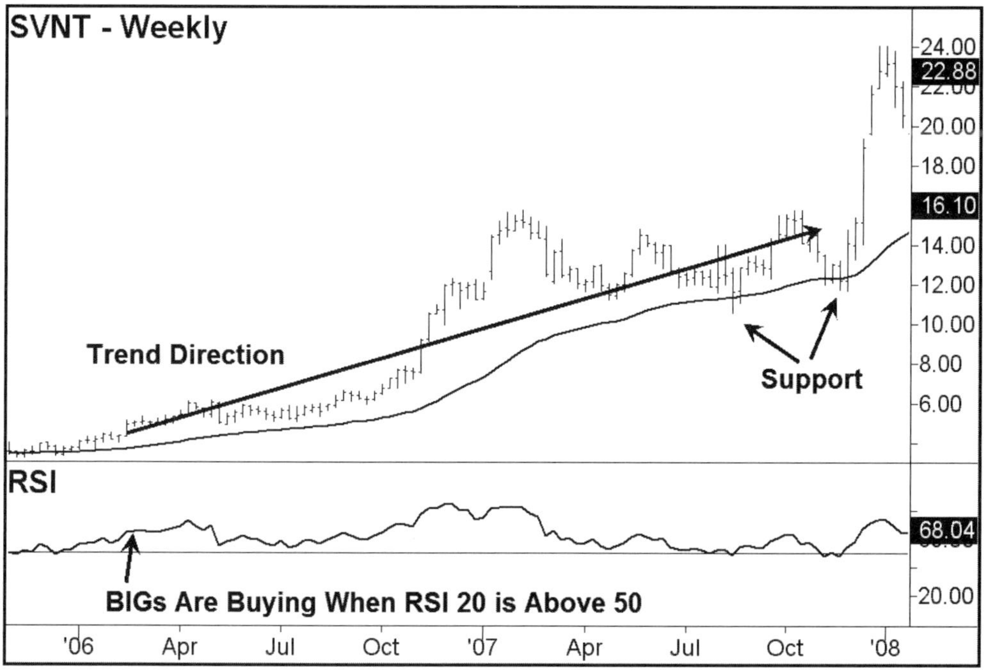

Figure 8.10 *The 50 MA shows the direction of the long-term trend and often provides a zone of support (arrows) for price during a price pullback. The RSI above 50 shows the trend is strong.* (Chart: TradeStation)

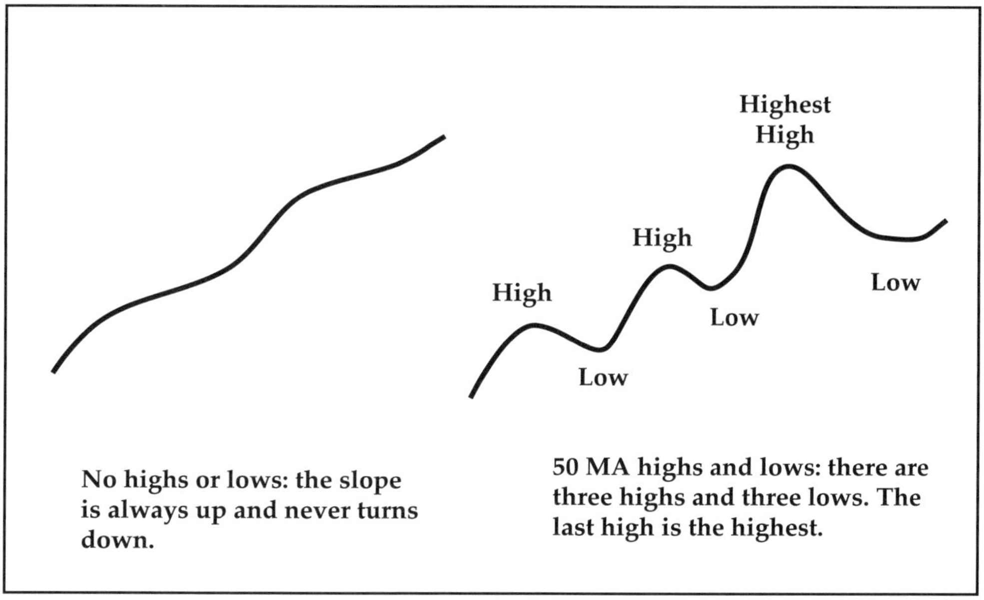

Figure 8.11 *When the 50 MA turns downward it forms a 50 MA high; when it turns upward, it forms a 50 MA low.*

RSI tells us if price is strong (above 50) or weak (below 50). An RSI above 50 means price is strong enough to trend upward. RSI is also used to see active buying and selling by the BIGs (Figure 8.10). When RSI is rising, the BIGs are actively buying; when RSI is falling, the BIGs are not actively buying. Now you know how to spot the BIGs. This information alone helps small investors become profitable.

No indicator is magic. The benefit of any indicator comes from the understanding of how to use it to interpret price. There are hoards of salespeople and software companies who will sell you their secret, proprietary indicator to make you rich. Salespeople love to create complicated indicators, so they have something to sell, and so you can pay them to "uncomplicate" it. If you become dependent on the indicator, then you'll have to subscribe to a service to get it.

The two indicators for the 50-50 Strategy are free and found on virtually all charting programs. They are not magic either. Their power comes from how you learn to apply them effectively with the 50-50 Strategy.

YOUR BEST CHANCES ARE 50-50

Technical analysis uses stock charts to study patterns of price behavior. Reading charts is a huge advantage for investors. Price shows when a stock is trending up. Indicators help us interpret both price and trend. Charts provide visual signals which allow you to be objective about buy and sell decisions.

Some investors don't know what is important on a chart, so they clutter up their charts and minds with fancy indicators which they hope will tell them the secrets of when to buy and sell. It is easier for them to put their faith in a magic indicator than to put faith in themselves. This tendency can only be overcome by a practical knowledge of charts and how to use them with simplicity and efficiency.

ΔΔΔ

Price is the only opinion that matters.

9 TOP PROSPECTS

Is the stock going to go higher or lower? Investors love to make predictions and tell you their opinions. Humans have a need to declare themselves and be recognized. We get thrills from making bets and taking chances. It's not necessarily a bad thing, unless you want to build wealth in the stock market.

It is a myth that winning investors are those who can successfully predict which stocks are going to go up in price. Still, many investors spend their time searching for a method, or paying for a system, to predict which stocks will be winners. Predictions that come true are like magic. Some investors will follow anyone whom they believe has the magic to predict the future. Unfortunately, there are only two forms of magic in the stock market—luck and skill, and luck doesn't last.

We believe in magic because it is the mental path of least resistance. We think if we can just find some magic, we won't have to work hard, use our brain, or develop discipline. It is a paradox of human nature that we will pursue the magic with great effort and determination, believing it is the easy path to success, while making little effort to learn basic methods which are known to work. Some people search endlessly for the Holy Grail, instead of being wholly committed to using a simple plan for profit.

TOP PROSPECTS

To find top prospects for investing, I developed the **TOP SCORE** method of rapid analysis. TOP SCORE combines technical analysis (TOP) and fundamental analysis (SCORE), analyzing eight of the main variables which are often present in stocks that present profit opportunities. This chapter will cover the **TOP** part of the method which uses three technical criteria: **T** stands for Trend, **O** stands for **O**verhead supply, and **P** stands for Price. In Chapter 10, you'll learn how to SCORE.

Trend is the most important of the three TOP variables. Unless the stock, mutual fund, or ETF is in an uptrend, there is no point in looking at anything else. In this chapter, I'll show you how to identify two types of uptrend conditions which tell you to either buy a stock or put it on a watchlist. Overhead supply is a concept the crowd seldom knows about or considers, but it affects the trend. I'll explain why price plays a role in finding stocks that make big profits.

TOP will be part of the **checklist** (Chapter 10) you'll use to find top prospects. Pay attention to this chapter; the principles you learn are a major part of using the 50-50 Strategy to build wealth.

T = TREND

There are only three directions for trends—up, down, and sideways—but different trends can occur on the same chart. It is sometimes hard to tell if the trend of a stock is moving more up than down, or vice versa. This is part of the reason that some investors abandon reading trend, and gravitate toward pinning their hopes on magic chart indicators to make them money. Investors get frustrated and want someone or something else to make decisions for them. Many buy green light-red light systems to give them mechanical buy and sell signals, and then they lose all sense of what price is doing on the chart.

When investors take their eye off the price trend, they lose sight of the most important information on the chart. That would be like a baseball player taking his eye off the ball when he swings at a pitch. He's likely to strike out. The important thing about reading trend is to keep the process simple and don't over think.

To simplify trend analysis, I'll define two types of uptrends. When you see a trend that is *not* one of the two, ignore it, forget it, and don't try to define it. Delete it from consideration—there is no profit opportunity. For the 50-50 Strategy, you only need to identify two types of trends. One is a **50-50 High Riser,** and the other a **50-50 Low Riser** (Figure 9.1).

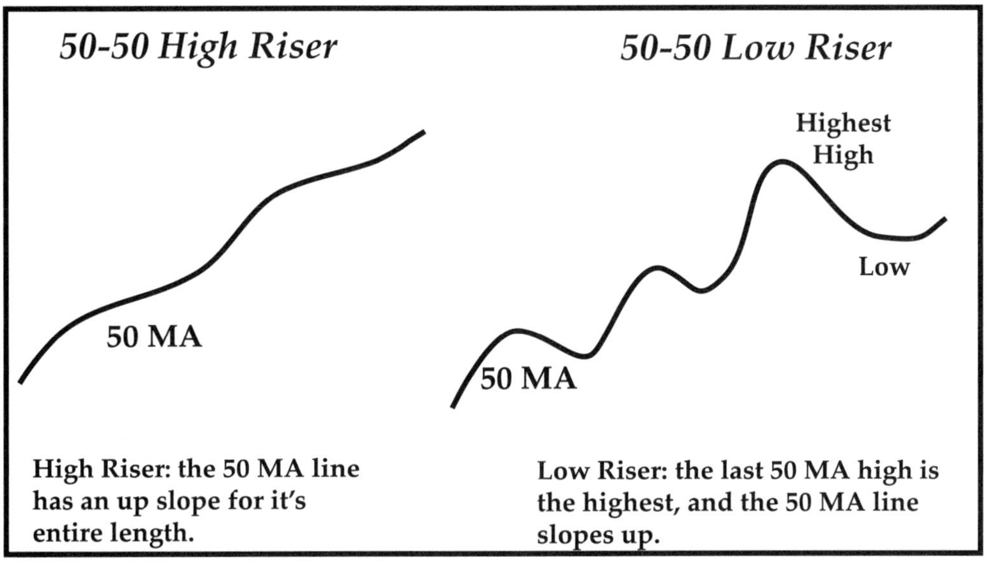

Figure 9.1 *The two uptrends for the 50-50 Strategy are the 50-50 High Riser and the 50-50 Low Riser.*

A **High Riser** is an uptrend where the 50 MA line rises for the entire length of the uptrend; it is the purest form of an uptrend (Figure 9.2). The 50 MA slopes upward from left to right on the chart. Price bars remain above the moving average about 90% or more of the time. They may drop under the 50 MA briefly. The RSI of a High Riser stays above the 50 level most of the time, but it too may drop briefly below the 50 level on price pullbacks. High Risers represent consistent buying by the BIGs without any major selling periods. Investors can buy High Risers at anytime when they meet the 50-50 Strategy criteria. The 50-50 High Riser is, by definition, a "rising 50 MA," so you can buy a High Riser anytime the price bar is above the 50 MA and RSI is above the 50 level.

The entire price bar must be above the 50 MA in order to buy the stock. A bar completely above the 50 MA means the buyers are strong enough to keep the lowest price of the week above the 50 MA. Sometimes, the stock's price closes above the 50 MA, but part of the price bar is below the 50 MA; this is harder to interpret and can cause confusion.

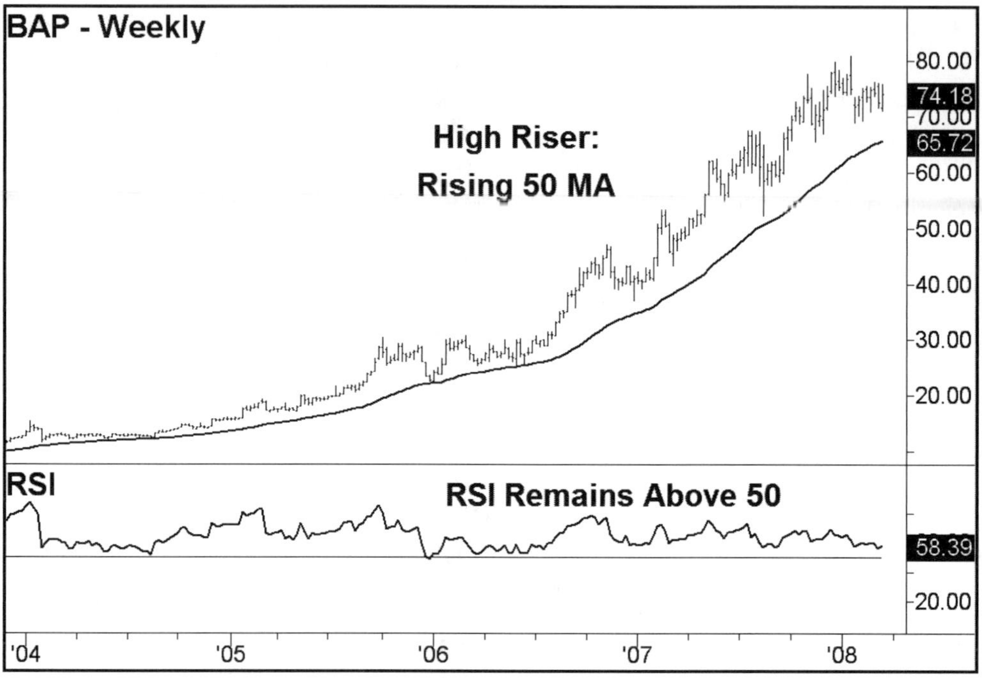

Figure 9.2 *Credicorp (BAP) is a High Riser where price remains above the 50 MA. The 50 MA is rising along the entire length of the trend.*
(Chart: TradeStation)

A **Low Riser** is an uptrend where the 50 MA periodically falls or moves sideways. This creates 50 MA highs and lows (Note: a sideways 50 MA is considered a "flat" low). A **50 MA high** occurs after the line changes its direction from up to down (or sideways). A **50 MA low** forms when a sideways or falling 50 MA line changes direction to up. During the periods when price is falling or moving sideways, price bars cross back and forth over the 50 MA, and RSI crosses above and below the 50 level. The frequent crosses make low risers more difficult to trade and more prone to being stopped out.

In a low riser, the 50 MA turns down, so how do you know the stock's price is not entering a downtrend? The answer is a key to identifying low risers as profit opportunities. The last 50 MA high must be the highest on the chart for the trend to be a Low Riser (Figure 9.1). If the last 50 MA high is lower, then it is a downtrend.

Low Risers represent periods of selling or lack of buying. If buying pressure resumes, the 50 MA turns up again. How can you tell when it turns up? The amount of time varies, but you should be able to tell within three months (12 weekly bars) after price crosses above the 50 MA and remains above it (Figure 9.3). Low risers take time for the 50 MA to turn from down or sideways to up, so there is no rush to enter the trade. It doesn't pay to anticipate when you want to participate in a profit opportunity.

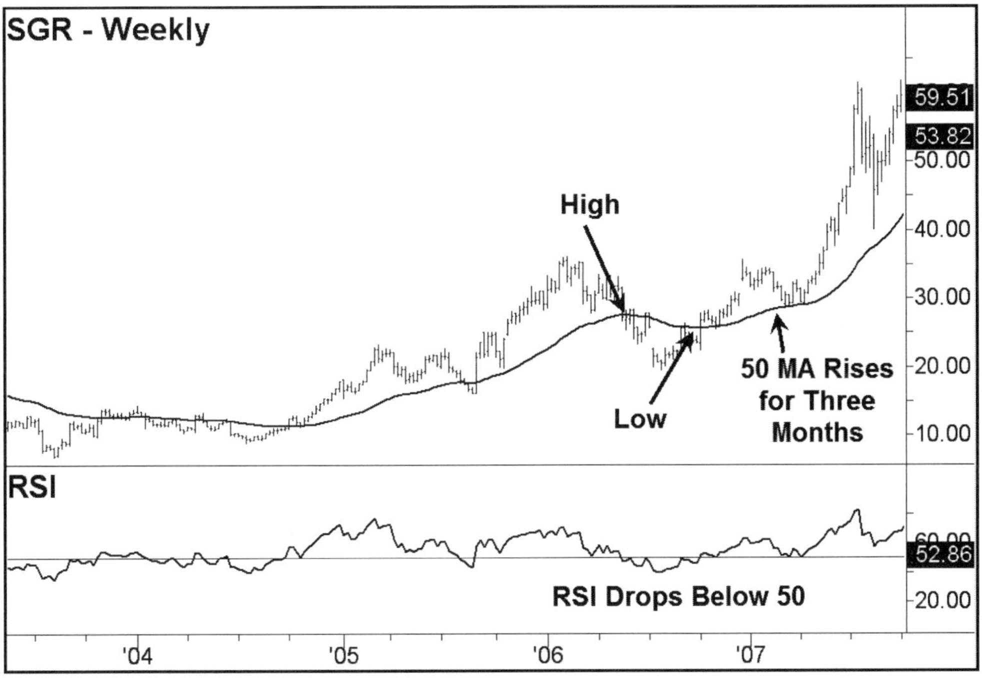

Figure 9.3 *Shaw Group (SGR) is a Low Riser. The last peak in the 50 MA was the highest on the chart. The 50 MA line turned up for three months.* (Chart: TradeStation)

Figure 9.4 is an example of a Low Riser where the 50 MA turned down in 2006; if you called this sideways, it doesn't matter because the result will be the same. In 2006, the last 50 MA was the highest 50 MA high (it was the only one). Price crossed above the 50 MA in late 2006, and RSI crossed above the 50 level. The 50 MA turned up in 2007; this gave an opportunity to buy.

The falling or sideways movement of a Low Riser 50 MA can last a few months to about a year. Be patient. Whether the Low Riser's 50 MA goes sideways or declines, you must wait for the moving average to turn up before you can buy. If not, you will likely be stopped out when price crosses back and forth over the 50 MA multiple times (Figure 9.4).

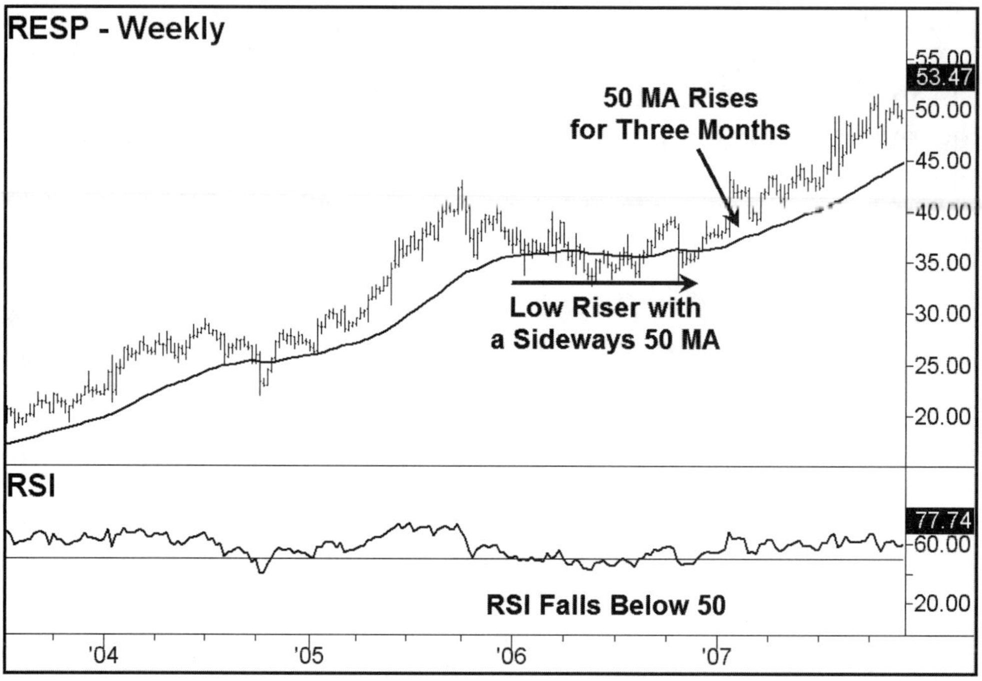

Figure 9.4 *Respironics (RESP) is a Low Riser where the 50 MA went sideways for a year. Price crossed over and under the 50 MA multiple times.* (Chart: TradeStation)

High Risers are stronger uptrends than Low Risers. High Risers have consistent, sustained buying by the BIGs. Low Risers represent periods where the buying pressure lessens significantly, and price falls or moves sideways. Low Risers must be entered carefully by waiting for the 50 MA to turn back up. If the moving average does not turn back up, then the buying pressure was insufficient to continue the uptrend. Once you see the 50 MA make a lower high, the long-term trend is down. If the stock was on your watchlist, delete it (Figures 9.5, 9.6).

Now it's your turn to rise to the occasion. Look at Figures 9.7-9.10 and determine if the stock is a High Riser or Low Riser (stock symbols have been removed, so you won't be influenced). If the stock is not a High Riser or Low Riser, what would you do with the stock? Would you ignore it or put it on a watchlist (answers are at the end of this chapter)?

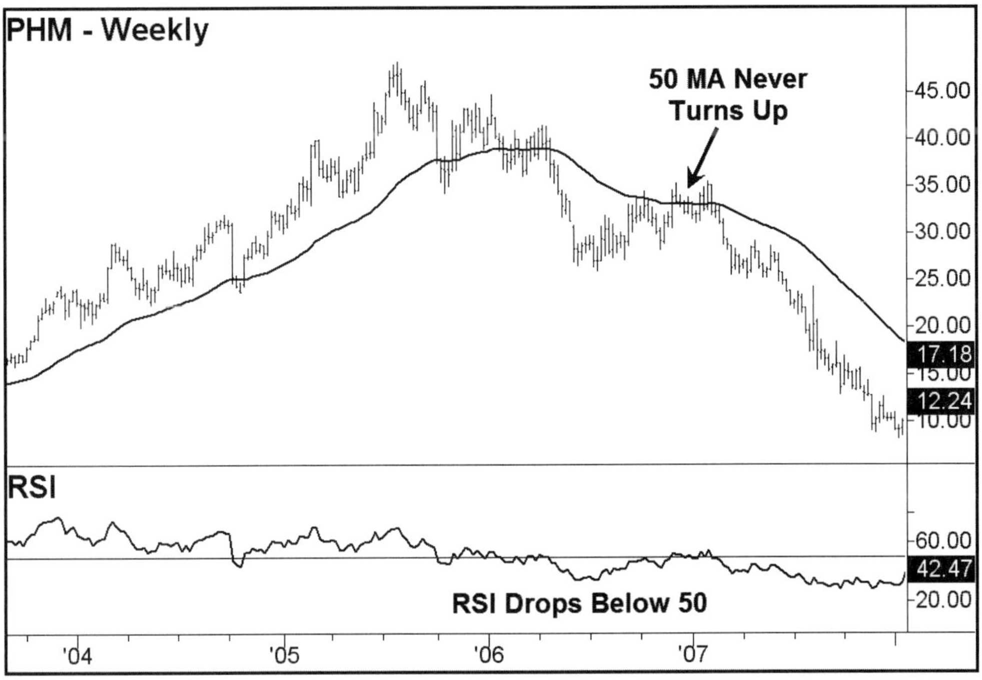

Figure 9.5 *Pulte Homes (PHM) was a Low Riser in 2006 until the 50 MA made a lower high ("flat" high). The stock entered a downtrend.* (Chart: TradeStation)

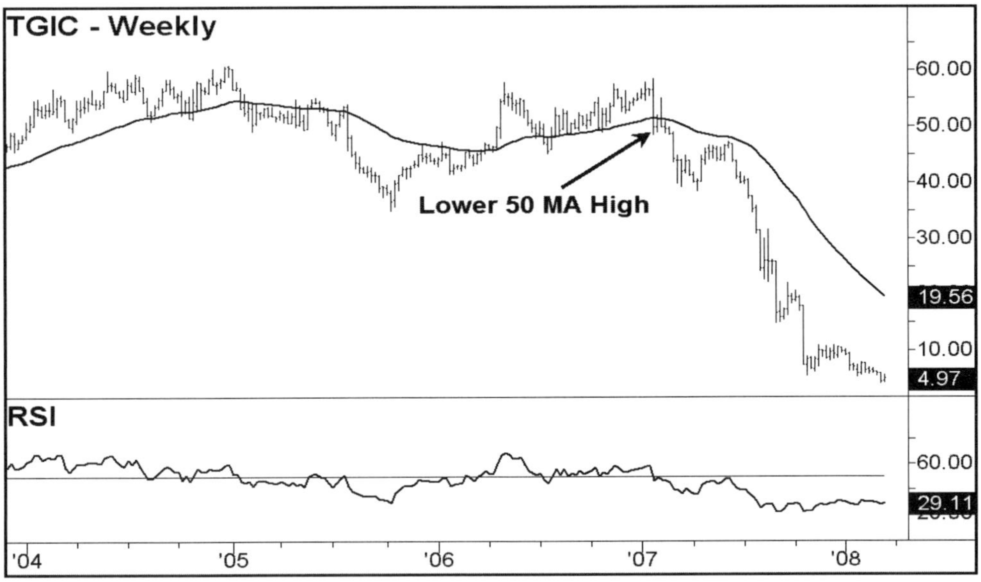

Figure 9.6 *Triad Guaranty (TGIC) is an example where the 50 MA made a lower high (compared to the high in late 2005) in early 2007 and entered a long-term downtrend.* (Chart: TradeStation)

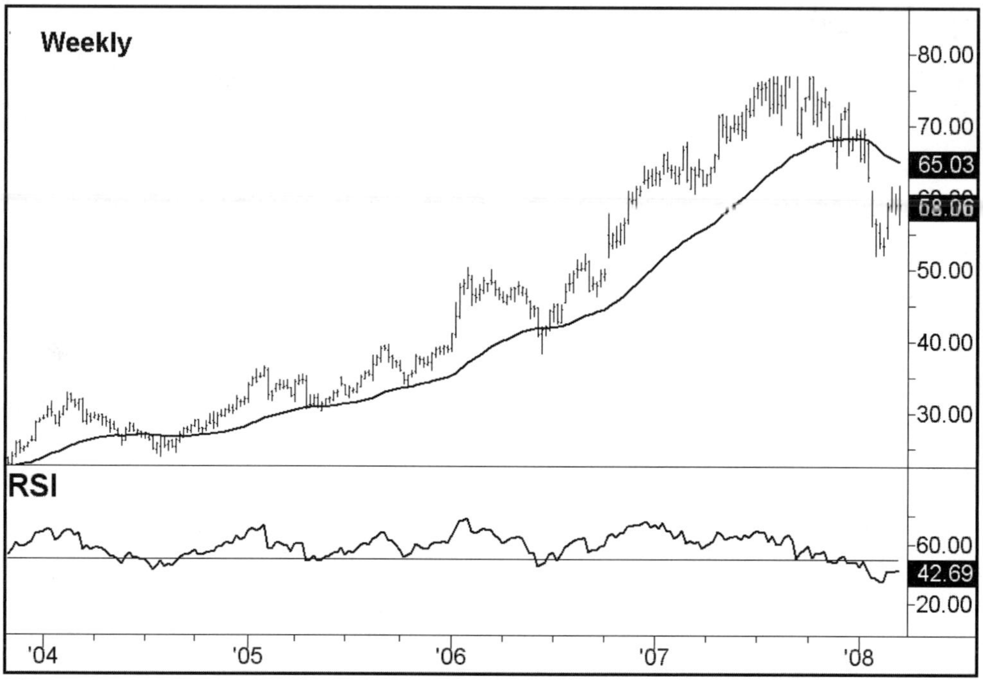

Figure 9.7 (Chart: TradeStation)

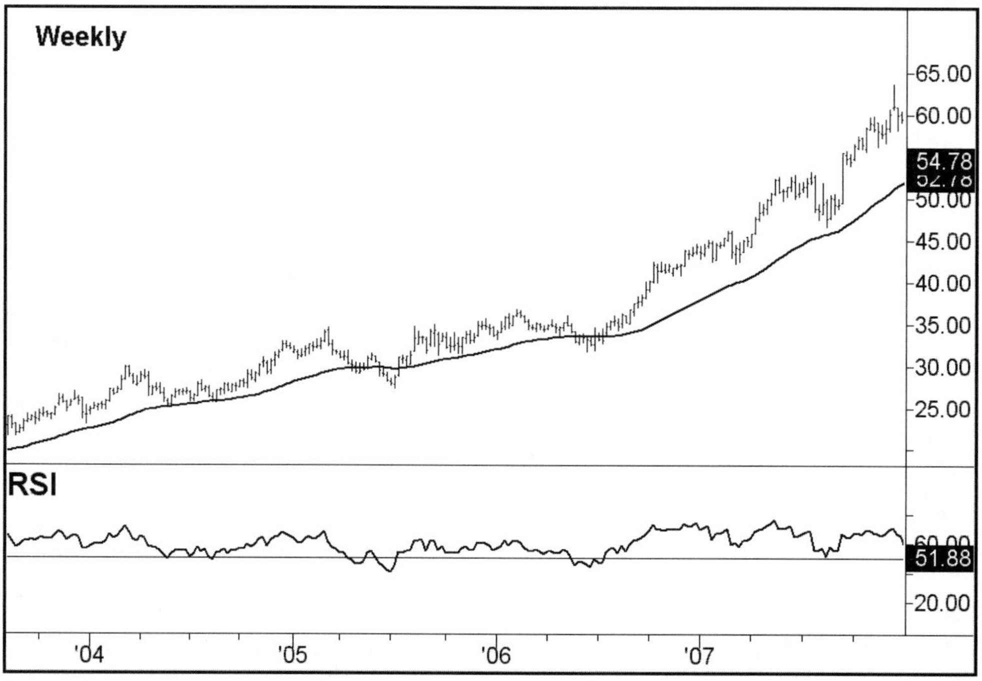

Figure 9.8 (Chart: TradeStation)

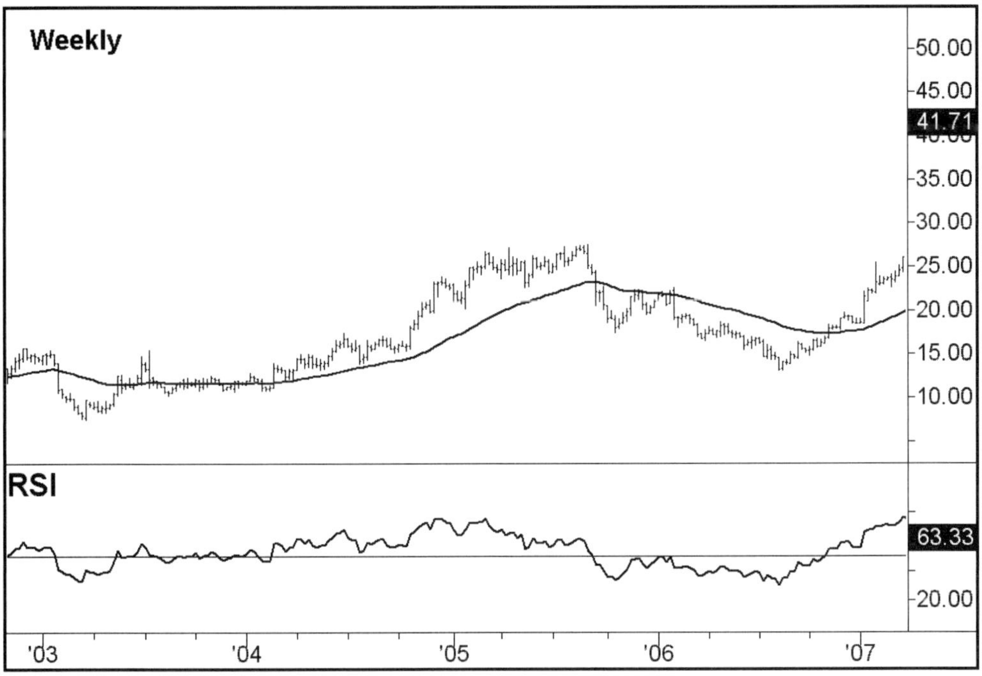

Figure 9.9 (Chart: TradeStation)

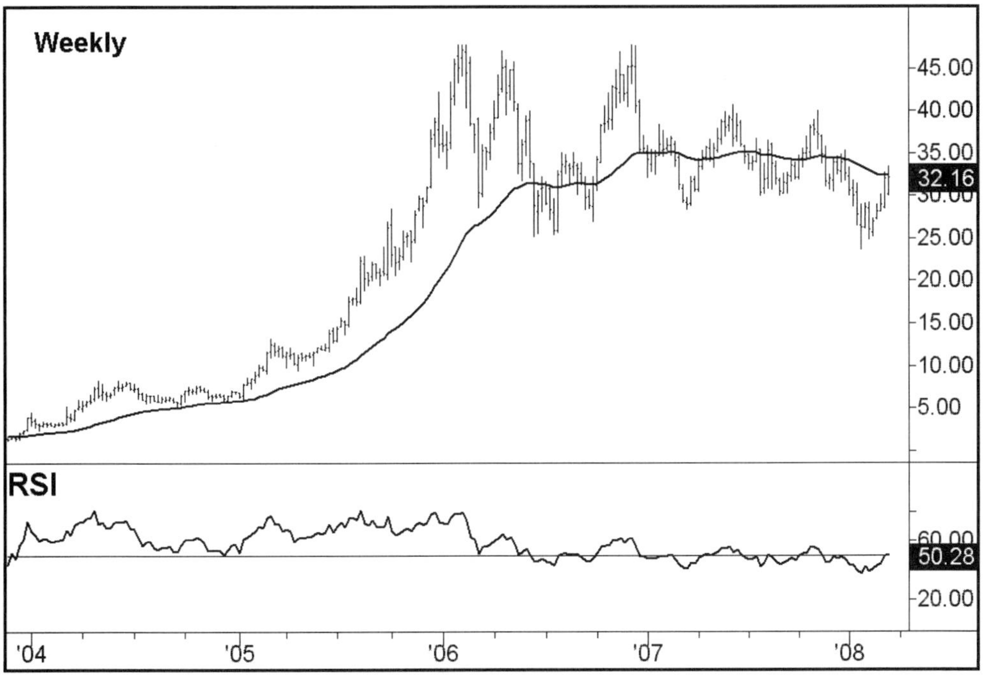

Figure 9.10 (Chart: TradeStation)

Why do we have 50-50 Strategy criteria and 50-50 High Risers and 50-50 Low Risers? They give us consistent, objective guidelines for buy and sell decisions. Without an objective system, investors are more likely to get confused, or they will see what they want to see. Why does this work? It works because of a major trend principle. *Trends are more likely to continue in the same direction than they are to reverse and go in the opposite direction.* It's a fact. If you invest in a stock already going up, you can be profitable because the stock is more likely to continue rising. This is a simple concept, but some investors still insist on buying stocks going down, and then they wonder why they don't make any money.

I was teaching a class in 2007 when one of the investors wanted to show me her trade. She had bought Starbucks at $30.

I said, "The stock is under the 50 MA, and RSI is below 50. Are you sure you want to own it here?"

"Well, I think it's headed to $60," she said.

"Hmmm....So you *wanted* to buy a stock under the 50 MA?"

She was quiet for a moment. "But I know it's going up. They say it's highly rated."

Look at Figure 9.11. What was the right thing for her to do according to the rules?

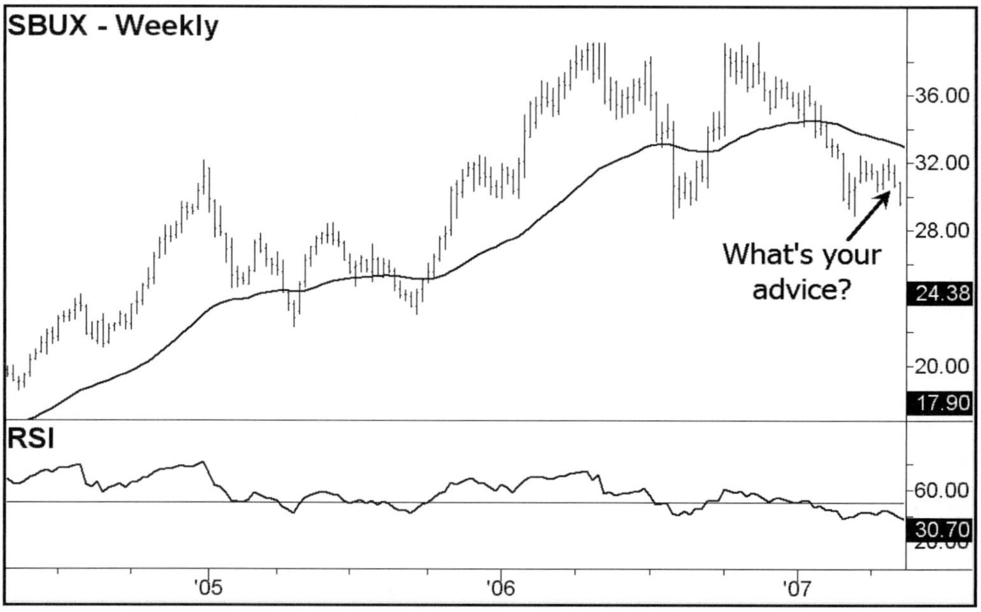

Figure 9.11 *What would you have told this investor about her purchase of SBUX at $30 (arrow)?* (Chart: TDAmeritrade)

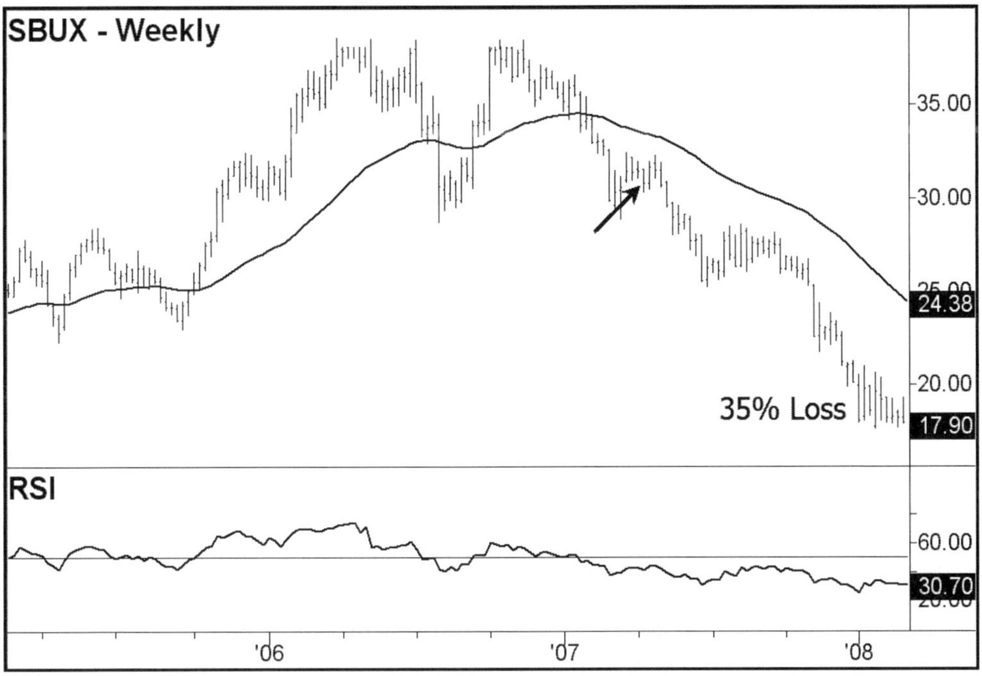

Figure 9.12 *Price was under the 50 MA and RSI was below 50, so SBUX did not meet the 50-50 Strategy criteria. The stock subsequently entered a downtrend.* (Chart: TDAmeritrade)

The price of SBUX was below a falling 50 MA, not above a rising 50 MA; RSI was below the 50 level, not above (Figure 9.12)! The 50-50 Strategy rules would have kept her out of trouble if she had followed them. SBUX was not a buy. I bet you got the answer right! Now you probably think you're a smarty-pants.

If you make a mistake and buy below the 50 MA, get out of the position as soon as you realize the error. Never sit in a trade that does not meet the 50-50 Strategy criteria. Suppose she had bought the stock back when it was above the 50 MA; she should have been stopped out when price crossed under the 50 MA. Here is the 50-50 *cry-tear-ia* rule: if you should have been stopped out, then you should get out. The right thing for her to do was to immediately sell the stock and put it on a watchlist. She could have bought it again if the 50 MA turned back up.

A trend has three directions, but only one direction makes money—up. If a stock is not rising, you cannot buy it and make money, and you certainly can't make big profits.

PASS THE POINTER

When I teach groups of investors, I like to do a 50-50 Strategy exercise with the class. I pass my laser pointer around the room, and each investor is asked about a different stock on the projector screen. Here's how it went the last time I did the exercise:

I passed the pointer to the first student and asked, "Is this a 50-50 Strategy buy? Yes or no?"

The first student said, "Well, the price is falling, but you had that big rise a month ago, and now there's a gap down on high volume, and ..."

"Pass the pointer," I said. I put up another chart and repeated my question to the next student, "A 50-50 buy? Yes or no?"

"It looks like it's going up, but I wouldn't buy it here," she said. "RSI is showing divergence, and price just made a key reversal."

"Pass the pointer." Another chart, and I asked another student, "Is this stock a 50-50 buy? Yes or no?"

"Well, it was going up, but then it went sideways," he said. "I think it's overbought, and momentum is slowing."

"OK, let's stop here."

I told the class that they were not trick questions. There were only two possible answers—*yes or no*--and not one of them answered the question right.

In our minds, we may think we understand a concept, but when put on the spot, we often over-think, over-analyze, and try to see too much. This is especially true if we have filled our heads with a lot of technical analysis that we don't know how to apply effectively. We think we have to be smart, when we just need to be observant. The pass-the-pointer exercise demonstrates a problem many of us have with learning technical analysis. We stray from rules and start thinking too much. Sometimes the most brilliant thing we can do is not try to act smart.

O = OVERHEAD SUPPLY

The concept of **overhead supply** refers to the situation where a stock fell in price after investors bought it, and the investor still owns it. These investors are expected to become sellers if the stock climbs back to their purchase price, or **breakeven**. They'll be anxious to dump the stock and move on, and they'll feel lucky if they can get out unscathed. When the investors get a chance to sell, it creates a supply of stock which resists the uptrend. The effect of overhead supply is not always significant. However, stocks without overhead supply have less resistance, and they often make better investment candidates. Figure 9.13 is an example of overhead supply.

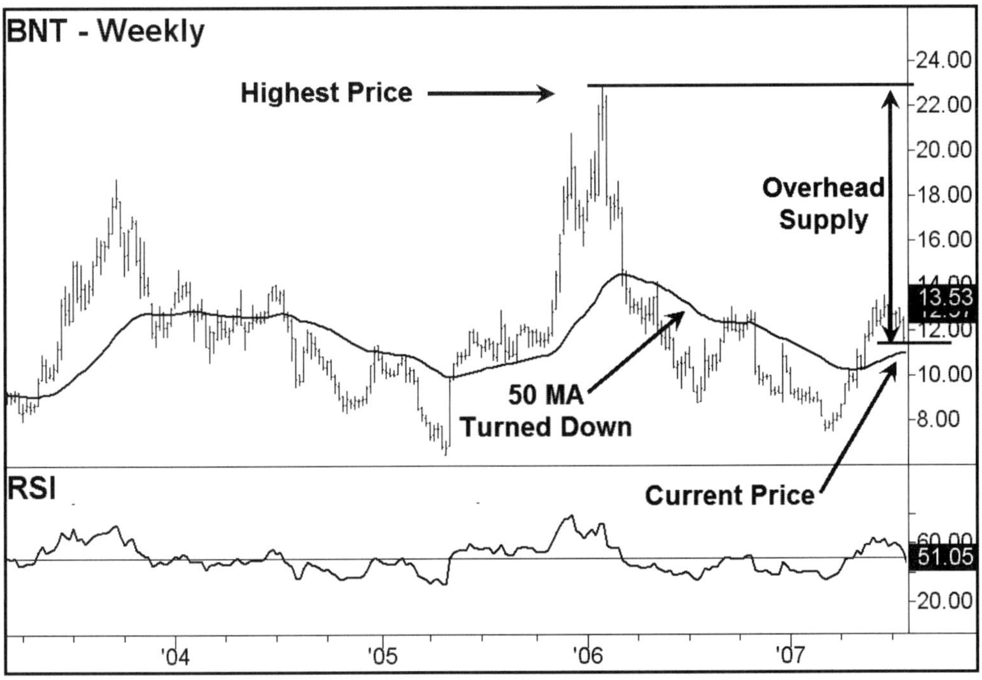

Figure 9.13 *Bentley Pharmaceutical (BNT) has overhead supply (arrow).* (Chart: TDAmeritrade)

Overhead supply can be quantified as the dollar amount between the current price and the highest price before the 50 MA turned down. In Figure 9.13, Bentley Pharmaceutical (BNT) topped out at around $23, and it fell to about $8 in the first quarter of 2007. Price is now at $14 and the 50 MA is rising. The overhead supply is $9; that's a lot for a $14 stock.

Overhead supply implies the stock may have a limited upside. Check for overhead supply before you consider buying a stock. The more overhead supply, the more difficulty the stock may have trending up. When choosing between stocks which meet the 50-50 criteria, it is generally better to choose the stocks with little or no overhead supply.

For Figures 9.14-9.15, answer the following two questions: (1) does the stock have overhead resistance, and (2) is the stock a High Riser or Low Riser, or neither (answers are at the end of this chapter)?

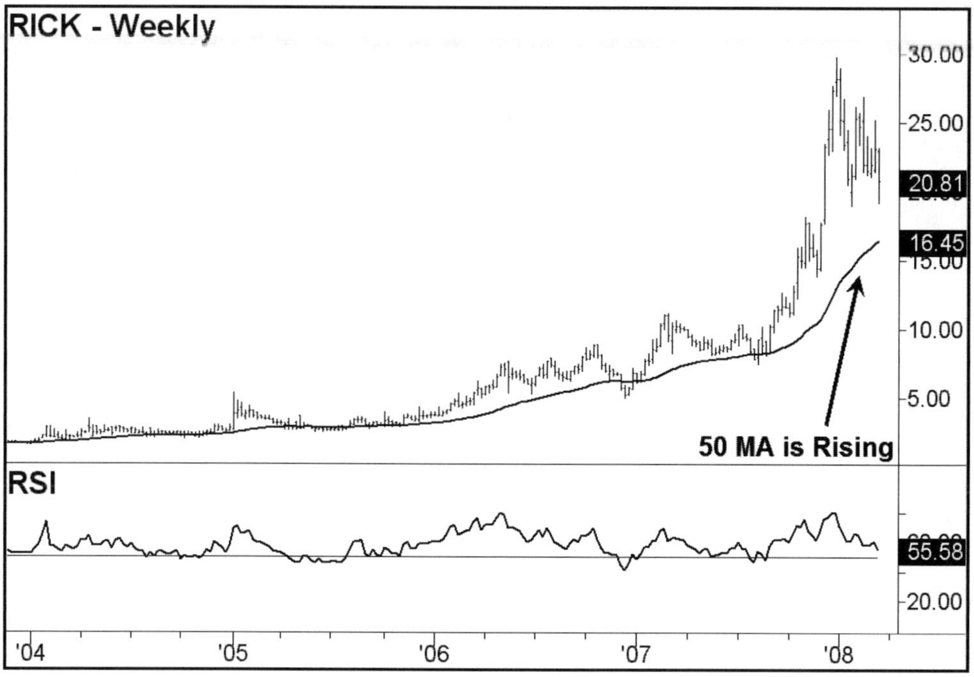

Figure 9.14 *Does Rick's Cabaret (RICK) have overhead supply? Is it a High Riser or Low Riser?* (Chart: TDAmeritrade)

Suppose you have a friend that is interested in buying stocks. She heard you talking about a new book, *Invest with Success,* which you had just started reading. She thinks you're pretty smart, so she shows you a stock chart to analyze. She wants a good stock pick, and she asks you to tell her if she should buy the stock. She mentions that she loves biotechnology stocks, and the chart is a biotech firm. What would you tell her to do after looking at the chart in Figure 9.16 (answer at the end of the chapter)?

Figure 9.15 *Does Family Dollar Stores (FDO) have overhead supply? Is it a High Riser or Low Riser?* (Chart: TDAmeritrade)

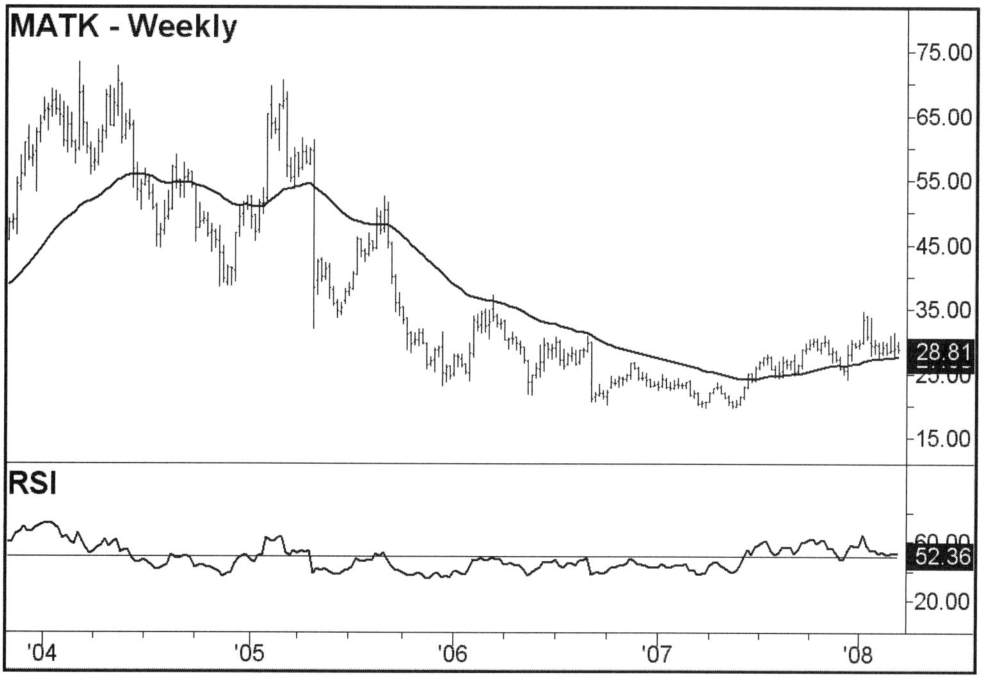

Figure 9.16 *What would you tell your friend?* (Chart: TDAmeritrade)

P = PRICE

One of the important considerations for stock selection is price. Stocks under $10 generally do not have strong institutional buying. If the BIGs were heavily committed to accumulating the stock, it would be hard for the price to remain under $10. The 50-50 Strategy avoids stocks under $10 because they are higher risk. Figure 9.17 shows how price will often rise faster after it reaches the $10 threshold.

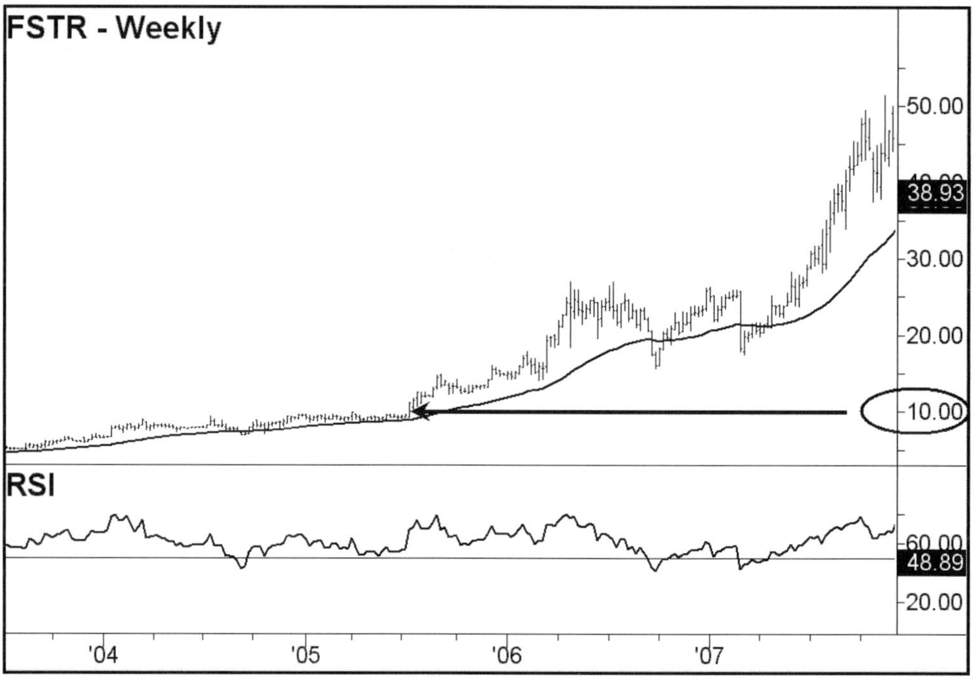

Figure 9.17 *Trends often attract more buying above $10.* (Chart: TradeStation)

In my experience, a good price range for growth stocks is between $10 and $40. That's not to say you can't find good growth stocks above $40, but most of the great opportunities occur at a lower price, when the company is still relatively undiscovered. Lower-priced stocks tend to rise faster than higher-priced stocks. For instance, it is easier for a $10 stock to go to $20 than for a $100 stock to go to $200. In both cases, the stocks have a 100% return.

Let's review the three criteria for the **TOP** method of rapid technical analysis (Figure 9.18). These will be on your checklist (Chapter 10).

TOP Method of Rapid Technical Analysis	
T = Trend	**Rising 50 MA (High Riser, Low Riser)**
O = Overhead Supply	**Low**
P = Price	**$10 to $40**

Figure 9.18 *TOP method of rapid technical analysis. TOP is the technical analysis part of the TOP SCORE method..*

THE EYES HAVE IT

Some investors do not bother to read a chart and analyze trend. They receive a recommendation from their broker, and they agree to purchase the stock without any further investigation. If you do nothing else, look at a stock chart before you buy a stock, mutual fund, or ETF. Trust what you see in the chart. Uptrends will develop irrespective of what news comes out about a company, how the analysts rate a company, or what the experts say about it on TV. You don't need to outsmart the market. Just use your eyes; they have what it takes to spot uptrends.

Stocks with a rising 50 MA represent the buying activity of the BIGs. We are only interested in buying stocks already going up, those with the proven ability to rise in value. Your job is to find stocks with a rising 50 MA and prepare to buy when the risk is low and the potential reward is high. Long-term uptrends can continue rising for a few years, resulting in big profits for the small investor.

Analyzing trends isn't always easy. You will get better with every chart you study. If you get the main direction right, everything else will seem a lot easier. If you get the direction wrong, you'll be left wondering why investing seems so complicated. Follow the TOP method of analysis to find good profit opportunities. If you have trouble, don't worry. The 50-50 Strategy will CYA (cover your analysis) most of the time.

ΔΔΔ

Answers for Figures 9.7-9.10, 9.14-9.16:

- **Figure 9.7:** The price of Shire Pharmaceuticals Group (SHPGY) is under a falling 50 MA. It is a Low Riser since the last 50 MA peak is the highest on the chart. Put it on your watchlist. Wait to see if the 50 MA turns up.

- **Figure 9.8:** McDonalds (MCD) is a High Riser and can be bought now. Both 50-50 Strategy criteria are present. Notice how price dropped below the 50 MA just briefly (twice) in 2005 and 2006. If you don't buy it now, put it on your watchlist.

- **Figure 9.9:** Owens Illinois (IO) is a Low Riser and can be bought because the 50 MA has turned back up. Notice how price remained above the 50 MA after RSI crossed above the 50 level. If you don't buy it now, put it on your watchlist.

- **Figure 9.10:** The price of GMX Resources (GMX) is below a sideways 50 MA. It is a Low Riser. The 50-50 Strategy criteria are not present, and the 50 MA has not yet turned up. Put it on your watchlist. Delete it if the 50 MA makes a lower high.

- **Figure 9.14:** Rick's Cabaret (RICK) is a High Riser. The overhead supply is not significant because the 50 MA is still rising.

- **Figure 9.15:** Family Dollar Stores (FDO) has about $18 of overhead supply, from the high of about $42 to the current price of around $24 ($42 - $24 = $18). It may have difficulty trending up. It is not a High Riser or Low Riser (the last 50 MA high is lower), so we don't care what it is. Delete it!

- **Figure 9.16:** You should tell her never to take tips from anybody (including you), and she should not fall in love with stocks. You can't tell her what to do. You look at the chart anyway and quickly see that Martek Biosciences (MATK) has about $42 of overhead supply; that's a lot for a $28 stock.

A company without earnings
is like a worker without a paycheck.

10 SCORE

Some people do research before they buy a car, camera, or new TV—all of which are depreciating assets. They may go to several stores to check prices and compare brands. They may read consumer magazines to search for the best values. In contrast, when people buy stocks, many do almost no research. Instead, they listen to a tip from a friend or a TV "expert," or they may notice a stock in a newspaper or magazine.

One reason investors shun stock research is they're not sure how to do it. We do not learn it in school. Even the word "research" may sound intimidating, reminding us of endless hours in the library doing term papers. It's much more exciting to pick the color of a new car or consider what kind of sound system we want.

There is another reason why investors may avoid stock research. People attach so much hope to stock picks that it blocks their reasoning and common sense. They become careless with money and are willing to just *take a shot.* This is gambling mentality, and it's irresponsible.

Many investors are unaware how easy stock research becomes once they know what to look for. With the help of a computer, it only takes a minute to complete the analysis. It may not be as much fun as picking out the color of your next car, but it may help you pay for the car in cash.

THE FUNDIES

Financial experts use **fundamental analysis** to make estimates of a stock's value. Fundamental analysis looks at the financial performance of companies; it is based on the concept that the price of a stock is determined by the company's past financial performance and future estimates of performance.

Company financials may be interesting to someone with an MBA in finance, but the average investor often finds it tedious and overwhelming. There are over 10,000 companies to analyze. There are so many variables that you can spend hours researching various companies and still end up with indecision about which stock to buy. The complexity of fundamental analysis causes some investors to abandon it in favor of pure technical analysis which is easier to see and interpret. In contrast, some investors don't believe technical analysis works, so they rely solely on fundamentals.

The best approach is to combine the two methods in a sensible approach, where each method complements the other. A company's fundamentals, or *fundies,* are easily accessed through the internet. My **SCORE** method of rapid fundamental analysis will give you five key numbers to review which tell you the majority of what you need to know; it only takes about 30 seconds to check. All we really need to know is whether or not the company is healthy and "fundamentally sound. If you want to dig deeper, you can, but it seldom adds much to the decision of whether or not to buy a stock.

YEARNINGS FOR EARNINGS

Fundamental analysis can be simple. The company is either making money or it isn't—there shouldn't be any mystery. To better understand fundamental analysis, imagine that your neighbor is going into debt, and he asked you to review his finances to help find out why. You would probably want to check and see if he has a steady paycheck from his job (earnings)? Does he have enough money in his checking account to pay his bills each month (cash flow)? Use this same common sense approach when analyzing the fundies of a company. It's not "stocket" science.

The most important thing to look for in the fundies is **earnings**. Does the company have earnings or not? Only invest in companies making money, because earnings growth is correlated with price growth (Figure 10.1). Be suspicious of any stock in an uptrend that does not have earnings

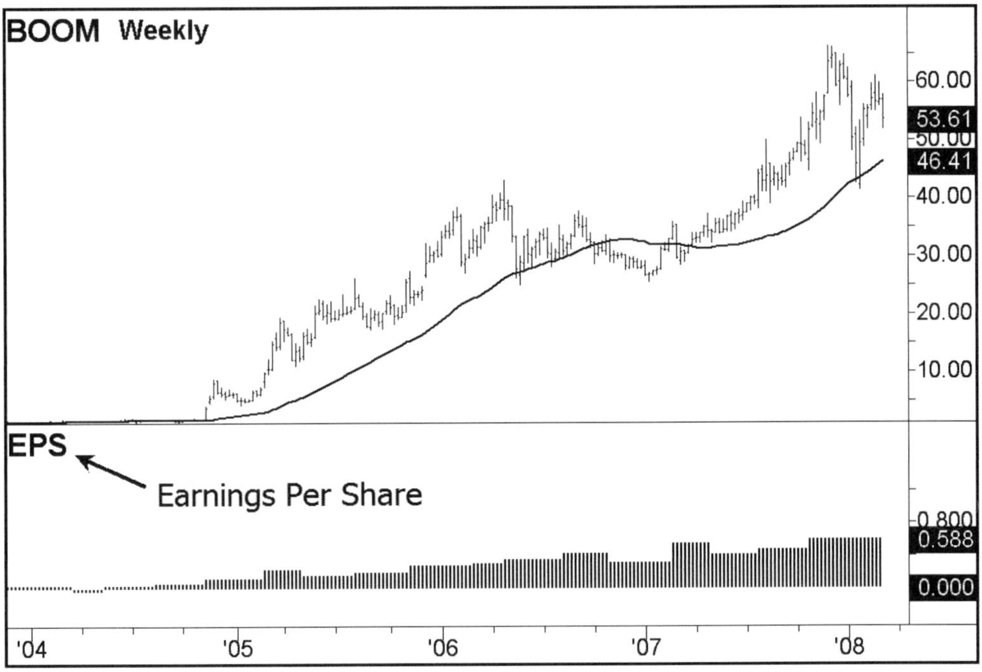

Figure 10.1 *Strong earnings attract buyers to drive up price. Quarterly earnings per share (EPS) are represented by the bars in the lower chart window.* (Chart: TDAmeritrade)

In Figure 10.1, the earnings for Dynamic Materials (BOOM) are shown in the lower window of the chart. As the earnings increased, so did the price of the stock. BOOM had a 600% rise in value. When a company's earnings grow, the perceived value of the company rises. Investors are willing to pay higher prices for the stock. Without earnings growth, the stock has little chance of trending up and making big profits. Big profits are not made on every investment, but every investment should be made with the *potential* to make big profits.

Earnings have a powerful role to play in risk. Stocks with strong earnings attract buying by the BIGs, and this inhibits the price from falling. A stock with poor earnings will not attract buyers, so there is less protection from it falling when the sellers step in (Figure 10.2). Circuit

City (CC) showed negative earnings in 2004, and earnings failed to grow in 2005-2006. Still, the stock went up, doubling in price. In late 2006, the lack of earnings finally took their toll, and price dropped over 80%! There was negative earnings growth in 2007, but the stock crossed below the 50 MA long before the negative earnings were apparent. This is why earnings are never a timing tool, even though the TV commentators report earnings as though every investor should have his finger on the computer mouse, just waiting to buy or sell the instant the earnings are released.

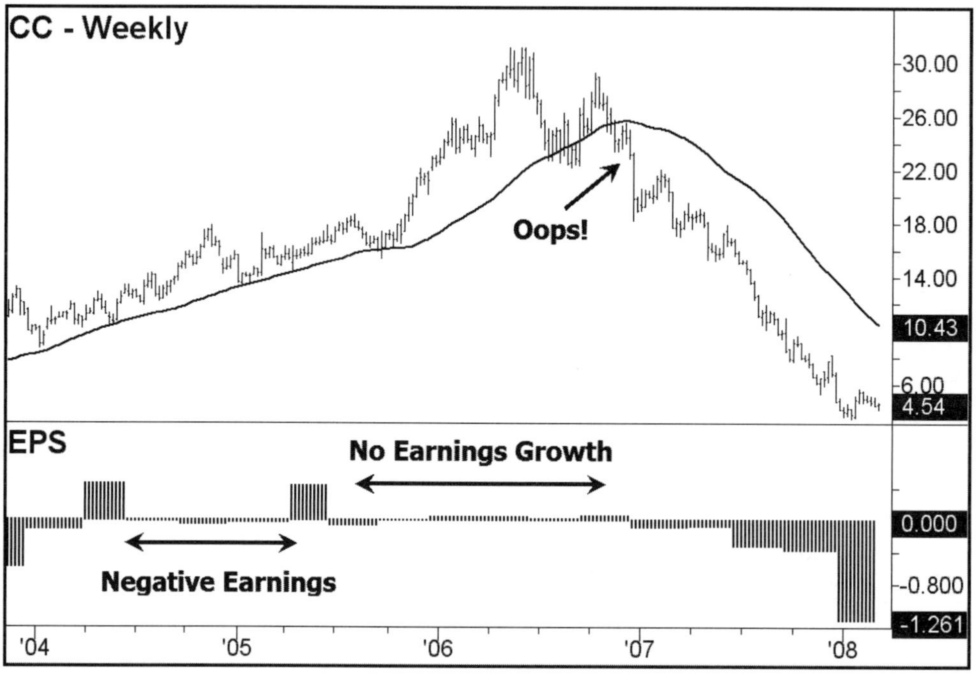

Figure 10.2 *A stock with poor earnings attracts fewer buyers and is more likely to fall in price.* (Chart: TDAmeritrade)

THE PAJAMA ANALYST

Some investors believe they can outsmart the BIGs by doing fundamental analysis and finding undiscovered gems. They think they can get up in the morning, sit at home in their pajamas, run computer searches, and find an undiscovered stock.

They may invest a great deal of money in the stock, expecting it to be the next Microsoft (MSFT). They will be "personally" invested too, because *they* found the stock nobody knew about. They tell themselves that it only takes one priceless gem to get rich. They imagine being able to brag their friends.

This scenario is highly unlikely, and it's not because your computer lacks memory, or because you shouldn't do the fundies in your undies. The BIGs are powerful financial institutions that employ legions of highly paid analysts with degrees in business and finance. They go to work in expensive suits and ties, and spend the entire day doing research. These analysts have access to the best professional software programs and better access to company information. They will speak to high level officers in the company to discuss future company growth and development, and they may be privy to information not released to the general public.

The price of a stock represents its fair value at any given time. As new information becomes known about a company, the price of the stock will adjust up and down based on the capital commitment of the BIGs. Much of the buying and selling by the BIGs is due to information we'll never have (Figure 10.3). Hovnanian Enterprises (HOV) was a housing stock that began a selloff in mid-2005, prior to the 2006 peak in earnings. The first negative earnings were not reported until 2007; by then, the stock had lost over 50% of its value.

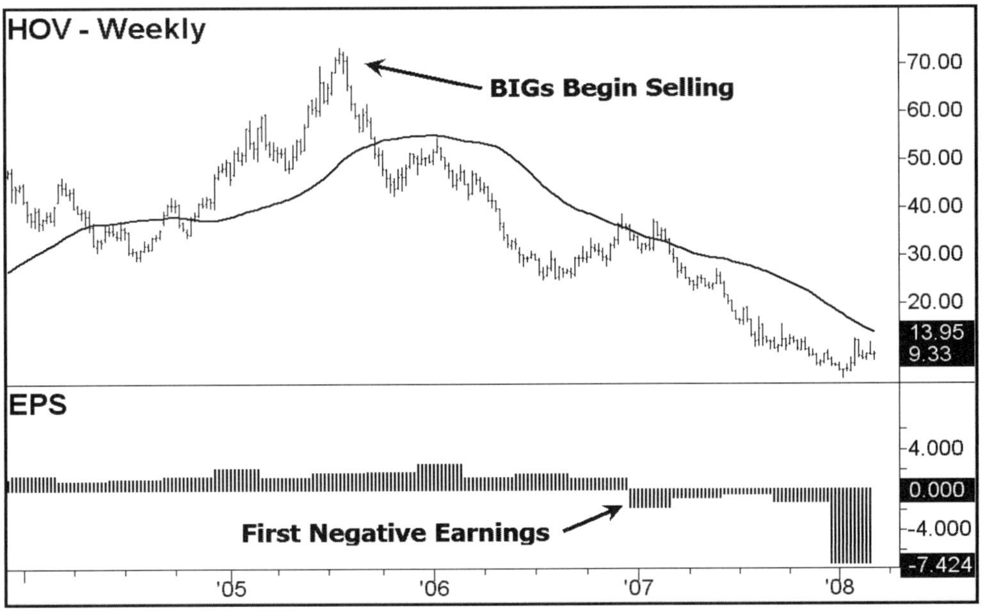

Figure 10.3 *The BIGs sold Hovnanian Enterprises (HOV) in mid-2005, but the first negative earnings were not reported until 2007.* (Chart: TDAmeritrade)

Information on expected future earnings growth is not as readily available to the small investor as it is to the BIGs. A company's earnings may be average, but its stock may be trending up due to something the BIGs know that we *don't* know. Conversely, a company may have above average earnings, but the stock may enter a downtrend. It pays not to think. Stick with what you know is irrefutably true: price is either above the 50 MA or below the 50 MA. When price drops below the 50 MA, successful investors get out of their stock positions; they don't wait for the earnings reports.

YAHOO! FINANCE

Most everything about a company's fundies is public knowledge and posted for free on the internet. My favorite two websites are (www.finance.yahoo.com) and (www.msn.money.com). There are many others, but they just repeat the same information with a different look.

Yahoo Finance has everything for the SCORE method on one webpage. If there's something more you need to know, there are several more web pages of more detailed information you can review. More research won't hurt, but too much research won't help. For example, suppose your neighbor is spending more money each month than he makes. You don't need to review a detailed list of expenditures to know he needs to cut back on his spending. Here are the steps to find the SCORE information at Yahoo:

Finding *Key Statistics* at Yahoo Finance (for SCORE analysis)

1. Go to the Yahoo site (www.yahoo.com)
2. Click on *Finance* in the left column.
3. In the upper left part of the Finance page, type the stock name (or symbol) in the small box to the left of *Get Quotes,* and then click on *Get Quotes.*
4. A page will open up to a *Quote Summary.* Look down the left column and find the heading of *Company.* Under it, click on *Key Statistics.*
5. The next page is the Key Statistics page (Figure 10.4). It's the only page you'll need. Now, get ready to SCORE!

Profitability	Stock: HOV
Profit Margin (ttm):	-14.88%
Operating Margin (ttm):	-13.16%
Management Effectiveness	
Return on Assets (ttm):	-8.08%
Return on Equity (ttm):	-45.91%
Income Statement	
Revenue (ttm):	4.73B
Revenue Per Share (ttm):	74.8
Qtrly Revenue Growth (yoy): R	-6.20%
Gross Profit (ttm):	231.54M
EBITDA (ttm):	-637.29M
Net Income Avl to Common (ttm):	-711.46M
Diluted EPS (ttm):	-11.259
Qtrly Earnings Growth (yoy): E	N/A
Balance Sheet	
Total Cash (mrq):	73.05M
Total Cash Per Share (mrq):	1.168
Total Debt (mrq):	2.37B
Total Debt/Equity (mrq):	1.997
Current Ratio (mrq):	6.633
Book Value Per Share (mrq):	16.790001
Cash Flow Statement	
Operating Cash Flow (ttm): C	215.83M
Levered Free Cash Flow (ttm):	617.17M

Average Volume (3 month)[3]:	4,158,760
Average Volume (10 day)[3]:	4,391,390
Shares Outstanding[5]: S	62.53M
Float:	37.83M
% Held by Insiders[1]:	11.29%
% Held by Institutions[1]: O	114.10%
Shares Short (as of 11-Mar-08)[3]:	27.16M
Short Ratio (as of 11-Mar-08)[3]:	8
Short % of Float (as of 11-Mar-08)[3]:	74.50%
Shares Short (prior month)[3]:	25.00M
Dividends & Splits	
Forward Annual Dividend Rate[4]:	N/A
Forward Annual Dividend Yield[4]:	N/A
Trailing Annual Dividend Rate[3]:	N/A
Trailing Annual Dividend Yield[3]:	NaN%
5 Year Average Dividend Yield[4]:	N/A
Payout Ratio[4]:	N/A
Dividend Date[3]:	N/A
Ex-Dividend Date[4]:	14-Apr-87
Last Split Factor (new per old)[2]:	2:1
Last Split Date[3]:	29-Mar-04

Figure 10.4 *Here we see the key statistics for Hovnanian Enterprises (HOV) (refer to HOV chart in Figure 10.3) showing all five fundamental criteria for the SCORE system of rapid analysis. (Note: this is only a portion of the Key Statistics page)* (Source: Yahoo Finance)

SCORE is used for stocks, not mutual funds or ETFs. You only need to check *five* things with the SCORE method (Figure 10.4). Notice that Hovnanian's recent revenue growth was negative (-6.2%) (Figure 10.4, "**R**") and the earnings growth was "N/A" (no earnings) (Figure 10.4, E). This makes sense for a stock that fell 85% in price. In the next sections of this chapter, I'll show you how to SCORE a stock's fundies. If it takes longer than 30 seconds to SCORE, you're working too hard.

LEARN HOW TO SCORE

SCORE is an acronym for **S**hares outstanding, **C**ash flow, **O**wnership by institutions, **R**evenue growth, and **E**arnings growth. You must know if the company is profitable and can attract buying by the BIGs. Not all of the SCORE criteria need to be fantastic; it's more of a pass/fail grading system. Companies, like people, are not perfect.

The two most important criteria of the SCORE system are earnings and cash flow. If these two are not positive, I move on to another stock. One of the reasons to avoid IPOs is they don't have a long history of fundamental data. Fundamentals are all about earnings; everything else is window dressing. Stocks may receive a great deal of hype in the media, but earnings growth is what creates sustained uptrends in price.

Learn how to SCORE and keep it simple. You can research until you have eye fatigue, but it may not improve your bottom line. Once you find a stock that fits the 50-50 Strategy criteria, you only need to know if the company has a good SCORE. If the company doesn't SCORE well, don't buy the stock. If the company SCOREs well, then consider it a profit opportunity.

S = SHARES OUTSTANDING

The concept of **shares outstanding** relates directly to the basic law of supply and demand. Outstanding shares represent the total supply of stock available to be bought and sold in the market. A low number of shares outstanding is less than 100 million shares. When a large demand meets a small supply of outstanding shares, the price of the stock is more likely to rise dramatically. This is why growth stocks have such big moves up in price compared to behemoths.

Think about the pool of outstanding shares as a small puddle of water and the BIGs as a big rock. When you throw the rock into the puddle, there's a big splash, causing large waves. Now think of throwing the rock into the ocean; you'll hardly notice a ripple. The smaller the pool of outstanding shares, the bigger the splash in price. Stocks with a low number of outstanding shares can have dramatic rises in price. Stocks with a high number of outstanding shares are less affected by buying pressure and less likely to make large moves. A big company like Microsoft (MSFT) will have outstanding shares in the billions. When the retail investor buys 500 shares of MSFT, it doesn't even cause a ripple in the price.

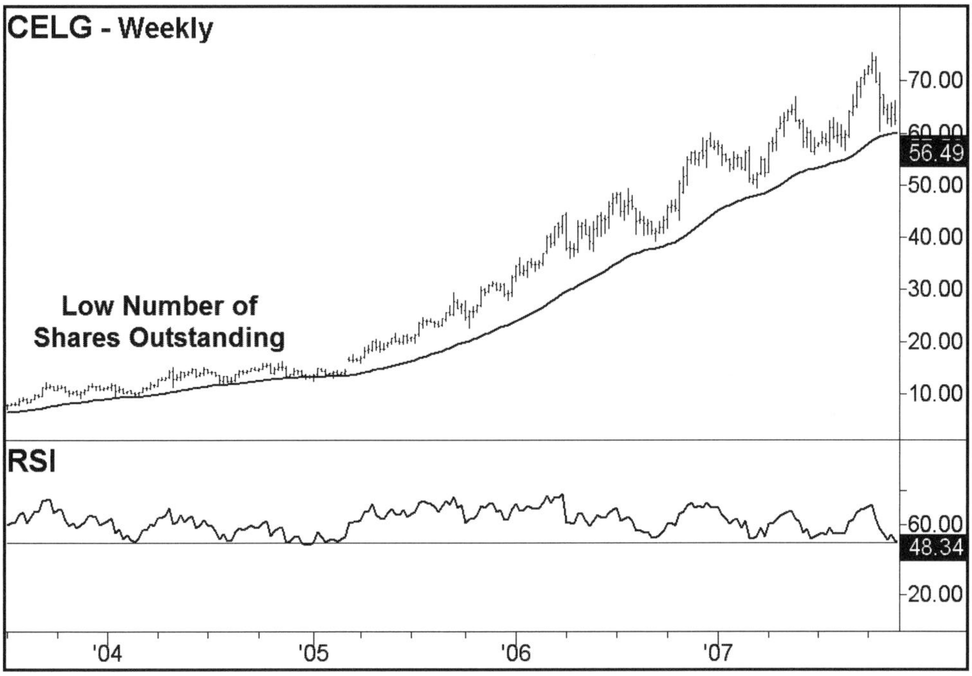

Figure 10.5 *Celgene (CELG) had less than 100 million shares in 2004 when it started a strong uptrend (price above a rising 50 MA and RSI above 50).* (Chart: TDAmeritrade)

In 2004, Celgene (CELG) (Figure 10.5) had about 100 million shares outstanding. As a result, the BIGs "rock" made a big splash, and shares of the stock rose nearly 400% over three years! By 2008, the number of shares outstanding had increased to over 400 million shares (Figure 10.6, "S"). Compare the rise in price of CELG in Figure 10.5 to the SCORE criteria in Figure 10.6. Could the rise have been because of earnings?

The year-over-year (yoy) quarterly earnings growth compares the earnings of this quarter to the same quarterly earnings one year ago. They are up over 200% in Figure 10.6! Combining technical and fundamental analysis gives the investor greater confidence in making well-researched investment choices, even if only takes about a minute.

I will refer back to Figure 10.6 during the rest of this chapter.

C = CASH FLOW

Cash flow is the amount of money the company has left over after meeting financial obligations. If the company doesn't have positive cash flow, then it is spending more money than it is making. The amount is not as important as the fact that the company is generating cash. We will only invest in financially healthy companies with a positive cash flow (Figure 10.6, **"C"**). A company with negative cash flow will have difficulty expanding, so there is limited upside potential. Negative cash flow is a red flag to avoid the stock.

Cash is important for company survival; it is a valuable, liquid asset which is used to pay daily expenses, pay dividends to shareholders, or pay off debt. A company also benefits by having cash flow to address emergencies rather than having to borrow money. Companies cannot grow unless they have cash to spend on expansion and new product lines. Expansion leads to more earnings for the company and higher prices for the stock.

O = OWNERSHIP BY INSTITUTIONS

One of the SCORE criteria is to look for the actual percentage of stocks shares owned by the institutions (BIGs). Stock prices rise from huge buying demand by the BIGs, so knowing how much they own is key information. The BIGs don't just buy stocks; they campaign into them, buying up to a 100,000 shares at a time. Without the BIGs, the stock just isn't going anywhere. Look for stocks with at least 20% ownership by institutions (Figure 10.6, **"O"**)

The trend is unlikely to reverse down when the BIGs favor a stock. Once they commit money, they are planning to hold it for 2-3 years.

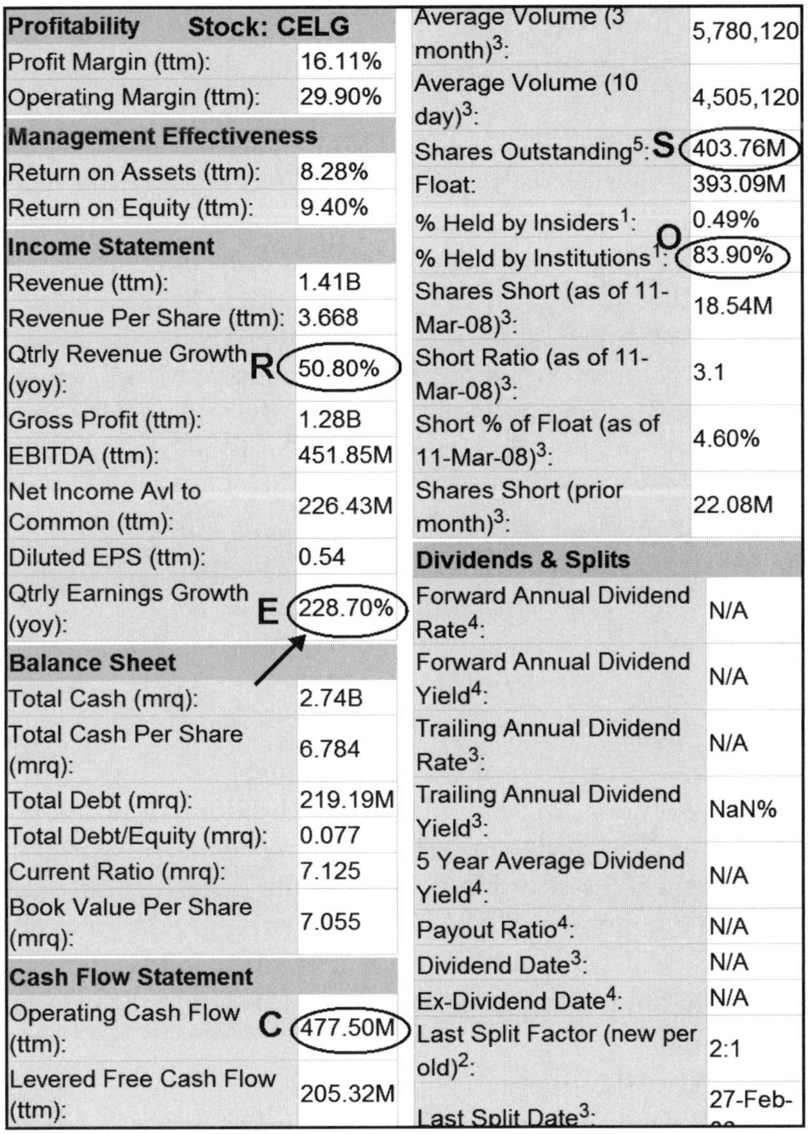

Profitability	Stock: CELG
Profit Margin (ttm):	16.11%
Operating Margin (ttm):	29.90%
Management Effectiveness	
Return on Assets (ttm):	8.28%
Return on Equity (ttm):	9.40%
Income Statement	
Revenue (ttm):	1.41B
Revenue Per Share (ttm):	3.668
Qtrly Revenue Growth (yoy):	R 50.80%
Gross Profit (ttm):	1.28B
EBITDA (ttm):	451.85M
Net Income Avl to Common (ttm):	226.43M
Diluted EPS (ttm):	0.54
Qtrly Earnings Growth (yoy):	E 228.70%
Balance Sheet	
Total Cash (mrq):	2.74B
Total Cash Per Share (mrq):	6.784
Total Debt (mrq):	219.19M
Total Debt/Equity (mrq):	0.077
Current Ratio (mrq):	7.125
Book Value Per Share (mrq):	7.055
Cash Flow Statement	
Operating Cash Flow (ttm):	C 477.50M
Levered Free Cash Flow (ttm):	205.32M

Average Volume (3 month)[3]:	5,780,120
Average Volume (10 day)[3]:	4,505,120
Shares Outstanding[5]:	S 403.76M
Float:	393.09M
% Held by Insiders[1]:	0.49%
% Held by Institutions[1]:	O 83.90%
Shares Short (as of 11-Mar-08)[3]:	18.54M
Short Ratio (as of 11-Mar-08)[3]:	3.1
Short % of Float (as of 11-Mar-08)[3]:	4.60%
Shares Short (prior month)[3]:	22.08M
Dividends & Splits	
Forward Annual Dividend Rate[4]:	N/A
Forward Annual Dividend Yield[4]:	N/A
Trailing Annual Dividend Rate[3]:	N/A
Trailing Annual Dividend Yield[3]:	NaN%
5 Year Average Dividend Yield[4]:	N/A
Payout Ratio[4]:	N/A
Dividend Date[3]:	N/A
Ex-Dividend Date[4]:	N/A
Last Split Factor (new per old)[2]:	2:1
Last Split Date[3]:	27-Feb-

Figure 10.6 *SCORE criteria are circled for Celgene (CELG).* The quarterly earnings growth was over 200% (arrow). (Source: Yahoo Finance)

That means a stock you own is less likely to suddenly fall in price and leave you with a loss. However, once the BIGs decide to sell, a stock can drop quickly. That's why we *always* use a **stop-loss** order to protect against losses. I will discuss how to use stop-loss orders in Chapters 15 and 16.

R = REVENUE GROWTH

Revenue growth is the gross income the company receives from the sale of goods or services. The investor is interested in whether or not the company is showing growth in revenues from year to year. Revenues are reported as quarterly growth year-over-year (yoy). In general, the revenue growth rate should be at least 25% from one year to the next, but the higher the number the better (Figure 10.6, **"R"**).

Revenue growth is essential to company analysis. A new company may be barely profitable, meaning its earnings are not great, but if the company has strong revenue growth, there is reason to believe the company will eventually be profitable and begin a growth phase. Conversely, a company with great earnings would be suspect if it shows declining revenue growth. When both revenues and earnings are growing, the company is usually going to do well.

E = EARNINGS GROWTH

The three rules of fundamental analysis are 1) earnings, 2) earnings, and 3) earnings. Again, think about your neighbor's finances. If he had received a raise of 25% per year for the last three years, he would likely be doing pretty well right now. He could probably pay his daily expenses, afford a house payment, and build up some savings. On the other hand, if his paycheck had been getting smaller the last three years, it would explain why he can't meet his expenses, and it would explain why he's in financial trouble.

Earnings growth differs from revenue growth. Revenue growth does not account for company expenses, while company's earnings do. Earnings mean profitability. Look for stocks with at least 25% earnings growth from one year to the next (Figure 10.6, **"E"**). Stocks struggle to establish an uptrend without long-term, accelerating earnings to fuel the rise. While some stocks may rise without earnings, the rise is usually short-lived. Stocks simply cannot sustain an uptrend without good earnings growth to attract the BIGs.

KEEPING SCORE

Now it's time to practice. Review the five criteria of SCORE analysis for LKQ Corporation (LKQX) using Figure 10.7. Then study the chart of LKQ in Figure 10.8. What kind of **TOP SCORE** does this stock have (answers at the end of the chapter)? To make it easier, follow the **TOP SCORE 50-50 Stock Evaluation** checklist (Figure 10.9). For now, you can ignore the parts dealing with sector/industry and overall market.

Profitability	**Stock: LKQX**
Profit Margin (ttm):	5.85%
Operating Margin (ttm):	11.08%
Management Effectiveness	
Return on Assets (ttm):	6.91%
Return on Equity (ttm):	10.54%
Income Statement	
Revenue (ttm):	1.13B
Revenue Per Share (ttm):	9.87
Qtrly Revenue Growth (yoy): R	102.80%
Gross Profit (ttm):	505.75M
EBITDA (ttm):	142.86M
Net Income Avl to Common (ttm):	65.90M
Diluted EPS (ttm):	0.55
Qtrly Earnings Growth (yoy): E	111.30%
Balance Sheet	
Total Cash (mrq):	74.24M
Total Cash Per Share (mrq):	0.552
Total Debt (mrq):	658.46M
Total Debt/Equity (mrq):	0.775
Current Ratio (mrq):	3.377
Book Value Per Share (mrq):	6.335
Cash Flow Statement	
Operating Cash Flow (ttm): C	54.37M
Levered Free Cash Flow (ttm):	-158.32M

Average Volume (3 month)[3]:	1,250,630
Average Volume (10 day)[3]:	1,188,820
Shares Outstanding[5]: S	134.50M
Float:	118.44M
% Held by Insiders[1]:	11.29%
% Held by Institutions[1]: O	94.10%
Shares Short (as of 11-Mar-08)[3]:	12.30M
Short Ratio (as of 11-Mar-08)[3]:	6.4
Short % of Float (as of 11-Mar-08)[3]:	10.30%
Shares Short (prior month)[3]:	12.42M
Dividends & Splits	
Forward Annual Dividend Rate[4]:	N/A
Forward Annual Dividend Yield[4]:	N/A
Trailing Annual Dividend Rate[3]:	N/A
Trailing Annual Dividend Yield[3]:	NaN%
5 Year Average Dividend Yield[4]:	N/A
Payout Ratio[4]:	N/A
Dividend Date[3]:	N/A
Ex-Dividend Date[4]:	N/A
Last Split Factor (new per old)[2]:	2:1
Last Split Date[3]:	04-Dec-

Figure 10.7 *SCORE for LKQX.* (Source: Yahoo Finance)

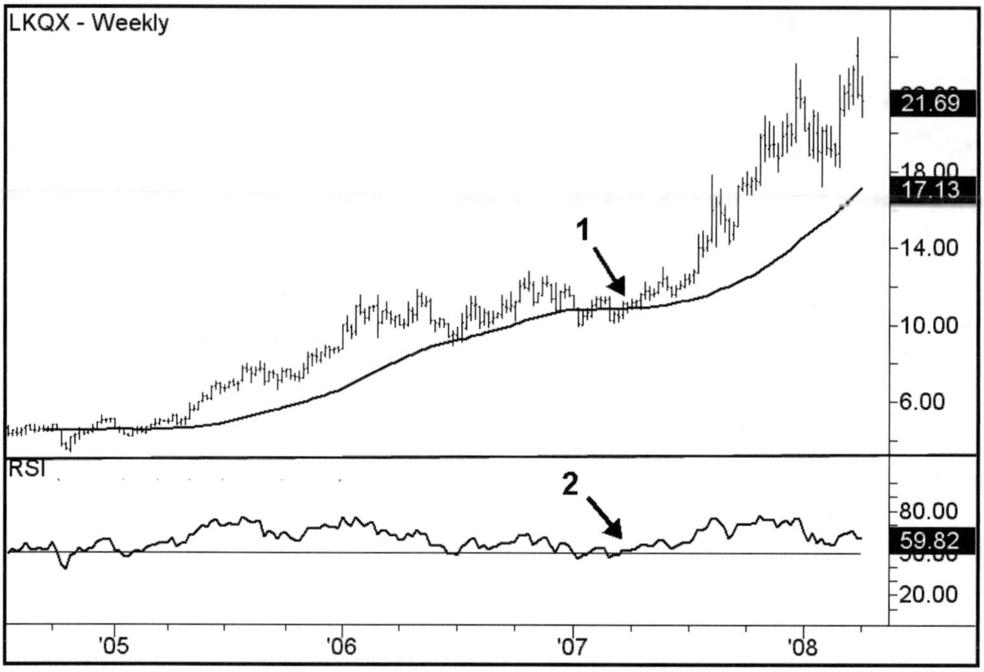

Figure 10.8 *LKQ Corporation (LKQX). What happened at (1) and (2)?* (Chart: TradeStation)

THE PRICE IS RIGHT

Sometimes, you study the fundies of a stock and they are strong, but the stock is in a downtrend. You may also find a stock in an uptrend, but the fundies are weak. Sometimes a stock with good fundies will be in a sideways trend for years. Why does this happen?

Why doesn't matter. We can think about it, but thinking won't make profits. Only uptrends make profits. Investors cannot know all that is going on with a company, and we must accept that there aren't answers for everything. Accountants determine earnings; the market determines price. Don't confuse the two. Always respect price; it is the best indication of the stock's real value.

TOP SCORE 50-50 Stock Evaluation			
Date			
Stock Symbol			
Sector/Industry			
Notes:			
Overall Market	**Condition**	**Yes**	**No**
SPY	Rising 50 MA		
Sector (optional)	Rising 50 MA		
Notes:			
TOP SCORE	**Criteria**	**Yes**	**No**
T = Trend			
O = Overhead Supply	Low		
P = Price	$10-$40		
S = Shares Outstanding	< 100 million		
C = Cash Flow	Positive		
O = Owner. by Inst.	>20%		
R = Revenue Growth	>25% yoy		
E = Earnings Growth	>25% yoy		

Figure 10.9 *Checklists are a handy way of of keeping stock research simple and focused. The references to "Sector/Industry" and "Overall Market" are from Chapter 12.*

GONE IN 60 SECONDS

One evening in Las Vegas, I went to a dinner party with friends. While enjoying an appetizer of *pizza quatro formaggi* and a glass of Brunello wine, a woman told me she wanted to invest in solar companies.

"Great," I said.

"Not so great, I'm losing money," she said.

"That's a different issue," I said. "You didn't say you wanted to make money. You said you wanted to invest in solar companies."

"But can't I do both?"

"Apparently not." We both laughed and drank more wine.

It's fine to have investment ideas, just be sure you have a plan for profit. The market doesn't care what we want, and it doesn't respect you for good intentions. Use objective criteria to screen stocks and make sure there is a profit opportunity.

The TOP SCORE 50-50 Strategy method is time efficient. After some practice, give yourself 30 thirty seconds to check for TOP stocks. Start with T (trend). If a stock is not trending up, do not proceed further; move on to another stock. If the stock is in an uptrend, check the O (overhead supply) and P (price).

Give yourself another 30 seconds to check the stock's SCORE. Use the same stepwise approach: start with S (shares outstanding) and proceed next to C (cash flow). If cash flow is negative, stop at C, and go no further. If the cash flow is good, then go on to O, R, and E. Use the TOP SCORE 50-50 Stock Evaluation checklist, and make it easy on yourself. Checklists build discipline by helping us to repeat the same steps of analysis for each stock.

There is no need to get lost in complicated, time consuming research. With some practice, you can do TOP SCORE analysis and be gone in 60 seconds.

ΔΔΔ

Answers to Questions about Figures 10.7-10.8

- **Figure 10.7:** LKQX had a good SCORE. Shares outstanding were over 100 million, but that's close enough. Cash flow was positive. Ownership by institutions was 94%. The earnings and revenues growth were both over 100%, far exceeding the minimum of 25%.

- **Figure 10.8:** The 50 MA is rising the entire length of the chart, so this is a High Riser. Price is above the 50 MA and RSI is above the 50 level. A 50-50 Strategy signal was given in early 2007 (1, 2). There is no overhead resistance, and the price is in the $10-$40 range. What's not to like? This stock could be bought now, or added to your watchlist.

A wealthy mind is one rich with knowledge.

11 The Stock Cycle

After reading Chapter 9, you know how to see TOP trends. Chapter 10 gave you the SCORE method of rapid fundamental analysis. These are two powerful tools. When you gain experience with this method of stock analysis, you will become more confident in your ability to find profit opportunities. Follow the checklist; it will guide you in the right direction.

Now, I want to provide you with an overview of how the BIGs campaign into and out of stocks, and how their activity plays out in the different types of recognizable trends. This information will give you a much larger perspective on how the market works, and how TOP SCORE stocks develop into profitable trends. You will gain valuable insight into why we have to buy and sell stocks, and not simply buy and hold them.

When beginners first look at stock charts, they often have trouble seeing any patterns to price movement. Price may appear to be moving up, down, and sideways. It may look erratic and lack a clear direction. While it might not be obvious at first, stocks generally move in recognizable cycles of supply and demand.

The **stock cycle** is the evolution of a stock's price, from an early uptrend to a price high and eventually to a downtrend. Stock cycles appear most clearly in growth stocks. Older companies, especially the behemoth stocks, do not have dramatic cycles, but they do cycle along with the economic conditions.

There is only one stage of the cycle where investors will make big money—the uptrend, or Markup Stage. Recognizing the Markup Stage is a huge advantage over less informed investors. Most of the crowd has no idea that stock cycles exist, and that's why they continue to hold onto losing stocks, thinking they eventually "come back."

BIG UPS AND DOWNS

Stock cycles are primarily influenced by the buying and selling of the BIGs. Small investors do not have any significant impact on the movement of stock prices. We may buy *hundreds* of shares of stock, but the BIGS are buying *hundreds of thousands* of shares.

The majority of stocks follow the same general path. A stock moves sideways as the BIGs accumulate shares. At some point, the stock starts rising. It goes up for a period of about 2-4 years, and then it tops out. Finally, the stock falls and finds a new price level to begin another sideways period. From this new level, the stock may never recover, or it might begin a new cycle. It all depends on the economy, company earnings, and interest of the BIGs.

Stock cycle is a grand buy-and-sell cycle occurring over several years. The cycle has four stages: **Accumulation, Markup, Distribution, and Markdown** (Figure 11.1). It's important to realize that stocks do not go up forever. They have an endpoint, and holding onto stocks after they have topped out can result in big losses when the stock enters a downtrend.

STAGE 1: ACCUMULATION

In the Accumulation Stage, stock prices move sideways within a relatively narrow range. A stock forms a **base** as the shares of stock are accumulated. The stock's fundamentals are usually unimpressive, so you won't see any big headlines about company profits.

Since the BIGs don't want to attract attention to their actions, Stage 1 may last several months to a year or more. Buying during the

Accumulation Stage could tie up investment capital for extended periods of time without any guarantee the stock will ever enter an uptrend.

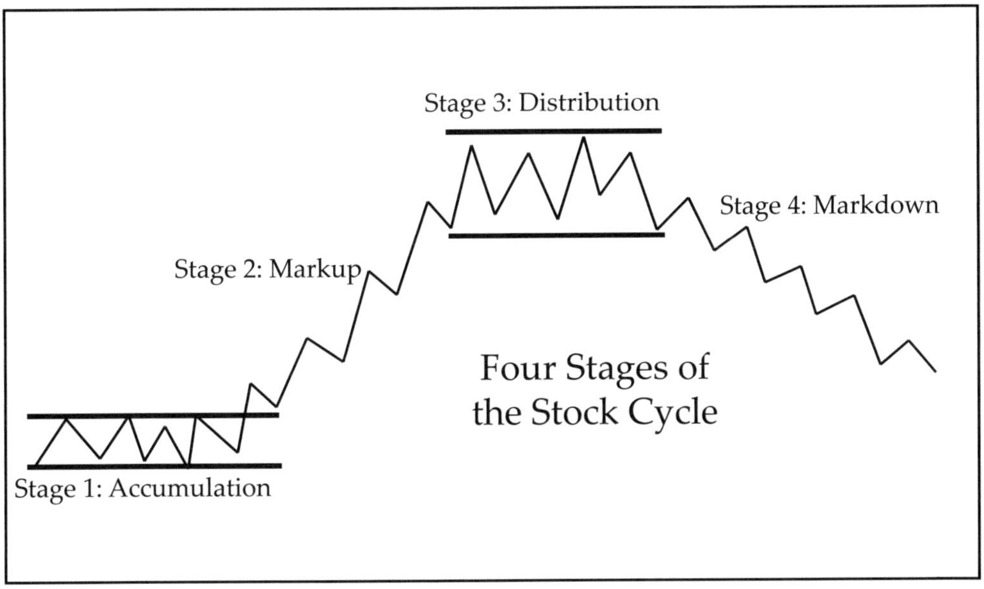

Figure 11.1 *The Four Stages of the Stock Cycle: Accumulation (1), Markup (2), Distribution (3), and Markdown (4).*

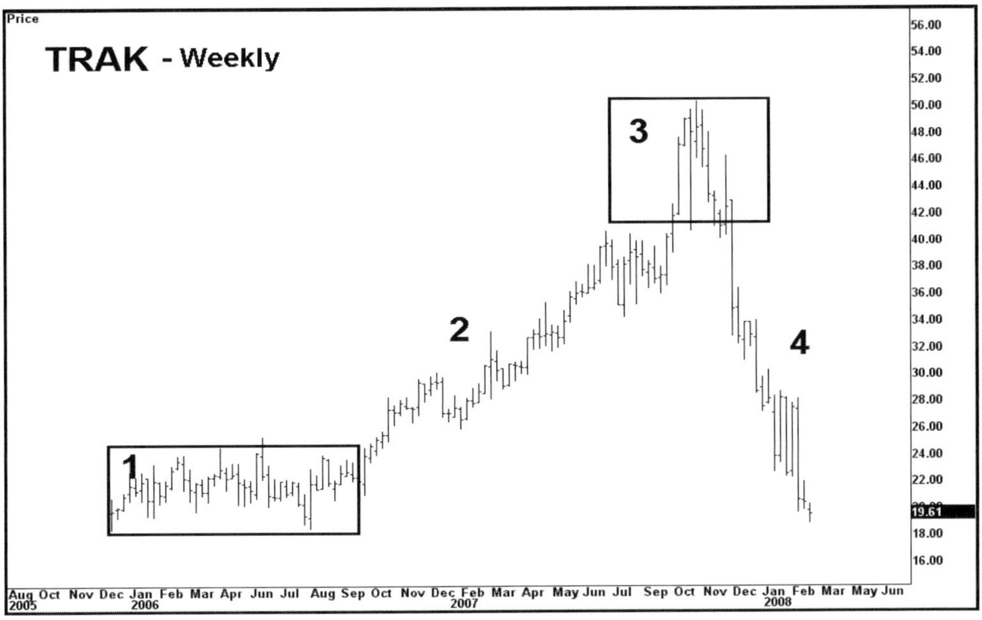

Figure 11.2 *The Four Stages of the stock cycle: (1) Accumulation, (2) Markup, (3) Distribution, and (4) Markdown.* (Chart: TDAmeritrade)

STAGE 2: MARKUP

When the BIGs are finished accumulating shares of the stock in Stage 1, they no longer want to hold down prices. The stock is advertised to the public through articles, analyst ratings, and "expert" endorsements. The CEO of the company may appear on TV to tout the company's bright future. The Markup Stage (Figure 11.2) begins when price begins trending up off the Stage 1 base. In Stage 2, the sudden rise in the stock's price makes news which attracts the attention of buyers. The Markup Stage is the *only* stage where investors should put their capital to work.

It is helpful to recognize the beginning of the markup phase *early* in order to capture the majority of the profits in the uptrend. Toward the end of the Markup Stage, price rises more rapidly, attracting the uninformed investor who listens to the media hype and decides to jump in and buy before it's too late!

In Stage 2, price remains above the 50 MA the majority of the time. There may be one or more periods where the trend pauses, and the stock moves sideways, forming a new base. The base allows further stock accumulation; the stock gathers energy before advancing up further (Figure 11.3) Bases during Stage 2 create excellent 50-50 Strategy opportunities.

STAGE 3: DISTRIBUTION

The Distribution Stage (Figure 11.2, Figure 11.4) begins when the Markup Stage ends. The beginning of Stage 3 is difficult to pinpoint. Price enters another range period, much like Stage 1, but this range has wider price swings and occurs at the end of the uptrend. During the Distribution stage, the BIGs distribute (sell) their shares to the investing public while a good earnings report reaffirms investor confidence.

Because there are a large number of shares to unload, the Distribution Stage often lasts several months. The stock will go sideways until the beginning of Stage 4. In Stage 3, price drops below the 50 MA; it may rebound, but eventually price goes lower and the 50 MA turns down. Do not buy a stock in Stage 3 once you recognize the range pattern developing. Not only will you tie up money, you are setting yourself up for losses. What if you make a mistake and buy in Stage 3? Don't worry—your stop-loss order will protect you.

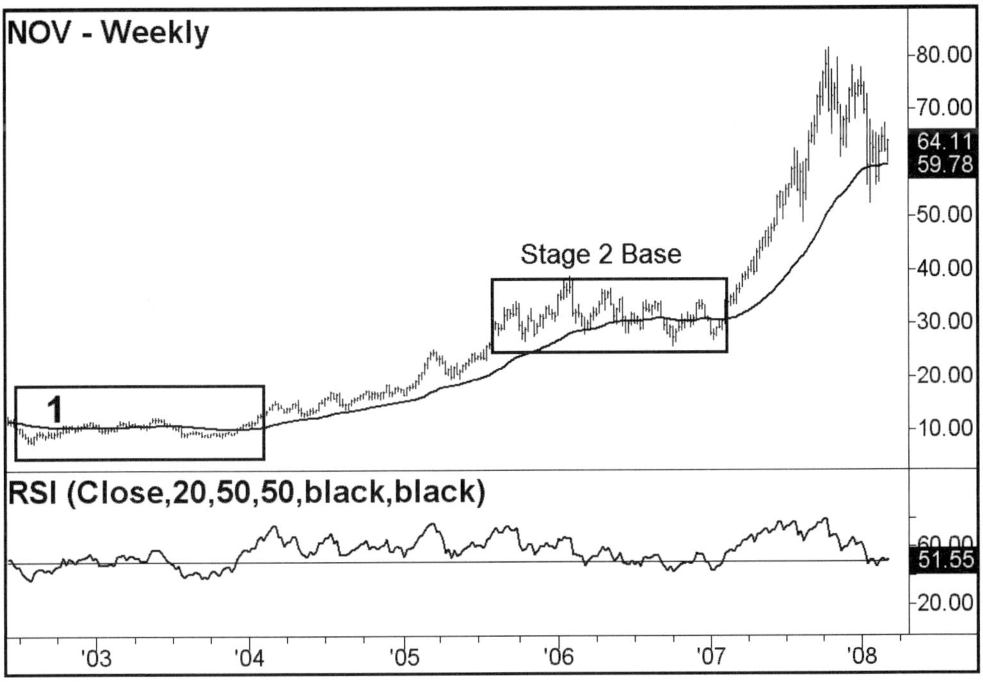

Figure 11.3 *National Oilwell Varco (NOV) is still in Stage 2. Note the Stage 2 base which formed after the uptrend period from $10 to $30.* (Chart: TradeStation)

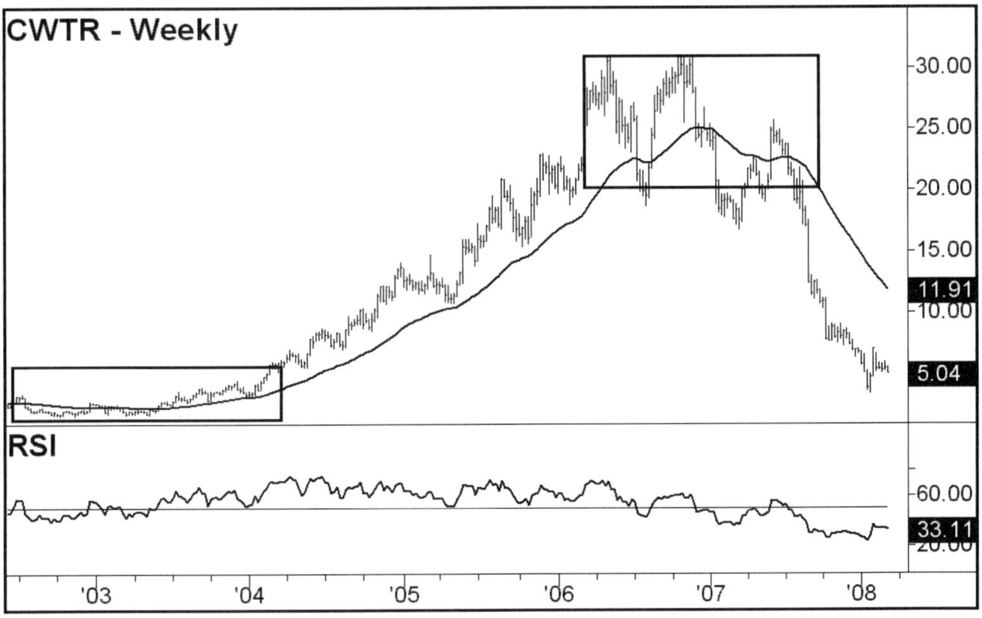

Figure 11.4 *Coldwater Creek (CWTR) shows the four stages of the stock cycle. Stage 1 and Stage 3 are marked with boxes.* (Chart: TradeStation)

STAGE 4: MARKDOWN

The Markdown Stage begins when price drops and the stock begins a downtrend. You will know the Markdown Stage has begun when price drops below the 50 MA and does not rise above it again. Without the BIGS to support price, the stock price falls, beginning a long-term downtrend.

Investors holding stock during Stage 4 (and who don't use a stop-loss) often enter a period of denial. The stock falls, but investors may see great company earnings and good news stories, and wonder how the stock could be falling. They tell themselves that the stock will rebound. As the stock continues to fall, they may freeze, not wanting to take a loss. Stage 4 is where buy-and-hold investors are put through emotional turmoil. In Figure 11.5, Travelzoo (TZOO) shows price moving sideways after the end of Stage 4.

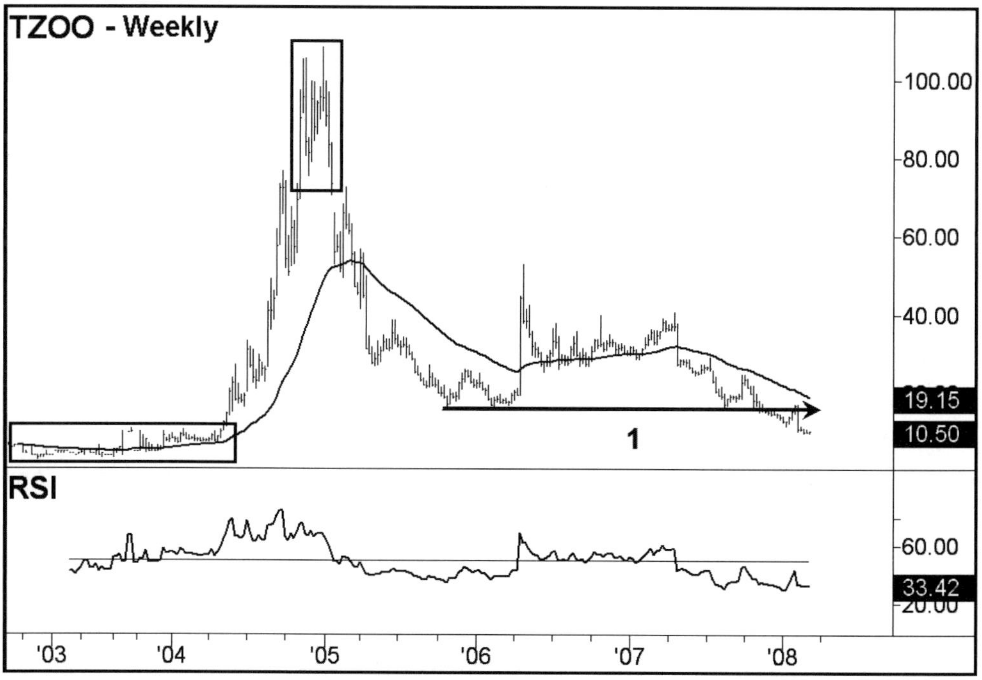

Figure 11.5 *Travelzoo (TZOO) shows the four stages of the stock cycle and a two year sideways trend (1) following Stage 4 which may eventually be a new Stage 1.* (Chart: TradeStation)

Part of the reason we invest with weekly charts that have 3-5 years of price history is to better see the stock cycle in action. The four stages are summarized in Figure 11.6.

CYCLE STAGE	STAGE NAME	CONDITION	ACTION
1	**Accumulation**	**Base**	**None**
2	**Markup**	**Uptrend**	**Invest**
3	**Distribution**	**Range**	**Take Profits**
4	**Markdown**	**Downtrend**	**None**

Figure 11.6 *Four Stages of the Stock Cycle.*

THE EMOTIONAL CYCLE

Emotions are always present when money is at risk. The stock cycle is closely associated to an **Emotional Cycle** which represents stages of investor emotion during the stock cycle (Figure 11.7). There is an upside and downside to investor emotions. The upside emotions won't hurt you, as long as you have a stop-loss in place for protection. The emotional cycle teaches an important lesson. When we are highly emotional, we make poor investment decisions. Unless you control your losses with a stop-loss order, you will eventually experience the downside emotions; they are unnecessary. To avoid the downside of the emotional cycle, follow the 50-50 Strategy and use a stop-loss.

A BUY-CYCLE BUILT FOR TWO

On the journey to success, many investors have a travel companion such as a spouse. Investing together can be rewarding, but it also poses special challenges. An investor's mindset is a major factor in success, and when two mindsets come together, there can be disagreement and disharmony. Nowhere is this more evident than when there are financial losses which challenge the strength of a relationship. Absence makes the heart grow fonder, but absence of money does not.

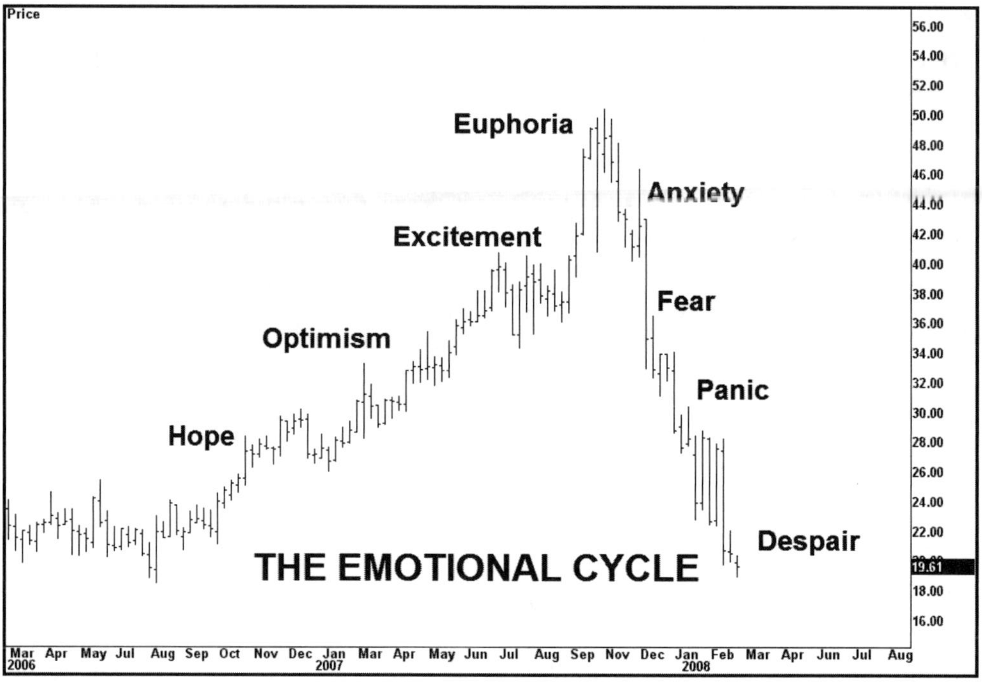

Figure 11.7 *The Emotional Cycle.* (Chart: TDAmeritrade)

It is common for one of the spouses to have the duty of handling investments, but both should be involved in setting investment goals. Avoid battles over which spouse is the better investor, which one is better at handling money, and which should have control of the finances. These attitudes are destructive to the bond of trust between you and your partner. Investing is a partnership, just like marriage. Don't let money damage your relationship, and don't let your relationship damage your money.

Couples have a joint interest in their personal wealth. Start by forming an alliance. Set goals, write them down, and be clear about the role each spouse will play in building wealth. Be open and honest, and never *hide* investment losses. Talk about the emotions you experience and be supportive. Many problems couples face have to do with childhood experiences and nothing to do with the love they have for their spouse. Take time to hold hands while you travel down the path together. Don't gamble with your love. Marriage is a lifelong investment.

ΔΔΔ

You can't predict when it will happen, and you can't trade it after it has happened; so you must recognize it when it happens.

12 The Business Cycle

The stock market and the economy generally move in the same direction. Stocks perform better when there is economic growth because businesses thrive during a rise in U.S. industrial manufacturing and production. A company sells more products and services, and earnings grow, resulting in higher stock prices.

Approximately three fourths of all stocks move in the direction of the overall market. By following the market's direction, investors gain insight into conditions which favor, or do not favor, investing in stocks. When the market rises, there is less risk and greater return. When the market falls, there is greater risk and less return.

The media enjoys endless debates as to the state of the economy, whether it gets to cheerlead an expanding economy or mournfully predict an impending recession. Successful investors tune out media exuberance and melancholy. Instead, they consult a chart of the stock market and use their knowledge of trend to quickly assess the state of the economy.

This chapter covers some economic material with which you may not be familiar. Don't worry; use the information as a resource for future reference. The main thing you need to know is how to tell when the stock market is rising, so you'll know that investment conditions are favorable for stocks.

WHY ARE YOU SO DEFENSIVE?

The U.S. economy goes through periods of expansion and contraction called the **business cycle**. The cycle is gauged by the **Gross Domestic Product (GDP)** of the U.S. economy. GDP is the broadest measure of economic performance and represents the total dollar value of all goods and services produced in the United States. GDP measures economic activity over the preceding quarter.

GDP is helpful for understanding the business cycle. Cycles vary in length and recur throughout history. Normally, the expansion phase is longer than the contraction phase. This means the U.S. economy has been expanding throughout history, reflecting the overall rise in U.S. wealth and standard of living. It is also why the average annual return of the stock market is a *positive* 12%. Each business cycle consists of two phases depicted in Figure 12.1.

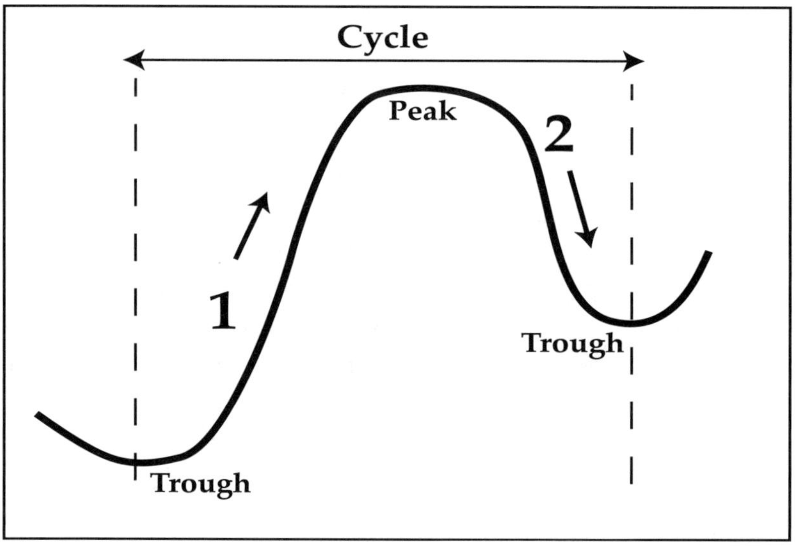

Figure 12.1 *The business cycle has two phases. The expansion phase (1) has a rising GDP, begins at a trough, and ends at a peak. The contraction phase (2) has a falling GDP, begins at a peak, and ends at a trough.*

The **expansion phase** begins at a **trough** in economic activity. The trough is a transition period at the end of a **recession,** a decline in GDP for two consecutive quarters. Economic conditions are not good; the economy is in a steady state, neither expanding nor contracting.

As the economy enters **recovery**, business activity steadily expands, and there is a rise in GDP. In the expansion phase, **cyclical stocks** generally perform well. Cyclical companies are those which produce goods needed by other companies to expand business activities. Cyclical stocks move up and down with the economic cycle.

The expansion phase ends at a peak. This is another transition period where economic conditions are good but not getting any better. Economic reports may be favorable, but fewer and fewer businesses are able to grow and expand services.

Eventually, the economy enters the **contraction phase** where GDP declines. Businesses generally experience decreasing demand for their products and services which leads to a recession. During the contraction phase, noncyclical, or **defensive,** stocks generally outperform the cyclical stocks. Defensive companies have products which are always in demand, such as food, drugs, and utilities. No matter how bad the economy gets, people still need to eat, take their medications, and use electricity.

SPYING ON THE MARKET

The business cycle is expressed in the movement of the stock market. The market rises during periods of economic expansion when GDP growth rates increase. The market falls during periods of economic contraction when GDP declines (Figure 12.2). Investors use the overall market as a proxy for the economy. This helps the investor recognize when economic conditions favor risking capital (bull market) or protecting capital (bear market). Knowing the phase of the economy also helps investors choose stocks in industries more likely to do well.

There are over 10,000 stocks in the stock market, and it would be difficult to track all of them individually. As a proxy for the overall market, investors use a stock market **index**. Indices are a representative sample of all the stocks in the U.S market. The three closely followed market indices are the **Standard & Poor's 500 (S&P 500), Dow Jones Industrial Average**, and the **NASDAQ Composite**. There are other indices which represent segments of the overall market, such as the **Russell 2000 Index,** which is composed of stocks from small companies.

Figure 12.2 *This is a chart of the S&P 500 ($SPX.X) from 1998-2003 showing a comparison to the growth rate of the Gross Domestic Product (GDP). During the bull market, growth rates were mostly above 4% per year, while during the bear market of 2001-2003, GDP growth declined to under 2% in 2001 and 2002. (Adapted from U.S. Department of Commerce GDP records)*
(Chart: TradeStation)

The S&P 500 is the best broad-based measure of market conditions (Figure 12.2). It is composed of 500 of the largest companies that trade on the New York Stock Exchange. The stocks represent different business sectors such as utility, industrial, financial, and transportation. To look at the S&P 500 on a chart, just type in "$SPX" the same way you would a stock symbol (Note: the symbol may vary depending on the charting program you use).

The majority of stocks move in the direction of the S&P 500 index. Investment conditions are favorable when the S&P trends up; there is money flowing into the overall stock market. A rising S&P demonstrates economic expansion, and the majority of stock industries will rise. There is an ETF which owns the stocks in the S&P 500. It is the **SPDR S&P 500 ETF (SPY),** and it lets you "spy" on the overall conditions of the stock market. The SPY can be bought just like a stock, allowing investors to own a small portion of the overall market.

Figure 12.3 shows the SPY during the bull market of 2003-2007. Notice that the SPY (stock market) gives the same 50-50 Strategy signals as a stock. See, I told you investing wasn't that hard when you know what to look for!

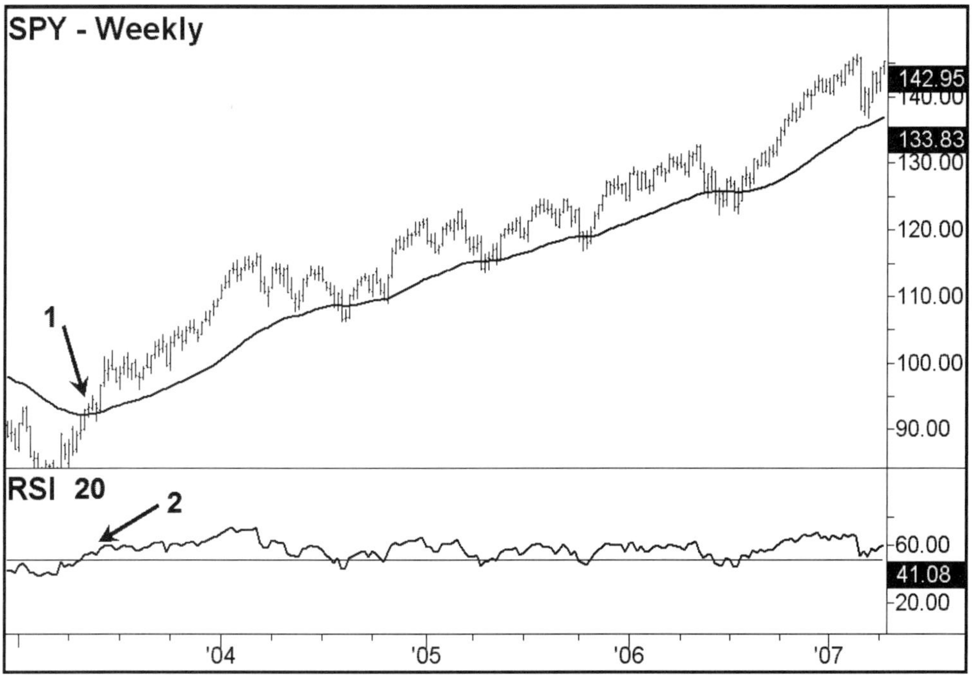

Figure 12.3 *The SPY is an ETF for the S&P 500 index. The 50-50 Strategy criteria are met when price crosses above the 50 MA (1) and RSI crosses above the 50 level (2).* (Chart: TradeStation)

STRIVING WITH THE TOP DOWN

Investors should always consider overall market conditions when striving to find good stock candidates. Some investors use a **top down** approach which has three basic steps, all of which help the investor drive profits to the bank. The first step begins with a snapshot of the overall economy. The S&P 500 is studied to see if price is above a rising

50-week moving average (bullish) or below the falling 50-week moving average (bearish).

The second step looks for top performing sectors and industries within the economy. Economists divide stocks into broad economic **sectors** representing major economic activities such as healthcare, technology, and energy. The sectors are further subdivided into **industries** which represent different, but related, business activities within a sector. For example, energy is a major sector of the economy, while two industries within the sector are oil & gas "equipment & services" and oil & gas "pipelines."

In Chapter 18, you'll learn how to use nine ETFs, representing major sectors of the market, for a big picture view of the market. You'll be able to find which sectors of the economy are trending up and which are trending down. The 50 MA is used as a reference, in keeping with the 50-50 Strategy principles.

The third step in top down analysis looks for top performing stocks in a strong industry. Once again, the investor uses the 50 MA for reference and applies the 50-50 Strategy for timing the stock purchase. Investing is easier with the repeated and consistent use of the 50 MA reference. It is used to analyze the S&P, sectors and industries, stocks, mutual funds, and ETFs. In Chapter 14, you learn how to find sectors, and then "drill down" further to study the top industries and stocks.

The top down approach is diagrammed in Figure 12.4.

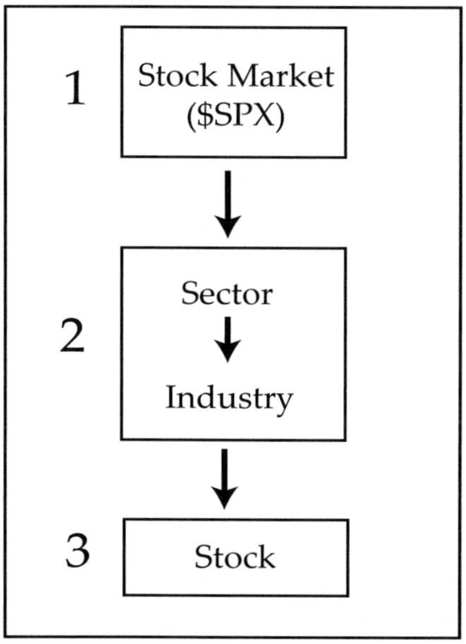

Figure 12.4 *The three steps of the top down approach to stock selection. The $SPX is used to represent the overall market.*

DON'T BE AFRAID OF SPYDERS

An easy way to follow the major economic sectors is with ETFs. State Street Global Investors created nine sector ETFs based on representative stocks from the S&P 500 index. The ETFs are named Sector Select SPDRs (pronounced "spiders") and are listed in Figure 12.5. Each can be used as investments if your trading plan invests in broad market sectors.

SECTOR SELECT SPDRs	
ETF Symbol	*Economic Sector*
XLY	**Consumer Discretionary**
XLK	**Technology**
XLI	**Industrial**
XLB	**Materials**
XLE	**Energy**
XLP	**Consumer Staples**
XLV	**Health Care**
XLU	**Utilities**
XLF	**Financials**

Figure 12.5 *Sector Select SPDRs represent nine major sectors of the U.S. economy.*

Imagine the pajama investor sitting at home at his computer, suddenly able to review the entire nine sectors of the economy and quickly assess the condition of the U.S. economy. In the time it takes the TV announcer to introduce an expert economist, the small investor can review a chart of the SPY and know whether the economy is expanding or contracting. Now you're a pajama economist. And where do you find these SPDRs? On a *web* page, of course (www.sectorspdr.com)!

Figure 12.6 is an example of the Select Sector SPDR XLI (Industrial) which gave a 50-50 Strategy signal in 2003. The 50-50 signal coincides with the beginning of an economic expansion phase from 2003-2008. The RSI crossed above the 50 level and remained mostly above 50 during the long-term uptrend. ETFs such as XLI can be used to invest in "sector" trends in the economy. This will be discussed further in Chapter 18 on mutual funds and ETFs.

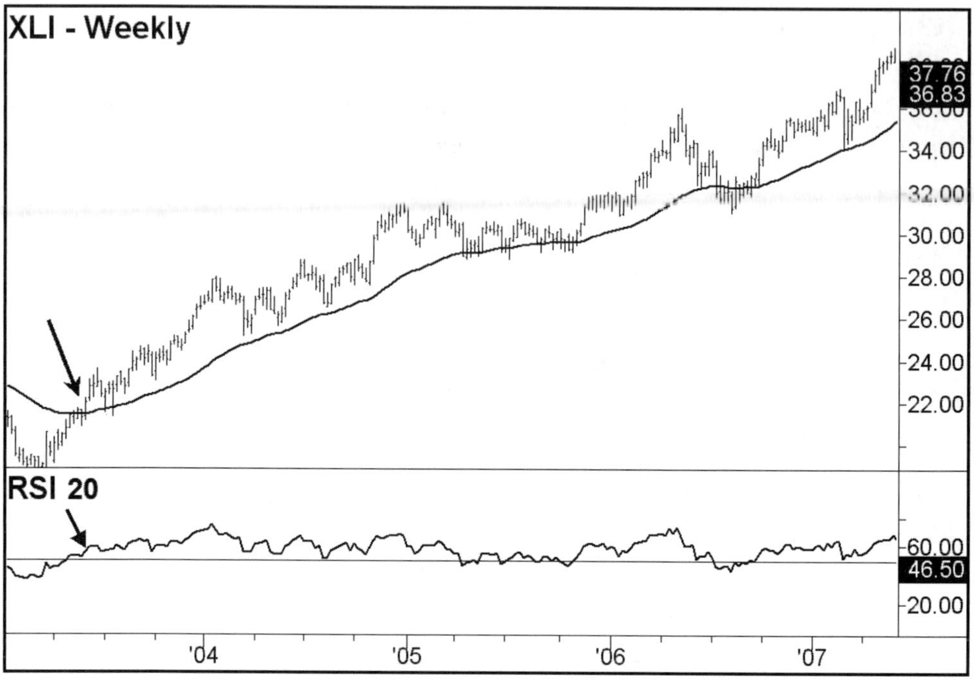

Figure 12.6 *The Select Sector SPDR XLI with a 50-50 Strategy signal (arrow) in 2003.* (Chart: TradeStation)

THE SPY IS FALLING!

The stock market is a **leading economic indicator**, meaning it will begin an uptrend before an economic recovery and begin to decline before an economic recession. At the early beginning of a new business cycle, the media will still report gloom and doom for the economy because economic indicators will not show growth. However, the market ($SPX) will already have begun an uptrend, and some of the best investment opportunities will occur. Buying stock during an economic expansion improves returns and allows the investor to hold some stocks for several years.

At the end of an economic expansion, the media will be exuberant over the economic indicators which show a strong economy; but the $SPX will already have begun a decline. Investors who spot the SPY under the 50 MA can preserve profits by selling some stocks. Successful investors never wait for the media to report a slow economy before taking decisive action to protect their capital.

This key principle of the market as a leading indicator of the economy has major implications for **market timing.** Market timing is making investment decisions based on the market trend. Market timing reduces risk and preserves profits. For instance, investors might be more invested in stocks during economic expansion when the SPY is in an uptrend. They might be less invested in stocks during an economic contraction when the SPY is in a downtrend. Market timing is natural for investors who have knowledge about the business cycle and can read price charts (that's you!). You won't have to run around screaming like Chicken Little that "the SPY is falling!"

BRAIN LAG

The crowd is slow to recognize and accept market changes, largely because of **sentiment**. Sentiment is the collective attitude of the majority of investors toward market conditions.

Before the economy turns and begins expansion, things seem the worst. The news compounds the problem by reminding us of how bad things are. It affects our mindset, and we might ignore any positive signs of market opportunity. When the market begins to turn up, we have the least evidence, but greatest opportunity. Likewise, things seem great before the economy begins to contract. The media personalities wear smiles and express great optimism. When the market begins to turn down, we have the least evidence, but the greatest risk.

The media reflects the sentiment of the crowd. The crowd is never confident about investing without a consensus of opinion. They need proof because they lack confidence in themselves to see the objective signs of market changes glaring at them on a chart of the $SPX or SPY. During the bear market of 2000-2003, the falling stock prices prompted the media to call it a market *crash*. When you drive a car, crashes usually occur when you don't see what's coming. That's why drivers should watch out for a swerving car, and investors should watch out for a swerving SPY. Don't listen to the media. Investors hear the truth by listening with their eyes.

I was at a sports bar with my buddies in 2000, watching a pro football game, when one of my friends switched the TV channel to a financial station. This act caught my attention, because no man with a healthy masculine mindset would interrupt a good football game to look at stock prices.

"What are you doing?" I asked.

At this point, my buddies were yelling for him to switch the channel back, which he did.

"Wanted to check my stocks," he said. I've been making a ton of money!"

"Really? I thought you just started learning how to trade."

"Yeah, but I'm following the methods of this guy that used to drive a taxi and then became a millionaire in the market."

"Well, good luck with that."

"I'm going to quit my job and trade for a living."

After talking to my friend, I decided the new highs in the market were making people nuts. Not long after our talk, the SPY was under the 50 MA and falling. About a year later my friend told me he had lost all his trading money and was still working at his job. The important lesson here is that money should never get in the way of a good football game!

Look at the SPY in 2000 and notice how it crossed under the 50 MA (Figure 12.7). My friend lost money because he traded against the trend.

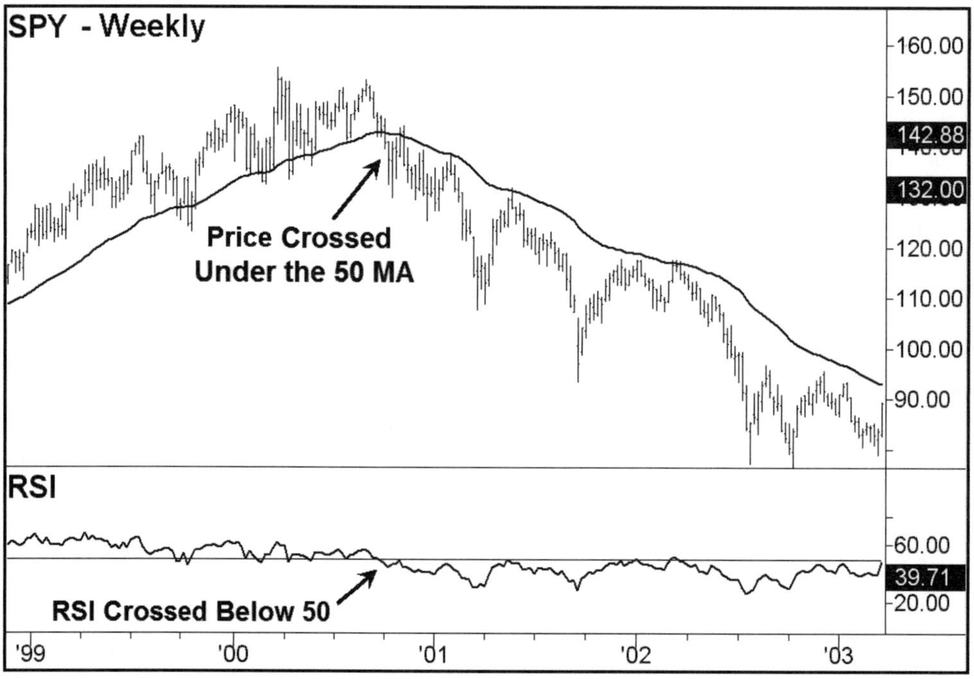

Figure 12.7 *In 2000, the SPY crossed under the 50 MA and RSI crossed under the 50 level. The market downtrend had begun.* (Chart: TradeStation)

CORRECT ME IF I'M STRONG

A bull market does not go straight up. Instead, there are periods of down movement called **pullbacks,** or corrections. Pullbacks are a normal part of market uptrends, and they represent changes in the balance of supply (selling) and demand (buying). Most pullbacks in price will remain above the 50 MA, but some will dip below it. Pullbacks in the market also lead to pullbacks in the majority of stocks, creating opportunities with the 50-50 Strategy. Figure 12.8 shows areas where the SPY dropped to the 50 MA. Investors can buy the SPY ETF after pullbacks, or they can look for great stock setups near the 50 MA.

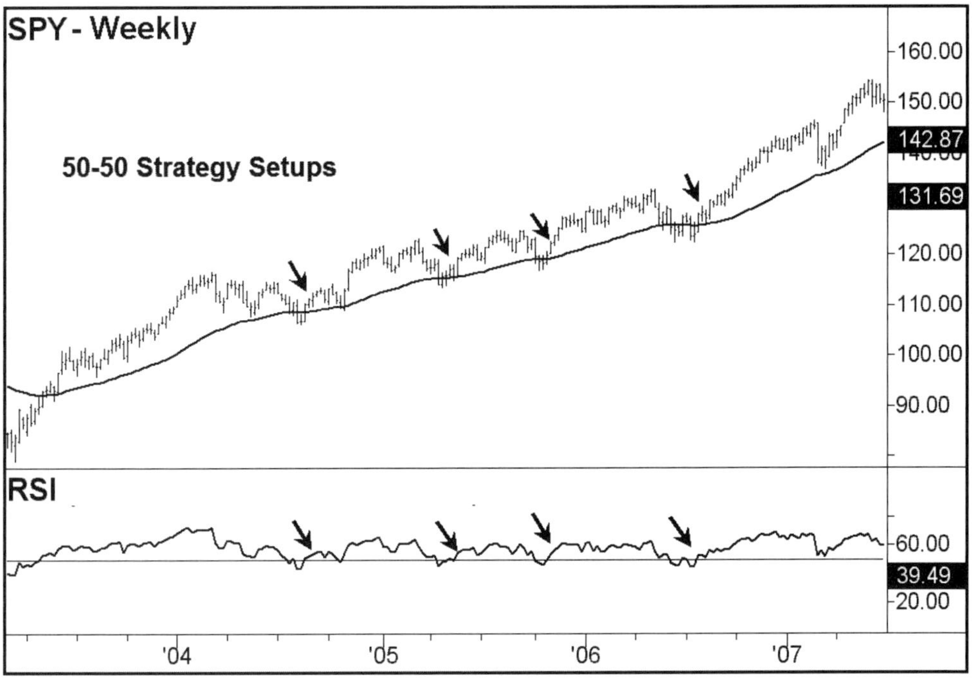

Figure 12.8 *The SPY pulls back to the 50 MA repeatedly (arrows) during economic expansion, giving great 50-50 Strategy setups.*
(Chart: TradeStation)

ECONO-ME

With a quick glance at a weekly chart of the SPY, you can tell if the economy is expanding or contracting (Figure 12.7 and Figure 12.8). You don't need to consult economists or pay for an advisory service. With knowledge of the business cycles, you are able to put the economy in its proper perspective.

Part of your investment plan will be to know the trend conditions of the stock market. When the price of the SPY (or $SPX) is above a rising 50 MA, the market is in a **buy zone** (Figure 12.9). You can buy stocks using the 50-50 Strategy and know you're not fighting against the overall trend of the market.

When the SPY is below a falling 50 MA, it is in the **no-buy zone** (Figure 12.10). Stock purchases using the 50-50 Strategy in the no-buy zone are fighting the trend of the market; trades are less likely to work out.

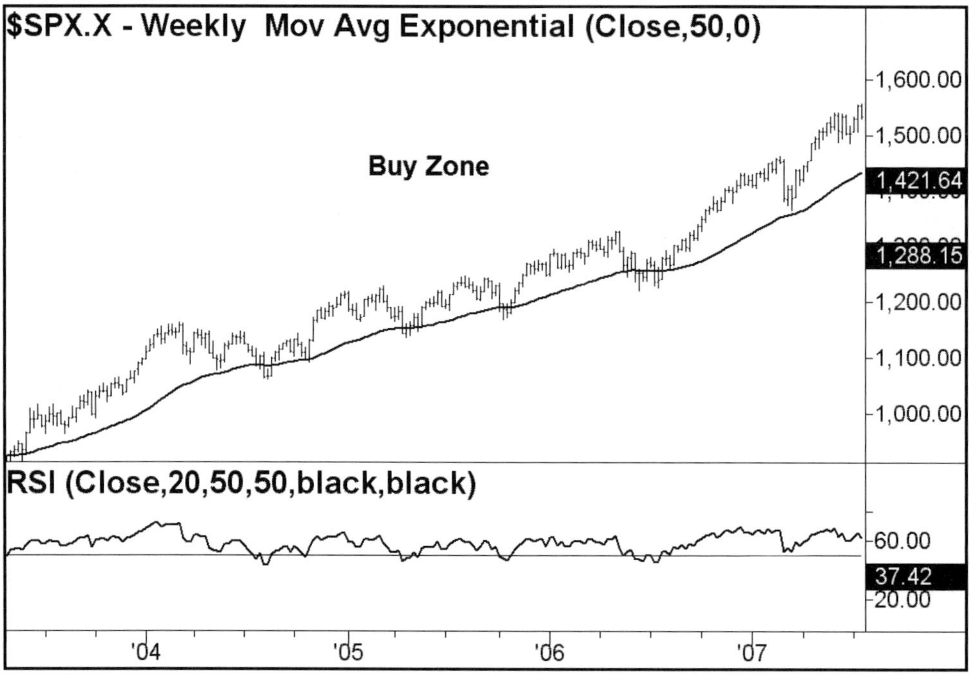

Figure 12.9 *In the buy zone, the price of $SPX (or SPY) is above a rising 50 MA. This occurred for most of 2003-2008.* (Chart: TradeStation)

You will experience the best investment conditions when the market is in an uptrend and the economy is expanding. Enter stocks early in market uptrends for big profits with small risk. Market downtrends require conscientious risk management. Using a top down approach, you can also look for strong industries and strongly performing stocks.

The 50-50 Strategy is used for market timing, as well as for timing stock, mutual fund, and ETF investments. Become your own economist and invest with success!

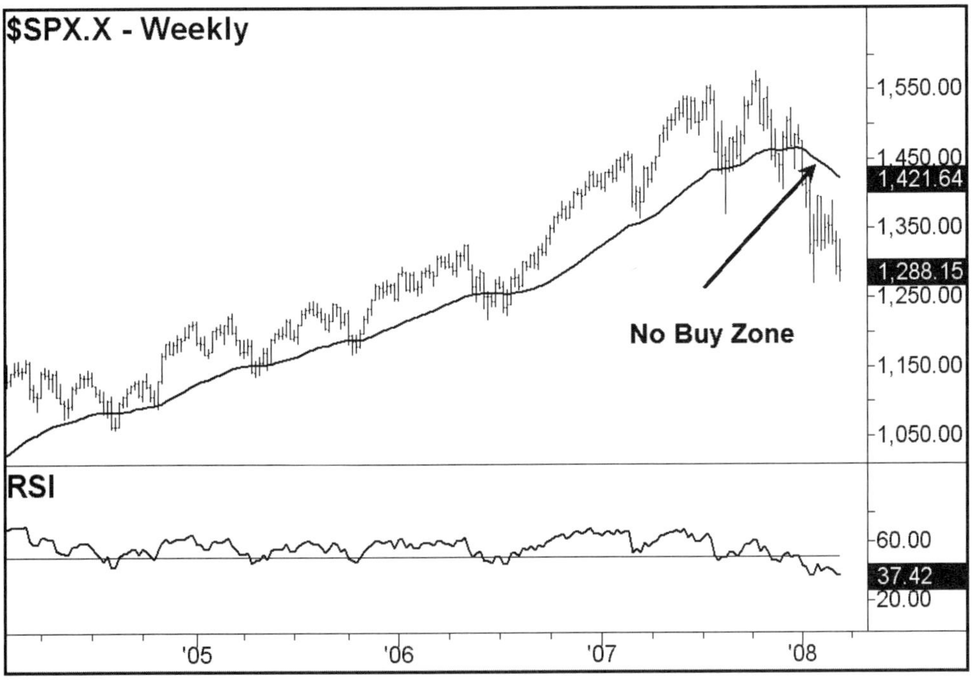

Figure 12.10 *In the no-buy zone, the price of the $SPX (or SPY) is under a falling 50 MA. This occurred in early 2008.* (Chart: TradeStation)

SIGNPOST

Knowledge is essential for your journey to investment success. Investors must make sense of how the market works, understand fundamental and technical analysis, and put important investment principles to effective use. Knowledge allows you to recognize the major landmarks along your path to success. When the investment topography is familiar, you will not lose your way.

You have now reached the third signpost on your journey—the end of Part Two on knowledge. All of the major investment principles have been presented, and Part Three will show how to use them. At this point, you have studied mindset and knowledge, but you still need a plan. Part Three will put your knowledge to practical use.

Having made it this far along your path, I'm certain you have the stamina to reach your final destination. The third signpost reads: *Summit of Knowledge*. The rest is "mostly" downhill.

ΔΔΔ

Part
THREE

*A plan puts thought into action
and action into thought.*

13 INVESTING ONLINE

In Part One of the book, you learned about the important qualities of a profit mindset. In Part Two, you gained useful knowledge about how the stock market works, how to read stock charts, and how to analyze stocks for potential investments. In Part Three, we'll put together the various parts of the investment plan. Plan is the third and final discipline in the Trilogy of Success.

The first decision of your investment plan is to decide who will manage your investments and where you will have your investment account. You must decide if you'll use a traditional stock broker, an investment advisor, or do your own investing online. **Investing online** is *do-it-yourself* investing. It puts you in control of your finances and gives you direct access to trading and portfolio tracking. It is easy, fast, and efficient. All you need is a computer and internet access.

Before there were computers, the investor had to phone a stock broker to make a trade. The stock broker then called the stock exchange to place the order. The stock broker would later call the investor back to tell him the purchase price of the stock. With the advent of computers, the broker was then able to enter orders from his office by using the brokerage's computerized **trading platform**. A trading platform is a computer software program used to place buy and sell orders. It can also be used to do research and monitor investments. Eventually, computer access to the stock market reached the small investor. By being able to invest online, small investors can work comfortably at their home computer; they can do their own research and buy their own stocks, mutual funds, and ETFs.

Investing online is not much different than paying bills online. You open an account with an **online broker** and fund the account. An online broker, or **discount broker**, is an electronic brokerage service with discounted commission fees (as opposed to a full-service broker). Online brokers provide a trading platform for the client to make his own stock choices and trades. Besides getting familiar with your broker's trading platform, you will need to learn how to enter buy and sell orders. This part is easy after you have done it a couple of times.

FOR RICHER OR BROKER

You must have a brokerage account if you plan to invest. There are two basic levels of brokerage services, **full-service and discount.** The main differences are the level of services provided and the commission fees charged. Many investors already use a personal, full-service broker. If you have a good investment relationship with your broker, there is no need to abandon his advice and service. You can still use the investing principles of this book to better interact with your broker. However, you may also decide to open an online account to manage some of your capital.

A full-service brokerage is a company with a physical office location. The stock broker sits at his desk and handles customer accounts. The full-service stock broker is the traditional broker that existed before online companies. Investors meet one-on-one with the broker to open an account and discuss your investment goals. The stock broker will make stock recommendations and execute all the trades on behalf of the investor. The client may also receive professional research and investment advice. Clients can call up the broker and ask questions about their accounts whenever they feel the need. All this service costs money, so fees for full-service brokers are significantly higher than discount brokers; many full-service accounts also have annual account maintenance fees. Examples of full-service brokers are Smith Barney, Merrill Lynch, and Morgan Stanley.

Discount brokers are online brokers. If you are going to take control of your finances, you should have an online brokerage account. You want complete access to your investment capital and the ability to manage your investments. Over one-half of all Americans currently invest online, so chances are you already have an online brokerage account. An online account is accessed through a computer, and the investor does his own research and executes trades (you can also phone in an order, but an additional fee may apply).

Online brokers have a "help desk" you can call if you experience a problem placing an order. However, they can't tell you if you should buy or sell a particular investment; it's not their job to provide investment advice. Online brokers have the lowest commissions. This is important because commissions should never be a consideration for getting in or out of a trade. If you had to pay a full-service broker a large commission to get out of a losing trade, you might hesitate, hoping the stock would turn around. Always make buy and sell decisions independent of commission fees.

Discount brokers provide great online research tools, including stock charts and fundamental research. You can track your portfolio, access account statements, and do retirement planning. You can choose to invest in a combination of investment products, such as money markets, CDs, stocks, bonds, mutual funds, and ETFs. You can also set up an account for an **Individual Retirement Account (IRA).** Examples of online brokers are TDAmeritrade (www.tdameritrade.com) and Scottrade (www.scottrade.com).

Do not choose a broker solely based upon fees. Choose the type of broker which is the best match for your investment needs. Online brokers are the best choice for small investors who plan to do their own research and make their own investment decisions. Online investing is a great hobby to keep your mind active and engaged, even if you're not out to make a million bucks. If you are retired, you may have extra time to spend online, so take advantage of it. If your goal is to invest for retirement, there are calculators to tell you how much money you must save between now and the time you retire. If you choose to use a full-service broker, you'll still want to use online websites to track investments and do research. Do what fits your lifestyle and investment goals.

DON'T LIMIT YOURSELF

Entering buy and sell orders on the trading platform is simple, but it can look intimidating if you're not familiar with the terms used. You can study different types of orders at your online account website, but let me simplify it for you. Use **market orders** for all your trades. Don't use **limit orders** (for more information on order types, see Appendix A).

There are three situations where you'll enter orders. First, you'll need to put in a buy order to make your initial investment. Second, you'll need to enter a **stop-loss order** right after you buy the stock. This will sell the stock if price drops to your stop-loss price. Third, you'll need to put in a separate sell order to take profits (if you aren't stopped out). All of these orders are placed in the same order window on a trading platform. Figure 13.1 is an example of how to place a buy order for 200 shares of Savient (SVNT) using the TDAmeritrade trading platform.

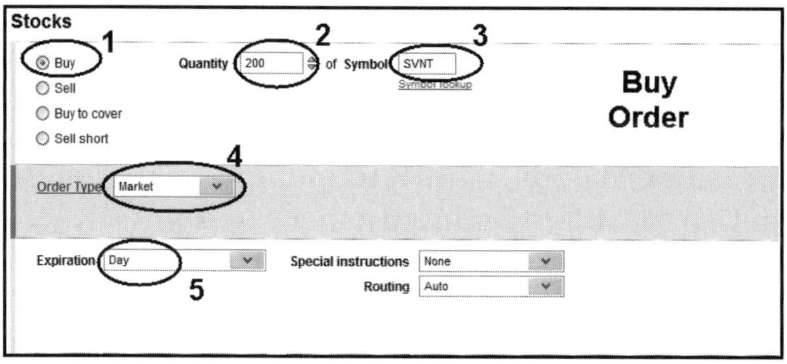

Figure 13.1 *This is an example of a buy order.* (Source: TDAmeritrade)

The five steps for a buy order are as follows: (1) Click the button that says "buy," (2) enter the quantity of shares you are buying, (3) type in the stock symbol, (4) choose "market" order, and (5) choose "day" for the expiration time of the order. The sell order is entered just like a buy order, except for step 1, where you enter "sell" instead of buy. Figure 13.3 is an example of a sell order. Figure 13.2 shows the five steps for the three main types of orders—buy, sell, and stop-loss.

STEPS	BUY ORDER	STOP-LOSS ORDER	SELL ORDER
1. Order Type	Buy	Sell	Sell
2. Quantify	200	200	200
3. Symbol	SVNT	SVNT	SVNT
4. Order Type	Market	4a: Stop Market 4b: Stop-loss price (activation price)	Market
5. Expiration	Day	5a: GTC (Good 'til Cancelled) 5b: Date you want order cancelled	Day

Figure 13.2 *This is an example of the five steps for a buy order, stop-loss order, and a sell order for 200 shares of SVNT.* (Source: TDAmeritrade)

The stop-loss order has two parts for steps 4 and 5 (Figure 13.4). In step 4-a, choose "stop market." This means your "resting" stop-loss order will turn into an "activated" market order to sell if the stop-loss price is hit. In 4-b, you type in the price at which you want the stop-loss order to activate. You'll learn how to figure out the activation price in Chapter 15. In step 5-a, choose **GTC (Good 'til Cancelled)**. This means the order will remain in effect until the date entered in 5-b. If you use a different trading platform, the basic steps will be the same, but there may be some variation in how the stop-loss order is placed.

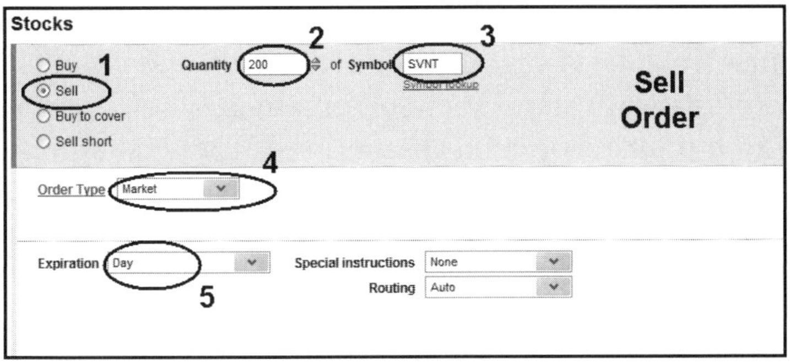

Figure 13.3 *An example of a sell order.* (Source: TDAmeritrade)

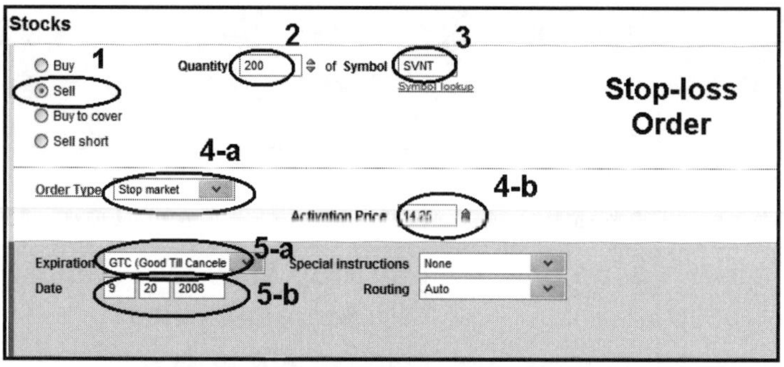

Figure 13.4 *An example of a stop-loss order.*
(Source: TDAmeritrade)

COOL TOOLS

Online brokers have investor tools for **screening** for all types of stocks, as well as mutual funds, ETFs, bonds, and CDs. Screening is a process where the investor chooses specific criteria for an investment, and the computer sorts through the hundreds or thousands of possibilities and tells you exactly which stocks (mutual funds, ETFs, etc) meet your criteria. For example, suppose you want to invest in an ETF composed of growth stocks. You can use online tools to find choices instantly. Perhaps you want to find ETFs that pay a dividend. Figure 13.5 is an example of the results for an ETF screen based on the annual distribution **yield** (Appendix A) from dividends. The distribution yield is the annual **percent return** based on the total dividends paid out during the year and the current price of the ETF.

At TDAmeritrade (and other brokers), you can set up your account to send yourself a daily "portfolio update" email, and you can use "price alerts" to automatically send yourself an email when a stock reaches a certain price (you set the price). TDAmeritrade (www.tdameritrade.com) has a special tool, called StrategyDesk™, which I use weekly to screen for stocks; I'll discuss stock screening in Chapter 14. If you already have a TDAmeritrade account, download the free StrategyDesk™ tool; it will save you hours of time. There are many more investment tools available to the investor, and you'll have fun exploring them.

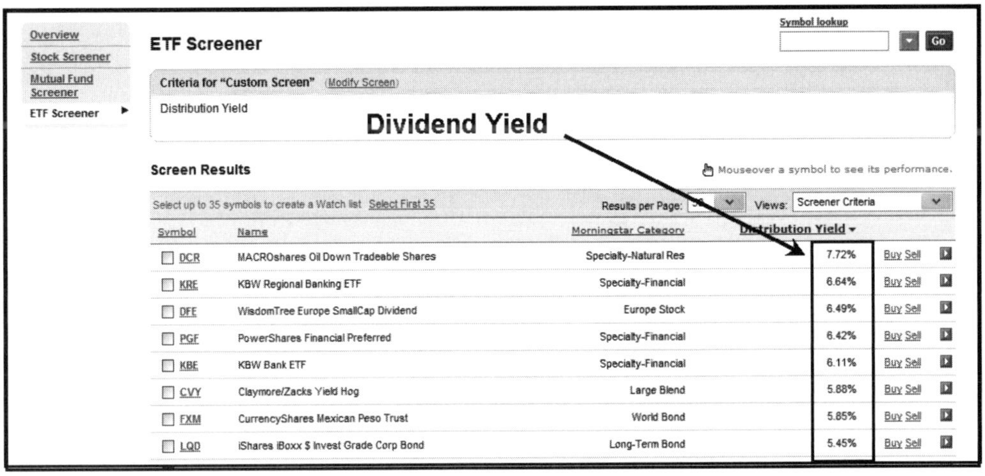

Figure 13.5 *This is an example of a screen for dividend-paying ETFs based on the distribution yield. The distribution yield is the percent return based on the dividends paid during the last 12 months and current price of the ETF.* (Source: TDAmeritrade)

IT'S A SETUP

If you currently can send emails and perform internet searches, then you already have the skills necessary to use online trading platforms. An online account can be created in about ten minutes. It's a simple, two-step process. First, you fill out account forms online, and second, you deposit (or transfer) money to the account. If your online broker has a branch office in your city, you can open up your account in person.

Most accounts can be opened with as little as a few hundred dollars. To fund the account, you'll need to send a personal check or make an electronic transfer of funds from your bank. If you already have a full-service brokerage account and want to transfer some or all of your assets to a new online account, you can fill out a one-page form to transfer assets to the account. The form can be downloaded from the online brokerage's website and printed out. Your full-service broker may have the option of allowing you online access to an established account.

It's not necessary to put all your money into a brokerage account, only the portion that you want to invest in stocks, mutual funds, or ETFs. You may choose to let someone else manage the bulk of your assets, but you can still learn to invest by starting a small account for yourself to manage. If you don't have a lot of money to invest at first, it doesn't matter. Consider investing as a learning process that you will use the rest of your life. Whether you buy 10 shares of a stock or 100 shares, it doesn't matter; the process is what matters. Your knowledge and money can both grow over time.

The type of account you choose is important. You can open a simple **cash account,** which means all your stocks are bought with money from the account. You can also open a **margin account**, which allows you to buy stocks by borrowing part of the money from the broker (they charge an interest fee). You do not need a margin account, since borrowing money to buy stocks is higher risk.

Likewise, you do not need to set up an **option account,** which would allow you to trade options. Options are an advanced skill and not recommended for most investors. That doesn't mean you can't learn how to trade options, but they are not part of the 50-50 Strategy. You can always add account privileges at a later time. I recommend investors have at least five years of investing experience before considering options.

CROWD CONTROL

Successful investing is not a group sport, and following the investor crowd will usually lead you down the wrong path. Making the journey alone can leave you feeling isolated and unsure about whether or not you're headed the right way. You may decide to reach out to other investors for support. It is natural to want direct contact with other investors, and some people join **investment clubs** and **groups**. As I said in the beginning of the book, mindset is the hardest part of investing. You must be careful about what sort of information you let get inside your head.

Investment clubs are formed as a partnership by a group of investors who pool their money and choose investments by a majority vote of the members. At club meetings, the investors review stock ideas and portfolio results. Some clubs place emphasis on investor education and speakers may be invited to do presentations. In my opinion, investment clubs are a waste of time and can get you off your path to success. Clubs are often run by a dominant personality who likes to feel important. Egos invariably exert themselves, and some members want to act like experts. In reality, you usually have novices teaching novices how to invest like a novice. Investment clubs have a crowd mindset. They are not for independent thinkers or the successful investor.

Investment groups are informal gatherings of investors who hope to share investment ideas. There is no pooling of funds, and the investors have varying levels of experience. These groups can be enjoyable for the social interaction, but they suffer from the same pitfalls as investment clubs. They usually lack a knowledgeable leader and a specific strategy on which to focus. The meetings are filled with many opinions and little truth, so nothing much gets accomplished. Enjoy the coffee and cookies, but save your learning appetite for the 50-50 Strategy. Do not veer off your path.

One of my students once wrote to my wife and said her investment group had divided into three smaller groups, and each was given the challenge of making a mock portfolio to manage. This was a competition to see which group was the smartest. The student used the 50-50 Strategy, and her group won the contest. However, when it was discovered that the student had been using the 50-50 Strategy, her group was disqualified. It didn't matter that the 50-50 group had the highest profits; they were accused of using a trading strategy when the group was considered an "investment" group. This is the sort of nonsense I talked about in Chapter 2 (Who Are You?). The goal is to make profits, not to be stuck in the adhesive of personal labels. If you join a group, you too may be disqualified because you make money.

Even if you don't join a group, you'll probably decide to watch financial programs on TV. TV shows are probably the worst source of information. The opinions expressed are highly biased, yet the commentators and guests project an air of authority and expertise. I had one student tell me she bought a stock because it had been recommended by an expert on TV.

"Did the expert give you the entry signal?" I asked.

"Well, no." she said. "It was just a pick."

"Did the expert give you the stop-loss?"

"No, but the stock is going to double in price."

"Are you going to call up the expert to find out when you should sell?"

"He's just a guy on TV."

"Exactly. What was your investment plan for the stock?"

"I guess I didn't have one."

A pick is not a plan. Don't listen to hot tips on TV, and ignore any stocks recommended on the show. The successful investor does his own research, checks a stock chart, and follows a plan with specific criteria for getting in and out of investments.

I didn't learn to become a doctor by watching ER on TV. You won't become a successful investor by watching financial TV shows. I remember one day, when I had the TV on to watch the ticker (stock prices), a commentator had a rare moment of honesty. He said, off-the-cuff, "If people can't tell the difference between entertainment and news, that's their problem." Follow common sense, not the crowd (Figure 13.6), on the way down your path to success.

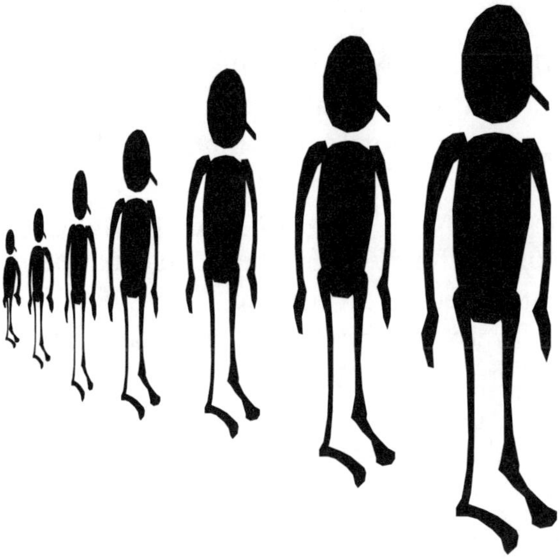

Figure 13.6 *Don't follow the crowd. Be an independent thinker.*

ASSETS AND LIE ABILITIES

Online public **chat rooms** are another way you can get lost on your journey. You will find investment chat rooms at various sites on the internet. Chat rooms are online forums where you can read and post comments about the stock market. The rooms are usually free, and some rooms run live discussions. The definition of chat is to talk socially about unimportant matters without exchanging too much information. Chat room chatter is just opinionated gossip.

Public chat rooms are much like investment groups, except there is total anonymity. People can say anything they want. You will find a lot of people who know only a little about the stock market, yet they act as if they are authorities. People can say anything they want because there is no way to differentiate truth from fiction. Chat rooms are a waste of time and dangerous to your mindset; they are laden with liars, braggers, and salespeople. Since you have no idea who these people are, they can tell all sorts of lies about what great investors they are, and brag about how much money they're making.

An important part of investing is staying away from bad information which can disrupt your mindset. Keep your mind free to learn the knowledge which really matters. By avoiding chat rooms, you'll eliminate the stress of constantly wondering how to keep up with the crowd.

DON'T SIGN ME UP

There are thousands of websites where you can go to research stocks, study charts, and get investment ideas. Most everything you will need is found free online. Websites give free information just so they can generate revenue from paid ads. Have fun exploring, but keep in mind that you will only need one main website to follow the TOP SCORE 50-50 Strategy, one such as Yahoo Finance (www.finance.yahoo.com). Yahoo has great research tools. For charts, you can use your online broker's charting program. If you don't use an online broker, then you will need a second website for free charts. Yahoo Finance is easy to use (example in Chapter 8). The best free online charts are at StockCharts (www.stockcharts.com). An example of their charts is shown in Figure 13.7, and it shows the settings for the 50-50 Strategy.

StockCharts also has exceptional free education on technical analysis. You may find other websites you want to explore, but the few I give you are all that are necessary. Most websites will want you to sign up with your email address to gain access to some of their web pages. Signing up means you'll also get lots of email ads from them to buy their products, so pick and choose your websites carefully. Everyone gets too much spam as it is. It's a good idea to create a separate (free) email account (yahoo, hotmail) just for such investment site signups. While it's tempting to explore the many different investment websites, try to do most of your research at one site; becoming familiar with a website increases your research efficiency and reduces stress.

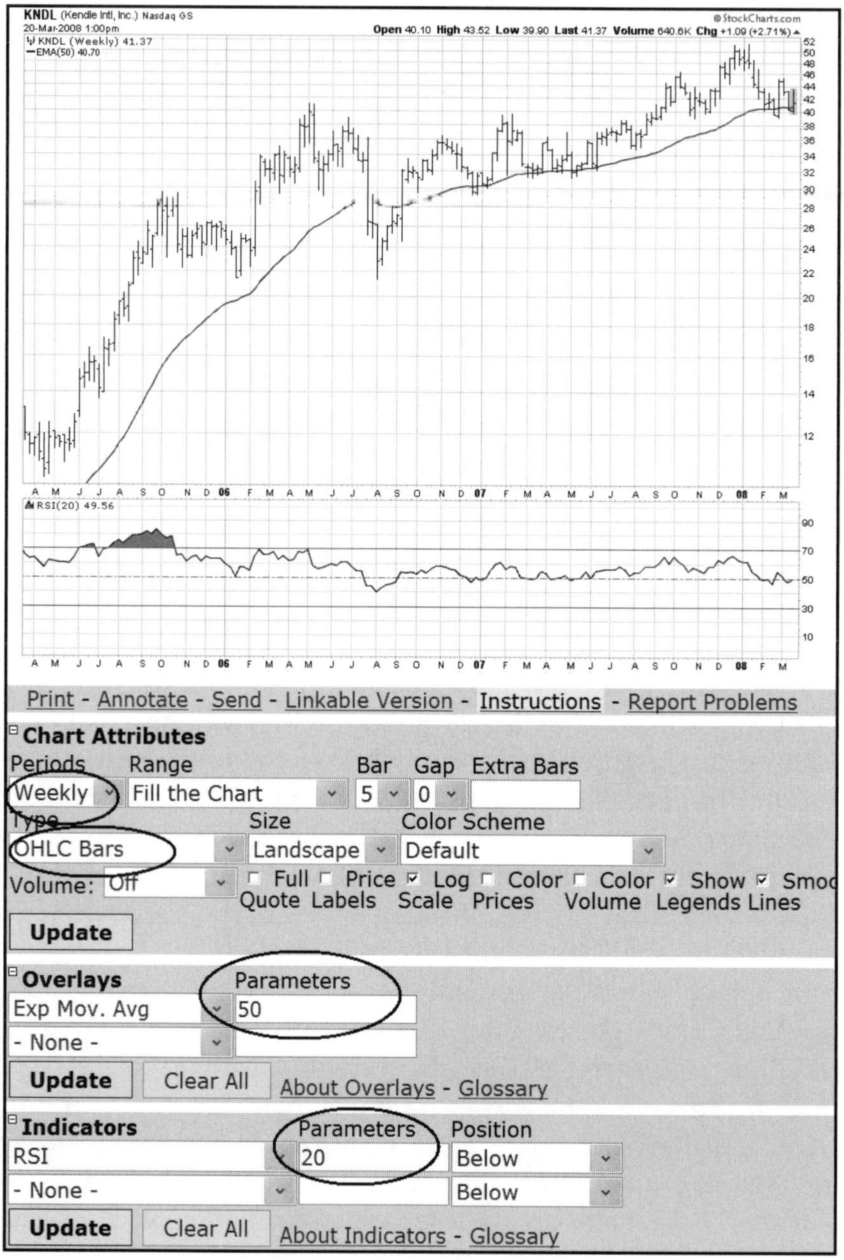

Figure 13.7 *StockCharts (www.stockcharts.com) has the best free online charts.*

WEBBED FEAT

Some websites do web-based seminars, or webinars. Websites use an online conferencing platform that allows investors from all over the world to sit in on a presentation about investing or trading. It's quite a technical feat. Webinars can be informative, but any new approach can take you off your path and lead you into all sorts of directions, away from your intended destination.

Your journey is not to become an expert in all aspects of investing; your journey is to become successful and profitable in one approach (50-50 Strategy). The path I show you is not the only way to get there, but I will guide you the entire way. Being exposed to different approaches may be interesting, but it won't help you become successful unless you study the entire investment method.

One reason I want to mention webinars is that I have done several on the 50-50 Strategy. TDAmeritrade sets up webinars to educate investors, and they asked me to be a presenter. My webinars offer a practical look at how I analyze stocks using the 50-50 Strategy. They are free, purely educational, and will support the material you learn in this book. The webinar moderator also demonstrates how to use the StrategyDesk™ tools (for those with TDAmeritrade accounts). The webinars are recorded and archived; you can view them at the TDAmeritrade website. You don't need an account with TDAmeritrade to view them. Just go to the TDAmeritrade website (www.tdameritrade.com) and click on the *Research & Ideas* tab; then, in the left column, click on *Webcasts*. Watch for live webinars where you'll have a chance to ask me questions. A list of my scheduled events can be found at www.5050Strategy.com (click on *Calendar*).

PAPER TIGER

With all of the knowledge you gain, you may feel like an investment tiger, ready to roar and pounce on any profit opportunity that crosses your path. Be a paper tiger instead. Tiger Woods doesn't win championships by the swings he takes on the golf course. He wins because of the thousands of practice swings he takes off the course. To be proficient at anything takes practice. Don't begin investing until you have had a chance to practice on paper, without risking money.

One of the best practices for an investor to do is simulated trading, or **paper trading**. Paper trades are trades you make on paper and not in your account. No money is at risk. You write down the price where you would buy and the price where you would put your stop-loss order. You can track ten or more stocks at the same time to test how the 50-50 Strategy works and to get comfortable with the mechanics of trading. To paper trade, simply use the trading log form (Figure 13.8). When you finish with Chapter 16 (Trade Management), you will be able to fill in all the blanks and know what each of them means.

Trade #	Buy Date	Stock Symbol	# of Shares	Buy Price	Stop Risk	Stop Price	$ Invest	$ Risk	Sell Date	$ +/-	% Rt +/-
1											
Trade Lesson:											
2											
Trade Lesson:											
3											
Trade Lesson:											
4											
Trade Lesson:											
5											
Trade Lesson:											
6											
Trade Lesson:											
7											
Trade Lesson:											
8											
Trade Lesson:											
9											
Trade Lesson:											
Total Stock Capital ________ Lot Amount ________ Shares Bought = Lot Amnt/Stock Price											

Figure 13.8 *Paper trading log. From left to right, the first eight blanks are filled out when you buy a stock, and the last three are completed after you sell a stock.*

I also like to track my trades by entering the trades into an online portfolio tracker. My favorite site for this is ClearStation® (www.clearstation.com).You can enter purchase prices and the numbers of shares bought; it keeps an ongoing record of your gains or losses. If you get stopped out of a mock position, you can enter the selling price in the portfolio and it will automatically calculate the gain or loss and percent return (+/-). If you want, you can receive daily emails with an update of your stocks. Go to the home page of the ClearStation® site and click on *Portfolio* (upper left), then click on *Add a Portfolio,* and follow the instructions (Figure 13.9).

Long positions in '50-50 Strategy' sorted by **Bought** in **descending** order

Symbol	Last	Change	% Change	Volume	Position	Bought	Value	Net	% Change	% Total
WDC	30.12	0.48	1.61%	2,817,209.	500	07/06/2007	15,060.00	4,495.00	42.54%	13.43
CHK	44.69	0.60	1.37%	4,242,662.	300	04/03/2007	13,408.79	3,777.79	39.22%	11.96
CALM	32.86	0.44	1.35%	230,120.	1000	01/29/2007	32,860.00	22,800.00	226.64%	29.31
ADM	43.84	0.95	2.21%	2,985,562.	400	01/13/2006	17,536.00	6,810.00	63.49%	15.64
KNDL	41.54	0.38	0.92%	58,375.	800	05/26/2005	33,232.00	24,126.00	264.94%	29.64
						Total	112,096.79	62,008.80	123.79%	

Figure 13. 9 *This is an example of a portfolio with five stocks.* (Source: ClearStation)

You can also set up a portfolio to paper trade at Yahoo Finance. Just go to the Yahoo Finance main page and run your mouse arrow over the *My Portfolios* tab at the top; a dropdown menu will appear. Click on *New Portfolio* and follow the instructions.

One of the main activities of investing is to create and follow a **watchlist.** A watchlist is a list of about 20 stocks that have already met the requirements of the TOP SCORE screening process. These are not stocks you own yet. You are waiting for the 50-50 Strategy criteria to buy one or more of them. You can set up a watchlist at ClearStation®. Go to the home page of ClearStation®, click on *Watchlist,* and then add stocks according to the directions (Figure 13.10).

ONLINE AND ON TRACK

At this point, you know about mindset, you've gained valuable knowledge, and now you are starting to plan for success. Starting an online account is the first big step most beginners will take. Go at your own pace. Investing is a process which can be adapted to anyone's

Symbol	Last	Change	%Change	Volume	Vol % Change	Added	How	%Change		
CHDX	32.97	1.40	4.43%	122,802	669.90%	03/11/08	your Watch List	0.09%	□Del	Trade
GMCR	25.72	0.47	1.86%	263,843	1,436.68%	03/11/08	your Watch List	0.47%	□Del	Trade
HEI	44.69	1.10	2.52%	50,400	402.47%	03/11/08	your Watch List	-0.71%	□Del	Trade
VIVO	29.31	-1.18	-3.87%	480,657	518.05%	03/11/08	your Watch List	-0.10%	□Del	Trade
LIFC	38.68	0.11	0.29%	163,638	72.08%	03/11/08	your Watch List	0.42%	□Del	Trade
PTEC	15.74	0.79	5.28%	158,838	156.60%	03/11/08	your Watch List	0.51%	□Del	Trade
RICK	20.69	-0.49	-2.31%	121,632	190.77%	03/11/08	your Watch List	3.09%	□Del	Trade
SWN	63.74	1.46	2.34%	899,025	306.43%	03/11/08	your Watch List	0.19%	□Del	Trade
ULBI	12.15	0.14	1.17%	28,128	45.20%	03/11/08	your Watch List	-0.08%	□Del	Trade
WDC	30.20	0.56	1.89%	2,705,909	77.49%	03/11/08	your Watch List	-0.03%	□Del	Trade
GEOI	12.79	-0.01	-0.10%	29,797	-26.98%	03/11/08	your Watch List	-1.56%	□Del	Trade
CALM	32.83	0.41	1.26%	222,515	276.94%	03/11/08	your Watch List	0.98%	□Del	Trade
EMKR	9.74	0.64	7.03%	1,082,200	254.81%	03/11/08	your Watch List	0.41%	□Del	Trade
DAR	12.98	0.56	4.51%	532,075	183.53%	03/11/08	your Watch List	0.00%	□Del	Trade
FSTR	39.52	3.09	8.48%	113,467	228.92%	03/11/08	your Watch List	0.18%	□Del	Trade
CNQR	26.14	0.47	1.83%	434,441	131.64%	03/11/08	your Watch List	0.93%	□Del	Trade
CYBS	12.27	-0.43	-3.39%	479,804	470.15%	03/11/08	your Watch List	-0.89%	□Del	Trade
GAIA	18.62	-0.73	-3.77%	231,915	334.68%	03/11/08	your Watch List	0.81%	□Del	Trade
SVNT	19.18	0.39	2.08%	1,289,466	332.74%	03/11/08	your Watch List	0.05%	□Del	Trade
QGEN	20.02	0.02	0.10%	520,789	100.04%	03/11/08	your Watch List	-0.10%	□Del	Trade

Figure 13.10 *An example of a watchlist from ClearStation®.*

lifestyle. Always stay focused on the ultimate destination of success. Once you achieve success, you will make big profits.

Investing principles are more important than the dollar amounts you invest. Executing a good plan is the way to find success. Whether you make 10% on $5,000 or 10% on $50,000, the investment strategy and money management principles are the same. Once you learn the skill, you will only get better. Even if all you do is manage a few mutual funds (or ETFs) or track your retirement plan at work, learning to invest will serve you well throughout life.

ΔΔΔ

How you trade is more important than what you trade.

14 Stock Selection

No matter where I lecture, I always get the most questions about finding good stock picks. I may have told the audience some of my secrets of technical analysis and showed them insights it took me many years to discover. I may have showed them how to enter stocks with the lowest risk and greatest potential for gain. It doesn't matter; they want to know how to find picks, picks, and more picks.

Some investors believe the magic is in the pick. They say, "If I only had a great pick, then I could make some serious money." This attitude is a waste of time and energy, and it feeds into a crowd mindset. In my experience, most investors spend about 90% of their time searching for a pick, and about 10% of their time managing the pick. Once you learn how to quickly find stocks that meet the TOP SCORE criteria, you'll have more picks than you'll have money to invest in them.

Investors search so hard for great picks because they are not so great at trading them. Stock picks are easy to find; it's the management that is hard. That's why the 50-50 Strategy is there to guide you. Investors only need to spend about 10% of the time finding investment opportunities. They should use another 20% of their time putting their investment plan to work. The remaining 70% of the time should be spent living a rich life.

You can easily get lost while searching for stocks. There are numerous ways to go about it, which is why you should find one or two ways that work and stick with them. There is no *best* way. Computers make the process easy. However, some investors get the notion they can program their computers with twenty different criteria, and then the computer will spit out a few gems. It just isn't that simple; the more criteria you use, the less likely a stock can meet all of them.

When you look at stock charts, it's easy to see which stocks are going up. You don't need a complex computer scan. When stocks in an uptrend also SCORE well, your search is done; put the stock on a watchlist as a potential investment. The hard part is the patience to wait for the right timing. It doesn't matter how you search for stocks; what matters is what you do once you find them.

A NEEDLE IN A STOCK STACK

There are over 10,000 stocks to consider as investments. Some investors search endlessly, hoping to find the next Apple (AAPL) or Starbucks (SBUX). It's like trying to find a needle in a stock stack. Stock selection is a daunting task that eats up time unless you have a simple, efficient way to go about it.

To be successful, you don't need to find the perfect stock, but you do have to prevent yourself from being overwhelmed by the task of sorting through all the stocks in the market, hoping to find the *one* stock that can make you rich. You will develop your own favorite method to screen for stocks. Later in this chapter, I will present three ways to use the computer for fast and efficient screening. Find a way that you like and which fits with your experience level.

When I do research to select stocks, I have no predilection to buy any particular stock. I don't want to own stocks; they are merely profit opportunities.

Think of finding stocks like you would hire employees to work for you. First you go through a pile of resumés to whittle down the list to just a few candidates. This is the same as scanning for stocks. All you're doing is taking 10,000 job applicants and narrowing down your search to a hundred or less. Then you'll apply the SCORE criteria which tell you if they have quality credentials. Finally, the TOP criteria represent their past and present work history. The face-to-face interview is where you apply the 50-50 Strategy to time your investment. You want to know if you have a candidate that's just too good to let get away. If so, you'll want to make a job offer and fill the position.

CAPITAL IDEAS

Stocks can be screened for profit opportunities based on the type of stock classification. One of the ways to classify stocks is by **market capitalization** which tells us if the company is small, mid-sized, or large. Market capitalization refers to the total dollar value of the stock shares issued—the price of the stock multiplied by the number of shares outstanding .

Figure 14.1 shows the relationship between classification and market value.

STOCK CLASSIFCATION	MARKET CAPITALIZATION
Small-cap	**Less than $1 billion**
Mid-cap	**$1-5 billion**
Large-cap	**Greather than $5 billion**

Figure 14.1 *Stock types classified by market capitalization.*

Large-cap stocks are the big companies that everyone has heard of, such as General Electric (GE), Wal-Mart (WM), Exxon Mobil (XOM), and Microsoft (MSFT). Microsoft's capitalization is over $280 *billion*. The large-cap group of stocks is the smallest in number, representing only 5% of stocks in the U.S. market; they are the largest with respect to total market value, accounting for about 75% of U.S. stock market value.

In the stock market, bigger is not better. While large-cap stocks are well known, they generally don't make the best investments if you are looking for growth and big profits. Large-cap stocks are older, well-established companies that have already gone through their main growth cycle. At one time, they were small start-up companies, providing opportunities to build wealth. Now, the opportunities have been lost. While these big companies dominate the market and are unlikely to go out of business anytime soon, the successful investor should look for stocks that are small and growing.

Even though large-caps are only 5% of U.S. stocks, the crowd flocks to these well-known stocks because there is a comfort level with them. They are in our psyche. Who doesn't shop at Wal-Mart? Most large-cap stocks follow the economy, but seldom have breakout growth. Unfortunately, the crowd will often ignore the other 95% of the market where most of the opportunities can be found!

Figure 14.2 is a chart of Wal-Mart, showing its lackluster performance during a period when the stock market rose over 70% percent. Wal-Mart is the largest retailer in the world with sales which exceed the second, third, and fourth largest retailers combined. One might think this stock should perform well, but that's why we shouldn't think when investing. We should follow price.

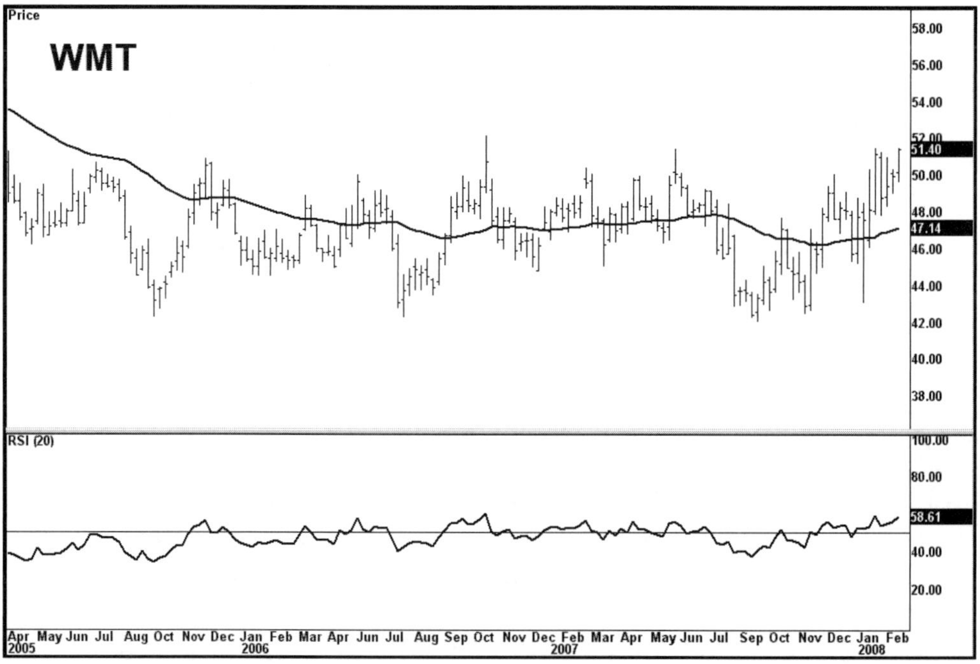

Figure 14.2 *Wal-Mart remained in a $42.00 to $52.00 range for four years during a strong bull market between 2003 and 2007. Can you see how the stock is just going sideways? Large-cap stocks are often well-known but are not good choices for investors seeking growth.* (Chart: TDAmeritrade)

Mid-cap stocks represent about 15% of the stocks in the U.S. market and account for about 15% of total market value. Mid-cap stocks can make good investments and may experience periods of growth.

Small-cap stocks account for about 80% of U.S. stocks but are the smallest category with respect to total market value. Growth stocks are often small-cap stocks. Since small-cap growth stocks are the way to big profits, the next section will cover them separately.

THE WILD BUNCH

When I talk to beginning investors, they sometimes act as if the stock market is foreign to them. People tend to forget that the stock market is all around us, every day of our lives. If you look at the world around you, you will find you know more about the stock market than you might think.

When I wake up in the morning, I turn on my TV (Sony, SNE). I then go and brush my teeth with Colgate toothpaste (Colgate-Palmolive, CL). I shower and wash my hair with Herbal Essence shampoo (Procter & Gamble, PG). I put on Mitchum underarm deodorant (Revlon, REV). Then I get dressed in slacks and a dress shirt (Jos A Bank Clothiers, JOSB) and go downstairs to eat Cheerios (General Mills, GIS) with sliced banana (Chiquita Brands, CQB) and milk from the grocery store (Safeway, SWY).

If you remain observant, you can learn a lot about U.S. companies. My wife hates to shop, but I dragged her out in 2002 to a shopping mall. By accident, we walked into an unfamiliar women's apparel store. The store was packed with women. Their hands fluttered through racks of brightly colored clothing. Several women stood in line to pay at the checkout register; each cradled a stockpile of clothing in her arms. Some ran their fingers through the jewelry rack while they waited to pay.

I took refuge in an overstuffed leather chair and found the sports page of a newspaper. My wife soon slipped into the dressing room with an armful of clothes.

After a while, another man sat down in the chair next to me.

"Have you seen the sports page?" he asked.

"Here, I'm done with it." I handed him the paper. "What's this place called?"

"Chico's," he said. "Have you ever seen a bunch of women go this wild over clothing?"

"No. Pretty amazing. Does it trade publicly in the stock market?"

"I don't know. But maybe we should buy some."

"Yeah, this many wild women can't be wrong."

My wife tried on clothes for at least an hour. Every time she emerged from the dressing room, she had a smile on her face. We left the store with two bags of clothing, and the wife who hates to shop became an official member of the wild bunch.

When we got home, I looked up the company on the internet. The symbol was CHS and it was trading for about $8. My wife looked at the fundamentals and they showed earnings growth. I saw the stock had built a price base for about a year, and it met the 50-50 Strategy criteria for an uptrend. I called my stock broker on Monday and asked him to buy some. He said he had never heard of the company, and recommended we not buy it. We bought the stock in our own trading account. In about a year and a half, the stock rose to $21, gaining over 150%. The stock eventually rose to over $45.

We take many products and services for granted in our daily lives. If we look around, we can see new companies emerging, others disappearing, and some staying the same. Staying aware of the products and services around you is one way to get stock ideas; it also gives you a closer connection to the stock market, making it seem more relevant to your daily life. Paying attention may also lead to some great investments, like Chico's was for us.

Now my wife drags me out to Chico's when she needs to go shopping. I learned a powerful lesson. Be observant and remain objective in your analysis of stocks. Some of the best ideas come from unfamiliar sources and when you least expect them. I got a wild hunch from the wild bunch, and I officially joined the hole-in-the-wallet gang.

THINKING-CAP SCREEN

You learned in Chapter 7 that big profits come from growth stocks and small company (small-cap) stocks. Small-cap stocks have the greatest growth potential and produce the highest historical returns. This should get you thinking "cap," as in capitalization. Now put on your thinking cap and combine small-cap stocks with growth stocks to get small-cap growth stocks.

You can use a simple scan to find small-cap growth stocks to study further. Start at the YAHOO! website (www.yahoo.com).

Thinking-cap Screen (Yahoo)

1. In the left column, click on *Finance.*
2. At the top, run your mouse over the *Investing* tab to bring up the hidden menu. Click on *Stocks.*
3. In the left column, click on *Stock Screener.* A page will come up. Find the *Preset Screens* section (left side of the page).
4. At the lower part of the Preset Screens section, click on *More Preset Screens.*
5. Go down the list and click on *Small Cap Growth.* A window will pop up (give it about a minute) with the screener, listing all the stocks that meet Yahoo's criteria for small cap growth (Note: make sure to disable your "pop-up blocker if you have it turned on). The screen will return 25 stocks in about fifteen seconds.
6. Click on *Earnings* (Figure 14.3, right) to sort the stocks and bring those with the highest earnings to the top. To this point, you have made six mouse clicks and taken 30 seconds to screen the entire stock market for small-cap stocks with the highest earnings growth (this is where you should say, "wow" to the power of computers).
7. Next, click on a stock symbol to bring up the *quotes* window.
8. In the left column, under Company, click on *Key Statistics.* At this point, you have added two clicks to see everything there is to know about the company's fundamentals. Apply SCORE analysis.
9. If it has a good SCORE, scroll down to the bottom of the page and click on *Add to Portfolio.* This will put it on a list for you to go to later when you look at the charts of the stocks on the portfolio list (notice that you haven't even had to pick up a pencil to write anything down yet!).

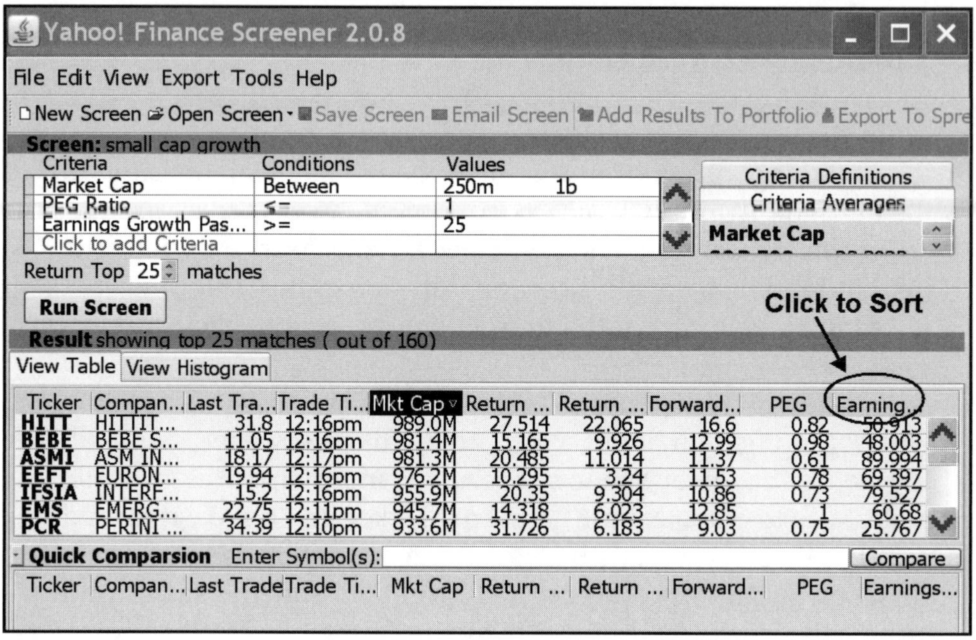

Figure 14.3 *This is an example of a small-cap growth screen.*

This is probably the easiest approach for the beginner (Figure 14.3). The screen selects the top 25 small-cap stocks (based on earnings) out of the 10,000 stocks in the market. The list gives the investor some solid prospects. This is a simple "six-clicker"; six clicks of the mouse and you have a great list to work with. Let the crowd struggle to find stock picks. Let them listen to tips and be misdirected by experts. Let them become lost in endless searches for the magic pick. You'll be on your own path, a path with the knowledge of how to make six simple clicks to find good stock prospects.

Normally, you'll find some good SCORE stocks within the first ten stocks on the list. The day I did the screen, the stock market was in a long-term decline, so I wasn't expecting too many of the stocks to pass the SCORE analysis. The *Key Statistics* of the fourteenth stock on the list, Iconix Brand Group (ICON), are shown in Figure 14.4. Study it for SCORE (refer to Chapter 10, if needed). Does ICON pass the SCORE test (answer at the end of the chapter)?

Do the Thinking-Cap screen once a month, and spend some time each week to go over stocks from the list until you build your watchlist of stocks to follow. You can easily study ten stocks each week which will take you about 15 minutes a study session. Add the SCORE stocks to your watchlist and later study their stock charts to see if they are TOP stocks. If they aren't, delete them from your watchlist. One or more of the stocks may already meet the 50-50 Strategy criteria. If so, you'll be ready to paper trade them at first, and later learn to buy them with the 50-50 Strategy as a guide for entry and risk management.

(mrq):	07
Profitability	
Profit Margin (ttm):	39.85%
Operating Margin (ttm):	72.34%
Management Effectiveness	
Return on Assets (ttm):	7.12%
Return on Equity (ttm):	12.84%
Income Statement	
Revenue (ttm):	160.00M
Revenue Per Share (ttm):	2.822
Qtrly Revenue Growth (yoy):	76.20%
Gross Profit (ttm):	160.00M
EBITDA (ttm):	121.55M
Net Income Avl to Common (ttm):	63.76M
Diluted EPS (ttm):	1.04
Qtrly Earnings Growth (yoy):	117.20%
Balance Sheet	
Total Cash (mrq):	48.07M
Total Cash Per Share (mrq):	0.838
Total Debt (mrq):	702.16M
Total Debt/Equity (mrq):	1.33
Current Ratio (mrq):	1.255
Book Value Per Share (mrq):	9.24
Cash Flow Statement	
Operating Cash Flow (ttm):	83.69M

Share Statistics	
Average Volume (3 month)[3]:	979,852
Average Volume (10 day)[3]:	1,864,680
Shares Outstanding[5]:	57.39M
Float:	49.88M
% Held by Insiders[1]:	14.26%
% Held by Institutions[1]:	105.20%
Shares Short (as of 26-Feb-08)[3]:	6.45M
Short Ratio (as of 26-Feb-08)[3]:	7.5
Short % of Float (as of 26-Feb-08)[3]:	11.30%
Shares Short (prior month)[3]:	6.07M
Dividends & Splits	
Forward Annual Dividend Rate[4]:	N/A
Forward Annual Dividend Yield[4]:	N/A
Trailing Annual Dividend Rate[3]:	N/A
Trailing Annual Dividend Yield[3]:	NaN%
5 Year Average Dividend Yield[4]:	N/A
Payout Ratio[4]:	N/A
Dividend Date[3]:	N/A
Ex-Dividend Date[4]:	N/A
Last Split Factor (new per old)[2]:	2:9

Figure 14.4 SCORE for Iconix (ICON). Does it pass?

SILK SCREEN

This screening method is another quick way to find stocks using a top down approach (Chapter 12, Striving with the Top Down). It's slightly harder; instead of six clicks, you have to use seven! You already have knowledge of the top down approach; now you will learn to apply it in a practical way. Essentially, you start at the top of the market and work down to industry leaders and the best performing stocks. It may sound overwhelming, but it's simple.

Imagine a beginning investor able to find stocks like the experts with just a few clicks of the mouse! With the right plan, it only takes a few seconds to reach the stock level. Then you will need just a few minutes to check the TOP SCORE on each stock that interests you. This method is free, fast, and very smooth; that's why I named it the **SILK Screen**: *Stock **I**ndustry **L**eaders to **K**eep.*

First, you look for top sectors in the market and choose one to study further. Next, you find the top industries within that sector and choose one of them to study further. Finally, you search for the best performing stocks in the top industry you chose to study. Start at the ClearStation® site (www.clearstation.com) (set up a user name and password, if needed).

SILK Screen (ClearStation®)

1. In the upper left, click on *Markets*.
2. Under Markets, click on *Sectors* (second from right). This will bring up a list of 12 market sectors and a bunch of numbers.
3. Click on *RS Rank* (about the middle of the headings). This will sort all the sectors in the market from the top (best) to the bottom (worst) performers (1 = top, 12 = bottom). Cool, huh?
4. Click on the name of the best **sector**. A new page will appear with a list of industries within the top sector.
5. Click on *RS Rank* to sort the industries from top to bottom (1 = top).
6. Click on the name of the top **industry**. A new page appears with a list of stocks within the top industry.
7. Click on *RS Rank* again. This sorts all the stocks in the top industry, but the numbers, or rankings, are reversed. Now, 99 is the high, and 1 is the low. Steps 1-7 should take 20 seconds. Is this smooth as silk, or what? You have now gone from top

sector to top industry, and top industry to top stock in seven mouse clicks. Why work harder than this? Choose any of the stocks with an RS rating over 80 (preferably 90) to study with SCORE analysis.

Sector: Transportation **Industry:** Railroads (1 - 17 of 17) (Technical View) ☑ Hide stocks less than

Symbol	Last	Change	%Change	Volume	13-week vs Ind.%	RS Rating (1)	Vol % Change	52-week High	52-week Low	% Off High
TRN	41.92	0.25	0.60%	1,117,900	10.97%	97	-2.12%	47.72	12.73	12.16%
GWR	34.66	1.37	4.12%	733,805	13.06%	95	50.75%	36.75	21.82	5.69%
CSX	54.62	1.57	2.96%	4,979,386	11.90%	94	-41.96%	55.00	29.81	0.69%
GBX	27.39	2.28	9.08%	373,200	8.12%	93	128.68%	38.99	16.21	29.75%
PRPX	11.16	0.10	0.90%	3,400	-0.98%	89	0.35%	18.64	8.21	40.13%
BNI	91.61	0.91	1.00%	3,820,991	-0.36%	89	-32.59%	95.47	67.24	4.04%
PWX	18.50	-0.25	-1.33%	1,480	-3.65%	86	-26.00%	21.61	14.35	14.39%
ARII	19.95	0.37	1.89%	232,967	-5.11%	85	1.78%	43.46	12.95	54.10%
NSC	53.33	0.92	1.76%	4,059,851	-4.92%	85	-41.74%	59.77	41.35	10.77%
RAIL	35.43	-0.17	-0.48%	303,290	-7.72%	82	7.75%	55.21	27.00	35.83%
KSU	37.47	0.42	1.13%	665,697	2.82%	82	25.78%	43.00	26.04	12.86%
FLA	62.51	0.00	0.00%	0	-8.34%	58	0.00%	85.75	55.33	27.10%
WAB	35.14	-0.34	-0.96%	1,063,000	-8.47%	54	141.76%	41.99	25.77	16.31%
CP	63.15	-0.46	-0.72%	636,600	-9.94%	52	-9.02%	90.15	46.65	29.95%
CNI	48.02	0.46	0.97%	1,403,215	-10.79%	50	-49.80%	58.49	40.77	17.90%
UNP	122.06	-2.24	-1.80%	5,801,294	-16.38%	41	86.52%	137.56	82.71	11.27%
GSH	25.03	-0.38	-1.49%	60,600	-36.48%	13	-37.43%	45.59	19.90	45.09%

Figure 14.5 *This is what you see after seven clicks. In this example, the top industry was railroads.* (Source: ClearStation®)

The day I did the SILK Screen, the top sector was transportation and the top industry was railroads. The railroad stocks are listed in Figure 14.5, with the top stocks at the top of the list. The second stock chart on the list had a recent 50-50 Strategy signal; a chart of the stock, Genessee & Wyoming (GWR), is seen in Figure 14.6. The next step would be to check the stock's SCORE (not shown).

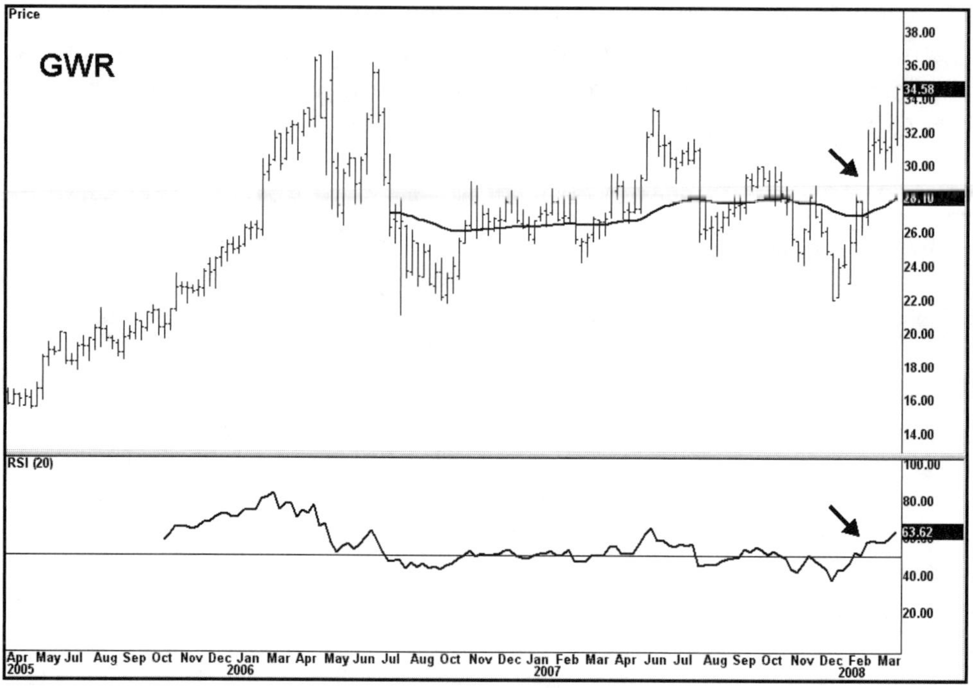

Figure 14.6 *Genessee & Wyoming (GWR) shows a recent 50-50 Strategy signal (arrows).* (Chart: TDAmeritrade)

This is a powerful seven-clicker for the small investor who is on the path to big profits. It's "top down" at its best (don't forget to check the overall market by looking at a chart of the SPY)! After you study the top-rated stocks from the SILK screen list with TOP SCORE, put the ones that pass in your watchlist. Do this once a week, once a month, it won't matter. The cream rises to the top and tends to stay there, waiting for you to whip up some creamy profits.

DESK-JOB SCREEN

Here's another way to make stock selection easy, although it's a little more advanced. It is something you can learn, and it's also a good teaching tool for the 50-50 Strategy. This strategy only works if you have the StrategyDesk™ tool which comes free with a TDAmeritrade account. It is hard to duplicate the power of this scan with any other free websites or trading platforms. (Disclaimer: this method uses my screening formula for the 50-50 Strategy; the strategy is not endorsed by TDAmeritrade. I only use their StrategyDesk™ software to do the stock screening).

The 50-50 Strategy formula should come as a built-in strategy in StrategyDesk™. The formula is entered into the StrategyDesk™ screener tool with a couple of mouse clicks (Figure 14.7) (For more information about the 50-50 Strategy formula, see Appendix A). I run the scan on the Russell 2000 Index of small-cap stocks. It can just as easily be used to screen stocks from the NASDAQ, S&P 500, or the Dow Jones Industrial Average.

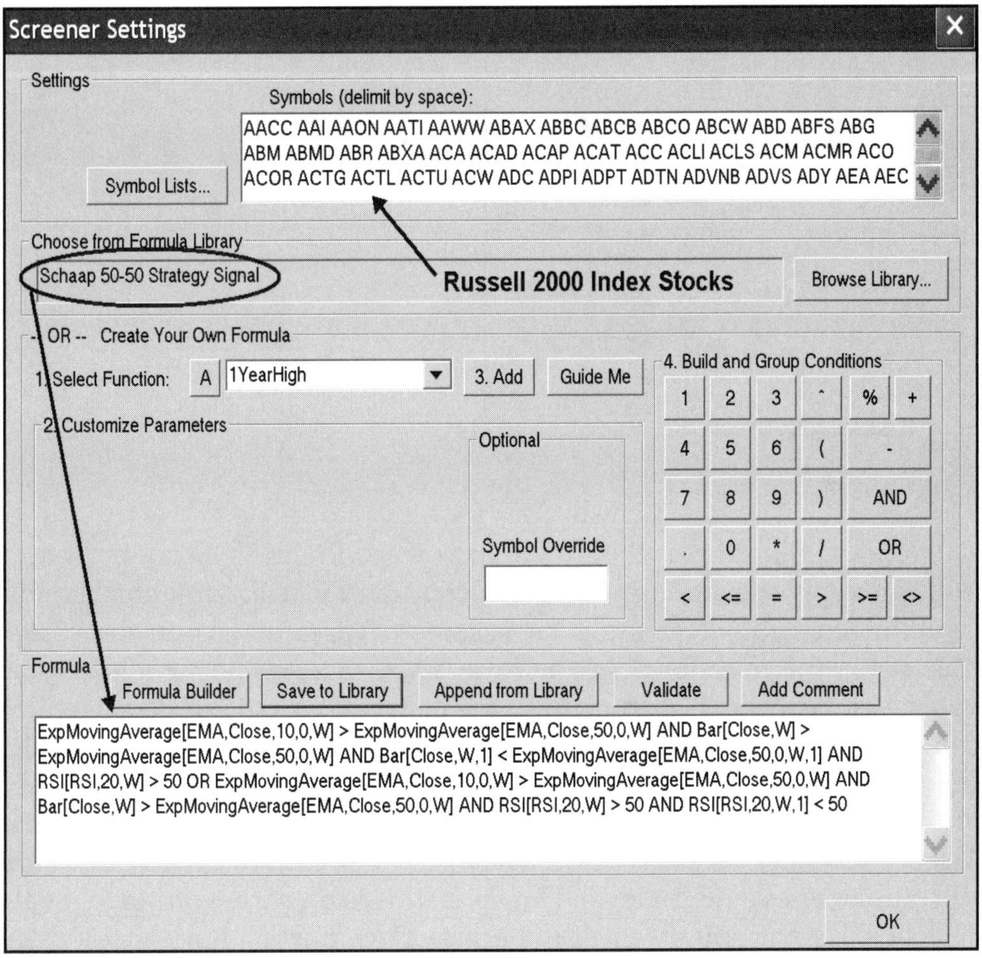

Figure 14.7 *Screening of the Russell 2000 Index stocks using the 50-50 Strategy formula.* (Source: TDAmeritrade, StrategyDesk™)

It takes a few minutes, but the screener will scan the entire list of 2000 stocks and find those where price recently closed above the 50 MA and where RSI recently closed above the 50 level (together or separately) (Figure 14.8). You can run the screener every weekend to check for stocks which gave new signals; it's a huge timesaver. You'll still have to look at charts to see if there is a rising 50 MA, and you'll want to look at the Key Statistics to see how the stocks SCORE.

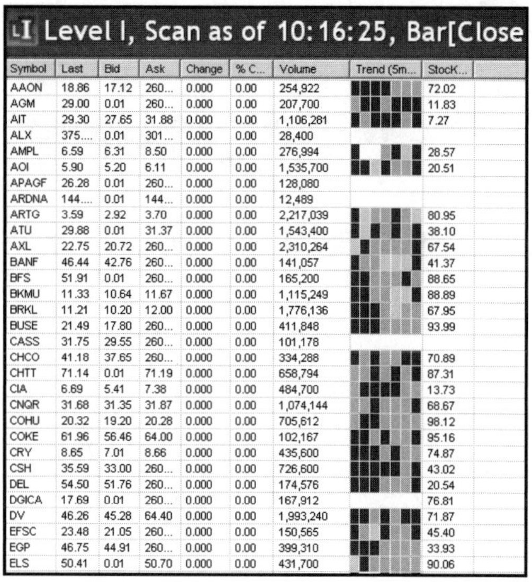
LI Level I, Scan as of 10:16:25, Bar[Close

Symbol	Last	Bid	Ask	Change	% C...	Volume	Trend (5m...	StocK...	
AAON	18.86	17.12	260...	0.000	0.00	254,922		72.02	
AGM	29.00	0.01	260...	0.000	0.00	207,700		11.83	
AIT	29.30	27.65	31.88	0.000	0.00	1,106,281		7.27	
ALX	375....	0.01	301...	0.000	0.00	28,400			
AMPL	6.59	6.31	8.50	0.000	0.00	276,994		28.57	
AOI	5.90	5.20	6.11	0.000	0.00	1,535,700		20.51	
APAGF	26.28	0.01	260...	0.000	0.00	128,080			
ARDNA	144....	0.01	144...	0.000	0.00	12,489			
ARTG	3.59	2.92	3.70	0.000	0.00	2,217,039		80.95	
ATU	29.88	0.01	31.37	0.000	0.00	1,543,400		38.10	
AXL	22.75	20.72	260...	0.000	0.00	2,310,264		67.54	
BANF	46.44	42.76	260...	0.000	0.00	141,057		41.37	
BFS	51.91	0.01	260...	0.000	0.00	165,200		88.65	
BKMU	11.33	10.64	11.67	0.000	0.00	1,115,249		88.89	
BRKL	11.21	10.20	12.00	0.000	0.00	1,776,136		67.95	
BUSE	21.49	17.80	260...	0.000	0.00	411,848		93.99	
CASS	31.75	29.55	260...	0.000	0.00	101,178			
CHCO	41.18	37.65	260...	0.000	0.00	334,288		70.89	
CHTT	71.14	0.01	71.19	0.000	0.00	658,794		87.31	
CIA	6.69	5.41	7.38	0.000	0.00	484,700		13.73	
CNQR	31.68	31.35	31.87	0.000	0.00	1,074,144		68.67	
COHU	20.32	19.20	20.28	0.000	0.00	705,612		98.12	
COKE	61.96	56.46	64.00	0.000	0.00	102,167		95.16	
CRY	8.65	7.01	8.66	0.000	0.00	435,600		74.87	
CSH	35.59	33.00	260...	0.000	0.00	726,600		43.02	
DEL	54.50	51.76	260...	0.000	0.00	174,576		20.54	
DGICA	17.69	0.01	260...	0.000	0.00	167,912		76.81	
DV	46.26	45.28	64.40	0.000	0.00	1,993,240		71.87	
EFSC	23.48	21.05	260...	0.000	0.00	150,565		45.40	
EGP	46.75	44.91	260...	0.000	0.00	399,310		33.93	
ELS	50.41	0.01	50.70	0.000	0.00	431,700		90.06	

Figure 14.8 Result *(partial) of the 50-50 Strategy screening of the Russell 2000.* (Source: TDAmeritrade, StrategyDesk™)

Here's another great thing to help you see the 50-50 Strategy better. You can apply the strategy to a stock chart and it will mark buy signals (you'll need another formula for sells; see Appendix A) on the chart. This helps the investor see when the 50-50 Strategy is signaled, so it becomes an excellent learning tool. For instance, one of the stocks which came up on Figure 14.8 was Nuance Communications (NUAN). In Figure 14.9, the strategy is applied to the chart of NUAN (buy signals are circled). The signals are small and hard to see, so I have circled them. The 50-50 Strategy signal shows when price closes above the 50 MA and RSI crosses above the 50 level. However, this is an early warning signal. The stock is not bought until the entire price bar is above the 50 MA (explained in Chapter 15).

Keep in mind, these are not automatic buy signals; all of the TOP SCORE 50-50 Strategy criteria must be met before the stock is bought.

The screen gives you a timely starting point for analyzing potential investment opportunities.

Have fun. The tools are cool.

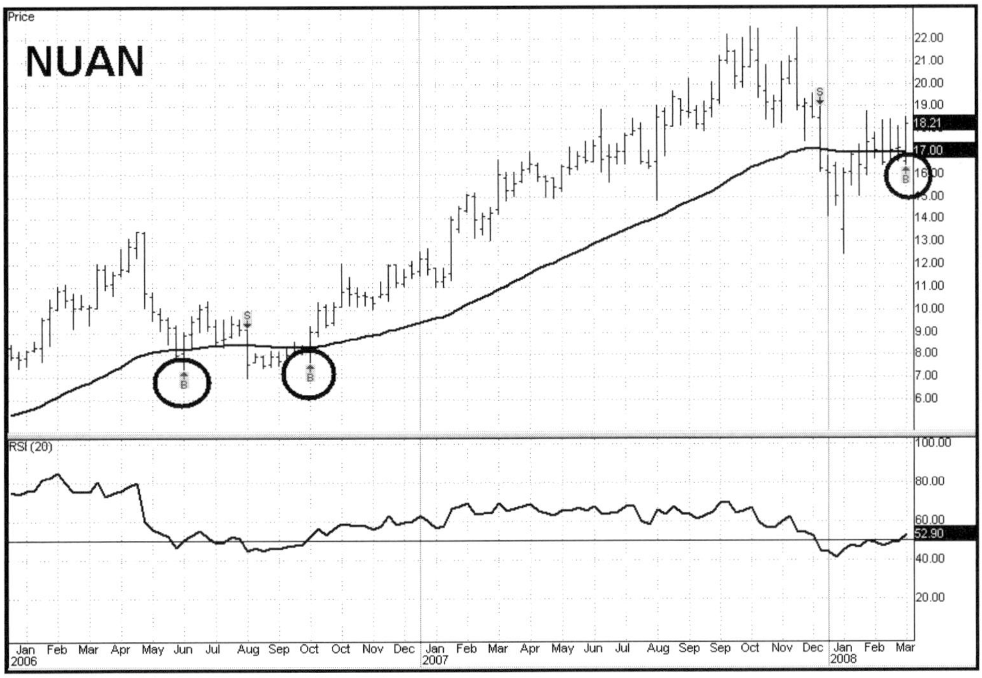

Figure 14.9 *A weekly chart with buy signals (circled because they are hard to see) based on the 50-50 Strategy. StrategyDesk™ marks the signals below the price bar; but the buys are always made when price is above the 50 MA.* (Chart: TDAmeritrade)

PICKS-ELATED

At one of my seminars, I taught the 50-50 Strategy. At the end of the class, I showed them five TOP SCORE stocks which I had previously screened. It was time to show the power of the method. I spent time pointing out rising 50 MA and RSI above the 50 level. I continued talking about the good fundamentals and the big upside for the companies.

Investors in the audience nodded their heads in agreement. At this point, I knew it was all making sense to them; they were finally getting it! After the seminar, we all went home to wait for an entry in one or more of the stocks I had presented.

A few weeks later, I discovered that most of them had completely ignored the stocks from the seminar presentation. Instead, they bought stocks without a TOP SCORE. Some of the stocks were in downtrends. Yikes!

Still, these investors were downright elated with their stock picks, and they defended their choices with "50-50 Strategy" reasoning. When I pointed out that their stocks did not meet the 50-50 Strategy criteria, they were embarrassed, for I had caught them with their brain in the "kookie jar."

This type of decision making always flabbergasts me. There is no rational explanation for picking poorly-rated stocks when you are aware of highly-rated stocks. Maybe the nodding of their heads in class was because they were *nodding off!*

After talking with them about their thought process, I realized that there is no glory for the ego in using someone else's stock pick. The glory is in finding your own stock pick, a pick no one else has found, and then having it become a stock-rocket, headed off to the moon. To the ego, goes the bragging rights. It's much like prospecting for gold. We want to be the one who discovers the gold. We want to strike it rich and stake our claim to fame as well as riches.

ΔΔΔ

Answer for Figure 14.4

Figure 14.4: Yes, the stock meets the SCORE criteria. It is added to your watchlist.

A novice with a plan is better than an expert without one.

15 The 50-50 Strategy

The 50-50 Strategy almost never happened. I had developed the strategy while looking for a method to trade strong trends. I studied thousands of stock charts to see what the strong performers had in common; I noticed that price was only able to establish a sustained trend when it was above a rising 50 MA. The RSI indicator was compared to price and adapted (the default setting was changed from 14 to 20) to better represent the strength of price in trending conditions.

For my own benefit, I documented the strategy and attached charts showing the signals for entry. I put the strategy in my desk drawer and left it there, but I continued to use the strategy with good success. My wife read the strategy and was impressed with its simplicity and effectiveness. Without telling me, she sent the strategy to *Technical Analysis of Stocks & Commodities* magazine, and they published my original work in the March 2004 edition.

Since then, investors from all over the world have profited with the 50-50 Strategy. The strategy has been refined over time as a result of teaching it and getting feedback. I have continued to simplify the strategy, removing every detail that wasn't essential. The result is the current strategy presented in this book. I have taught the 50-50 Strategy to groups for several years. It has been a favorite strategy for building wealth, especially by those who have busy, full-time jobs and a family.

The purpose of an investment **strategy** is to give the investor directions for when to buy and sell. The criteria for the strategy should be easily understood and contain objective signals. An objective signal means anyone who looks at the signal will see the same thing. For instance, a traffic stoplight gives objective signals. Unless you are color blind, you will see green when I see green and red when I see red. We both know when to go or stop. Even the ego knows the light is red, but the ego likes to beat the red light.

If you give your strategy to another investor, he should be able to understand it and use it in the same way. If he can't, then you don't have an effective strategy. An effective strategy leaves no room to insert opinion, intuition, or bias. Why do some people succeed with a strategy while others fail? They may not have the mindset to apply the strategy, they may lack the knowledge of how to use the strategy, and/or they may not have an overall plan to give context to the strategy. This is why I have emphasized the Trilogy of Success.

BLANKS FOR THE MEMORIES

It's been awhile since you read Chapter 1, and you've come a long way. In Chapter 1, I presented the Trilogy of Success—mindset, knowledge, and plan. I demonstrated the 50-50 Strategy, so you would understand the basic approach of the book. I also promised you something:

> *"The 50-50 Strategy is the method you will use to know when to buy a stock. I will go over the strategy in more detail in Chapter 15, but the basic strategy will be the same from here on out. Throughout the rest of the book, the charts will be similar to the ones you just studied. I won't make them any more complicated."*

I've kept my word; I've repeated the 50-50 Strategy signals over and over on charts throughout the book. Repetition is how we learn, and investing is simple if we don't complicate it with what we think.

The 50-50 Strategy should be very familiar to you by now. You should be seeing uptrends in your sleep. Now it's time to test your memory and show me that you have paid attention since Chapter 1. Fill in the following blanks:

The Two 50-50 Strategy Criteria are:

1. **Price is __________ a __________ 50 MA.**
2. **RSI 20 is __________ the _______ level.**

As they say in Italy, *fantastico!* Now it's time to go over the 50-50 Strategy in more detail.

RETURN TO TRENDER

The 50-50 Strategy is based on the principle that price always returns to the 50 MA (Figure 15.1). A stock may stay above it for several months, but eventually the stock pulls back to the 50 MA. The first consideration of applying the 50-50 Strategy is to find stocks that are already trending up. Start with a 3-5 year history of price on the chart. This lets you see the long-term trend of the stock, mutual fund, or ETF.

As you study a stock chart with a price uptrend, look for areas where price pulls back to the 50 MA. If price drops below the 50 MA and stays below it, the stock will not meet the 50-50 Strategy criteria. In this case, the stock is not a buy, but it may be placed on your watchlist. Only after price crosses back above the 50 MA will there be a 50-50 Strategy signal; RSI must cross back above the 50 level, too. When price crosses back above the 50 MA, it means there is enough buying pressure to continue the uptrend. The 50-50 Strategy won't give you the signal to buy until conditions are right; that's why the strategy can have instant success with beginners—it compensates for any lack of technical expertise.

The majority of stocks are likely to return to their 50 MAs when the overall market makes a pullback. The natural response of many investors is to avoid stocks with falling prices. However, market pullbacks create some of the best 50-50 Strategy setups! Successful investors stick to their plan and use the 50-50 Strategy to guide them. When the market resumes its long-term uptrend, you'll also find several TOP SCORE stocks resuming uptrends and meeting the 50-50 Strategy criteria.

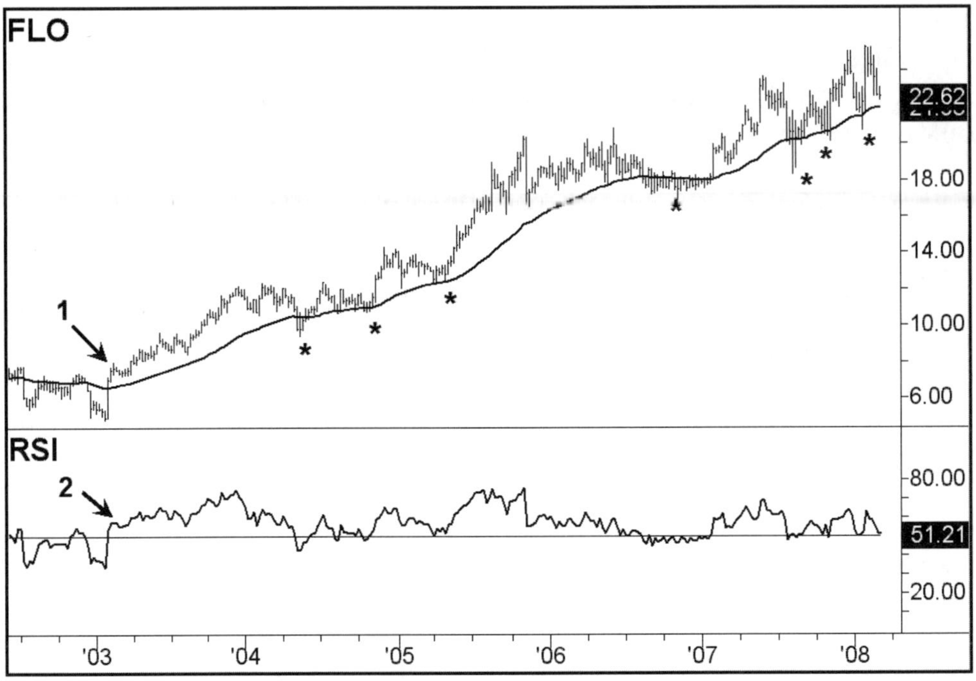

Figure 15.1 *Flowers Foods (FLO) is an example of how price returns to the 50 MA (asterisks). By now you should recognize what happened at (1) and (2).* (Chart: TradeStation)

PURTY DOUBLE CROSSER

The purpose of the 50-50 Strategy is to signal the moment when price resumes an uptrend following a pullback. After the signal occurs, investors can buy a stock if the 50 MA has turned up. High Risers can be bought as soon as the 50-50 signal is seen because the 50 MA is already rising. Low Risers need the 50 MA to turn up for about three months (after a 50-50 Strategy signal) before they are a buy. Once the moving average turns up, there is less risk of price dropping below it and stopping out a position.

The classic signal of the 50-50 Strategy is the double cross: 1) price crosses above the 50 MA and 2) RSI crosses above the 50 level. It's a purty sight to see! They may cross together, or cross separately, but both must meet the 50-50 Strategy **criteria** before risking capital. Figure 15.2 shows two 50-50 Strategy signals for Amphenol (APH), one in 2004 and another in 2005. To better see the detail in the crosses, zoom in and look at 1-2 (or less) years of history (Figure 15.3).

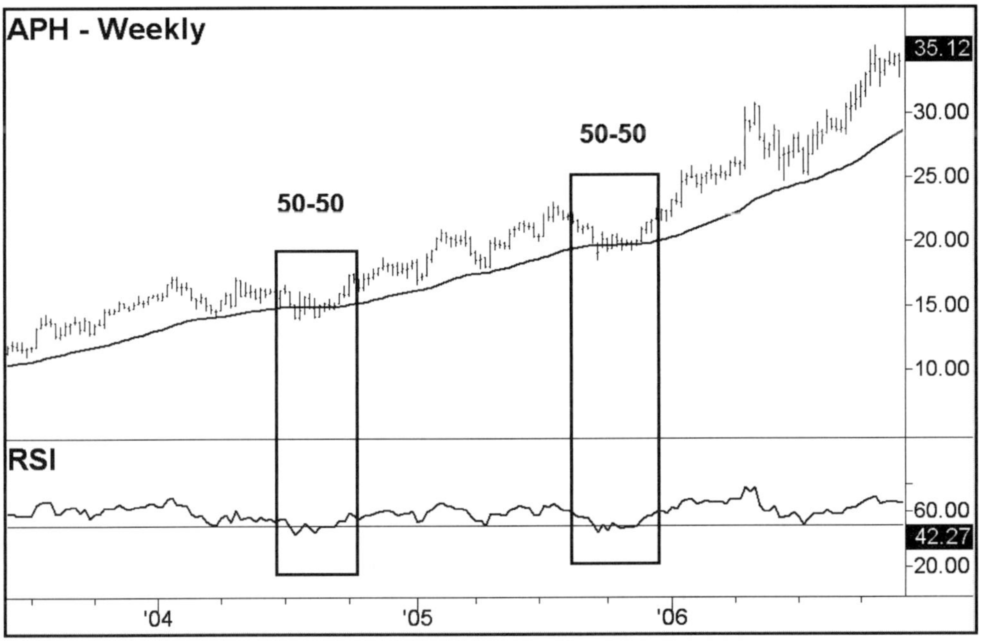

Figure 15.2 *Aphenol (APH) shows two 50-50 Strategy signals. It may be hard to see the first price bar that is above the 50 MA or when the RSI line is above the 50 level. See Figure 15.3 for comparison.* (Chart: TradeStation)

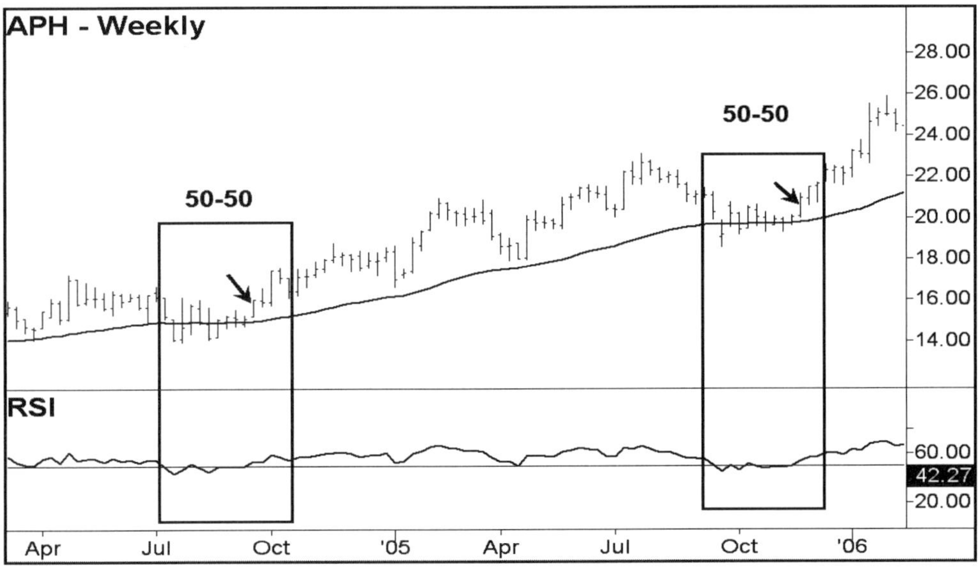

Figure 15.3 *By zooming in on the chart of Aphenol (APH), the 50-50 signals are more easily seen. This chart covers about seven months of price history. The first price bars above the 50 MA are shown (arrows).*
(Chart: TradeStation)

ANOTHER UP RISING

One of the biggest problems for investors is knowing when to enter a trade; it is often a source of stress. If you enter a stock position too early and get stopped out, you'll get mad at yourself for not having entered later. If you enter late and miss out on profits, you'll get mad at yourself for not entering earlier. You may start believing you just can't win no matter what you do. These are common emotions which can lead to a revolt against your trading plan. By providing specific criteria for buying a stock, the 50-50 Strategy eliminates a great deal of emotional stress which can result from weighing investment decisions.

In Chapter 2, I talked about Yin and Yang and the importance of knowing who you are as an investor. Trade entry is one area where this is important. For instance, you can enter a stock anytime price is above a rising 50 MA (and the 50-50 Strategy criteria are met). For some, this may sound simple. Others may be uncomfortable with it because there isn't a specific signal for when to enter. If you like specificity, then enter High Risers when price drops under the 50 MA and reverses back up above the 50 MA; you enter exactly on the first bar entirely above the 50 MA after the 50-50 Strategy signal is given. This type of entry can be programmed into software if you are an engineering-minded person. If you are more of a free-spirited person, enter the High Riser anytime you want, or enter the Low Riser about three months after the 50-50 Strategy signal. Do what works best for you. Both ways make money, and both ways have about the same risk.

Figure 15.4 summarizes how to use the 50-50 signal to enter a stock position. What do the two "risers" have in common? The entry for both occurs when the 50 MA is rising, and not before. That should make sense by now, since the first of the two 50-50 Strategy criteria is: price is above a rising 50 MA. The consistency of the 50-50 Strategy allows beginners and advanced investors to easily apply the strategy in a way that suits their investing personality.

ENTER AT YOUR OWN RISK

Investors frequently want to know exactly where they should enter a trade using the 50-50 Strategy. This attention to the "perfect entry," while important, is not as important as paying attention to the perfect exit. You have some wiggle room on entry, but all investors must exit trades when price closes below the 50 MA. It is up to your own discretion whether you enter a High Riser or Low Riser and on which bar you buy. You don't get to use your discretion about when to exit a trade. A stop-loss order will be in place to take you out of a trade automatically; it is your protection against a big loss. It is also your protection against yourself. You are more likely to make an emotional decision about when to exit a bad trade if you don't set a stop-loss order in advance.

TYPES OF 50-50 UPTRENDS	WHEN TO ENTER TRADE
High Riser **(Rising 50 MA)**	**Price above a rising 50 MA:** The 50-50 Strategy signal is not needed. Enter on any bar above the 50 MA. **Price below a rising 50 MA:** Enter on the first 50-50 Strategy signal (when price is above the 50 MA).
Low Riser **(Sideways or Falling 50 MA)**	**Price above the 50 MA:** Enter after the 50 MA has turned up (about 3 months) if price is above the 50 MA. **Price below the 50 MA:** Enter when the 50 MA turns up (about 3 months) after a 50-50 signal with price above the 50 MA.

Figure 15.4 *Summary of how to enter High Risers and Low Risers.*

The stop-loss price is determined before you buy a stock. It is important to assess the risk of a trade before you enter it, just as you would want to know the risk of surgery before you go under the scalpel. No matter where you decide to buy a stock above a rising 50 MA, the risk is always the distance (in price) back to the 50 MA. The stop-loss order is placed under the 50 MA (less $0.25 cents); the trade is exited if price drops below the 50 MA and activates your stop-loss order.

To determine the stop-loss, you need to know the current price of the stock and the price of the 50 MA (Note: the actual entry price may be different). For example, look at Figure 15.5. Suppose you bought Western Digital (WDC) in December, 2006, and the closing price was $20.61 (now's the time to grab your calculator). The 50 MA is at about $18.20. We'll plan to put the **initial stop** (initial stop-loss order) $0.25 cents under the 50 MA, or at $17.95 ($18.20 - $0.25 = $17.95). This ensures that price must clearly drop under the 50 MA (by $0.25 cents) before the stop-loss is activated.

A **trailing stop** is a stop-loss order that "trails" price. A trailing stop is just a stop-loss order that is placed after price moves in your favor; the price of the stop-loss is raised periodically to protect profits. In general, you would place a trailing stop $0.25 cents under the 50 MA and move it about once a month, following along under the rising 50 MA. I'll explain more on how to use a trailing stop in Chapter 16.

Next, you'll want to calculate the **initial risk** (initial stop-loss risk) per share of stock you buy, so you know exactly how much money you'll lose if you are stopped out. The initial risk per share of stock is the distance between your entry price and your initial stop under the 50 MA. The stop-loss risk for WDC is $2.66 per share ($20.61 entry price - $17.95 stop-loss = $2.66). If you had bought 200 shares of WDC stock, and then you had been stopped out, you would have lost $532 ($2.66 risk per share x 200 shares = $532).

Much of the stress associated with investing comes from what is unknown, and not from what is known. Calculating the initial risk of a trade in advance allows you to be fully informed of the potential loss *before* you buy a stock. Accepting the amount of the loss helps you invest with the proper mindset—there will be no surprises, and you'll be less likely to react emotionally in the event you are stopped out.

Many investors think of investments as *all-or-none* events—you either have winners or losers. Your ego will declare you right or wrong. This is the way the crowd thinks about the decision to buy a stock, and it is the wrong mindset. Price can never make you a winner or loser. Trades result in a gain or a loss for the portfolio, and that's all.

The market will pitch you many investment opportunities, but sometimes it throws curve balls and sliders. The successful investor keeps his eye on the ball and waits for his favorite pitch. Often, getting stopped out sets up an even better opportunity to buy a TOP stock (Figure 15.6). How will you know? You won't until you see the next "50-50 pitch" coming right over the plate (rising 50 MA), and you swing the same way you did in practice (paper trade).

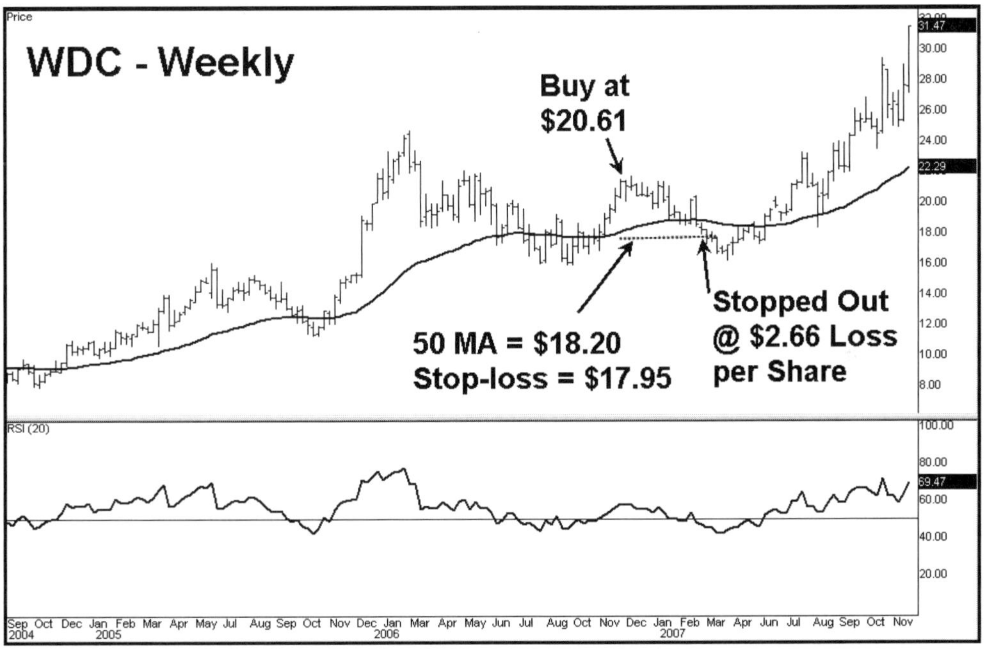

Figure 15.5 *The stop-loss risk (per share) of any trade is the price distance from the entry price to the stop-loss price ($0.25 below the 50 MA).* (Chart: TradeStation)

Don't chase after a bad pitch just because you're anxious to score. My grand-uncle played with the Chicago Cubs, and he used to pitch to Babe Ruth. My uncle told me that when the Babe retired, he had struck out more times than any other baseball player in history. Babe Ruth is better known for having held the all-time home run record which was unbroken for nearly 40 years after his 1935 retirement.

In Figure 15.6, Central European Distribution (CEDC) was a Low Riser in 2006. If the investor had entered at the first signal (1, 2), he would have been stopped out (3) with little or no loss. The next signal (4, 5) occurred after the 50 MA had turned up for at least three months. The second trade was successful and gained about 100% in a year. By proper management of your stop-loss, your plan is to take small, calculated losses when a trade is stopped out. You also let the successful trades work hard and long to make big profits which greatly outweigh the small losses.

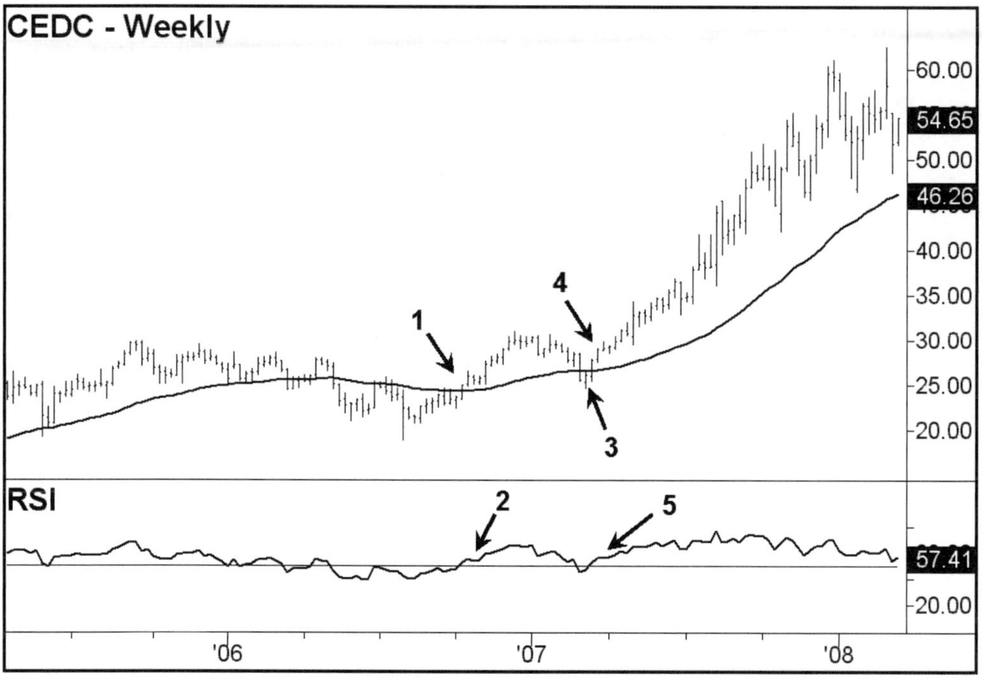

Figure 15.6 *Some of the best 50-50 trades occur on the second attempt to buy a stock. Central European Distribution (CEDC) gave a 50-50 signal in 2006 (1, 2), but the 50 MA was not rising, and the trade was stopped out (3). The next 50-50 Strategy signal (4, 5) came with a rising 50 MA, and the trade resulted in a 100% profit.* (Chart: TradeStation)

YOUR CHANCES ARE 50-50

Part of mindset is your expectation of what will happen after you buy a stock. The name "50-50" also refers to your chances of any one trade getting stopped out, which is about 50%. This is often hard for beginners to comprehend; they tend to think that a strategy must be successful most all the time in order to make money. A shift in mindset is important for keeping your expectations reasonable.

It is normal to expect to "win" on trades most of the time. In our society, winning is revered and lauded, while losing is frowned upon. Would you go to a surgeon who had reportedly lost 50% of his patients during surgery? We are conditioned from childhood that a high score in school is 90% ("A" grade), a good score is 80% ("B" grade), and an average score is 70% ("C" grade). Now you have to think differently.

Babe Ruth had a lifetime batting average of .342, which means less than 40% of his swings resulted in a hit. You can learn the skills necessary to invest successfully, but you must have reasonable expectations. Your goal is to make profits on 50% or more of your trades; some of these trades will have big profits. On the other 50%, you will accept small losses. Like Babe Ruth, you won't hit home runs all the time, so be mentally prepared in case you step up to home plate and strike out.

At first, you may think investing is just a toss of the dice, but that is far from the truth. How would you like to go to the casinos in Las Vegas and win 50% of your bets at the craps table? You could retire in one night of gambling! The best professional traders can make a living by winning on 40% of their trades. How is this possible? The reason is that losses are limited by a stop-loss (the 50-50 Strategy will use a 15% stop-loss). Conversely, your gains are *not* limited and can produce much higher returns, some over 100%.

Expectation is part of your mindset as well as your investment plan. Before you learn how to make a big profit, you must learn how to take a small loss. There is no guarantee a stock will continue to rise after you buy it, and that's why we use a stop-loss to manage risk. If you aren't prepared for the losses, you will naturally be frustrated and disappointed. As long as you accept the small losses as part of doing business, the winning trades and big profits can build great wealth over time.

WATCHING THE WATCHLIST

By now you should understand the mechanics of the 50-50 Strategy entry. The main stocks to follow with the 50-50 Strategy will come from your watchlist. Your watchlist has about 20 stocks which have been screened using the TOP SCORE method of rapid analysis. Where did the TOP SCORE stocks come from? I gave you three different methods for selecting stocks in Chapter 14. All of the methods require that stocks meet the TOP SCORE criteria. The TOP criteria are checked on a chart such as StockCharts (www.stockcharts.com) and the SCORE criteria are checked at Yahoo Finance (www.finance.yahoo.com). If a stock has a TOP SCORE and fits the 50-50 Strategy criteria, you can buy the stock—

it's as simple as that. If a stock has TOP SCORE credentials but doesn't meet the 50-50 Strategy criteria, it is placed on the watchlist for you to follow.

Keep your watchlist limited to about 20 stocks; more than 20 are too many to review each week (or month). If one of the stocks makes a lower 50 MA high (Chapter 9), it is taken off the list and another stock is added. By reviewing the same 20 stocks each week, they become familiar, and it's easy to see when price and RSI make crosses above or below the 50 MA and 50 RSI level, respectively. Watchlist stocks need no further analysis; that work has already been done. The only thing you need is a stock to show the 50-50 Strategy criteria to buy it.

USE "ESP" TO SEE FUTURE PROFITS

There is no way to predict which stocks are going to generate big profits, so don't waste any mental energy on trying to see the future. Use **ESP** instead. **E** is for **E**ntry price, **S** is for **S**top-loss price, and **P** is for **P**osition size. These are the only three things to think about when you put a stock to work for you. You'll periodically have to evaluate your worker's performance, but don't be a micromanager. Predicting which stock will be employee of the year is not going to make you more money.

On the weekend, find a watchlist stock that meets the 50-50 Strategy criteria. Buy the stock on the next day the market is open; use a market order (see Appendix A for a discussion of order entry types). If you don't get around to buying the stock for a week or two, it probably won't make that much difference. Again, enjoy your life; don't let investing be stressful. Look at Figure 15.7 for an example of using ESP to buy a stock with the 50-50 Strategy.

To use ESP, start with the entry price and the 50 MA price. For entry price, let's make it easy by assuming the stock is bought at the closing price for the day. Your **E**ntry price in Figure 15.7 is the closing price of the day which is $23.45. The closing price of the last price bar and the price of the 50 MA can usually be found on a stock chart. The charts at StockCharts have the information in the upper left corner of the chart. The "interactive" charts at Yahoo Finance display the information if you run your mouse over the last price bar on the chart. In the TDAmeritrade chart in Figure 15.7, prices are in the upper left.

The next step is to determine your **S**top-loss price. To do this, you must know the approximate price of the 50 MA on the day you buy the stock. In Figure 15.7, the 50 MA price is $21.47. The stop-loss would be placed at $21.22 ($21.47 50 MA price - $0.25 = $21.22) which is $0.25 cents below the 50 MA. Now, you have your **E** (Entry = $23.45), S (Stop-loss = $21.22), and the next thing is to calculate the **P**, or **P**osition size (number of shares to buy).

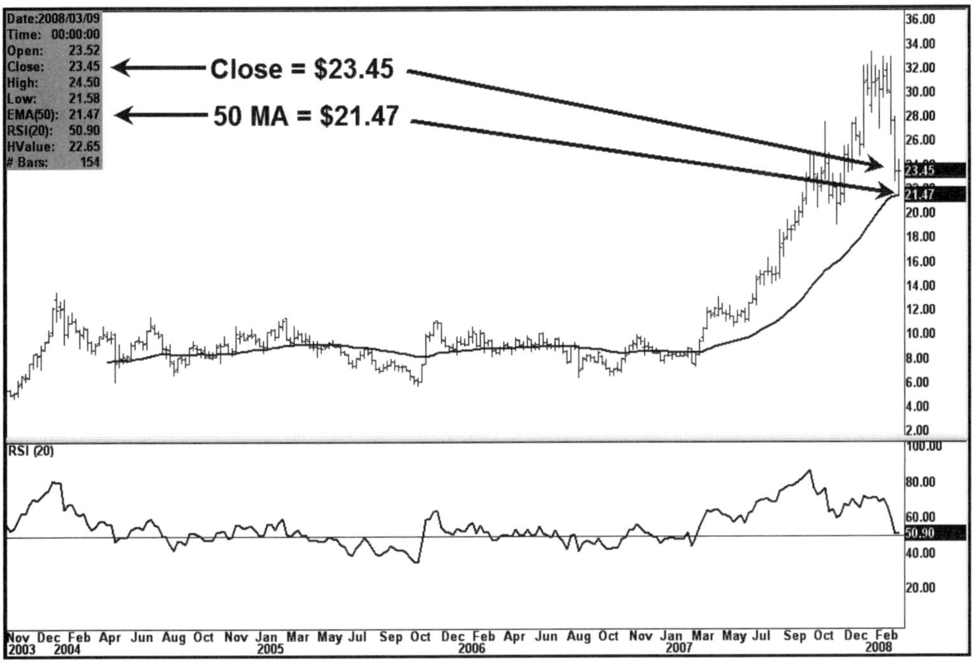

Figure 15.7 *The weekly chart shows the closing price of the last price bar and the price of the 50 MA.* (Chart: TDAmeritrade)

Imagine you're on wine-tasting vacation with friends in Sonoma County, California. You and your friends decide to have a hotel pool party with chips, salsa, and guacamole. You go to the Farmers Market on Fourth Street in Santa Rosa to buy some fresh avocados; they're selling for $2 each. You have a $20 bill in your pocket. How many avocados can you afford? You can afford 10 avocados. The party will be a success! Now, suppose you wanted to invest $5,000 in the stock in Figure 15.7. The number of shares you could afford is determined by dividing $5,000 by the stock's price. In this example, the number of shares would be 213 ($5,000/$23.45 per share = 213 shares). More than likely, you would round off the number to an even 200 shares.

How much money can you lose if you get stopped out? To find out, we need to calculate the initial risk, or the initial stop-loss risk per share of stock. As you will recall, the initial risk per share is the distance between your entry price and your stop-loss price. In Figure 15.7, notice how the stock price is relatively close to the 50 MA (currently) and below the highest price of about $33. This means the **stop-loss risk** will be relatively small compared to the risk if you had bought at $33). The initial risk per share, or stop-loss risk, is $2.23 ($23.45 entry price - $21.22 stop price = $2.23 per share). You're probably way ahead of me by now. The amount of money you would lose on the trade (if stopped out) is $446 (200 shares x $2.23 initial risk per share = $446).

Carnac the Magnificent is done with ESP (aka Extra-common **S**ense **P**lanning). Now, it's your turn to use your ESP and foresee where the stop-loss should be placed in a trade. Concentrate..."don't" close your eyes...you should begin to visualize an image any time now. I'm sensing it, are you? I see it now! It's Figure 15.8. In late 2007, was the stock a High Riser or Low Riser? Use your ESP to determine the entry price (closing price), the stop-loss price, and the number of shares you could have bought using $5,000 to enter at the current closing price? Don't expect me to ESPlain it to you, Lucy!

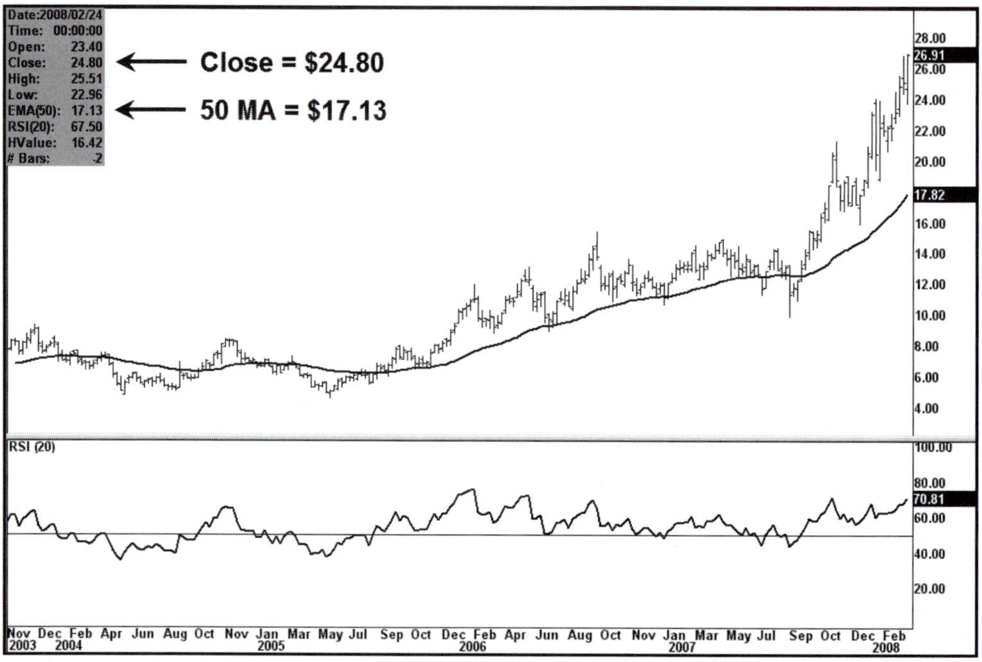

Figure 15.8 *Don't guess; use your ESP.* (Chart: TDAmeritrade)

TAMING OF THE SHREWD

I meet many investors everywhere I go. Some of them are pretty shrewd, and some of them only *think* they are shrewd. When asked, they cannot clearly explain their investment strategy. You should be able to tell someone your basic strategy in one or two sentences. For example, "I buy stocks with earnings growth when they are above a rising 50 MA, and I put my stop-loss under the 50 MA." That's simple enough. It's not necessary to sound like a "shrewd" investor who uses a complicated system that no one could possibly understand, let alone use. We all have to tame any shrewdness of ego we might have. Egos trade for dollar thrills, investors trade for dollar bills.

I have covered a great deal of information to this point in the book. Don't let it overwhelm you. My wife and I always talk about the need to stick with the basics of the 50-50 Strategy. If you can learn the basic steps to the strategy, you can make money, no matter how much else there is to know about investing. That's the benefit of a good strategy.

If your strategy works and you don't get stopped out, you'll make a profit. If you get stopped out, it will be with a small loss. How do you calculate the total dollar gain on a trade? The gain (or loss) is the sell price minus the buy price multiplied by the number of shares bought.

Profit = (Sell price – Buy Price) x Number of Shares

Now, look at the following four charts (Figures 15.9-15.12); they are all charts of the same stock. I'll ask you some questions underneath each chart (answers are at the end of the chapter). If you understand these charts, you have 80% of what you will need to know to make big profits. Take your time. Assume you have $10,000 to invest in a stock. You found the stock in Figure 15.9 (symbol absent) and the fundamentals passed the SCORE analysis. It was placed on your watchlist a couple of weeks ago. Today, you looked at it again.

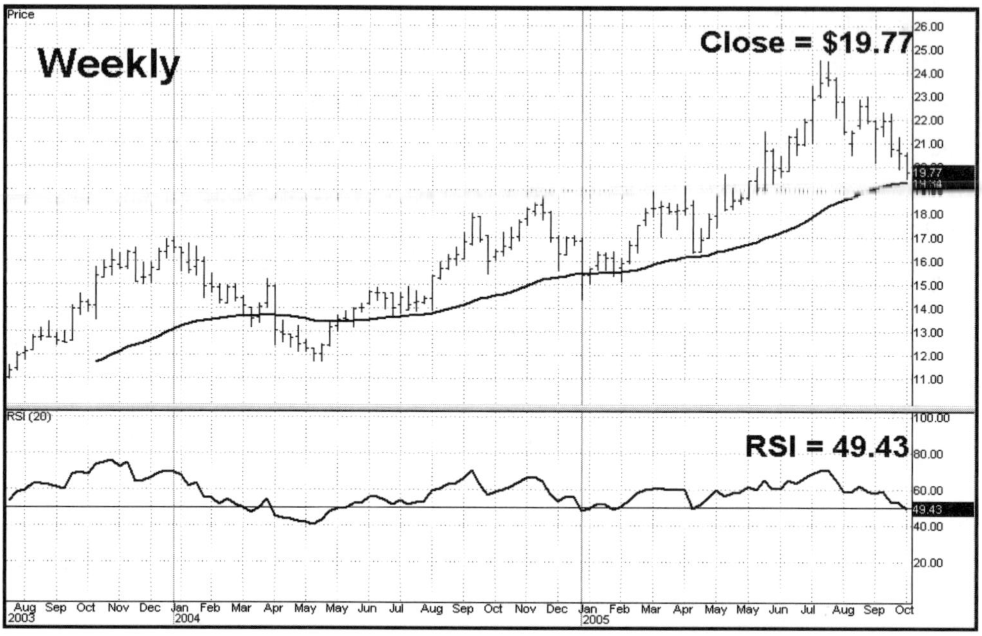

Figure 15.9 *What kind of trend is this (High Riser or Low Riser)? Could you buy the stock on the last bar on the chart (look carefully at the numbers for price and RSI)?* (Chart: TDAmeritrade)

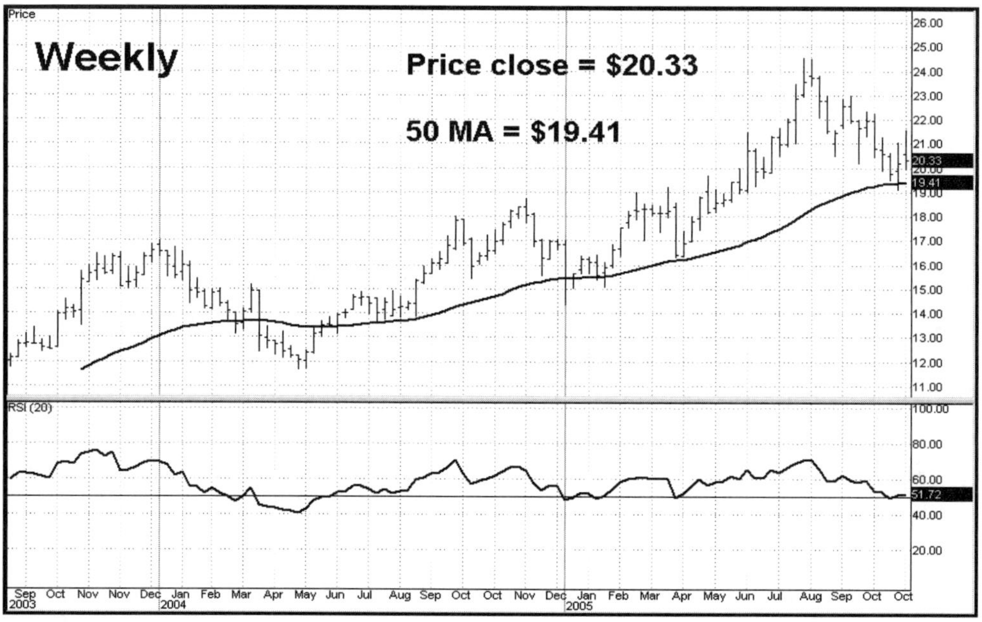

Figure 15.10 *This is the same chart two weeks later. Could you buy now? If so, what is the price (based on the last close) for your entry and stop-loss? Could you afford 200 shares?* (Chart: TDAmeritrade)

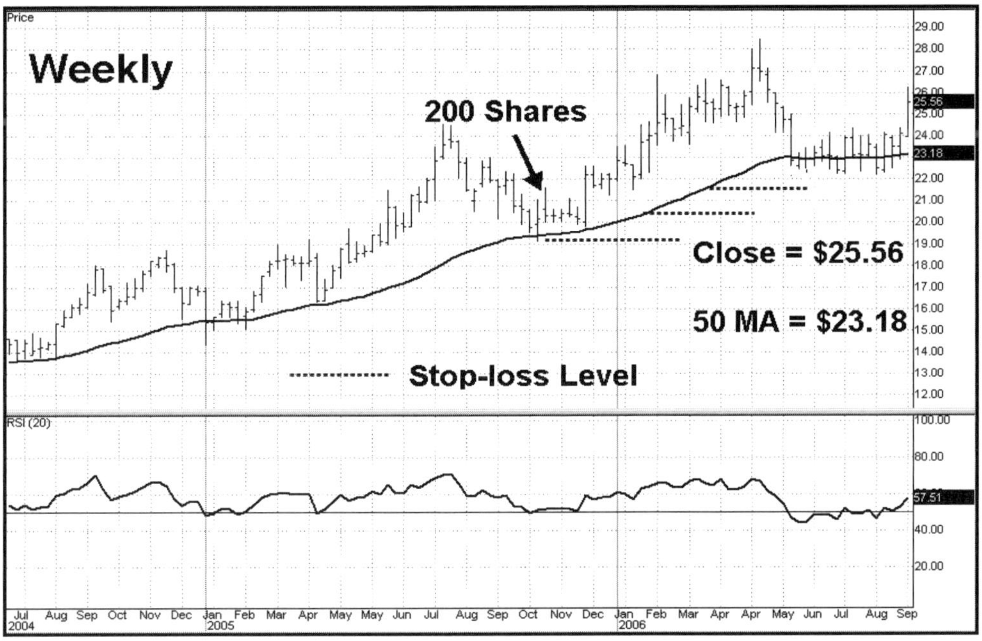

Figure 15.11 *This is the same stock as in Figure 15.10, almost a year later. The entry is shown (200 shares). The low price in June 2006 was $20.12. If you used stop-loss levels as shown (dotted lines), were you stopped out? Could you afford to buy 200 more shares at the close ($25.56)?* (Chart: TDAmeritrade)

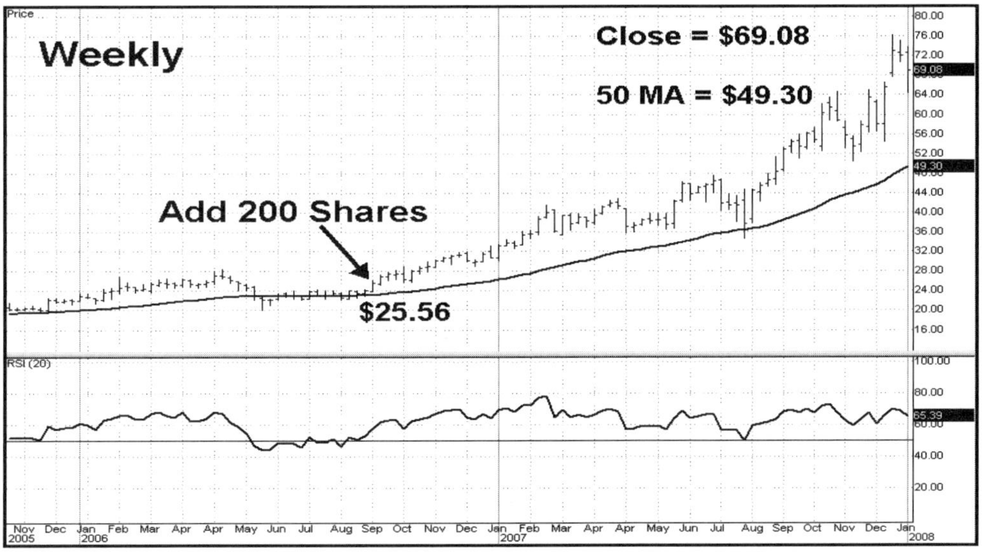

Figure 15.12 *This is the same stock as in Figure 15.11 about a year and a half later. Assuming you were not stopped out, and assuming you sold all your shares of stock at the last price shown, what was your profit on the first 200 shares? What was your profit on the second 200 shares?* (Chart: TDAmeritrade)

To make these two trades, did you need to know the name of the stock? Did you need to hear it recommended by an "expert" on TV? Did you need to hear any news about the stock? Did you need to pay for any special software to tell you when to buy? All you needed was your eyes, your brain, and the 50-50 Strategy. If you're like me, you also needed a small calculator!

THE PSYCHIC POWER OF PATIENCE

I am often asked, "How did you know that stock was going to go up?" To the untrained eye, it looks like I have psychic powers. The truth is, I am just patient. I spend most of my time watching for the 50-50 Strategy signal. I have a plan for success. I don't just buy a stock and hope it mysteriously starts going up.

Investing requires patience more than hard work. It is normal to become impatient. We see a stock we like, it has great ratings, and it's above the 50 MA. It appears poised to start an uptrend. Why not take a shot? Why not just go for it? This is our ego wanting some excitement! Patience is boring to the ego because it wants everything now.

The successful investor learns that it pays to be patient, and it usually costs to be impatient. He does not buy a stock randomly, hoping it will make him rich. That puts money at unnecessary risk, and it also ties up money that could be working in a profitable investment elsewhere. In a way, you have to learn to not care what price does. It takes a certain amount of emotional detachment. Just be consistent about reviewing your watchlist, finding a stock to buy, and doing a little ESP. After that, let the trade work and go on with your life. Make a batch of fresh guacamole and invite over some friends for a little wine tasting.

ΔΔΔ

Answers to Figures 15.8-15.12

- **Figure 15.8:** The stock is a High Riser. The entry price was $24.80, assuming you bought the stock on the close of the last bar on the chart. The 50 MA is $17.13. Your stop-loss would be placed at $16.88 which is $0.25 cents below the 50 MA ($17.13 - $0.25 = $16.88). The number of shares you could afford is 201 ($5,000/$24.80 entry price = 201 shares). You would round that off to 200.

- **Figure 15.9:** The chart is a High Riser. You could not buy here, because the RSI is below 50, even though the price bar is entirely above the 50 MA.

- **Figure 15.10:** You can buy High Risers as soon as there was a 50-50 Strategy signal which is present on the last bar on the chart. The entry was 20.33 and the stop-loss was $19.16 ($19.41 - $0.25 = $19.16). You could afford to buy 200 shares. They would cost a total of $4,066 (200 shares x $20.33 per share = $4,066), and you have $10,000 to invest.

- **Figure 15.11:** You were not stopped out. You had an initial stop-loss, and you moved up your stop twice. When price started to pull back to the 50 MA, you stopped moving up your trailing stop. The first 200 shares cost $4,066 (200 shares x $20.33 per shares = $4,066). The second 200 shares would cost $5,112 (200 shares x $25.56 per shares = $5,112). You had $10,000 to start with, and the 400 shares cost a total of $9,178 ($4,066 + $5,112 = $9,178). You could afford 200 additional shares.

- **Figure 15.12:** The current price is $69.08, and the purchase price of the first 200 shares was $20.33. The total profit per share is $48.75 ($69.08 - $20.33 = $48.75). The first two hundred shares would have made a profit of $9,750 (200 shares x $48.75 profit per share = $9,750). The profit per share on the second trade would have been $43.52 ($69.08 – 25.56 = $43.52). The second 200 shares would have made $8,704 ($43.52 x 200 = $8,704). (Note: Your total profit on the two trades was $18,454 ($9,750 + $8,704 = $17,885).)

All investors lack some discipline,
and some investors lack all discipline.

16 Trade Management

Many investors are not profitable because they don't use good **trade management**, don't use it consistently, or don't use it at all. While not the most exciting subject, trade management will be a major factor in your profitability. It won't matter how good you are at stock selection if you fail to manage your trades well. Trade management includes all of the procedures you follow to enter a trade, manage risk, and take profits. By trade management, I'm not talking about being a "trader." I mean the trading activities related to your investments.

Trade management is usually not explained in "investment" books which tend to cover the subject of investing, but don't give specific guidelines for how to safely enter and exit an investment. You can't control anything the stock market does, but you have the power to control everything that *you* do. The one thing you have absolute control over is the amount of risk (loss) you are willing to accept. Whether you are a beginner or advanced investor, trade management will be the same. It will involve some basic calculations. Fortunately, I will give you checklists to follow, so you don't have to strain your brain more than is necessary.

The biggest challenge of trade management is personal discipline. Discipline is the most difficult thing to learn in most any area of life.

You can improve your investment discipline to some degree, but it is a difficult task because discipline is part of our character. Lack of discipline is the biggest reason why investors make the same mistakes over and over. They vow to change their habits, but year after year, they keep sabotaging their own chances of success.

The best way to improve discipline is by following a routine. The less discipline you have, the more you should rely on checklists. The checklist is a short outline or worksheet with each part of the routine clearly written out. It tells you exactly what to do for calculations. It protects you from getting off track and cutting corners. Of course, you still need discipline to use the checklist!

By the way, for this chapter, you'll want to have a small calculator close by.

LOOT CAMP

You can improve your discipline with a trading partner or trading coach, someone whom you trust and to whom you will agree to be accountable. Explain your plan to your partner and report back to them with your recorded results. Your partner's job is to make sure you stuck to your plan. Let your partner analyze your trades and give you feedback. While they give it, say nothing, just listen. If you stop to defend your actions, you will no longer be listening to what you need to hear. The more you try to defend yourself, the more your ego is in charge of the investment plan.

You don't need to pay for an expensive trading coach. Find a friend, preferably one who has read *Invest with Success*, and work together. You'll learn twice as much by coaching them. Like most topics in life, we are experts at telling others what they should do, but we often don't take our own advice. Often, the mere thought of accountability to your coach supplies the motivation to use more personal discipline. For example, a person may not have the discipline to do regular housecleaning, but it's amazing how fast he finds discipline on the day he has guests arriving for a party.

My wife is a great coach; she keeps students on track and tells them what they most need to hear when they least want to hear it. She is blunt, honest, and she cares. She's much like a drill sergeant at boot camp, so I often refer to her as the dollar-bill sergeant at "loot camp." Students can fool themselves, but they can't fool her. One student told me that, after a year of Candy's coaching, all he needs to do is ask himself, "What would Candy say to do?" The student realizes he'd rather just do it than have her tell him he should have done it. Another student complained that Candy was awfully hard on him. Candy has a familiar line with which I totally agree. She says, "I may be hard on you, but not as hard as the market will be if you don't learn to protect your capital."

YOU DESERVE A BREAK

The initial goal of every 50-50 Strategy trade is to protect capital. The second goal is to get the trade to **breakeven risk. Breakeven** is simply the price level of your entry. An investment with breakeven risk has had the stop-loss order moved up to the entry price level after the stock has made a gain roughly equal to the initial risk. Conceptually, if you buy a stock at $25 and your stop is under the 50 MA at $20, your initial risk is $5 per share ($25 entry price - $20 stop-loss price = $5). Your stop-loss could be moved to breakeven at $25, when the price of the stock has increased in price to $30. At $30, the stock is $5 above your entry, an amount equal to your initial risk. I prefer to wait until the 50 MA is at breakeven. It's easier, and fits better with the principles of the 50-50 Strategy.

You deserve a break after working hard to research a stock, follow it on a watchlist, and then make the investment. The break you may get is a breakeven trade. The point of getting a trade to breakeven risk is that the capital invested in the trade is no longer at risk. Imagine having an investment with no risk while still maintaining its upside potential! This is how successful investors think. When your risk goes to zero, so will the stress of investing. There is an exception to the "no risk" aspect of the breakeven stop-loss, but it seldom occurs, so I have put the explanation in Appendix A.

Just like your initial stop-loss, the breakeven stop-loss is placed below the 50 MA and never above it. Since we always place our stop-loss $0.25 cents under the 50 MA, we must wait until the 50 MA is $0.25 cents above the entry price before moving the stop-loss to the breakeven (entry) price. Using the 50 MA as our reference price for the stop-loss lets us follow the gradual movement of the moving average instead of trying to set a stop-loss based on the frequently fluctuating stock price. Figure 16.1 is an example of how to move an initial stop-loss to breakeven. The breakeven price for the 50 MA is simply the entry price plus $0.25 cents (to account for the stop-loss being placed $0.25 cents below the 50 MA).

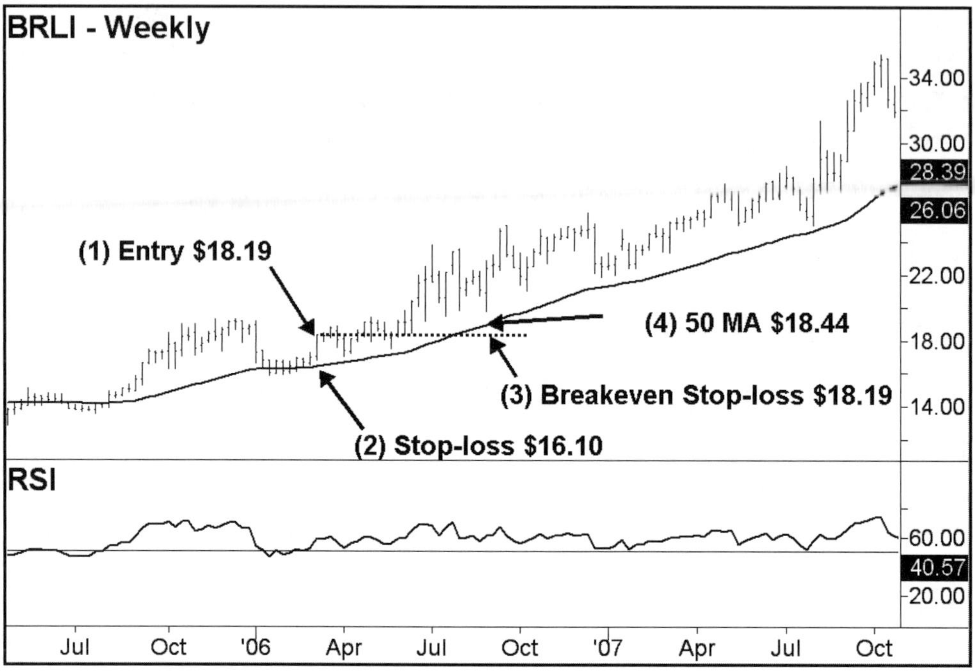

Figure 16.1 *This chart shows how the stop-loss can be moved to breakeven once the price of the 50 MA is $0.25 cents above the entry price.*
(Chart: TradeStation)

In Figure 16.1, consider the following price references for Bio-Reference Labs (BRLI):

BRLI Example
Entry Price = $18.19
50 MA Price = $16.35
Initial Stop Loss = $16.35 - $0.25 = $16.10
50 MA Price (at Breakeven Stop-loss) = $18.19 + $0.25 = $18.44
Breakeven Stop = $18.19

Suppose BRLI was entered at $18.19 (1). The stop-loss was placed $0.25 cents below the 50 MA at $16.10 (2). The initial risk was $2.09 per share. The stop-loss is moved to breakeven ($18.19) when the 50 MA price equals the entry price plus $0.25 cents, or $18.44 (4). This is an easier way to manage your stop-loss, always keeping it below the 50 MA level. If price drops below the 50 MA when your stop-loss is at breakeven, the trade is exited at no loss. This is like a foul ball in baseball. You don't get on base, but you can't strike out.

Now it's your turn since I did the last one. Figure 16.2 is a chart of the iShares MCSI Brazil Index Fund ETF (EWZ). Determine the initial stop-loss, the breakeven price, and the price of the 50 MA when the stop-loss is moved to breakeven (answers are at the end of the chapter).

EWZ Example
Entry Price = $16.20
50 MA Price = $14.25
Initial Stop Loss = **?**
50 MA Price at Breakeven = **?**
Breakeven Stop-loss = **?**

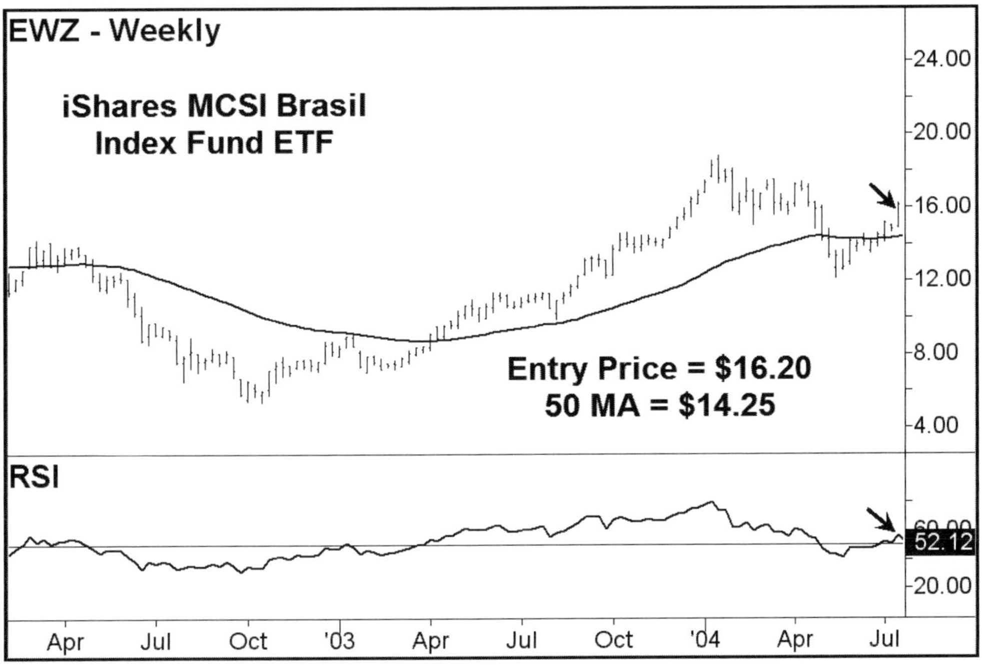

Figure 16.2 *EWZ is an ETF which represents an index of Brazilian stocks.* (Chart: TradeStation)

A trailing stop-loss order, or **trailing stop**, is a stop-loss order which trails, or shadows, the 50 MA. The trailing stop is raised up to a higher level under the 50 MA about once a month. The stop-loss is always placed $0.25 cents under the 50 MA for consistency. If you notice, when price bars turn down toward the 50 MA, it usually takes three to five weeks (bars) to reach the 50 MA area. So relax, don't worry about getting stopped out every day. The stop-loss is there so you *don't* have to worry. Why is a trailing stop better than an initial stop-loss or breakeven stop-loss? A trailing stop will stop you out at a profit!

Figure 16.3 is the same ETF (EWZ) as in Figure 16.2. The initial entry from Figure 16.2 is shown at the arrow in Figure 16.3. Did your breakeven stop-loss survive the trade? Assume you moved your trailing stop up every first of the month. Would you have been stopped out? If so, at about what price? Approximately how much money would you have made per share of stock purchased (answers are at the end of the chapter)?

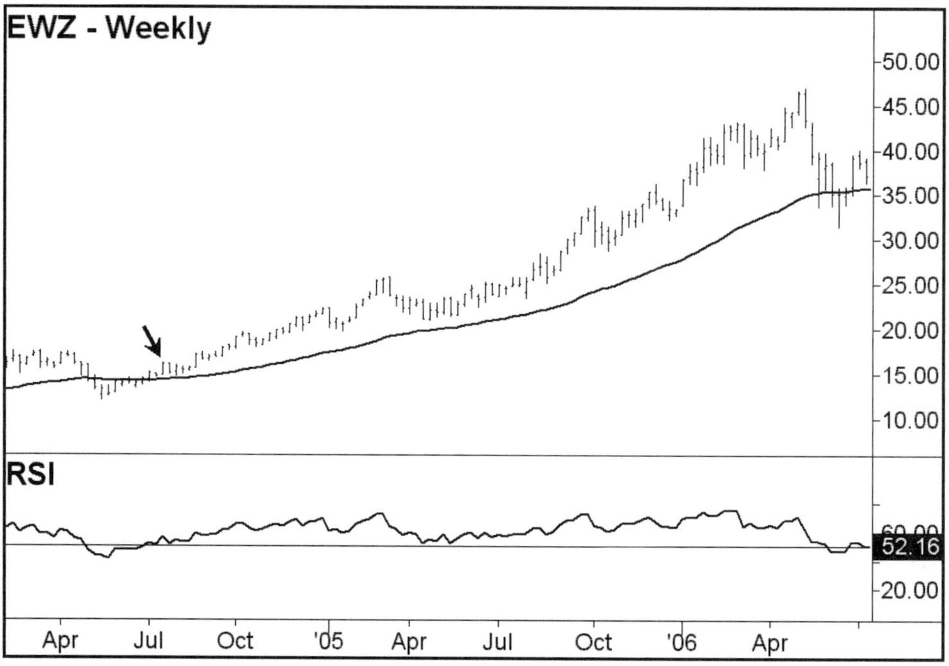

Figure 16.3 *Would this ETF have been stopped out according to the 50-50 Strategy rules for trade management?* (Chart: TradeStation)

To review, the first stop-loss price is the initial stop-loss, the second stop-loss price is the breakeven stop, and the third stop-loss price is the trailing stop. They serve to protect capital (initial), create a risk-free trade (breakeven), and protect profits (trailing). The trailing stop is adjusted up as the 50 MA rises. This is how successful investors should think. No matter how well you manage your trades, you have no control over the price of a stock, and some trades will have small losses. In fact.... oops! It appears I just got stopped out of this topic.

LOTS OF MONEY

Suppose you have $50,000 to invest in stocks. How do you determine how much money to put into a particular stock? Many investors make this decision based on how much they like a stock or by how confident they are that the stock will go up. If they're feeling confident, they might go for the big score with a big wager. If they're not so confident, they'll invest less money and hope the stock surprises them. This approach to investing often reflects the mindset of the crowd, and it can get you in a whole lot of trouble.

The successful investor always has a plan, and he decides how much money to invest in each stock well in advance. For the 50-50 Strategy, divide up your stock capital into equal amounts, or **lots** of money (I don't mean a generous amount). Lots are bundles of cash, or units of profit-making potential. This makes investing a whole "lot" of fun!

The best plan is to divide up your stock capital into ten equal amounts. (This also makes the calculations easier—yeah!). With $50,000 of capital, you would have ten lots, each in the amount of $5,000 ($50,000/10 = $5,000). You will have $5,000 to buy as many shares as you can afford of any given stock. Dividing your capital into 10% lots means you can own a maximum of 10 different stocks; this allows the small investor to achieve **diversification** (discussed in Chapter 17) in the stock portion of his portfolio.

Why only 10% allocation to each stock? Why not just "go for it" with 50% and make all your money at once? Suppose a stock goes bankrupt tomorrow; the maximum amount of money you could lose with one 10% lot is 10% of your stock capital. You can survive that. If you put 50% into one stock and lost all of it, you would lose 50% of your stock capital all at once; that's not the way to build wealth or promote mental health. Learning to use equal lots is a great way to keep your risk low and improve portfolio returns. Learn before you earn.

By forming lots, you equalize the amount of money put at risk in each stock. Different stocks have different prices, so the number of shares you can afford will vary depending on the price of the stock you buy, but the total amount of money invested in each stock will remain equal. Equal lots are also important for a profit mindset; it keeps the investor more neutral toward expected stock returns. The investor is less likely to sink a large amount of money in a stock they "think" is going to be a real winner.

What if you only have $10,000 to invest in stocks? Does that mean you shouldn't bother with lots? No; you use the exact same process. Divide the $10,000 into ten lots; each lot will be $1,000. You won't be able to buy as many stock shares with $1,000 (compared to $5,000 above), but it doesn't matter. Should you buy cheaper stocks under $10 to compensate for having less money? No. With each $1,000 lot, you can buy 100 shares of a $10 stock; that's fine. What matters is that you follow the same plan no matter how much money you have. You learn by following the plan, not by how much money is in your account.

DIVE-10-15-20

Dividing your stock capital into 10% lots is part of reducing your risk through diversification (I'll talk more about portfolio diversification in Chapter 17). The DIVE-10-15-20 is an easy way to remember how you can diversify your stock investments; it stands for **DIVE**ersification into **10**% lots with **15**% risk per lot and using a maximum of **20**% in any one stock. This is the method used for the 50-50 Strategy. Let's go through the steps; they are fairly straightforward.

First, you divide up your stock capital into 10% lots (already discussed). Second, you limit the amount of dollar risk per trade to 15% of the lot amount (not the stock price). Third, you limit the amount of money invested into any one stock to 20%, or two 10% lots. This allows you to use one lot to establish a position in a stock and a second lot to add to the position after the stock price is above breakeven on the first lot. The result is you will have twice as much money invested, but with no more initial risk than you had when you entered the position with the first lot.

If you start out with $50,000 in capital for stock investments, the calculations are as follows:

<u>DIVE-10-15-20 for $50,000 Capital</u>

Stock Capital = $50,000
One 10% Lot = $5,000 (.10 x $50,000 = $5,000)
Maximum 20% of capital in any one Stock = Two 10% Lots
= $10,000 ($5,000 + $5,000 = $10,000)
Maximum 15% Lot Risk = $750

The purpose of the 15% lot-risk rule is to limit the total amount of money you are willing to risk (lose) on any trade; this applies to any stock at any price. If you enter a stock at $25, you risk the same amount of money (15% of the lot amount) as you would if you entered the same stock at $30. The 20% limit per stock keeps you from becoming too invested in any one stock, while still allowing you to add a second lot to a stock that has proven itself and is making profits. You'll invest no more than $10,000 in any one stock.

In the example above, you will risk no more than $750 on any one trade. You don't care how great a TOP SCORE a stock has or how much you think it can make big profits. You risk $750 per trade, period. This is how you take control of risk and become profitable.

SHARE AND SHARES ALIKE

A principle of the 50-50 Strategy is that entries near the 50 MA are relatively low risk compared to entries high above the 50 MA (Figure 16.4). In an uptrend, the distance from the stock's price to the 50 MA is the amount of initial risk per share the investor has if the stock is bought. Why? The stop-loss for the 50-50 Strategy is placed just below the 50 MA ($0.25 cents below). When you buy a stock anywhere above the 50 MA, you will likely be stopped out if there is a pullback that drops below the 50 MA. When a stock is high off the 50 MA, you will have more initial risk per share because the stock has farther to fall to hit the stop-loss under the 50 MA.

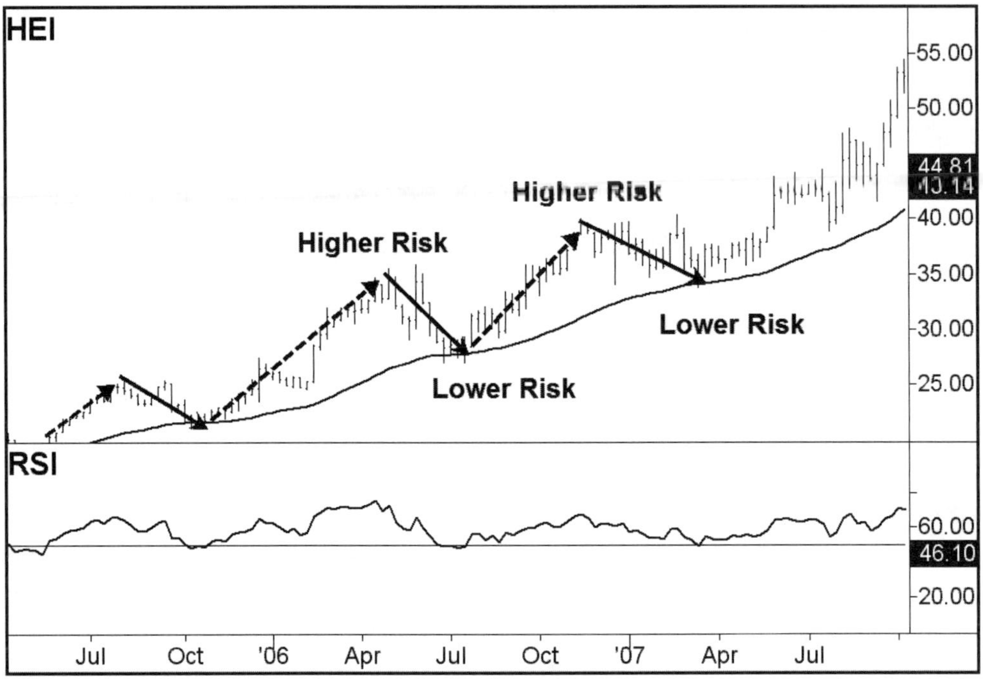

Figure 16.4 *Stock entries high above the 50 MA have a higher initial risk per share than an entry closer to the 50 MA.* (Chart: TradeStation)

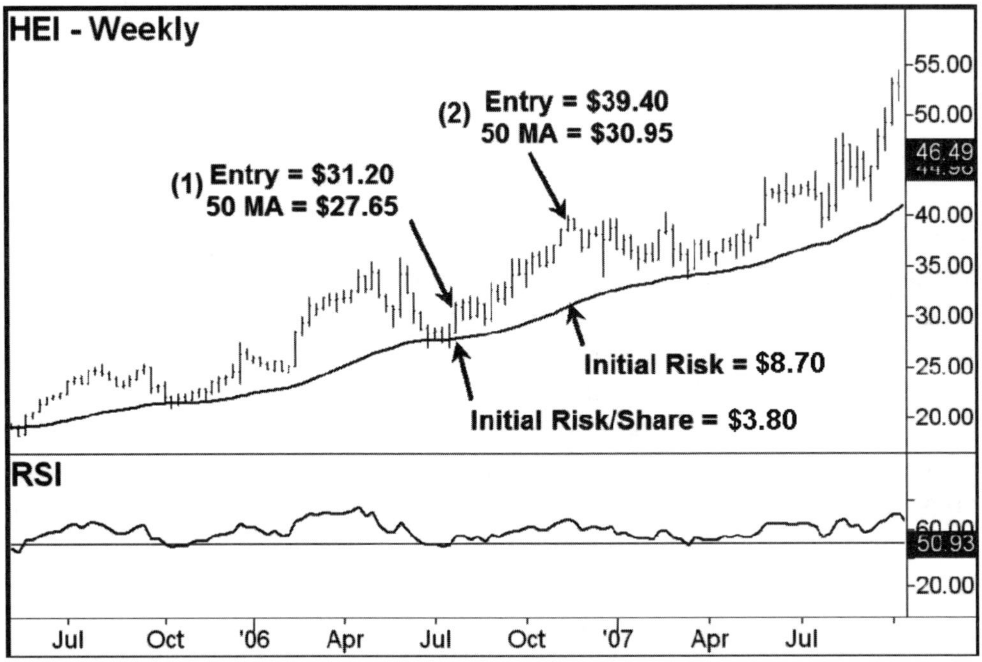

Figure 16.5 *A comparison of the initial risk per share for an entry high off the 50 MA versus close to the 50 MA.* (Chart: TradeStation)

Now look at Figure 16.5. First, what kind of 50-50 Strategy riser is this? Right, it is a High Riser because there are no 50 MA lows. According to the rules of your plan, you can enter anytime you want, as long as the entire price bar is above the 50 MA. Maybe you caught the trade early, or maybe you were sunbathing on a beach in Italy and had to enter the trade a little later. The first entry (1) is close to the 50 MA and has an initial risk of $3.80 per share. The second entry (2) is farther above the 50 MA and has an initial risk of $8.70 per share. Neither trade would have been stopped out, but the risk per share was higher for the second entry. Let's figure out what would have happened if you had invested in both trades (entries).

First, you have to determine how many shares of stock to buy. Why? Because your initial risk "per share" of a trade depends on the number of shares you buy. The formula to determine the number of shares sets the maximum amount you can "afford" to buy. Of course, you can always buy less if you want. Let's assume your total capital is $50,000 and your lot size is $5,000.

<u>Maximum Shares per Lot</u>

= Lot $ Amount / Entry Price

= __________________ Shares*

<u>Trade (1)</u>
Entry Price = $31.20
50 MA Price = $27.65
Initial Stop Loss = $27.40 ($27.65 - $0.25 = $27.40)
Initial Risk (per share) = $3.80
($31.20 entry - $27.40 stop-loss = $3.80)
***Number of Shares** = 160 shares
($5,000 lot/$31.20 entry price = 160)

<u>Trade (2)</u>
Entry Price = $39.40
50 MA Price = $30.95
Initial Stop Loss = $30.70 ($30.95 - $0.25 = $30.70)
Initial Risk (per share) = $8.70
($39.40 entry - $30.70 stop-loss = $8.70)
***Number of Shares** = 126 shares ($5,000 lot/$39.40 entry = 126)

First, notice that the risk per share in trade (2) is $8.70 and the risk in trade (1) is $3.80. The risk per share in trade (2) is more than twice the risk per share for trade (1). Let's figure the loss for buying 160 shares of Trade (1) and 126 shares of Trade (2), assuming both trades were stopped out.

Loss if Stopped Out = Initial Risk per Share x Number of Shares

Trade (1) Loss = $3.80 initial risk/share x 160 shares = $608

Trade (2) Loss = $8.70 initial risk/share x 126 shares = $1,096

Trade (1) lost $608 while Trade (2) lost $$1,096—that's quite a difference! The trade entered high above the 50 MA lost nearly twice as much as the trade entered lower, near the 50 MA. In general, the higher you buy above the 50 MA the greater initial risk per share you will have. How do you avoid taking the bigger loss? Look back to the previous section showing the DIVE-10-15-20 approach for $50,000 capital.

We accounted for the 10% lot amount ($5,000) in Trade (1) and Trade (2). The 15% risk per lot ($750) was fine for Trade (1), but it was violated in Trade (2). Trade (2) went over the limit by $345 ($750 limit - $1,096 loss = -$345). Does that mean you can't take the trade? Absolutely not. You're always in control of your risk, remember? You simply need to reduce the number of shares you buy for Trade (2). You don't have to make it complicated. Just cut the number of shares you buy in half and err to the safe side (a more thorough discussion is presented in Appendix A, Stop-loss Method #2). Let's assume we bought half as many shares of stock in Trade (2). The amount of the loss would have been $548 (126 shares/2 = 63 shares; 63 shares x $8.70 risk per share = $548). This number is under the $750 limit. For getting through all these calculations, I have a surprise for you later in the chapter. You'll want to check it out.

The point of this discussion was to show you that buying closer to the 50 MA has less initial risk per share. One of the reasons for using the 50-50 Strategy signal is to tell us when price is crossing back above the 50 MA, so we can buy closer to the 50 MA after all of the 50-50 Strategy criteria are met. Do you always have to buy near the 50 MA? No, read on.

ARE YOU HIGH?

I don't want to leave you with the impression that you should never buy a stock high off the 50 MA. While stocks high above the 50 MA have greater relative initial risk per share, they often make good entries. One of the points of this section is that you don't have to worry about making the perfect entry. How you manage risk will take care of that for you.

We don't know what the price of a stock is going to do, and we shouldn't think too much about it or try to make predictions. We'll leave that to the crowd. Still, when you stare at a chart of one of your watchlist stocks, you'll naturally look at price and say, "are you high?" You can never tell for sure, so don't fall into the trap of making value judgments; they mess up your mindset. Focus instead on finding TOP SCORE stocks which meet the 50-50 Strategy criteria. Buy them, set a stop-loss, and get on with your rich life.

Figure 16.6 shows two entries for Mosaic Company (MOS), one close to the 50 MA and one relatively high off the 50 MA. Investors often think they missed the entry when price of a stock is high off the 50 MA, after there had been an opportunity to buy the stock closer to the 50 MA.

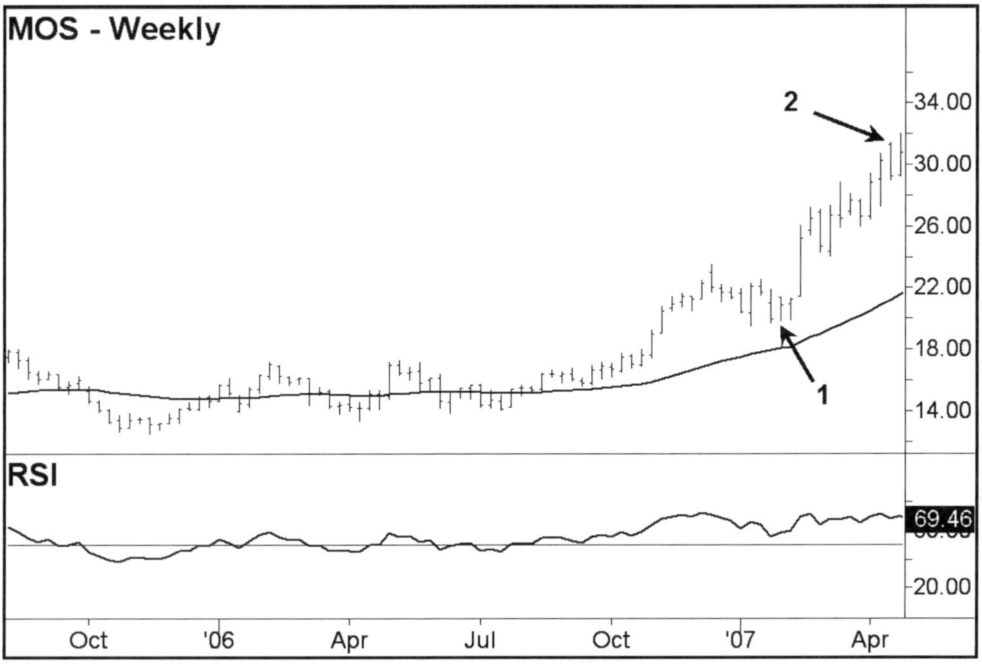

Figure 16.6 *The chart shows two entries for Mosaic Company (MOS). The first entry (1) is close to the 50 MA, and the second entry (2) is relatively high above the 50 MA.* (Chart: TradeStation)

Some stocks have strong trends and will stay high above the 50 MA for six months to a year. If you always wait for a stock pullback under the 50 MA and cross back above it before you buy, you may miss out on some great profit opportunities. Figure 16.6 is a High Riser. You can buy the stock anywhere above the 50 MA. In Figure 16.7, you can see that both entries worked. Price didn't pullback under the 50 MA. The lesson is manage your risk and don't form judgments about when a stock is too high. Of course, if you show the trade to a friend, *they* may think the stock looks way too risky. Don't be surprised if they ask, "Are you high?"

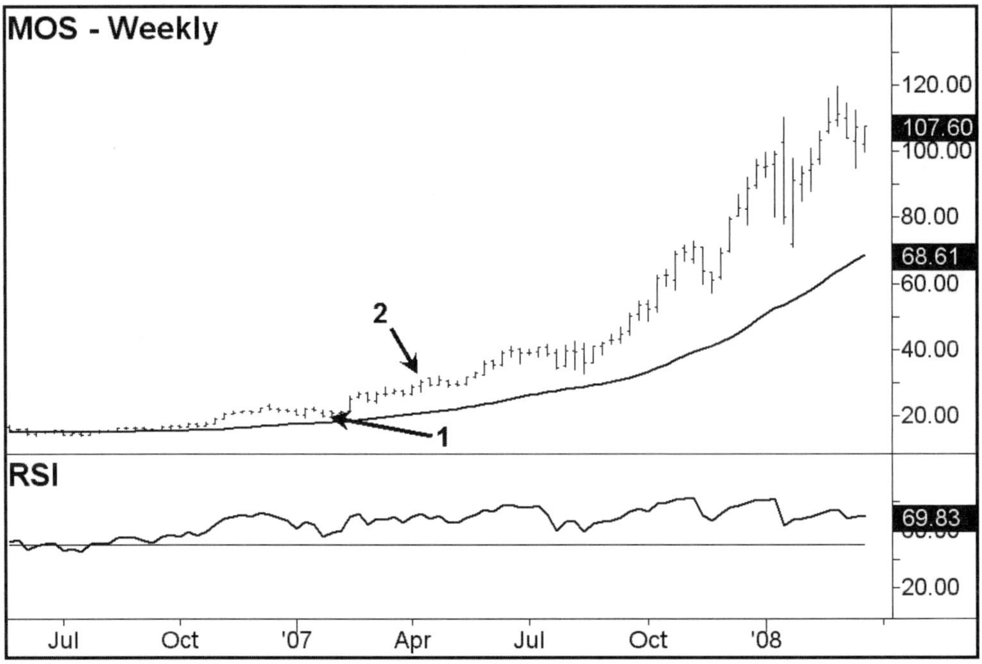

Figure 16.7 *This is the same stock as in Figure 16.6 showing that price did not return to the 50 MA again during a long rise in price.* (Chart: TradeStation)

The baseball analogy works here. The 50-50 Strategy criteria tell you when the market has served up a stock-pitch over the strike zone. Keep your eye on the ball, and swing the same way you did in practice. You'll fly out on some swings, hit a few singles and doubles, and sometimes you'll hit a grand slam.

CHECK IT OUT

Trade management involves calculations; did you notice? You can make it much easier if you use a checklist with all the formulae written down as reminders. Make the checklist part of your routine when buying a stock. If you buy five stocks in a year, that's five times you'll have to use the checklist. For your convenience, an example of a checklist for 50-50 Strategy trade management is shown in Figure 16.8.

The mere fact that you have considered risk will likely keep you safe. Many investors just say, "I think I'll buy 1000 shares this time," without any idea of the risks they are taking with their capital. As a matter of fact, many investors don't even use a stop-loss at all! For mindset, I like to think that the stress of doing trade management is always going to be less than the stress of a big loss.

When you calculate the number of shares you can afford, you'll usually get an odd number of shares. You'll want to round off the number to shares of 50 or 100 to keep all your future calculations simple. For instance, 117 shares would be rounded down to 100 shares; 139 shares could be rounded down to 100 or up to 150. Keep those calculations as simple as possible!

TIPPING THE SCALES IN YOUR FAVOR

What? There's more?

Scaling is a method of trade management you should consider as part of your investment plan. Scaling into a trade means initially buying a portion of the total amount of shares you want to accumulate and adding additional shares later, after the stock proves itself. Suppose you want to buy (and can afford) 400 shares of a stock. You scale in by buying 200 shares on the first entry. If you get stopped out, you lose only half of the money you would have lost if you bought all your shares at once. If you are not stopped out, and price rises to the point where you can enter a breakeven stop, you can then buy the other half of the shares you want to accumulate.

Scaling allows you to commit less money in the beginning, before the stock has proved itself. You could also scale in with ¼ lot amounts,

50-50 Strategy Trade Management (ESP)	
Stock Symbol: **Date:**	
Lot Amount: $ ***15% Lot Limit: $*** **Δ**	
Entry Price	
Stop Price	**Stop Price = (50 MA __________ - .25)** **= $ __________________ (Stop-loss Price)** **Stop-loss Risk = Entry Price - Stop Price** **= $ ________________ (Stop Risk)[A]** **Initial Risk per Share**
Position Size	
<u>Maximum Shares based on Lot $Amount</u> **= Lot $Amount / Entry Price** **= __________________ Shares[B]** **Total Risk Amount = Shares[B] x Stop-Risk[A] = __________________ Δ** ***ΔCompare to 15% lot limit above; adjust shares as needed.***	

Figure 16.8 *Example of the 50-50 Strategy trade management (ESP) checklist.*

but ½ lots is less management. If a stock is high above the 50 MA, scaling in offers some risk protection.

One final consideration is the number of stocks to own in your portfolio. You have 10 lot amounts with which to invest. That's a maximum of ten stocks you could own. Don't be in rush to buy several stocks; add stocks slowly. You will generally have about 4-7 stocks at any one time. The number of stocks will change as you are stopped out, take profits, and add new stocks.

Is this chapter over yet?

FOUR WEDDINGS AND A FUNERAL

One of the worst things an investor can do is fall in love with his stocks. This is something I see investors do repeatedly, and it can lead to unnecessary losses. Bob was a beginning investor who I knew was getting ready to buy a stock we had discussed. He knew how to manage risk and set a stop-loss. At one point, I checked back to see if he had made the trade.

"How's it going?" I asked. "Did you ever buy that stock?"

"Sure did," he said.

"Great."

"And three others."

"Three others? When?"

"The same day. I had good signals for all four, and the market looks really strong."

"Is that what I taught you to do?"

"Yeah, you said 4-7 stocks is a good number for a portfolio."

"I said 4-7 total in the portfolio, not 4-7 in one day."

"What's the difference? Four is four."

"Are any of them at breakeven?"

"None. I almost got stopped out in two of them, but I took off my stops."

"That's too much risk to take at one time."

"No way. I love these stocks. Been watching them for some time now."

"Don't fall in love with stocks. Treat each stock like a date. If the date doesn't go well, you don't keep dating. Let yourself get stopped out of a bad relationship. Then get another date. Don't date four women at once."

"I did in college!"

The investor did not listen. Several weeks later, he was still not profitable, and he was still married to all four of his stock positions. A few weeks later he decided to finally put stop-loss orders on all four positions, but at much lower prices than his original stops. Then the market had a big down day, and all of his positions were stopped out at once.

"What happened?" he asked.

"You fell in love with your stocks," I said. "You had four stock weddings and one portfolio funeral. I don't know what to tell you."

"I thought my stocks would bounce. That's okay; I can make the money back."

"Don't think. Start over, but buy one stock at a time. If you can't make money with one stock, you can't make money with four stocks. Besides, people should marry spouses, not stocks."

Because of Bob, I teach investors to enter one stock position at a time. Sometimes they balk at this advice, so I tell them the story of four weddings and a funeral. Get the first stock to breakeven or better; then add a second stock. This way, you have two stocks, but no more risk than you had with one stock. After the second stock is at breakeven, add a third stock, and so on. If you have three breakeven stocks and one that is still at risk, a sudden downturn in the market will only create one small loss since the other three stocks are considered risk free.

Bob is now remembered every time I teach trade management. When you want to add a stock to your portfolio, remember to ask, "What about BOB?" BOB stands for **B**reakeven **O**r **B**etter. Investing losses can create a great deal of anxiety. Instead of going to a shrink, learn to take baby steps, adding one stock at a time. Pretty soon you will be shouting, "I'm investing, I'm investing!"

STOP SIGN

A lack of discipline in trade management will keep you from making big profits. Discipline means waiting for a signal to enter a trade, routinely placing a stop-loss order, and following your plan for trade management. Repeat the same things over and over. If you fail to follow the checklist, it is a sign that you should stop investing with real money. The greatest discipline for investors is the discipline to *stop* investing. If you don't have the discipline to stop investing and quit losing money, you'll never have the discipline to invest and make money. Go back to paper trading until you are able to follow the checklist.

Investors are often more afraid of being stopped out than of letting a trade turn into a big paper loss (a position with a big negative gain). They will often be tempted to remove their stop-loss order. Being stopped out is perceived by investors as final, while paper losses are perceived as temporary. Investors hope and think they can come back from a paper loss. They don't want to give up on the trade as long as there is a chance to make back their losses. This is a crowd mindset, and it's a losing mindset.

Changing your discipline requires that you understand the various impulses (or lack of impulses) and emotions that affect your mindset. Trade management is mostly self-management. Good trading discipline gives us the ability to choose between our best and worst investment qualities. When we lack discipline, our self-limiting qualities emerge. When we have good discipline, we are able to express our best qualities as investors. With discipline, you will invest with success.

ΔΔΔ

Answers to Questions for Figures 16.2and 16.3

- **Figure 16.2:** The initial stop-loss is placed $0.25 cents under the 50 MA at $14.00 ($14.25 50 MA - $0.25 = $14.00 stop-loss). The breakeven price for the 50 MA is the entry price plus $0.25 cents, or $16.45 ($16.20 entry price + $0.25 cents = $16.45). When the 50 MA rises to $16.45, the initial stop-loss is moved to breakeven at $16.20 (entry price).

- **Figure 16.3:** The breakeven stop would have survived the trade. Using a trailing stop, the trade would have eventually been stopped out at around $34.75 ($35.50 MA Price - $0.25 cents = $34.75). The amount of profit per share equals the exit price minus the entry price, or $18.55 per share of stock ($34.75 exit price – 16.20 entry price = $18.55). This is a 116% return in under a year.

Always diversify into stocks going up.

17 The Portfolio

The **portfolio** is the main tool for implementing an investment plan; it is the collection of assets you put to work to achieve your goals. The portfolio is also the feedback system for your success. Each investor constructs a portfolio to meet his unique needs; there is no right or wrong way because everyone has different levels of capital, skill, and interest. However, there are portfolio principles which every investor should follow as a guide.

To invest with success, you should take an active role in portfolio construction. Constructing a portfolio is the process of dividing up your capital into various assets which are consistent with your investment goals. You should consult an investment advisor if you are unclear about how this is accomplished. Even if you give an advisor the authority to manage all or part the portfolio on your behalf, you are still responsible for your investment plan.

The two main portfolio principles are **asset allocation** and **diversification.** Asset allocation is the way you divide up your capital into different asset types, or classes. For instance, you might divide your portfolio into 60% stocks, 30% bonds, and 10% cash. In contrast, diversification is choosing different investments *within* an asset class. In the previous example, the 60% stock portion of the portfolio might be diversified into five different stocks from five different industries. Allocation and diversification serve to preserve capital and reduce risk.

As you go through this chapter, don't get overwhelmed. I want you to have this information available for reference, but little of it will come into play when using the 50-50 Strategy to make investments. Become familiar with the general concepts, and refer back to this chapter whenever you need to refresh your memory. At least you won't have to do any calculations!

HARD BOILED PROFITS

Here's a way to conceptualize asset allocation and diversification. Suppose you have a portfolio containing three Easter baskets. Asset allocation is not putting eggs in all your baskets. You'll have one basket for eggs, one for chocolates, and one for jelly beans. Diversification is making sure your egg basket contains Easter eggs of different colors, your chocolate basket has both regular and dark chocolate, and your jelly bean basket has different colors of jelly beans.

Before we hop into this topic further, let me remind you that investment advisors spend a great deal of time learning portfolio construction. They'll have software which they'll use to enter information about your financial situation, such as your total assets, **time horizon**, and **risk tolerance**. The software will produce pie charts and graphs, and it will recommend an asset allocation plan. If you want to do this yourself, online brokerages have similar software at their websites where you can enter in your own information and get most of the same information. Online brokers usually have an entire area of their website devoted to retirement planning and portfolio construction (Disclaimer: you may want to consult a professional to make sure you have made prudent decisions concerning your portfolio).

Asset allocation chooses from broad asset types, or classes. The most common asset classes are stocks and bonds; others include foreign securities, cash equivalents (money markets, CDs, treasury bills), precious metals (gold, silver), and real estate. The number of assets in a portfolio is typically three to five. Most every portfolio is going to have a mixture of stocks, bonds, and cash equivalents. If you add another asset class, foreign securities can be considered. Until retirement, only a small portion of total capital is put into cash equivalents because the long-term effect of inflation (money is worth less) makes it hard to build any wealth from cash investments; cash is a safety net for emergencies and a form of capital preservation. The amount of capital allocated to each asset class will depend on the person; however, an example is provided in Figure 17.1 to give you the general idea.

INVESTOR TYPE	U.S. STOCKS	BONDS	CASH	FOREIGN STOCKS
Conservative (Income)	20%	50%	30%	0%
Moderate (Income and Growth)	45%	40%	10%	5%
Aggressive (Growth)	60%	25%	5%	10%

Figure 17.1 *Example of asset allocation for different investor types and goals. Foreign securities are an optional asset class; if they are not used, their percentage is added to U.S. stocks.*

If you are 25 years old, you have much longer to let your investments grow than someone nearing retirement, so you should have a large percentage of stocks and a low percentage of bonds and cash equivalents. Investors nearing retirement will be interested in assets which provide income, and they will have a low percentage of stocks and high percentage of bonds and cash equivalents. Individual risk tolerance is also considered. The emphasis of asset allocation is the preservation of capital. The major consideration is the percentage of capital allocated to stocks (high risk), bonds (lower risk), and cash vehicles (no risk). Allocation gives the portfolio protection in economic contractions while allowing for portfolio growth during economic expansion.

Asset allocation is a long-term approach. Once you decide on allocation percentages, let the portfolio work for you. Asset allocation allows some adjustments to the percentages of assets according to market conditions. For example, during economic expansion, stocks usually outperform bonds and cash vehicles; an investor might increase the percentage of stocks in the portfolio using the asset allocation model. In a period of economic contraction, one might reduce the percentage of stocks in a portfolio and increase the amount of cash. This keeps more money safe and ready to go to work for you when market conditions improve. Never forget that cash is an investment decision.

EGGS OF A DIFFERENT COLOR

Diversification is choosing different assets within the same asset class, such as choosing several different stocks within the stock asset class. The main goal of diversification is to reduce **company risk,** the risk that some negative event involving a company will cause a large drop in its stock price. For our basket of eggs, we don't want all the eggs to look alike. To avoid confusion in the following discussion, I'll limit the discussion of diversification to your basket of eggs; consider them differently colored stocks. You can go ahead and eat the chocolate and jelly beans!

Market risk is the risk of a stock price falling just because the overall market declines. Diversification reduces company risk, but it does not affect market risk. Company risk occurs when there is an untoward company event that has an immediate and negative impact on the value of the company's stock. The public usually has no prior knowledge of the event, so the resulting drop in the stock price can be sudden and significant. An example is a pharmaceutical company whose best-selling drug is suddenly pulled off the market due to safety concerns. Another example is a company recently reported to have been involved in accounting fraud.

Dividing up your stock capital into 10% lots, as I recommend, is a form of diversification. It reduces the risk that any one stock can negatively affect your portfolio returns. Company risk is usually isolated to the company involved, although it may have a lesser impact on other stocks in the same industry. Diversification cannot remove all company risk from a portfolio, and the benefit of diversification is greatly reduced after about 10 stocks, so buying 50 stocks won't help much (and is hard to afford).

ETFs are perfect examples of diversification. ETFs are indices composed of a large number of stocks, so they are already diversified. With so many stocks in an ETF, the effect of a single stock within the ETF has little impact on the entire ETF. ETFs are also cost effective for small investors. For example, if an investor wants to buy five growth stocks, he could instead buy a single growth-oriented ETF. The returns from a growth ETF will not be as high as the potential returns of buying a few of the best performing stocks in the ETF. However, it is harder to diversify with five stocks compared to one ETF.

Figure 17.2 (daily chart) is an example of how company risk will affect stocks differently than an ETF. WellPoint is one of the stocks included in the Select SPDR Healthcare ETF (XLV). WLP gapped down in 2008, losing 26% of its value in one day. The drop occurred after bad news came out about the company's future earnings. You can see how the price of XLV was not affected by fall in price of WLP because the stock is just one of many stocks that make up the ETF.

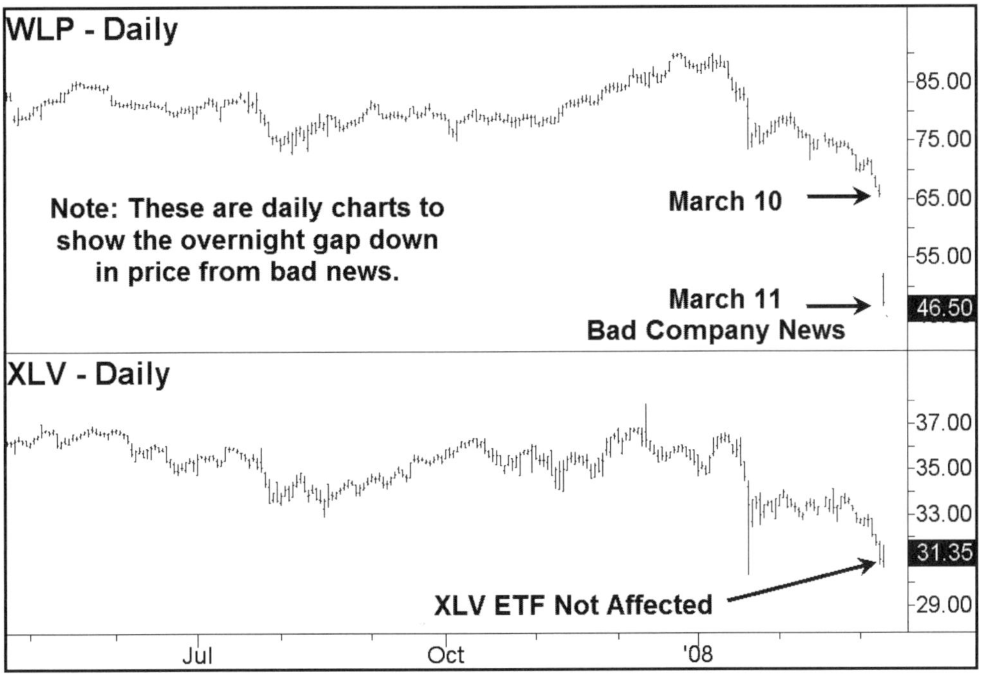

Figure 17.2 *On March 11, 2008, WellPoint (WLP), a health insurance company, reported that it was lowering profit expectations. The stock fell 26% in one day, while the ETF, of which it is a part, went up 1% ($0.30 cents) on the same day.* (Chart: TradeStation)

Did news affect the price of WLP? You learned in Chapter 6 (Myth: The News Moves Price) that price is poorly correlated with the news; WLP is an example. The stock had already been falling for two months before the news came out; it had fallen nearly 40% in 2 months. News may appear to affect price, but it's better to study the trend if you want to make big profits and avoid big losses. (Figure 17.3).

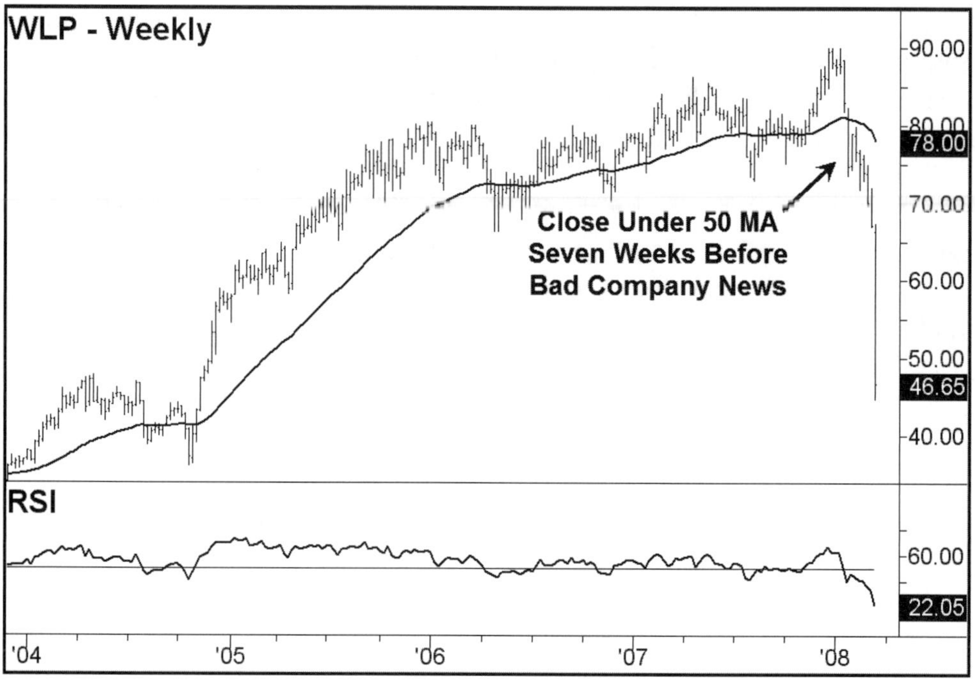

Figure 17.3 *Price dropped below the weekly 50 MA seven weeks before the bad news came out about the WellPoint (WLP).* (Chart: TradeStation)

Notice that price dropped below the 50 MA seven weeks before the bad news came out about WLP. In addition, the stock was in a sideways trend for over a year before it began falling. Successful investors following the 50-50 Strategy would have been stopped out of this stock below the 50 MA, so they would not have experienced the big loss. If you follow the 50-50 Strategy rules, they will protect you most of the time.

BALANCING ACT

The concept of **correlation** is important for diversification (you only need to understand correlation as a concept, so diversification will make more sense). Correlation is the degree to which two different assets (stocks) move in the same direction at any given time. An example of correlation is the way in which different sectors of the economy rise and fall at different times during the business cycle. Diversification works on the principle that investment vehicles can move independently in response to market conditions. Two stocks are positively correlated if they move in the same direction and negatively correlated if they move in opposite directions.

A company that sells Easter baskets might have a negative correlation with a company that sells Christmas trees. The Easter basket company will do well at Easter but not at Christmas, and vice versa. In contrast, the Easter basket company might be highly correlated to a company that sells Easter egg dyeing kits. Keep this simple; there's no need to be an egghead about correlation.

How do we put this concept to use? When diversifying your portfolio, just choose stocks from unrelated sectors or industries. There is no benefit from buying two drug stocks that will generally move in the same direction and provide similar returns. It would be better to just buy one drug stock, and find another stock that isn't associated with drugs or healthcare. If you plan to buy five growth stocks, just make sure they are from a wide variety of sectors or industries. This creates a more balanced portfolio.

Figure 17.4 is an example of two ETFs which are not closely correlated; they move in different directions much of the time. GLD is a gold ETF (SPDR Gold Shares) and XHB is a homebuilders ETF (SPDR S&P Homebuilders). During economic contractions, homebuilder stocks often drop due to a slowing of the housing market. In contrast, gold stocks often rise during uncertain economic conditions.

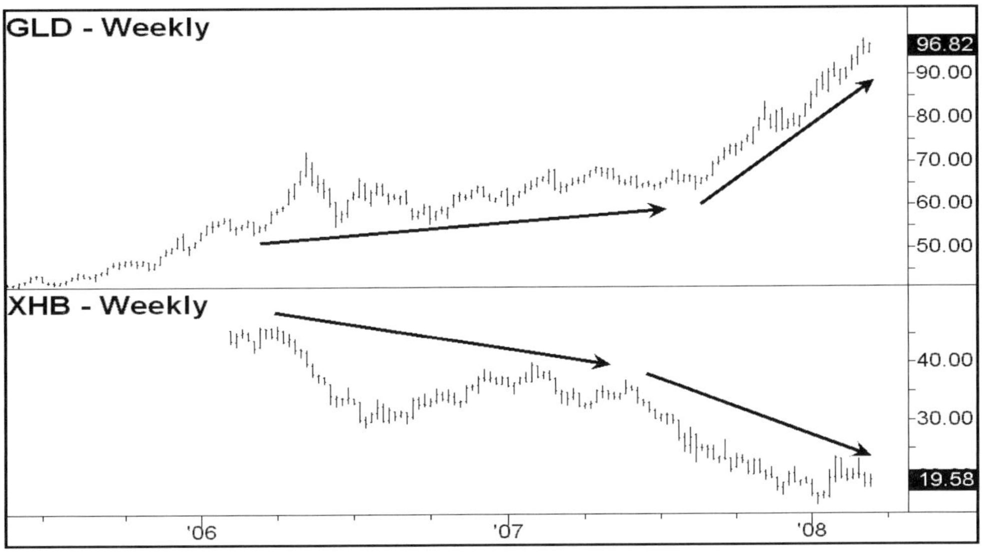

Figure 17.4 *GLD (SPDR Gold Shares) and XHB (SPDR S&P Homebuilders) are not highly correlated, and they tend to move in opposite directions.* (Chart: TradeStation)

How many shares of a stock will you buy from each sector or industry? You already know the answer. Instead of thinking in terms of shares, think in terms of **lots** of money (Chapter 16). When something is balanced, there is equal weight distribution, suggesting you put equal capital into each stock rather than being overweighted in any one industry. Using 10% lot amounts adds diversification to your portfolio and reduces risk.

A BASKET CASE

The stock basket is the riskiest basket of assets (except for real estate, options, and futures which are not being discussed). It's also where the small investor makes big profits and builds wealth. So how do you diversify the basket and still achieve high returns?

Simply choosing stocks from different industries provides diversification. However, when you buy stocks in different industries, always diversify into stocks going *up*. This concept fits with our 50-50 Strategy criteria. Trend is never diversified—you don't invest in some uptrends, some downtrends, and a few sideways trends. What is the point of buying a stock going down just so you can say you're diversified into a different industry? If you buy downtrends, your portfolio's assets will end up like a bunch of basket cases!

Don't let a stock broker or investment advisor put you in a stock going down just for the sake of diversification. There are plenty of industries with stocks in uptrends, so why invest in a stock where you know you're going to *start out* losing money? One of the first things I told you in the book is that you only make money with stocks going up; it's that simple. Sure, you can make money with dividend-paying stocks moving sideways, but you won't make big profits.

One way to find industries for investing is to use the method I gave in Chapter 14 where I showed you how to use ClearStation® to screen sectors, industries, and stocks. The **Basket Case Screen** is the same thing, except you will skip the sector part and just screen the industries from top to bottom in the market. It's a very fast way to find several top-performing industries. There are up to two hundred possible industry classifications, so don't worry, you won't run out of industry choices. There are always several industries going up, even in a bear market. Use the 50-50 Strategy criteria to tell you when to buy and you're all set. If you invest in a downtrend, you'll end up with egg on your face.

Figure 17.5 is the Basket Case screen, a simple "three-clicker" screen for top industries at ClearStation® (www.clearstation.com). With five clicks, you can find the top stocks in one of the top industries.

Basket Case Screen (ClearStation®)

1. At the ClearStation® site, click on *Markets* in the upper left of the main page.
2. The top section of the next page shows a Markets heading; go to the far right of the list and click on *Industries.*
3. A list of industries appears on the left. Along the top is a list of column headings showing % changes in price. Click on *RS Rank* (5th item from the left) to sort the industries (1=highest rank).
4. Choose one of the highest ranked industries (preferably ranked between 1-20) and click on it. This will take you to a list of stocks.
5. Click on RS Rank to bring the top stocks to the top of the list (they may already be ranked with 99 at the top). Have fun finding TOP SCORE stocks and add them to your watchlist (Note: stocks are ranked differently than sectors. The best stock has a rank of 99; the best industry has a rank of 1).

STYLE POINTS

Here's one more concept to know about. It has to do with your mindset and expectations for profit. There are two different styles of portfolio management—passive and active. The style you choose will depend on how active you are in choosing and managing your investments.

Passive management is used by investors with the mindset that they can't improve stock returns through individual stock selection. Passive management is often used by investment advisors since they are not paid a performance fee. They receive the same fee whether your account has gains or losses. Therefore, they are more likely to put you into investments that require less management since there is no incentive to work harder to try to make you money. To me, passive management is putting your mind in idle instead of shifting it into gear.

Passive management is widely used; investors buy investments and hold them for the long-term, casting their fate to the historical winds

Industry: All (Technical View)

Name	1-day % Change(1)	5-day % Change (1)	13-wk % Change(1)	13-wk % vs S&P (1)	RS Rank (2)
Non-Metallic Mining	-6.25%	-9.00%	22.14%	45.41%	1
Fish/Livestock	-1.99%	-6.19%	6.66%	26.97%	2
Oil & Gas Operations	-1.44%	-5.13%	4.96%	24.95%	3
Coal	-6.46%	-11.43%	1.44%	20.77%	4
Security Systems & Services	0.14%	-2.22%	1.02%	20.27%	5
Gold & Silver	-0.95%	-6.21%	-0.87%	17.83%	6
Advertising	-2.11%	-1.37%	-1.72%	17.01%	7
Crops	-1.97%	-2.70%	-1.93%	16.75%	8
Railroads	-0.92%	-3.22%	-2.80%	15.72%	9
Trucking	-2.71%	-2.12%	-5.03%	13.06%	10
Tobacco	0.54%	2.01%	-5.17%	12.89%	11
Retail (Department & Discount)	-1.90%	-3.27%	-5.59%	12.40%	12
Natural Gas Utilities	-1.08%	-2.92%	-5.86%	12.08%	13
Iron & Steel	-5.39%	-6.46%	-6.06%	11.83%	14
Business Services	-0.89%	-2.38%	-6.07%	11.81%	15
Chemical Manufacturing	-4.31%	-10.19%	-6.39%	11.39%	16
Biotechnology & Drugs	-2.44%	-4.96%	-6.90%	10.73%	17

Figure 17.5 *Screening for top industries at ClearStation®. This example shows 17 top industries on March 12, 2008. On the right side of the figure are the rankings (1 = top).*

of market performance. Since the markets historically provide a 9-12% return, one only has to buy stocks representative of the market and do nothing else to build wealth. The advisor generally uses a broad-based index fund of stocks. There are many mutual funds and ETFs which are used for this purpose. You can buy the exact same funds yourself.

Figure 17.6 is the SPY ETF and the $SPX (S&P 500 index) charted together, both of which represent the overall market. The SPY (price bars) tracks right along with the $SPX (solid line). If you buy the SPY ETF, it's like buying a small piece of the entire stock market. Over a decade or more, you can expect the returns to be similar to the historical returns of the overall stock market, about 9-12%.

Figure 17.6 *This is an example of the SPY ETF (price bars) which is like buying the overall stock market (S&P 500), shown here by the symbol $SPX.X (line). Notice how closely the ETF tracks the index.* (Chart: TradeStation)

The low cost of passively managed portfolios helps them provide stable returns over the long-term if you have a long time horizon (number of investment years until retirement). Passive management is better than *no* management. To make big profits, you have to be more active.

Investors who believe that stock selection plays a significant role in stock returns use **active management**; the time spent on management is worth the higher returns which can be achieved by finding better profit opportunities. The investor uses a strategy to time investments and manage risk. An example of active management is using a top down approach (Chapter 12) to stock selection; it finds the strongest performing stocks in the strongest performing industries. You can use the 50-50 Strategy to time entries and manage risk. Paying someone to select stocks for you does not ensure they will be able to produce higher returns than the overall market. In addition, higher returns are needed to compensate for having to pay the advisor.

Investors can combine active and passive management styles to some degree. For instance, investors can actively choose strongly performing mutual funds and ETFs instead of individual stocks. There are hundreds of funds that track industries, and you can buy only the strongly trending industries and manage them actively. That means getting out of the fund if it drops below the 50 MA and finding another fund above the 50 MA to replace it. I recommend this as a first step for beginning investors because it is easier and there is less risk.

What would you do if your investment advisor phoned you and told you it's the right time to buy the CGM Realty fund, a top-rated mutual fund? He said the fund made 40% over the last five years, and you just can't pass up that kind of return (Figure 17.7).

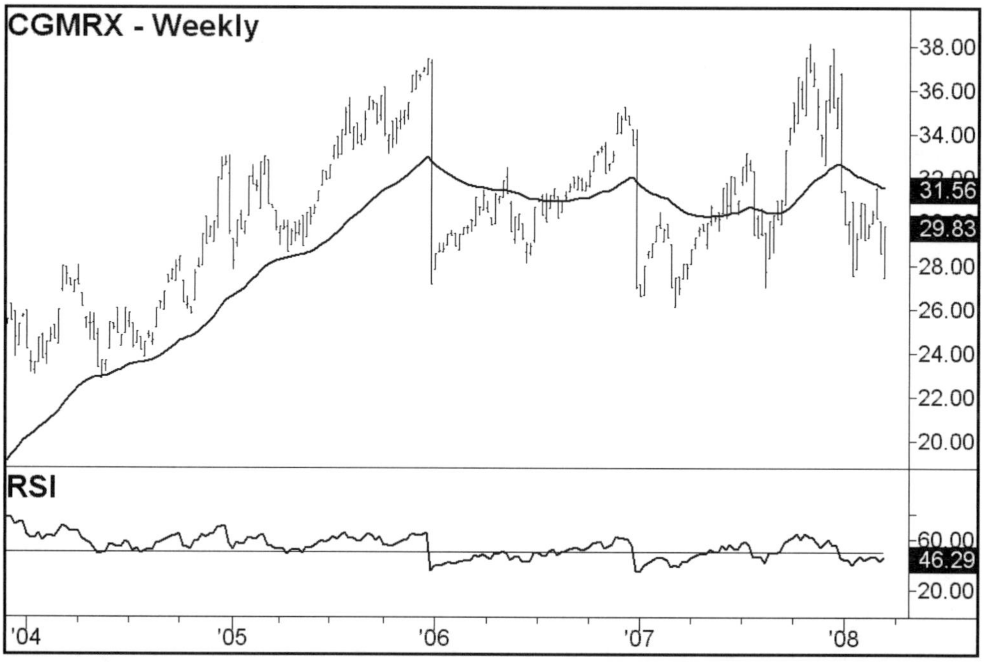

Figure 17.7 *Would you buy this mutual fund now?* (Chart: TradeStation)

Here's how the conversation might go after reading *Invest with Success*.

"What's the symbol for the fund?" you ask.

"Let me see... It's CGMRX."

As the advisor is telling you all the great benefits of the fund, you look up the fund on your charting program. You notice that the fund has gone sideways for the last two years. It's also below the 50 MA!

"The fund is in a sideways trend," you say.

"Well, uh…it's a top-rated fund."

"It's been sideways for two years. Does it pay a dividend, so I at least get paid to own it?"

"Let me look that up. I wouldn't worry too much about that trend stuff. You can't time the market. Investing is a marathon, not a sprint."

"While you're checking on the dividends, what's the year-to-date return?"

"Looks like a negative 5%, but you can't decide based on one year's performance."

"I really appreciate your help. Why don't you phone me back with a dividend-paying mutual fund that's in an uptrend. I like those better."

THE ENFORCER

In Chapter 2, I asked, "Who are you as an investor?" You must know what you are trying to achieve through investing. It's not a complex thing you have to figure out; you just need a basic idea of how to set up your portfolio with assets to meet your goals. No matter what goals you set for yourself, the first goal of any investor is to protect capital. Think of yourself as the "enforcer" of your family's financial laws of common sense. It doesn't matter if you're the new rookie on the force. Your motto is to *preserve and protect*.

Investors sometimes come to me for advice. I cannot give them advice, because I am not their financial advisor, but I can give them some common sense suggestions about what to ask or tell their advisor. A woman came up to me after a lecture I had given where I had showed how to make big profits in stocks trending up. The woman told me her stock broker had lost 50% of her money. At the time, the market was falling; she looked frantic and desperate.

"What was your plan?" I asked.

"What do you mean?" she replied.

"Have you talked to your broker about what you want him to do?"

"I called him up and yelled at him."

"Yelling is not a plan. Did you give him any direction?"

"What are you talking about? I yelled at him. He wasn't doing his job!"

"Your broker's job is to follow your plan. It's your responsibility to set goals for your plan and make sure your broker follows the plan."

"But I don't know anything."

"Then you should learn."

"But I don't have time."

"Well, then what do you expect from your broker if you can't even find the time to learn about investing?"

"At least I yelled at him."

I told the woman that she should talk to her broker about putting her money into risk-free cash assets (money markets, CDs) until she could sit down with him and develop a plan. At least that would remove the risk of losing more money, and she would be less stressed and able to think more clearly. It's better to be in a cash vehicle that's idling than a stock vehicle going in reverse.

The hardest time to make a plan is when you've already lost capital because you didn't have a plan in the first place. Keep your money free from risk (preserve and protect) until you have a plan to follow, one you've developed along with your broker or advisor. If you plan to manage your own portfolio, write down your plan on paper, and discuss it with your spouse (if you have one).

You have to police your own portfolio. A knowledgeable investor is the portfolio's enforcer, and someone to be reckoned with. When a broker or advisor tries to rob you of the opportunity to make money, you only have to point your barrel of knowledge at him and say, "Go ahead, make my day."

CAPITAL IDEA!

One of the overlooked areas of an investment plan is deciding how much money to save each month toward retirement. It's a good idea to build up capital with a regular savings program, putting away a small percentage of your paycheck into savings each month. Building wealth is not just about making big profits. It's also about making a big commitment to saving part of your hard-earned money, so it can work that second job for you.

When you make an investment plan, you want to start with the overall goal. Is it to build up the nest egg for retirement? Is it to generate income during retirement? Is it to build up capital for a special purpose, such as college tuition, a large purchase, or a special vacation?

Your capital is allocated within your portfolio by setting a main goal for the portfolio as follows:

Preservation of Capital: The investor wants to preserve his wealth and not risk losing it. He will want to have his money in treasury bills, money market funds, and CDs. These have virtually no risk, but they provide less return than more aggressive strategies. The main downside is inflation. If inflation occurs at a higher rate than the investment returns, the investor's buying power is decreased.

Current Income: The investor wants to generate an income stream for living expenses. He or she should consider interest-paying bonds and stocks with a high dividend. Choosing dividend-paying stocks in an uptrend can add to the overall return through capital appreciation.

Growth: The investor does not need to rely on investment income for living expenses. He wants to grow wealth over time and is willing to accept higher risk for the higher potential return. This is a good strategy for those who are younger and have a long time before retirement.

Growth and Income: The investor wants to generate income and also grow wealth through capital appreciation. Capital appreciation will help protect against inflation. The income assets can be a mix of bonds and dividend-paying stocks. Investors with lower risk tolerance can use this method rather than seeking pure growth.

Speculation: The investor is willing to accept high risk for high potential returns. Small-cap growth stocks are the best choice, especially technology stocks. Normally, speculation is done with only a portion of the portfolio capital. Stocks are usually chosen in industries of the economy which are performing exceptionally well.

LET'S GET PERSONAL

I encourage investors to set up their own brokerage accounts online. It's the best way to take control of your financial destiny. The journey to investment success will take time, so you may want to ease into it slowly. It is fine to use a full-service, personal **stock broker** for all or part of your investments. Understand that no one cares more about your money than you. You are ultimately responsible for investing your money, even if that means developing a plan with your broker or investment advisor.

We are often under the false impression that the job of the stock broker is to make us rich; it is not. The stock broker is a salesperson whose job is to generate commissions and sign up new investors. Brokers are employed by the brokerage company, not you. The company's goal is to get your money under management, so they can sell you products and services, as well as use your capital for lending. This is not a bad thing; brokers compensate the investor by their service and limited advice.

Brokers are knowledgeable about the stock market, but they are usually not skilled traders; if they were, their job would be trading for a large bank or mutual fund. They would also be able to trade and make themselves rich, in which case they would not need a job earning commissions as a broker. This is just common sense.

If you use a personal broker, remember that they are not there to be your friend. You may be friendly with them, but their job is to give you good advice on investments and help manage your portfolio. You can't worry about hurting their feelings; don't hesitate to go against their recommendations when you know better. For instance, if they suggest you buy a stock trending down, the enforcer in you should know exactly what to say: "Do you feel lucky? Well, do ya, punk?"

Whether your broker is a nice guy or not should not influence the decisions you must make to protect your family's finances. Be objective in assessing portfolio performance. Keep it simple: the balance of your account is either going up, down, or remaining about the same.

A stock broker can be an invaluable partner in helping you build wealth. A great broker is one who fully understands your investment objectives and does his best to meet your goals. You have to make sure he understands your objectives. A broker will only work as hard as you do to grow wealth. Never think you are so smart that you cannot benefit from the advice of an experienced stock broker. Remember, brokers do not control the market, and stock prices are out of their control. How the broker reacts to changes in the market is important. He should stay in tune with market uptrends and downtrends and discuss investment choices which are appropriate for the market conditions.

If you decide to use a full-service broker, you must know some basic questions to ask for each stock recommendation you receive. If you learn the methods in this book, you will be way ahead of the lady who can only call up her broker and yell at him. For any stock investment, ask your broker the following questions:

1. **What is the basis for your stock recommendation (what is it about the stock that makes it a buy)?**
2. **Why do you believe the stock is a buy *now* (timing)?**
3. **What is your price target for the stock in one year (must have reason to expect the stock will go up)?**
4. **At what price will you exit the trade if it does not work out (stop-loss risk)?**

Let me warn you. Stock brokers don't like using stop-loss orders, and they'll often try to talk you out of them. You already know my advice: have a stop-loss on *all* stock positions at *all* times. You may need to change brokers if they won't work with you to limit your losses to a specified amount.

PAYBACK TIME

Some investors have neither the inclination nor the time to do stock analysis or make investment decisions. They can turn to an **investment advisor (IA)** for advice or management of their investments. An investment advisor is someone in the business of giving investment advice and security recommendations for a fee or commission. Even if you use an investment advisor, you can still keep a portion of your assets to manage on your own with an online account.

Investment advice can be general or specific. General advice would be obtained from an advisory newsletter service. The investor would use the newsletter as a general guide for market conditions, economic concerns, and stock recommendations. Investment advisors can also provide specific advice to clients, beginning with an assessment of the investor's goals and risk tolerance; they will make individualized recommendations on asset allocation and stock selection. Some investment advisors can also take over management of your investments.

It is important to distinguish investment advisors from other persons or entities that might give you investment advice. A stock broker's job is investment sales, so he is not an investment advisor (unless separately registered). Brokers are compensated through commissions, so any advice they give is part of their overall service; they are not paid separately for advice. In addition, accountants, lawyers, and banks are not investment advisors, although they commonly provide incidental investment advice. Investment advisors are *registered* as advisors within a state. By being officially registered, they are responsible for following securities laws and rules of ethical conduct.

Investment advisors who take over management of your money are generally paid a percentage of the money under management. The fee is negotiable and generally decreases as the amount of money they manage increases. For accounts under $100,000, a 2% fee might be charged. For accounts over $100,000, the fees are usually 1% or less. If you give an investment advisor $100,000 to manage and the fee is 1%, it will cost you about $1000 per year for advice or management of capital.

Investment advisors must pass a standard written examination. Be aware that state regulation of investment advisors is geared toward fraud and unethical conduct. States do not regulate competence. While some advisors may have a great deal of experience and expertise, others may be novices who are unskilled at making your investments grow. If you have an investment advisor and he's not making you money, you have to find out why. Are your stocks under the 50 MA, for instance? Advisors may tell you to stay the course when things are going badly. Remember that they make money by how much total capital they have under management; they don't make more money with brilliant trading decisions.

Investment advisors are sometimes paid a fee by a mutual fund for putting you into that company's funds. It's not illegal or unethical, but you should ask whether the advisor is being compensated by the fund they recommend. It may affect their ability to make an unbiased opinion about which fund is best for you. Mutual fund "paybacks" to the investment advisor are not an issue if you insist on **no-load** funds (Chapter 18).

Managing money requires time, energy, and sometimes difficult decision-making. If your account is dropping in value, you may not sleep well. However, your advisor will probably sleep fine since it's not his money at risk. The advisor loses sleep when *his* account is falling in value. Be vigilant about your account performance and understand that, if you pay a 2% fee, your account must make at least 2% a year just to break even.

BIG COMMITTMENT

Successful investors are active investors, taking full responsibility for their investment plan and overseeing the process. They accept that they will make some mistakes, but they will learn from them. They understand that they are the best person to manage their money, for they have worked hard for the money, and no one can value money more than the person who created it. Investors make big profits when they make active choices about which stocks to buy or which mutual fund or ETF to buy. They use the amazing, free tools available to them online, to find stocks going up rather than stocks going down or sideways. Successful investors are always trying to make their money work hard for them. They have a plan, and they follow the plan.

ΔΔΔ

Investing requires a stronger backbone than a wishbone.

18 Mutual Funds & ETFs

You were already introduced to mutual funds and Exchange Traded Funds (ETFs) in Chapter 7, and I have mentioned them throughout the book. It's time to expand the definitions, provide greater detail about the funds, and discuss important things to consider before investing in them. This is another chapter that you can refer back to as a reference.

Constructing a successful portfolio is a two part process. First, you allocate capital between different asset classes (stocks, bonds, cash, etc.). Second, you diversify your assets classes by making individual investment selections. Since mutual funds and ETFs are already diversified, they are natural choices for portfolio construction (all or part). There are ETFs and mutual funds for practically any type of investment you might want to make. Funds are easy for a beginner to use because he or she only has to buy one fund instead of several individual stocks. I will go over three specific strategies which can be used with mutual funds and ETFs (Disclaimer: the strategies in this chapter are for educational purposes; make sure any fund you buy meets with your portfolio objectives, and obtain professional advice as needed).

There are several online screening tools for ETFs and mutual funds, so you can easily find what you want with just a few mouse clicks. Yahoo Finance has a good screener, and most online brokers also have screeners. The larger mutual fund companies, such as Fidelity (www.fidelity.com) and Vanguard (www.vanguard.com) also have great tools. The Yahoo finance site is especially good for getting a thorough, independent analysis of a fund.

In keeping with the 50-50 Strategy, you should review charts of any funds under consideration before risking investment capital. I recommend ETFs over mutual funds, and you'll soon find out why.

THE FEELINGS ARE MUTUAL

Mutual funds are financial companies that pool money from a large number of investors and then invest the money in a variety of assets. To invest in a mutual fund, investors buy shares of the fund. Mutual funds are professionally managed funds. Each mutual fund company has several types of funds, each with a stated investment purpose or allocation strategy. For instance, a growth fund would invest in growth stocks; an income fund would invest in dividend-paying stocks. The major benefits of mutual funds are **diversification** and **professional management**.

Mutual funds are an alternative to investing in individual stocks. The fund company hires professional money managers to make stock selections. The professionals decide what to buy, when to buy, and when to sell. All the investor has to do is decide how to allocate his capital to a few of the various types of funds available. With mutual funds, you can have the benefit of automatic reinvestment of dividends, capital gains, and interest. You can set up automatic monthly deposits (from your bank account) into a mutual fund. Mutual funds can be bought with minimal initial capital, making them accessible to small investors (minimum investment amounts usually apply). Mutual funds can make you money in three ways: dividend payments, capital gains distributions (when stocks are sold in the fund), and capital gains from an increase in the value of the fund.

Mutual funds are priced differently than stocks or ETFs. At the end of the trading day, the total value of the fund is determined based on the prices of the stocks in the fund. Then the value of the fund is divided by the number of shares owned to give a **net asset value (NAV),** or share value. Why at the end of the day? The reason is that the closing price for each stock in the fund must be known before the value of the fund can be calculated. The quotes you read for a mutual fund today are really the NAV as of yesterday's close of the stock market. If you bought a mutual fund today, you will not pay the NAV price you see quoted online; instead, you'll pay the NAV price at the end of today.

Mutual funds are common investment vehicles for retirement plans provided in the workplace. A plan administrator either makes investment decisions on behalf of the entire plan or gives you a limited choice of mutual funds from which to choose. Approximately half of American households own mutual funds, and they can be used for long-term growth of capital for retirement (or other purposes). There is a mutual fund to meet every investment need, including stocks, sectors, industries, bonds, market indices, international stocks, and money markets. Mutual funds are often named for the type of assets of which they are composed. For example, you might see a fund named a large-cap value fund or a small-cap growth fund.

When several mutual funds are offered from a single fund company, their funds are referred to as their "family of funds." You can buy mutual funds directly from any mutual fund company. Large mutual fund companies, such as Vanguard and Fidelity, will also sell funds from smaller companies, in addition to their own family of funds. Fidelity, for instance, lists over 4,000 mutual funds for sale. I ran a screen for small-cap growth funds at the Fidelity website and came up with over 200 (Figure 18.1).

	Fidelity Fund Name	Investment Category	Load Adjusted Returns[1] YTD	1 Yr	5 Yr	10 Yr/LOF
1	Fidelity Small Cap Growth Fund (FCPGX)	Small Growth	-13.48%	-1.56%	--	13.31%[2]
2	Fidelity Small Cap Independence Fund (FDSCX)	Small Growth	-15.50%	-11.20%	13.90%	4.78%

First 8 funds that match your criteria (1-8 of 249 funds available, including Fidelity funds)

	Fund Name(all matching funds)	Investment Category	Load Adjusted Returns[1] YTD	1 Yr	5 Yr	10 Yr/LOF
1	AFBA 5Star Small Cap CL I (AFCIX)	Small Growth	-15.88%	-16.35%	15.01%	8.11%[2]
2	AIM Small Cap Growth CL A (GTSAX) **	Small Growth	-16.61%	-9.87%	12.54%	8.45%
3	AIM Small Cap Growth CL B (GTSBX) **	Small Growth	-16.23%	-9.50%	12.72%	8.26%
4	AIM Small Cap Growth CL C (GTSDX) **	Small Growth	-12.72%	-6.18%	12.97%	6.44%[2]
5	AIM Small Cap Growth Instl CL (GTSVX) **	Small Growth	-11.66%	-4.23%	14.38%	5.77%[2]
6	Adams Harkness Small Cap Growth (ASCGX)	Small Growth	-15.72%	2.76%	--	6.13%[2]
7	Alger Small Cap CL A (ALSAX) **	Small Growth	-19.43%	-9.48%	17.04%	0.66%
8	Alger Small Cap CL B (ALSCX) **	Small Growth	-19.28%	-9.80%	17.28%	0.49%

Figure 18.1 *This is a small-cap growth screen for mutual funds. The two at the top are Fidelity funds and the bottom eight (partial list) are funds from other companies.* (Source: Fidelity)

GET A LOAD OF THIS

When I am done explaining the various costs associated with mutual funds, you'll see why I prefer ETFs. Still, if you own mutual funds or plan to buy them, you should understand their fee structure because fees affect their overall returns. Check the cost of buying a mutual fund before you invest in it; the amount will vary from company to company and from fund to fund.

Load charges are a commission, or sales charge, the investor pays to buy a mutual fund. The fund uses the load fee to pay the broker who sold the fund to the client. Some funds are called **no-load funds** which are commission free, and these are the only ones I recommend. There is little or no difference between the performance of load and no-load funds, so there is no reason to pay a commission.

Some brokerage companies require that you own a fund for about three months to get the no-load benefit. This really isn't a problem, since mutual funds are long-term investment products. In general, you would normally give a fund at least 6-12 months before you judge performance, unless it falls below the 50 MA. Vanguard (www.vanguard.com) and Fidelity (www.fidelity.com) are two companies which have a good selection of no-load funds.

A **front-end load** is a sales charge (purchase fee) which is paid up front, or as soon as you buy a fund. The load fees are usually in the 3-5% range, but they can be as high as 8.5%. If you invest $20,000 in a 5% front-end loaded mutual fund, you will be charged $1,000 in commissions (.05 x $20,000 = $1,000). Your $20,000 investment is immediately worth $19,000. The fund will have to make back more than 5% in the first year just to get you back to breakeven.

A **back-end load** is a commission you pay when you sell the fund; it is a deferred sales charge (redemption fee). The back-end load usually decreases over time, and it may be waived if you own the fund for 5-6 years. The charges can be waived because the company was able to get other fees from you while you owned the fund for several years. The back-end load makes it a disincentive to exit a fund, so it can be an issue if you want to get out of a poorly performing fund (especially if it falls below the 50 MA).

A **12(b)-1 fee** is a fee charged to the investor annually to pay for marketing and distribution costs. These fees can be about 1% of the assets under management. If you have $20,000 in a mutual fund, that would be a potential fee of $200 per year. The fee is charged regardless of the fund's performance. Many no-load funds will charge a 12(b)-1 fee to make up for the lost load commissions, making 12(b)-1 a hidden load. I recommend you only buy mutual funds which have no 12b-1 fees.

Figure 18.2 shows a screen for Vanguard mutual funds (partial list) based on their *expenses*. None of the funds shown have a front load, but a few have a 1% redemption fee if the fund is sold within the time period specified. Make sure you check the expenses of a fund before you buy it.

Domestic Stock - More Aggressive			Learn more about who should invest in this asset typ	
Name	Number	Expense Ratio	Purchase Fee	Redemption Fee
Capital Opportunity Inv	0111	0.45%	None	1% if held < 1 yr
Capital Value Fund	0328	0.53%	None	None
Explorer Fund Investor	0024	0.41%	None	None
Extended Mkt Index Inv	0098	0.24%	None	None
Growth Equity Fund	0544	0.68%	None	None
Mid-Cap Growth Fund	0301	0.56%	None	None
Mid-Cap Growth Index Inv	0832	0.24%	None	None
Mid-Cap Index Fund Inv	0859	0.21%	None	None
Mid-Cap Value Index Inv	0835	0.24%	None	None
PRIMECAP Fund Investor	0059	0.43%	None	1% if held < 1 yr
Selected Value Fund	0934	0.42%	None	1% if held < 1 yr
Small-Cap Growth Index	0861	0.22%	None	None
Small-Cap Index Fund Inv	0048	0.22%	None	None
Small-Cap Value Index	0860	0.22%	None	None
Strategic Equity Fund	0114	0.30%	None	None
Strategic Sm-Cap Equity	0615	0.38%	None	None
Tax-Managed Small-Cap	0116	0.13%	None	1% if held < 5 yrs

Figure 18.2 *This screen is for mutual fund expenses and it shows expense ratios, purchase fees, and redemption fees.* (Source: Vanguard)

TOTALLY FEES-ABLE

What? You thought you were done learning about fees? Funds can also charge a **management fee** which pays for professional money management. This is another annual fee which must be paid despite the fund's performance. There are also **administrative fees** which go to cover the fund's costs for buying and selling stocks in the fund. Both management and administrative fees are reasonable, and are necessary to compensate the professional managers for managing the fund.

The management costs for a mutual fund are listed in the **expense ratio**, a common gauge of management efficiency (Figure 18.2). The ratio compares the management fees to the total assets under management, and it ranges from about 0.5% to 2.5%. I recommend you find mutual funds with expense ratios below 1%, preferably around 0.50%.

Also be aware that some companies charge exchange fees and account maintenance fees. Exchange fees are sometimes charged for transferring from one mutual fund to another within the same family of funds. The fee is a disincentive for investors to jump in and out of funds. Account maintenance fees are sometimes charged to maintain the account. Most likely, you won't have to pay this, but check with the company where you buy your funds. A successful investor is an informed investor.

All of the charges and fees for mutual funds can be found listed under the *profile* page at Yahoo Finance. If your investment advisor recommends a fund to you, tell him you enjoy being well-informed about your investments. Get the name of the fund (or symbol) and tell your advisor you'll get back to him in five minutes. Then quickly go to Yahoo and check the fees (Figure 18.3). This is a *three-clicker* search which takes about ten seconds. By the way, if it takes more than seven or eight clicks to research a stock or fund, I consider it just too much work!

The Yahoo Three-clicker for Mutual Fund Expenses:

1. Go to the Yahoo site (www.yahoo.com).
2. Click on *finance* in the left column.
3. Enter the symbol for the mutual fund and click *get quotes*.
4. In the left column, click on fund *profile*. Scroll down to find the expenses.

NOT MY TYPE

One of the jobs of a mutual fund company (or ETF company) is to continually create products for customers to purchase. Consequently, there is an overload of funds, and most mutual fund companies offer similar types of funds. For instance, if you screen for small-cap growth funds, you'll get a list of over 700 at Yahoo.

Some of the terms used by fund companies seem as though they are meant to intentionally confuse the small investor. For instance, a "value" fund is described by one company as having characteristics of "low

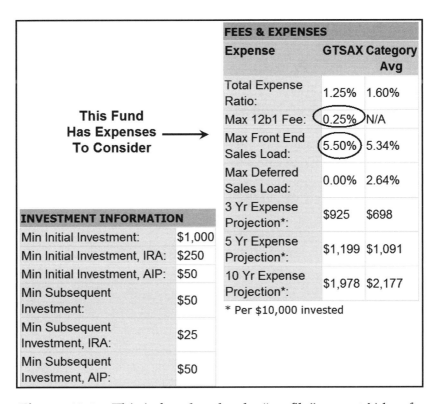

This Fund Has Expenses To Consider →

FEES & EXPENSES		
Expense	GTSAX	Category Avg
Total Expense Ratio:	1.25%	1.60%
Max 12b1 Fee:	0.25%	N/A
Max Front End Sales Load:	5.50%	5.34%
Max Deferred Sales Load:	0.00%	2.64%
3 Yr Expense Projection*:	$925	$698
5 Yr Expense Projection*:	$1,199	$1,091
10 Yr Expense Projection*:	$1,978	$2,177

* Per $10,000 invested

INVESTMENT INFORMATION	
Min Initial Investment:	$1,000
Min Initial Investment, IRA:	$250
Min Initial Investment, AIP:	$50
Min Subsequent Investment:	$50
Min Subsequent Investment, IRA:	$25
Min Subsequent Investment, AIP:	$50

Figure 18.3 *This is found under the "profile" page at Yahoo for AIM Small Cap Growth Fund A (GTSAX). It shows a 5.50% load and a 0.25% 12b-1 fee. Is the total expense ratio high (look and see)?* (Source: Yahoo Finance)

price-to-book, price-to-earnings, price-to-sales, and price-to-cash flow ratios." Does that make sense to you? What they mean is they buy stocks that are worth more on paper than they are currently selling for. This is not my type of fund. As I have said, price is determined by supply and demand, and not facts and figures. I prefer to buy funds in uptrends because I can see it becoming worth more.

I categorize stock mutual funds by their two main components: size and strategy. Funds can be composed of small-cap, mid-cap, or large-cap stocks; and their strategy can be growth, income, or both (blend). Why make it any more difficult? If an advisor gives you a complex name for a stock fund, you can come right back and say, "Is that a small, mid, or large-cap fund? And is it designed for growth, income, or both?" Make advisors explain things in terms *you* understand.

COMMAND PERFORMANCE

The performance of mutual funds tends to follow the general economy. If you owned mutual funds during the bull market of the nineties, you probably did well and had a favorable opinion of them. If you owned them during the 2000-2003 bear market, you may have lost a lot of money. Mutual funds are long-term investments, but that doesn't mean you must remain in a fund when it enters a downtrend. You should take command of your funds and expect reasonable performance (Figure 18.4).

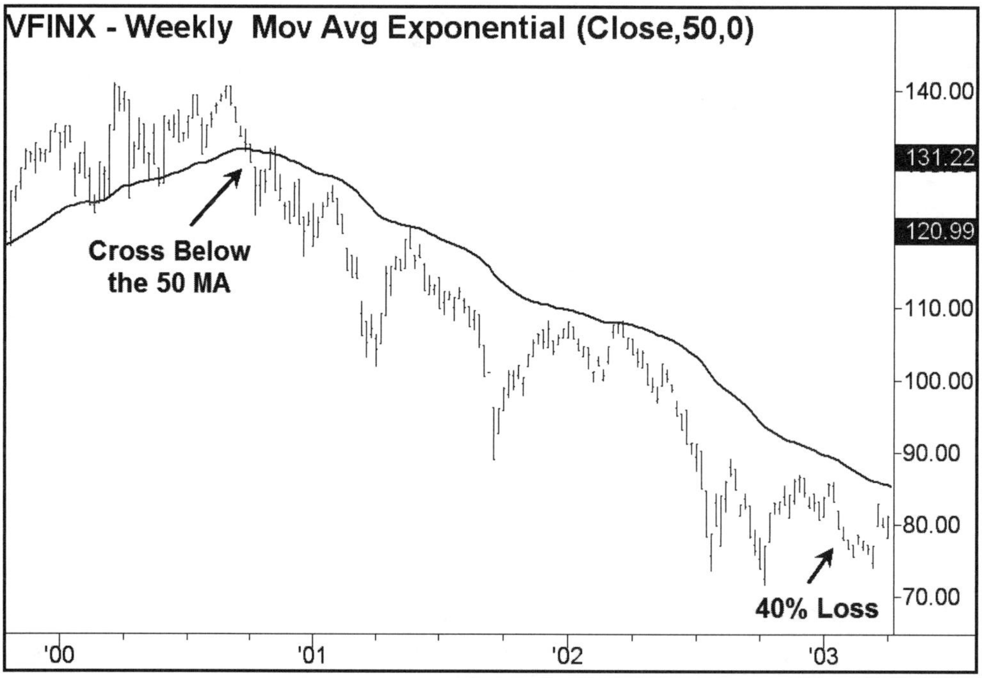

Figure 18.4 *The Vanguard Index Trust 500 (VFINX) is a fund which tracks the S&P 500 ($SPX).* (Chart: TradeStation)

Figure 18.4 shows the Vanguard Index Trust 500 (VFINX). It went from $140 down to $80 during the bear market of 2000-2003, losing 40% of its value. By 2008, it was back to $140, but that was 3 years of emotional stress going down, four years of hope and optimism going back up, all just to breakeven. Over the long term, the fund should grow at the rate of about 9-12% per year, but you must have a 10-20 year horizon for this to play out.

Most funds market themselves based on past performance. Many investors end up chasing performance records rather than looking at a chart of the fund to see if it is rising in value. If it is not, the fund's performance will be poor, no matter what the *past* performance has been. Some of the best opportunities in funds will present themselves after a few years of lackluster performance, when the fund goes from a sideways trend to an uptrend. As always, use your eyes to make sense of price. Chase profit opportunities, not past performance.

LET'S EXCHANGE TOPICS

Exchange Traded Funds (ETFs) are similar to mutual funds; they are composed of a collection of stocks, and investors buy shares of the ETF rather than individual stocks. ETFs also provide diversification for the investor, and they are great for investing in individual sectors or industries of the economy. The general types of ETFs are similar to mutual funds.

ETFs are different in that they are based on stock indices which already have an established composition of stocks. Therefore, ETFs have fewer expenses; they are passively managed, and they do not have to pay a fund manager a huge salary to choose individual stocks. There is very little buying and selling of stocks in the ETFs, so there are less transaction costs. This keeps the expense ratios smaller for ETFs than for mutual funds.

ETFs have some major differences from mutual funds which make them perfectly suited for the small investor. Unlike mutual funds, ETFs trade on stock exchanges and you can buy as little or as many shares as you want in your online account. There is no minimum investment amount. You can short ETFs (not recommended) and buy them on margin (not recommended), both of which you can't do with mutual funds. ETFs have minimal stock turnover, so they do not generate significant taxable income. Capital gains are realized when you decide to sell the ETF. However, ETFs do not allow dividend reinvestment or monthly investment programs.

ETFs trade like a stock on a stock exchange; you can buy them at any time throughout the market day at the quoted market price. To buy ETFs, the investor pays the same commission that is paid to buy a stock. There are no "load" fees or 12(b)-1 fees for ETFs. Most online brokerages charge $10 or less in commissions which is not a big concern compared to front-end loaded or back-end loaded mutual funds. Because they trade like stocks, you can place stop-loss orders on ETFs which you can't do on mutual funds. This alone is a reason to buy ETFs over mutual funds. You can control the price at which you enter and exit the investment.

There are ETFs for practically everything—market indices , market sectors and industries, bonds, currencies, real estate, stock categories (large-cap, growth, income, etc), and foreign stocks and currencies. With so many possibilities, ETFs offer a flexible, low-cost way to adjust asset allocation with diversified investment vehicles.

MIRROR, MIRROR, ON THE WALL STREET

Indexing is a passive investment approach which uses market index funds to mirror, or match, the performance of a market index (S&P 500, DJIA, NASDAQ, etc.). You can use a mutual fund or ETF for indexing. A fund that matches the S&P 500 will hold the same 500 stocks that are in the index. Index funds can be used to construct all or part of a portfolio. Indexing simply follows the performance of the overall market. It works because of the historical performance of the U.S. markets over time, which is about 12% per year for the S&P 500.

Indexing can be accomplished with index mutual funds such as the Vanguard 500 Index Fund (VFINX) or the Fidelity 500 Index Fund (FSMAX), both of which mirror the S&P 500. SPY is the SPDR S&P 500 ETF (www.statestreetspdrs.com) which mirrors the S&P 500 index; QQQQ is the PowerShares QQQ Trust ETF (www.powershares.com) which represents the NASDAQ-100 index; and DIA is the Diamonds Trust ETF (www.statestreetspdrs.com) which matches the Dow Jones Industrial Average. Figure 18.5 is an example of how DIA tracks the Dow Jones Industrial Average, shown here in a rising market.

Indexing makes money during periods of economic expansion, and it loses money in economic contractions. Over time, there is a positive, upward bias to the U.S. markets which is why indexing is considered a long-term investment method. To index on a shorter-term basis, you would invest in index funds when the index is above the 50 MA and get out of the fund (go to cash) when it is below the 50 MA. Sound familiar?

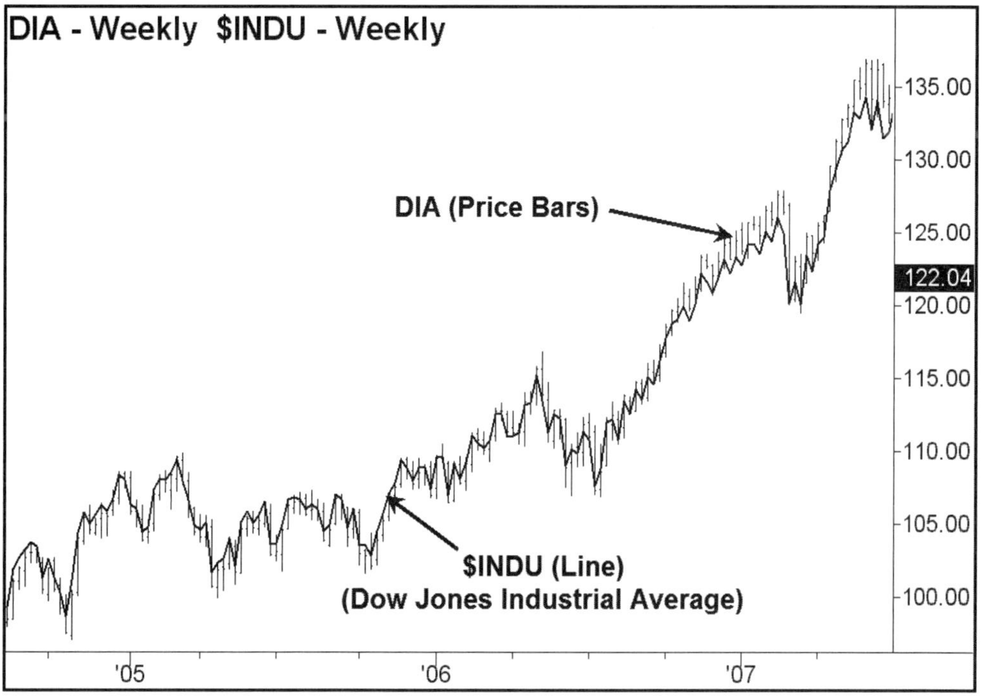

Figure 18.5 *The DIA ETF (price bars) mirrors the Dow Jones Industrial Average (Line)* (Chart: TradeStation)

ONE FOR THE ROAD

If you're on the road a lot, or just can't seem to find the time at home to do any research, you can buy one mutual fund that automatically combines different percentages of assets. These funds are called balanced, or hybrid funds, because they combine both stocks (growth) and bonds (income). For instance, the Vanguard Balanced Index Fund (VBINX) is a mix of 60% stocks and 40% bonds. It is a no-load fund with no 12(b)-1 fees and a low expense ratio at 0.20% (average is 1.0%). Since portfolios usually have a mix of stocks, bonds, and cash, you can construct a portfolio by simply buying VBINX (stocks and bonds) and a money market fund (cash). Balanced funds do not perform as well as the overall market during economic expansion, but they perform better than the market during economic contractions. They are long-term investments intended to ride out market cycles.

Another one for the road is an asset allocation fund; it combines all three asset types—stocks, bonds, and money markets— into a single fund. The Vanguard Asset Allocation (VAAPX) fund is a no-load fund with no 12b-1 fees and an expense ratio of 0.37%. With VAAPX, it is possible to buy one mutual fund to construct a portfolio. Investing can be simple once you have some basic knowledge.

Finally, you can buy funds that have a mixture of assets based on time horizon. These funds are often referred to as life-cycle funds. For instance, if you plan to retire in 2025, you can buy the Vanguard® Target Retirement 2025 Fund; if you plan to retire in 2030, buy the Vanguard® Target Retirement 2030 Fund. I guess we'd have to call this type of fund something different, such as "one for the *end* of the road."

I have one word of caution. The one-for-the-road strategies are like driving with cruise control. There's not much to do, but you'd better not fall asleep at the wheel. Any strategy needs some monitoring.

TRIPLE PLAY

This strategy is only slightly more difficult. You pick two index ETFs, one to represent stocks and one to represent bonds. Cash can be put in money markets or CDs at a bank, or you can buy a money market mutual fund. You only have to determine how much money to allocate to each asset class (Figure18.6). Total fees for this plan are under $50. It doesn't get much easier.

ASSET CLASS	FUND
Stocks	VTI Vanguard Total Stock Market ETF
Bonds	IEI iShares Lehman 3-7 Year Treasury Bond ETF
Cash	FDRXX Fidelity Cash Reserves Mutual Fund

Figure 18.6 *Triple Play Strategy with two index funds and a money market fund.*

VTI made over 100% in returns during the bull market of 2003-2007 (Figure 18.7). That's roughly 20% per year which is very respectable. During the same period, the S&P 500 (overall market) made about 75%, so VTI outperformed the S&P. VTI is based on a different market index (MSCI Broad Market Index) which accounts for the difference.

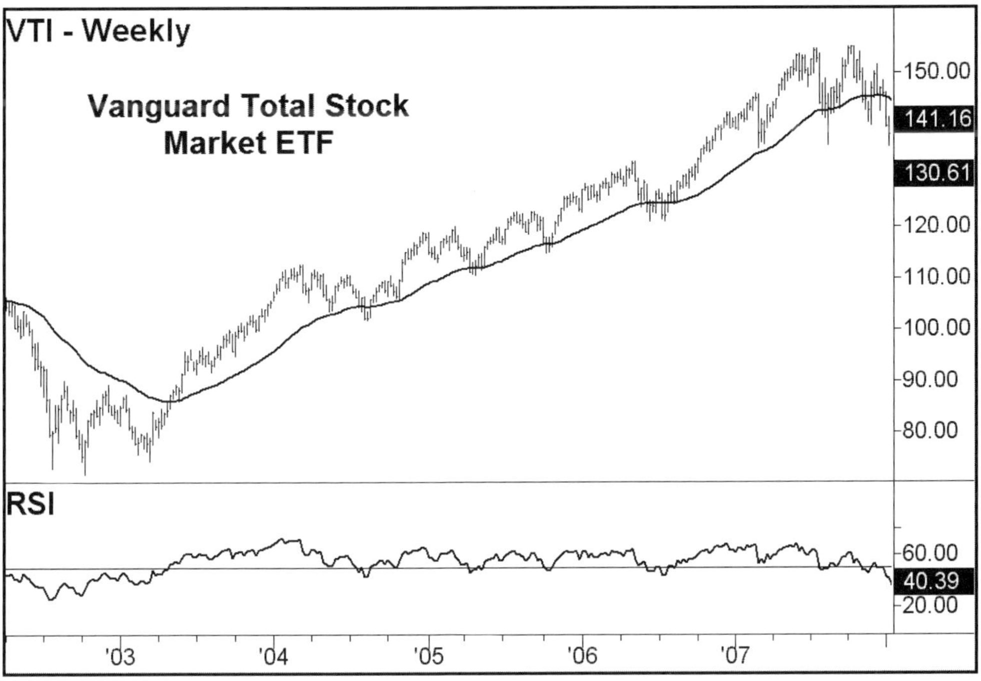

Figure 18.7 *The Vanguard Total Stock Market (VTI) tracks the overall market and will perform well during bull markets.* (Chart: TradeStation)

SPIDER WEB

Sector rotation involves the relationship between business sectors and the business cycle. The concept is that different sectors of the economy go in and out of favor at different times during the expansion and contraction phases of the business cycle (Chapter 12). Sector rotation can be the basis for considering investments in the stock portion of a portfolio.

In theory, the various sectors rotate in a certain order. This is generally true, but in reality, the order is variable and the sectors overlap one another. Every business cycle is a little different. For this strategy, we use the **Select Sector SPDRs** (S&P Depository Receipts) ETFs, called "spiders," which divide the S&P 500 into nine sector funds (Figure 18.8). You can find more information on the funds at the SPDR website (www.sectorspdr.com).

SECTOR SELECT SPDRs	
ETF Symbol	*Economic Sector*
XLY	**Consumer Discretionary**
XLK	**Technology**
XLI	**Industrial**
XLB	**Materials**
XLE	**Energy**
XLP	**Consumer Staples**
XLV	**Health Care**
XLU	**Utilities**
XLF	**Financials**

Figure 18.8 *Sector Select SPDRs for nine sectors of the economy.*

For reference, I have matched the nine SPDR ETFs with the four phases of the business cycle (Figure 18.9). The strategy is simple: determine which sectors are in uptrends and divide your allocation of stock capital evenly among the rising sectors. You have 10 lots of capital for stocks, and there are nine sectors in which to invest, so that makes a nice fit.

During economic expansion, all of the nine sectors may be in uptrends. During economic contraction, it is possible that none of the sectors will be in uptrends. As always, use the 50 MA to determine if the ETF of the sector is a High Riser or Low Riser, and buy according to the 50-50 Strategy criteria. Why change a good thing?

CYCLE PHASE	SECTOR ROTATION	SPDR ETF
Early Expansion	**Industrial** **Technology**	**XLI** **XLK**
Late Expansion	**Materials** **Energy**	**XLB** **XLE**
Early Contraction	**Consumer Staples** **Health Care**	**XLP** **XLV**
Late Contraction	**Utilities** **Consumer Discretionary** **Financial**	**XLU** **XLY** **XLF**

Figure 18.9 *Four phases of the business cycle are shown with sector rotation and SPDR ETFs.*

Let's test out part of the strategy. Figure 18.10 is a chart of the XLE SPDR ETF which represents the energy sector. What kind of trend is it (High Riser, Low Riser)? Would you consider buying this ETF now? Do price and RSI meet the 50-50 Strategy criteria (answers are at the end of the chapter)?

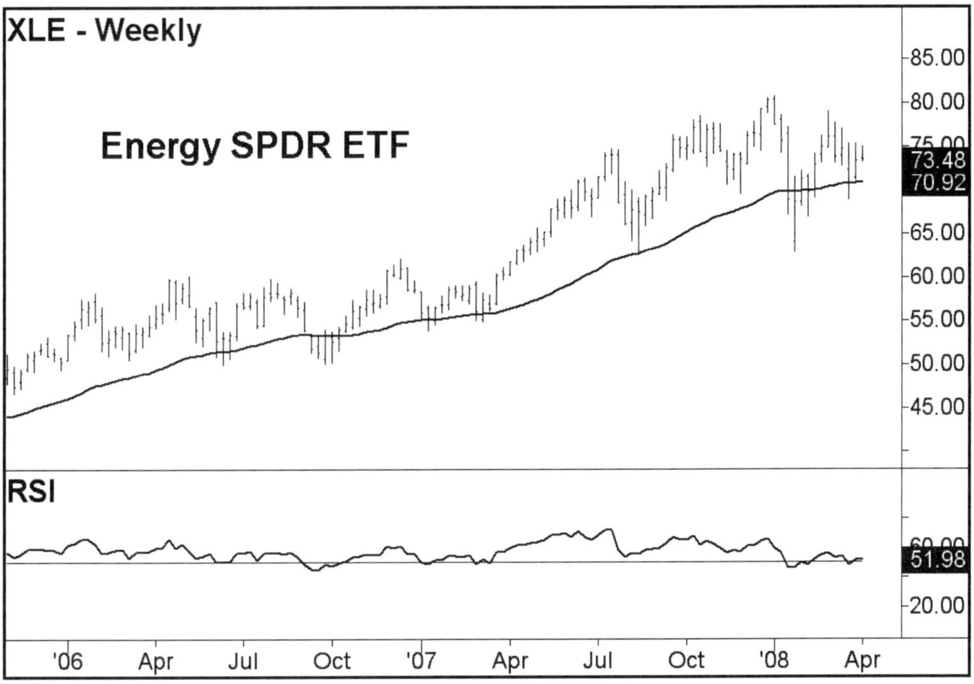

Figure 18.10 *The XLE SPDR ETF for the energy sector.* (Chart: TradeStation)

Now look at Figure 18.11 which is a chart of the XLF SPDR ETF for the financial sector. What kind of trend is it (High Riser, Low Riser)? Would you consider buying this ETF now? Do price and RSI meet the 50-50 Strategy criteria (answers are at the end of the chapter)?

You should always wait for the 50-50 Strategy criteria before you buy a sector ETF. Remain in the sector ETFs as long as price remains above a rising 50 MA. You don't need a financial expert to tell you how the economy is doing. You can simply follow the nine SPDR sector ETFs. Put all of them in a watchlist at your brokerage account, at Yahoo Finance, or at ClearStation®. Check them about once every quarter. Major sectors of the economy trend for years at a time.

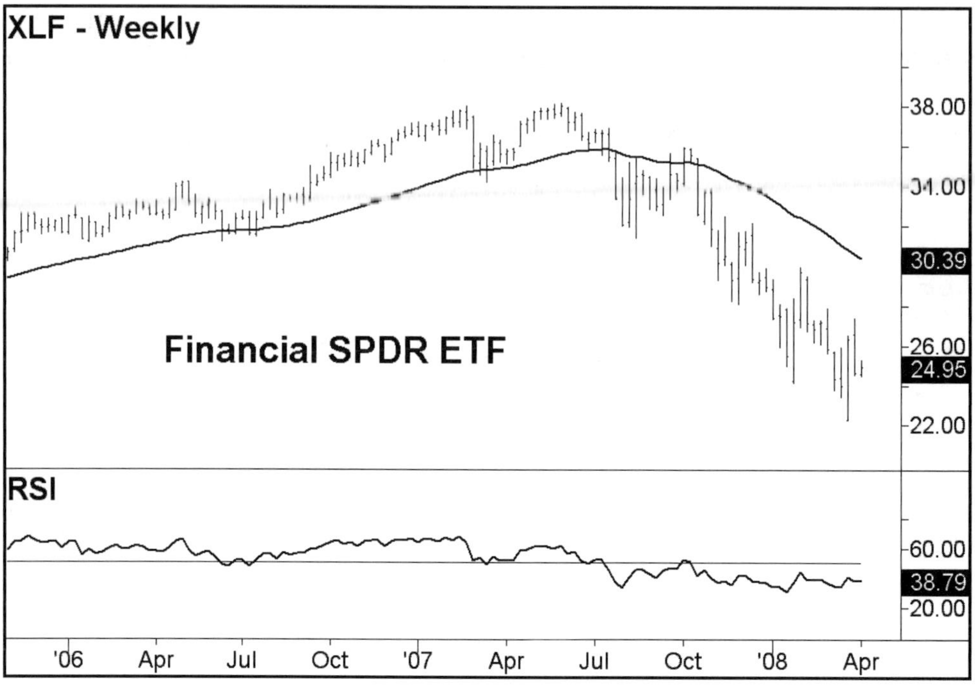

Figure 18.11 *XLF SPDR ETF for the financial sector.*
(Chart: TradeStation)

After this section, you should no longer need to be afraid of spiders.

ΔΔΔ

Answers for Figure 18.10-18.11:

- **Figure 18.10** XLE is a High Riser. It is a buy. Price is above the 50 MA (entire price bar) and RSI is above the 50 level (51).

- **Figure 18.11** XLF shows price below a falling 50 MA and RSI is below the 50 level. It does not meet the 50-50 Strategy criteria, so it is not a buy.

Poor discipline is knowing what to do and not doing it, knowing what not to do and doing it, or not knowing what to do and doing anything.

19 THE MASTER PLAN

The investment **plan** is a structured outline of how you will manage your investments. The plan should be specific, simple, and written. It should describe what actions will be taken and how the results will be monitored. A good plan takes into consideration the investor's overall goals and how they will be achieved. The investment strategy and risk management rules should be included. The plan should have reasonable expectations in terms of investment returns and the activities expected of the investor. It will also designate who will manage the plan—you or your investment advisor.

There are many online tools to help with portfolio planning, and the market offers plenty of investment vehicles to meet the goals of the portfolio. Professional advice is usually a good idea to make sure the plan follows generally-accepted portfolio principles. Some investors will want to let an investment advisor manage everything, but the investor is still responsible for the plan. He should monitor the progress of the plan the same as if he were managing his own investments.

The more complicated the plan, the less likely it is to be carried out effectively. Keep the plan simple and straightforward. If you need ten pages to explain the plan, it is too complicated (1-2 pages is plenty). In this chapter, I will provide an overview of questions to ask yourself (or your advisor) when making a plan. The first time you put together a plan, there are many things you must consider. Once you have a plan, it doesn't change much from year to year.

THE CFO OF FARBUCKS

Many investors do not have a specific plan for success. They only have a general idea of what they want to accomplish, such as to get rich, retire early, or buy low and sell high. If you ask them to explain their plan, they have difficulty even outlining the basic points. This is because most of us are not taught about investment plans in school; then one day we are expected to make a plan that will determine the financial security of our family's future. It's no wonder that investing can seem overwhelming.

Building wealth is like forming a business for the purpose of making money. Consider yourself the CFO (Chief Financial Officer) of your family's finances. You won't need the newly-made bucks until far into the future, so you name your startup business Farbucks. The portfolio is your office and you have a business plan for how to put your money to work. You will interview job candidates (assets) by looking at their qualifications (fundamentals) and past work history (chart patterns), and you will hire workers that meet your criteria. The business has different departments, so you must hire different assets for different jobs—stocks to make big profits, bonds to make regular income and CDs for short-term cash (temporary workers). Your business will have its ups and downs, but some years you'll make big profits, and all the efforts of forming Farbucks will have been worth it. The gossip around the water cooler is "there's a new sheriff in town," and he thinks he's Clint Eastwood.

Not everyone wants to be the CFO of Farbucks. Not long ago, my wife and I worked with an investor who came to us because he just wanted to learn about how the stock market worked. He spent time studying our methods, including the 50-50 Strategy. The investor practiced investing for awhile and came to the conclusion that he didn't really want to handle his own investments. Instead, he gave his stock broker a list of ten stocks, along with specific instructions to buy according to the 50-50 Strategy. Not all of the stocks did well, but two of the ten made big profits. In a period of one year, the investor had made as much money from his stocks as he had made working the entire year at his regular job! He was successful, not because he was a financial genius, but because he gave his stock broker a specific plan of action. He also continued doing what he enjoyed, which was working at his job.

MIND OVER WHAT MATTERS

Investing losses can negatively affect your mindset. Part of being a successful investor is sticking with your plan when trades don't turn out the way you had planned. As long as you manage your risk according to the plan, let the plan work. If you add one stock at a time (Chapter 16, "What about BOB?"), you will keep your risk to a minimum while you build a valuable portfolio. Remember that the first goal of portfolio management is the preservation of capital.

If you have a string of losses, you will invariably experience a portfolio **drawdown**. A portfolio drawdown is the maximum percentage of money lost from the highest account balance in any given time period. It's much like drawing money out of a bank account; you draw down the balance to a lower level. You expect the level to go back up when you deposit your paycheck. If your expenses in one year are more than your paycheck deposits, you'll have a drawdown of your account balance at the end of the year.

It's the same concept with investing. For instance, if you start out the year with $50,000 capital, and you lose $5,000 by the end of the first year of investing, then you had a drawdown of 10% for the year ($5,000/$50,000 = .10 x 100 = 10%). To have a 10% drawdown, you would need a string of about seven straight losses; about 14 straight losses if you scale into trades one half-lot at a time. A string of 14 losses with the TOP SCORE 50-50 Strategy System is not likely, especially during a long-term market uptrend. The 50-50 Strategy, applied randomly, has positive results. My research has shown that if you bought every stock in the S&P 500 during the period from 2003-2007 (making no choices based on earnings and/or trend conditions), the returns would have been 6% per year (a positive number). Of course, our goal is to *make* choices, so we can make bigger profits.

Drawdowns matter because it is harder to recover losses than it was to incur them. I recommend that investors, especially couples, set a **drawdown limit**. The couples should agree that, if the limit is reached, no further investments are entered until the plan is reviewed and trading errors are analyzed. It is important that couples agree on this number, so both feel comfortable about the family's finances. Each spouse may have a different set of values toward money. While you may not agree on how to value money, you can agree on a drawdown limit. Married or not, every investor should set a drawdown limit and stick to it. The drawdown limit should be clearly stated in the investment plan.

PROFIT OR PROPHET?

When to take profits in a successful trade can be a challenge, especially for beginning investors. Some investors are much more tolerant of losses than gains, meaning they are mentally slow to take a loss and quick to take a profit. Often, beginners have a nice gain on a stock, and they want to take profits and declare a winning trade; they don't want to risk the trade turning into a loser. To build wealth, you must be able to let profits accumulate. Place your stop-loss under the 50 MA and let your trades work. Then what do you do? That's right, go live your life.

Here's the basic **stop-loss rule** for entries: how much money are you willing to lose (initial risk) in order to see if the stock will trend higher? Once a stock is profitable, we have a different question: how much profit are you willing to give back in order to see if you can make even more profits? The answer will influence how long you stay in a trade (investment). There is no way to predict how high a stock will go; still, some investors want to be prophets. They think they know when a stock looks too high. No one knows, so don't try to predict. Be a profit investor, not a prophet investor.

The amount of profit you will definitely give back is the amount you'll lose if you are stopped out during a pullback. **Pullback risk** is the amount of dollar risk from the current price of a stock to the trailing stop-loss under the 50 MA. It is totally acceptable to put on a trade, and then use a trailing stop until you get stopped out. This **trailing-stop exit** approach is easy and it doesn't create stress from wondering if you should or shouldn't exit a trade. Beginners will find this method the easiest. Use the trailing-stop exit method when you paper trade.

A profit is not a profit until you put it in the bank. Another approach is to take profits periodically instead of waiting to be stopped out. Taking periodic profits reduces the risk to your capital. For most investors, the less you tinker with your investments the better. As a general rule, take partial (half) profits when you have a 50% gain. That means you would sell half of the shares you own. If one of your stocks reaches a 100% gain, you have doubled your money. Sell another half of the remaining shares, and let the rest of them ride until you get stopped out. This approach is called **scaling** out of a position. In general, never take profit on your entire position when the 50 MA is still rising—give price a chance. Figure 19.1 is an example of scaling out of an investment.

In Figure 19.1, The Knot (KNOT) shows an initial entry at $10 (1). After a 50% gain in price, one half of the shares are sold (2). After a 100% gain in price, (from your entry), one-half of the remaining shares are sold (3). The remaining one-fourth of the shares would have been stopped out at (4). If you had bought 100 shares of the $10 stock, your initial investment would have been $1,000. Your total profit would have been $800, or 80% in about a year and a half.

KNOT Trade Analysis

Entry Price: $10
Number of shares: 100
Initial investment: $1,000
Profit on ½ shares: $250 (($15 exit - $10 entry) x 50 shares = $250)
Profit on ¼ shares: $250 (($20 exit - $10 entry) x 25 shares = $250)
Profit on ¼ shares: $300 (($22 exit - $10 entry) x 25 shares - $300)
Total Profit: $800
Percent Return: 80%

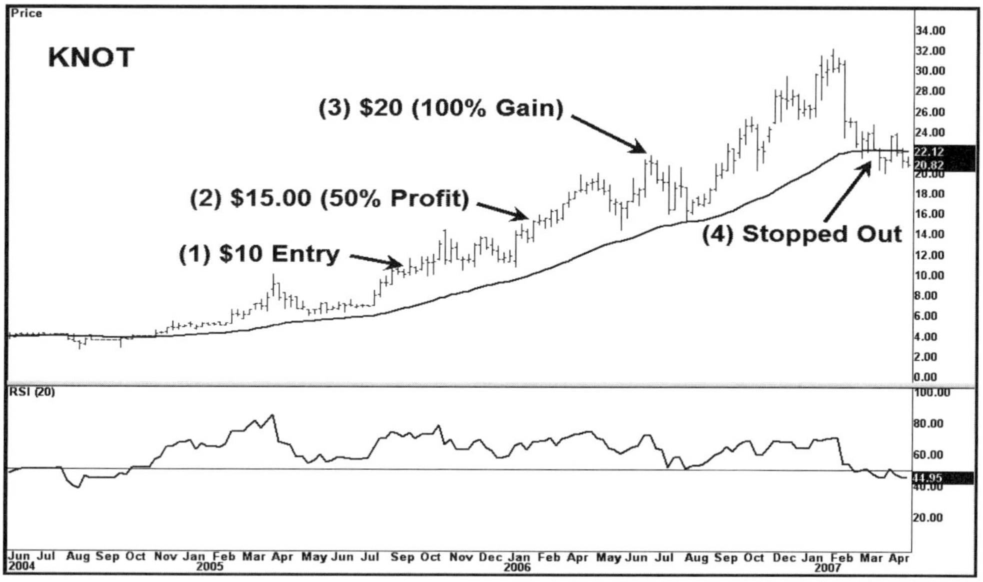

Figure 19.1 *This weekly chart of The Knot (KNOT) is an example of scaling out of an investment.* (Chart: TDAmeritrade)

MASTER OF YOUR DOUGH-MAIN

It's recommended that every investor have a plan, but what does a plan look like? By now, you probably realize there are several things to consider. How do you keep it all straight? Don't think too hard. The plan can be developed by asking a list of questions; the answers will define your plan. The plan organizes your objectives into a list of actions you will take on behalf of your household.

If you want to be master of your "dough-main," then you'll need a master plan. In the next several sections, I will give you a **MASTER Plan** for wealth. MASTER stands for ***M**arkets, **A**llocation, **S**trategy, **T**rade Management, **E**xpectations,* and ***R**eassessment.* It is your CFO's guide to planning wealth. Every investor is different, so only you can set the financial goals for Farbucks.

For the sake of discussion, I will assume the investor is going to manage his own assets. The same plan applies if you are managing a financial advisor. The only difference is that the advisor will take most of the actions. A MASTER plan takes into consideration stocks, bonds, cash, and other assets. However, I will place the main emphasis on the stock portion of the portfolio.

M = MARKETS

There are several different types of markets, or assets, in which you can invest. The big three are stocks, bonds, and cash equivalents. You must decide if you will invest in other types of assets. For a fourth asset, consider foreign stocks (ETFs); they have been shown to add value to a portfolio. Asset types are your different Easter baskets (Chapter 17).

- Who is responsible for the portfolio?
- What markets will you trade?

Markets

Stocks: stocks, mutual funds, or ETFs.
Bonds: U.S. bonds and corporate bonds, or bond funds.
Cash Equivalents: CDs, money market funds, treasury bills.

This is not a complete list of every type of asset; others may be considered more speculative. Other types of assets include foreign securities, agricultural commodities (wheat, corn, soybeans, etc.), metals (gold, silver), currencies, collectables, and real estate. Most investors will stick with stocks, bonds, and cash equivalents, but I mentioned these because some investors may have more experience in certain types of investments. Never invest in anything with which you are not familiar.

A = ALLOCATION

Once you decide on which markets you want to trade, you then decide on allocation, or how much capital you want to put into each type of asset type (Easter basket). There are online financial calculators you can use to figure this out, or you can use a general reference guide (see Chapter 17).

Asset allocation takes into consideration the amount of money you have to invest, your time horizon (the number of years to retirement), and your risk tolerance. The longer your time horizon, the greater percentage of stocks you will have in your portfolio. As you get closer to retirement, you will generally increase the percentage of bonds and cash equivalents and decrease the percentage of stocks.

- What percentage of capital will you put into each asset basket?
- What is the total amount of money allocated to stocks? The amount of money allocated to stocks includes stock-based mutual funds and ETFs.
- How many stocks (mutual funds, ETFs) will you buy, or how much money will you put into each investment lot (example: 10%)? It is easier to think in terms of **lots**. I recommend dividing the stock capital into ten equal amounts. This allows diversification and lowers portfolio risk.
- What different types of stocks (mutual funds, ETFs) will you buy? You might use four lots for small-cap stocks, two lots for large-cap, and four lots for mutual funds or ETFs in sectors. Do what fits your financial goals.

S = STRATEGY

For stocks, you also have to decide how to buy and sell them. This part of the MASTER plan is the most detailed. It is essentially the **TOP SCORE 50-50 Strategy**.

- How will you select stocks? Will you use both technical (TOP) and fundamental (SCORE) analysis?
- What timeframe will you use for investing (weekly charts are best for wealth building)?
- What strategy will you use for timing entries (50-50 Strategy)?
- Will you consider the condition of the overall market?

T = TRADE MANAGEMENT

For each stock investment, you must know how to manage each trade.

- How will you manage risk with a stop-loss (15%)?
- Will you buy stocks one at a time (What about BOB?)?
- Will you buy stock shares in full or half-lots (scale in)?
- How will you take profits (scale out)?

E = EXPECTATIONS

Your expectations are your goal for the portfolio. How much do you expect to make per year in returns? It is important to be reasonable based on how you allocate capital to assets and what strategy you pursue. Set minimum goals for your plan, so you can tell if the plan is working.

- Do you expect to get rich overnight? If you do, stop right now and save your money.
- Will you work with a partner or coach (a great idea)?

- Do you plan to make a higher return than 12% historical return of the stock market (possible with TOP SCORE stocks and the 50-50 Strategy)?
- At what amount of drawdown will you stop investing and review your errors and/or paper trade (10-15%)?
- What will you do for ongoing investment education (www.5050Strategy.com)?
- Will you have someone review your plan (trades)?
- How long will you paper trade?
- Will you make regular contributions to your portfolio?

R = REASSESSMENT

The investment plan results must be reassessed periodically.

- How often will you readjust your portfolio for total asset allocation due to a changing time horizon (every 5 years)?
- How often will you rebalance the assets to maintain your percent allocation to each asset class (yearly)?
- How often will you readjust the total capital in your stock basket (annually)?

You should review your returns for each asset class. If your plan is working, don't mess with it. If it needs to be adjusted, you can increase or decrease the percentages of assets in each group. About every three months, make adjustments to lot amounts if needed (drawdown will decrease your lot amount).

Every year, it's a good idea to review your allocation for your stock categories. Suppose you want to invest in 60% growth stocks and 40% income stocks. After a year, growth stocks account for 80% of the value of your portfolio and income stocks account for 20%. You may want to take profits in your growth stocks to get back to the desired ratio of 60% growth stocks and 40% income stocks.

The same applies for each asset class in your portfolio. The portfolio should be rebalanced every five years or so. For instance, suppose you want to have 60% stocks, 30% bonds, and 10% cash equivalents. Over the year, your stocks make some big profits. Now the value of your portfolio is 75% stocks, 15% bonds, and 10% cash. You would then take money from the stock returns and distribute it into the bond and cash categories to get back to a 60%/30%/10% balance.

Readjust your plan anytime something changes in your life that might affect your goals. You may get a salary increase at work. You may have a child and want to plan for college tuition. Maybe you inherited money, and you want to put it to work. Unfortunately, divorce will greatly affect your portfolio, and you'll need to create a new plan.

Reassess your goals at the same time every year, so it becomes routine. I like to reassess my plan in December, so I can start each new year fresh and focused. This is also the time to set personal goals, travel goals, marriage goals, etc.

DR. SCHAAP HANDS OUT A SAMPLE

MASTER Plan for I.C. Franklins
CFO, Farbucks

Markets

- I will be responsible for managing the portfolio, but I will obtain professional advice. I will fire myself and hire a new CFO if I do not follow my plan.
- I will read my plan once a month, so I keep it in mind.
- I will invest in stocks, bonds, and cash equivalents.
- I will buy stocks and ETFs for the stock basket, ETFs for the bond basket, and a money market fund for the cash basket.

Allocation

- I have $100,000 to invest in the portfolio
- I will allocate $60,000 to stocks, $30,000 to bonds, and $10,000 to cash equivalents. My long term goal is to build wealth for retirement.

- The stock capital will be divided into $6,000 lots (total of 10 lots = $60,000))
- I will invest four lots in small-cap growth stocks with emphasis on making big profits; two lots will be used for dividend-paying stocks; two lots will be used for an index ETF (SPY) during market uptrends.
- I will find small-cap stocks by using the Yahoo Finance Thinking-cap Screen, Chapter 14). I need to research how to find good dividend-paying stocks.

Strategy

- I will invest using weekly charts to trade long-term uptrends.
- I will use Dr. Schaap's TOP SCORE method to screen for stocks.
- I will create a watchlist of 20 TOP SCORE stocks to follow.
- Screening will be done once a week using the SILK SCREEN until I have 20 stocks in my watchlist.
- I will use Dr. Schaap's 50-50 Strategy for timing my investments, and I will use his checklists to guide me. I will look for potential stock buys once a week (on the weekend). During football season, I'll cut back to once a month, so I don't miss out on getting together with my buddies to watch football on TV.
- I will also consider the overall market, using the weekly SPY as my reference.

Trade Management

- I will use a stop-loss on all trades at all times. I will allow a maximum loss of 15% of the lot amount.
- My stop-loss will be placed $0.25 cents under the 50 MA; I will calculate the number of stock shares for each lot, so that all stocks have about the same initial dollar risk.

- I will move my stop-loss to a breakeven stop-loss according to the method I learned, and I'll set a trailing stop once a month.
- I will buy stocks one at a time (taking "baby steps" with BOB). Once a stock is at breakeven, I will add another stock.
- I will use half lots during the first year of my investing and reevaluate this at the end of the year.
- For the first year of using capital (not paper trading), I will let the stop-loss take me out of profitable trades. I will further study how to take profits because I don't fully understand it yet. I will study the scaling method more before I use it.

Expectations

- I don't plan to get rich overnight. I plan to build wealth over time. My goal is to have at least $1 million dollars by the time I retire.
- My goal in the first year is to make a positive return.
- If I have a drawdown of 10%, I will stop investing and paper trade for six months, or until I have more confidence.
- I will paper trade this plan for six months before I risk capital.
- I will continue to learn about trend, since Dr. Schaap said it was important.
- I plan to contribute 10% of my net earnings each month to savings, so I have money for emergencies.
- I will find a friend who is using *Invest with Success* and try to work together, coaching each other.
- I will expect myself to make mistakes, but I will correct them.
- I will make sure my spouse agrees with my plan.

Reassessments

- I will reassess my portfolio allocation every five years, or sooner, if my plans change. I will do more online research about retirement.
- Each year, in December, I will review my plan and rebalance my assets as needed.
- Every three months, I will monitor the returns of my stock basket and make adjustments to my lot amount.
- Every three months that I follow my plan, I'll treat myself to something special as a reward.

"YES, MASTER"

Don't make the plan too detailed, or you will have difficulty following it. Don't try to spell out every minute detail, anticipate every possible event, or catch every possible investment opportunity. A plan must be simple and straightforward. Reward yourself every year with a nice vacation, paid for with your profits.

Do not put more into the plan than you will actually do on a regular basis. Doing more is not necessarily better. Stay relaxed, but follow the plan. The most important thing is that the plan makes sense. The investment plan is a contract with yourself to follow an established set of rules and take specific actions. The plan should be tailored to your individual goals and level of investing ability. Make sure you are clear about who is going to implement the plan—you or an investment advisor. You have to know who to fire if he doesn't follow the plan!

Tape the plan to the wall or the shelf next to your computer. Review it each week or month when you study your watchlist candidates. You must not only master the plan, you must master yourself in order to achieve ultimate success. Don't sabotage your own plan. When your MASTER plan instructs you to carry out certain actions, don't resist or override the plan. Simply say, "Yes, MASTER."

ΔΔΔ

It takes money to make money, but it takes a plan to not lose money.

20 Try Angles

After you develop your investment plan, you can start paper trading the 50-50 Strategy. It is a good idea to paper trade the strategy for at least six months before you risk capital. If the strategy is not working on paper, don't risk your capital until you figure out why it is not working. Paper trading is not a final test that you pass. You should continue to paper trade stocks, mutual funds, and ETFs throughout your investing life. You will likely find more stocks to trade than you have money, so practice with the ones you don't buy. I still paper trade new ideas and strategies; it's free, and it provides experience and feedback.

You may hear it said that you can't really know what it is like to invest until you use "real bullets" (real money). This is the ego talking. Paper trading is mechanically the same as actual trading; the difference is the emotional aspect. The stock market is not a place to go and test your emotional fortitude. The purpose of using the 50-50 Strategy is to train yourself to take much of the emotion out of trading. You won't want to start losing real money, and then wish you were still trading with blanks.

In this chapter, you will meet three investors who read *Investing with Success* and made a plan to either trade or test the strategy. Each has a different goal for investing, and each tries a different angle to integrate mindset, knowledge, and plan. Their stories are different, but all have the same goal—to invest with success!

MEET MOMMY FARBUCKS

Mommy Farbucks is relatively new to investing. She is a stay-at-home mom with two children. Her husband works for the City of Las Vegas and has a 401K plan. She stumbled across *Invest with Success* while browsing through the investing section of a bookstore. Mommy pays all the bills, and she liked the idea of being the CFO of her family's finances. Mommy paper traded the 50-50 Strategy for several months before she started an online account. She and her husband won't be retiring for at least 30 years, and her goals are to build wealth over time and put away some money for her kids' college tuition. If her investments go well, perhaps she and her husband will be able to retire sooner than they think.

Mommy Farbucks

Online Account: Scottrade
Capital for stocks: $30,000 (Lot Amount $3,000)
Fundamental Research: Yahoo Finance
Charts: Yahoo Finance
Stock Selection: Basket Case Screen (ClearStation® site)
Strategy: TOP SCORE 50-50 Strategy
Risk: 15% of lot amount
Scaling In: Yes
BOB: Yes

Mommy Farbucks ran the **Basket Case Screen** (Chapter 17) for top performing industries in the economy. She went to the ClearSation® site and completed the "five-clicker" in about 20 seconds. Fish/Livestock was listed as number eight out of over 200 industries. She looked for stocks in that industry which scored greater than 80 in relative strength (RS rank). One of the stocks she found was Cal-Marine Foods (CALM). She checked the stock's SCORE (fundamentals) at Yahoo Finance (Figure 20.1).

Profitability	**Stock: CALM**
Profit Margin (ttm):	15.71%
Operating Margin (ttm):	23.30%
Management Effectiveness	
Return on Assets (ttm):	29.13%
Return on Equity (ttm):	69.01%
Income Statement	
Revenue (ttm):	850.18M
Revenue Per Share (ttm):	35.959
Qtrly Revenue Growth (yoy): R	58.70%
Gross Profit (ttm):	118.62M
EBITDA (ttm):	222.49M
Net Income Avl to Common (ttm):	133.59M
Diluted EPS (ttm):	5.64
Qtrly Earnings Growth (yoy): E	228.60%
Balance Sheet	
Total Cash (mrq):	85.80M
Total Cash Per Share (mrq):	3.618
Total Debt (mrq):	101.94M
Total Debt/Equity (mrq):	0.408
Current Ratio (mrq):	1.765
Book Value Per Share (mrq):	10.525
Cash Flow Statement	
Operating Cash Flow (ttm): C	142.53M
Levered Free Cash Flow (ttm):	126.05M

Average Volume (3 month)[3]:	793,210
Average Volume (10 day)[3]:	1,281,280
Shares Outstanding[5]: S	23.71M
Float:	14.23M
% Held by Insiders[1]: O	45.38%
% Held by Institutions[1]:	81.30%
Shares Short (as of 11-Mar-08)[3]:	12.44M
Short Ratio (as of 11-Mar-08)[3]:	21.2
Short % of Float (as of 11-Mar-08)[3]:	75.10%
Shares Short (prior month)[3]:	11.99M
Dividends & Splits	
Forward Annual Dividend Rate[4]:	0.05
Forward Annual Dividend Yield[4]:	0.20%
Trailing Annual Dividend Rate[3]:	0.04
Trailing Annual Dividend Yield[3]:	0.10%
5 Year Average Dividend Yield[4]:	0.70%
Payout Ratio[4]:	1%
Dividend Date[3]:	15-May-08
Ex-Dividend Date[4]:	19-Nov-07
Last Split Factor (new per old)[2]:	2:1

Figure 20.1 *The SCORE for Cal-Marine Foods (CALM). All five of the SCORE criteria were met.* (Source: Yahoo Finance)

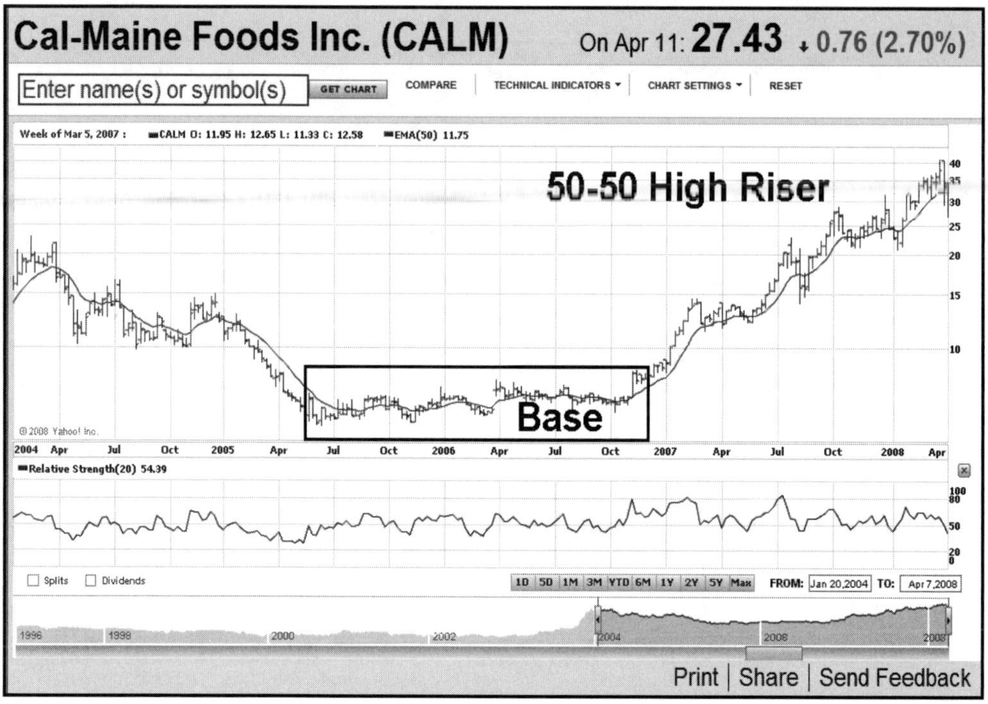

Figure 20.2 *TOP analysis for Cal-Marine Foods (CALM).*
(Chart: Yahoo Finance)

She made a few more clicks and brought up a Yahoo chart of CALM (Figure 20.2). The trend was a High Riser. However, price was below the 50 MA and RSI was below the 50 level. Overall, she thought the stock was a profit opportunity, but the 50 MA signal was needed before she could buy it. The stock was added to her watchlist.

MEET JOHN DOUGH

John Dough is a 56-year-old architect who plans to retire in ten years; he would like to build up more capital in his IRA. He is a long-time investor who has had mixed results. John said he did pretty well during the nineties, but since 2000, he hasn't made a penny in stocks. He has paid for several different trading systems, and none of them have worked. He's read over 100 books on investing. He recently finished reading *Invest with Success*, but he's leery of "yet another" method. He plans to paper trade the strategy for the next three months before he risks any of his retirement capital. He plans to screen for small-cap stocks once a month at Yahoo Finance (Thinking-cap screen), and each weekend, he will paper trade (buy) a stock that meets the 50-50 Strategy criteria. John says the 50-50 Strategy looks so easy, he's not so sure it will work. However, he knows he has nothing to lose by paper trading the strategy. Who knows? He might finally become successful.

John Dough

Online Account: Fidelity
Capital for stocks: $100,000 (Lot Amount $10,000)
Fundamental Research: Yahoo Finance
Charts: StockCharts
Stock Selection: Thinking Cap Screen
Strategy: TOP SCORE 50-50 Strategy
Risk: 15% of lot amount.
Scaling In: No
BOB: No

In March, 2008, John started by checking the overall market (SPY), since it had been going down for several weeks (Figure 20.3). He looked at a chart at StockCharts (www.stockcharts.com) and noticed that price was under the 50 MA, and conditions were less favorable for investing. That was okay, since he was going to paper trade anyway.

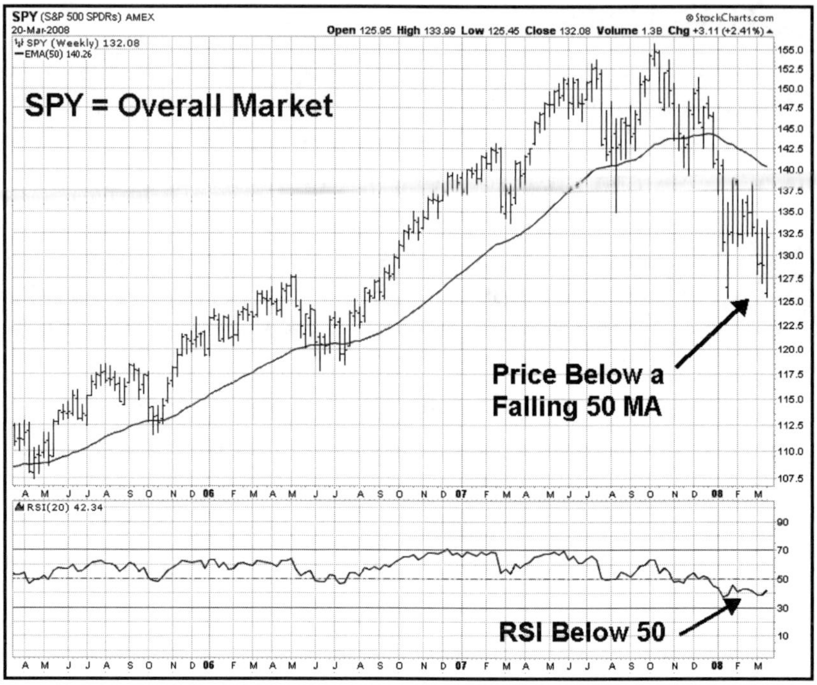

Figure 20.3 *The SPY ETF is used to study the overall market.* (Chart: StockCharts)

Next, he ran the Thinking Cap screen (Chapter 14) at Yahoo Finance which brought up 25 growth stocks. He decided to look at charts before he checked fundamentals. John noticed a recent 50-50 Strategy signal in the stock chart of Pricemart (PSMT) (Figure 20.4, arrows). PSMT was a High Riser with low overhead resistance, and it was in the $10-$40 price range.

Figure 20.4 *TOP analysis for Pricesmart (PSMT).*
(Chart: StockCharts)

John went to Yahoo Finance to check the stock's SCORE. He recorded his TOP SCORE findings on a checklist (Figure 20.5). John decided to paper trade PSMT; he entered the mock buy in his trading log (Figure 20.6).

TOP SCORE 50-50 Stock Evaluation	
Date	3/20/08
Stock Symbol	PSMT
Sector/Industry	Con. Staples / Retail

Overall Market	Condition	Yes	No
SPY	Rising 50 MA		✓
Sector (optional)	Rising 50 MA		✓

TOP SCORE	Criteria	Yes	No
T = Trend	High Riser	✓	
O = Overhead Supply	Low	✓	
P = Price	$10-$40	✓	
S = Shares Outstanding	< 100 million	✓	
C = Cash Flow	Positive	✓	
O = Owner. by Inst.	>20%	✓	
R = Revenue Growth	>25% yoy	✓	
E = Earnings Growth	>25% yoy	✓	

Figure 20.5 The *SCORE checklist for Pricesmart (PSMT).*

Trade #	Buy Date	Stock Symbol	# of Shares	Buy Price	Stop Risk	Stop Price	$ Invest	$ Risk	Sell Date	$ +/-	% Rt +/-
1	3/20/08	PSMT	375	26.76	2.50	24.26	10,035	938			
Trade Lesson:											
2											
Trade Lesson:											
3											
Trade Lesson:											
4											
Trade Lesson:											
5											
Trade Lesson:											
6											
Trade Lesson:											
7											
Trade Lesson:											
8											
Trade Lesson:											
9											
Trade Lesson:											
Total Stock Capital 100 K			*Lot Amount* 10 K				*Shares Bought = Lot Amnt/Stock Price*				

Figure 20.6 *Trading Log with entry for PSMT.*

MEET DESPERATE MOUSEWIVES

Robin and Donna are both married and have kids in college. Robin works part-time from home as a graphic designer; Donna isn't working, but she used to be a computer programmer. Both of them spend several hours a day on the computer and are used to a lot of mouse clicks. Now that the youngest of their kids has left for college, the women are desperate for a romantic vacation with their husbands. After reading *Invest with Success,* they decided to plan a trip to Italy.

Their husbands want to wait until the kids are out of college, so Robin and Donna made a deal. The men agreed to take the trip sooner if the wives could make enough money with investments to pay for the trip. Robin and Donna paper traded for three months, and felt like they were ready. Because of their computer background, they liked using the 50-50 Strategy formula in StrategyDesk™ which comes free with their

TDAmeritrade account. They found the formula for the Desk Job screen as a built-in formula (Schaap 50-50 Strategy) in StrategyDesk™. Once they were done clickin', they were ready to do some pickin'.

Desperate Mousewives

Online Account: TDAmeritrade
Capital for stocks: $50,000 (Lot Amount $5,000)
Fundamental Research: Yahoo Finance
Charts: TDAmeritrade
Stock Selection: Desk Job
Strategy: TOP SCORE 50-50 Strategy
Risk: 15% of lot amount.
Scaling: No
BOB: Yes

In December of 2007, Robin and Donna used StrategyDesk™ to run the 50-50 Strategy screen on the Russell 2000 Index of stocks. The screen finds small-cap stocks which have just given a 50-50 Strategy signal (price is above the 50 MA and RSI is above the 50 level). Robin and Donna looked at stock charts until they found one they liked. They noticed that AZZ Inc (AZZ) was a High Riser (Figure 20.7). The women noticed an excellent 50-50 Strategy signal back in December of 2005 (Figure 20.7; arrows 1, 2). The recent signal in December, 2007 (arrows 3, 4), met the 50-50 Strategy criteria. They checked the SCORE at Yahoo Finance and it passed.

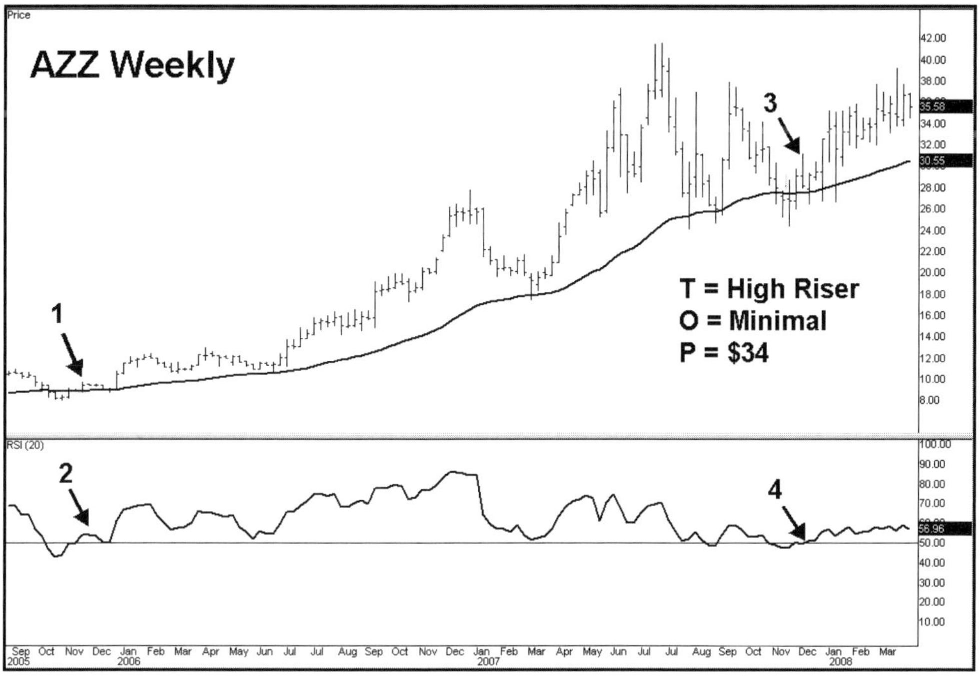

Figure 20.7 *TOP for AZZ. Note the recent 50-50 Strategy signal in late 2007 (3, 4).* (Chart: TDAmeritrade)

The women determined the number of shares they could afford was 147 shares using the 50-50 Strategy Trade Management (ESP) checklist as shown in Figure 20.8. However, the total risk amount was $951, which was more than the $750 allowed by their rule (15% lot limit). They wisely cut back the number of shares to 100 and bought the stock at $34 in early January, 2008. When Robin clicked the mouse and the order was filled, Donna shouted, "Brava!"

50-50 Strategy Trade Management (ESP)

Stock Symbol: AZZ Date: 1/9/08

Lot Amount: $ 5,000 *15% Lot Limit:* $ 750 Δ

Entry Price	34.00
Stop Price	Stop Price = (50 MA 27.78 - .25) = $ 27.53 (Stop-loss Price) Stop-loss Risk = Entry Price - Stop Price = $ 6.47 (Stop Risk)[A] Initial Risk per Share
Position Size	100

Maximum Shares based on Lot $Amount

= Lot $Amount / Entry Price

= 147 Shares[B]

Too High!

Total Risk Amount = Shares[B] x Stop-Risk[A] = 951 Δ

ΔCompare to 15% lot limit above; adjust shares as needed.

Figure 20.8 *Trade Management for AZZ Inc. (AZZ).*

YOUR FALTER EGO

The investors you just met were presented to show you that everyone invests differently. Each person has his own goal, his own preference, and his own way of doing things. Find *your* way. Investing is a great way to learn about yourself—how you think and how you process information. I also wanted to point out that all of the investors used the same objective criteria to analyze stocks and make decisions; only their screening tool was different. While you have some latitude in your plan, the 50-50 Strategy has objective criteria which must be followed to invest with success.

I like to think of the 50-50 Strategy as my alter ego, an investing persona that tells me exactly what to do. I try to separate myself from the decision of when to buy and sell; I let my alter ego tell me what to do. Thinking is how an investor falters; instead of using the 50-50 Strategy for signals, his "falter ego" takes over the plan and does what *it* wants to do. Your falter ego doesn't want to follow the rules and doesn't care if you make money.

One investor I know sent me an email saying he had been losing a lot of money. He said he had finally figured out why. The way he wanted to invest didn't follow the 50-50 Strategy rules, so he expected the rules to fit the way *he* wanted to invest. We all think differently, but we should all see the same 50-50 Strategy signals. No matter what you know, think, feel, believe, or hope about a stock, price must always prove itself before risking your capital. Price proves itself worthy of taking risk when it meets the 50-50 Strategy criteria.

LAST SIGNPOST

You have come to the end of this book, but not the end of your investment journey. The end of one path is always the beginning of another. Thank you for letting me be your guide on the path to success. Perhaps our paths will cross one day. Maybe you'll see me and Candy on a ferry boat in Italy. We'll be the ones sipping espresso and devouring bars of dark chocolate.

A journey is a passage from one place to another; it has the power to change you. It has been a long journey, and I congratulate you on your hard work and determination. A new signpost is in view. This signpost says, *Financial Freedom Trail: This Way to a Rich Life.*

I hope that your new knowledge brings you wisdom, your mindset brings you truth, and your plan for success brings you purpose. I wish you the best of success!

Ciao.

Charles and Candy, *Rapallo, Italia*

ΔΔΔ

APPENDIX

How to Calculate Capital Gains/Losses

The investor profits when he sells a stock (mutual fund, ETF) at a higher price than the price at which he bought it. The amount of money received from selling the stock, less the initial investment, is the **capital gain.**

Profit or Loss per Share = Sell price – Buy Price

Capital Gain or Loss = # Shares x Profit or Loss per Share

If you buy at stock at $20, and a year later it is worth $50, you will have a $30 per share gain ($50/share sell price - $20/share buy price = $30/share gain). If you owned 200 shares of the stock, your capital gain would be $6,000 (200 shares x $30/share = $6,000) (Note: this does not include commissions).

If you sell a stock at a price lower than your purchase price, the amount of your original investment not returned back to you is your loss. If you buy a stock at $20, and a year later it is worth $10, you will have a loss of $10 per share ($10/share sell price - $20/share buy price = $-10/share loss). If you owned 200 shares of the stock, your capital loss would be $2,000 ($-10/share x 200 shares = $-2,000).

Stock gains/losses, or **returns**, are often reported as a percentage of the original investment. This is figured by dividing your profit by the amount of your original investment.

$$\textbf{Percent Return} = \frac{\textbf{Capital Gain or Loss}}{\textbf{Amount Invested}} \times \textbf{100}$$

In the first example above, you would have invested $4,000 (200 shares x $20/share = $4,000) to make a $6,000 profit ($10,000 sell price - $4,000 buy price = $6,000). Pull out your calculator and divide your gain by the original investment and multiply by 100 to find out your percentage gain over the year. Your gain would have been 150% ($6,000/$4,000 x 100 = 150%).

How to Calculate Dividend Yields

Dividends may be reported on a dollar basis. For example, a stock may pay a $1.05 dividend every quarter. The annual dividend is $4.20 (4 quarters x $1.05 dividend per quarter = $4.20). The dollar basis does not take into account the price you pay for the stock in order to receive the dividend. To calculate your annual income, you multiply the number of shares owned by the annual dividend amount. For example, if you own 400 shares of a $25 stock, and the company pays a quarterly dividend of $1.05, you will receive $420 in income (400 shares x $1.05 /share = $420) every quarter.

The dividend **yield** assesses the dividend as a percentage of the stock's price. The yield represents the rate of income from the investment. The dividend yield is calculated by dividing the annual dividends received per share by the current price of the stock.

Dividend Yield (%) = <u>Annual Dividend per Share</u> x 100
Current Stock Price

Suppose you own a $25 stock that pays a $1.05 quarterly dividend. The dividend yield for the stock would be calculated by dividing $4.20 (4 quarters x $1.05 per share) by $25 (stock price), for a yield of 16.8% ($4.20/$25 = .168 x 100 = 16.8%).

What if you wanted to compare the $25 stock to a $45 stock that pays the same $1.05 dividend. A $1.05 dividend for a $25 stock will provide a different return, or profit, than a $1.05 dividend for a $45 stock. The dividend yield for the $45 stock would be 9.3% ($4.20/$45 = .093 x 100 = 9.3%). Knowing dividend yield tells you the $25 stock has a higher return than the $45 stock, even though they pay the same dividend amount.

What happens if you own a dividend-paying stock, but the price of the stock falls?

You can lose money. Suppose you pay $50 for a stock paying a 5% dividend, and the stock falls to $40. Your real return is -15%. The value of the stock will have dropped 20% ($-10/$50 = -.20 x 100 = -20%) while your dividend only paid 5% of the purchase price. When you subtract the -20% loss from your 5% gain, you end up losing 15%. This is why it is important to always buy stocks in an uptrend.

<u>Order Entry Types</u>

The **market price** of a stock is quoted with a **bid** price and an **ask** (or offer) price. The bid is the highest price that someone is willing to pay for a stock, and the ask price is the lowest price someone is willing to accept to sell the stock. These numbers fluctuate throughout the day. At the stock exchanges, the bids and asks are matched to one another which creates the "market." If you buy a stock with a **market order**, you will pay the ask price (higher). If you sell using a market order, you will receive the bid price (lower).

The difference in price between the bid and ask prices is called the bid-ask spread. Normally, it will be within about $0.01 to $0.05 cents. It's not much of a difference if you're only buying about five stocks a year. For the 50-50 Strategy, I recommend using market orders. Market orders are filled immediately at the market price, and they are easier to use than setting limit orders. Sometimes, a stock will have a wide bid-ask spread, maybe $0.25 cents. If you want to buy the stock today, use a market order.

If you use a **limit order**, you may not get your order filled, or you may get a partial fill. A limit order is an order to buy or sell at a specific price (or better). Suppose a stock is quoted at 34.55 bid/34.60 ask. You can place an order to buy the stock at 34.55 or lower, using a limit order. The order is not filled unless the limit price is hit.

A **stop order** is an "activation" order; when the stop price is reached, it activates a buy or sell order. The buy or sell order can be a limit or market order (some trading platforms also have a "trailing" stop type). Sell stop orders are entered below the current bid price, and buy stop orders are entered above the ask current price. Stop-loss orders are **sell stop orders** which are placed below the price of the stock. If price falls to the stop level, the sell order is automatically entered to exit the position with a small loss. If you use a **market sell stop** (stop-loss), the order will be filled. If you use a **limit sell stop** (stop-loss), the order may or may not be filled. The limit price must be entered separately from the stop price when using a limit sell stop.

All orders remain in effect for a specified duration. A **day** order is active for the trading day. A **good 'til cancelled (GTC)** order remains in effect until it is cancelled, or until a date which is set at the time the order is entered.

The 50-50 Strategy Formula

The 50-50 Strategy formula was shown for use with StrategyDesk™. The 50-50 Strategy signal is when price closes above the 50 MA and RSI crosses above the 50 level. These two events may occur together or separately. There is a triad of signals.

50-50 Strategy Triad of Signals	
1.	Price crosses above the 50 MA and RSI crosses above the 50 level at the same time.
2.	Price crosses above the 50 MA first, and then RSI crosses above the 50 level.
3.	RSI crosses above the 50 level first, and then price crosses above the 50 MA.

Each of these conditions is accounted for in the 50-50 Strategy formula. Below is the formula for StrategyDesk™. If you use another type of trading platform, you can adapt the formula for use.

Entry (this is the weekly scan which is the timeframe used for building wealth with stocks):

ExpMovingAverage[EMA,Close,10,0,W] >
ExpMovingAverage[EMA,Close,50,0,W]
AND Bar[Close,W] > ExpMovingAverage[EMA,Close,50,0,W]
AND Bar[Close,W,1] < ExpMovingAverage[EMA,Close,50,0,W,1]
AND RSI[RSI,20,W] > 50 OR
ExpMovingAverage[EMA,Close,10,0,W] >
ExpMovingAverage[EMA,Close,50,0,W] AND
Bar[Close,W] > ExpMovingAverage[EMA,Close,50,0,W]
AND RSI[RSI,20,W] > 50 AND RSI[RSI,20,W,1] < 50

Exit (this is a simple weekly exit on a close $0.25 cents below the 50 MA which is the recommended stop-loss):

Bar[Close,W] < (ExpMovingAverage[EMA,Close,50,0,W]-.25)

The 50-50 Strategy entry **signal** is given when the weekly bar closes above the 50 MA; however, the 50-50 Strategy **criteria** are not met until the entire weekly bar is above the 50 MA (and RSI is above the 50 level). The close above the 50 MA may, or may not, occur at the same time that the entire weekly bar is above the 50 MA. Usually, the close above the 50 MA (50-50 Strategy signal) precedes the entrie bar above the 50 MA (one of the 50-50 Strategy criteria).

This differentiation between "signal" and "criteria" is intended. Since the signal usually occurs earlier, it alerts the investor, so he can buy the stock on the first weekly bar that meets the 50-50 Strategy criteria (for High Risers), instead of the next bar afterward. Sometimes this is helpful to reduce the intial stop-loss risk per share. The 50-50 Strategy signal alone is not a signal to enter the trade. There must be a weekly bar which is entirely above a rising 50 MA and the RSI 50 must be above the 50 level.

Breakeven Stop-loss Exception

Normally, you will be stopped out of a trade when price bars cross down below the 50 MA. However, it is possible for a stock to **gap down** under the 50 MA instead. In this case, the stop-loss order will exit your trade at a price lower than it was set. This is because the stop-loss order will be activated at the opening price (lower) on the day the stock gaps down rather than the stop-loss price (higher) at which it was set.

A *weekly* gap down is a situation where the entire range of prices for the week is below the range of prices for the previous week, leaving a gap between the price bars (See figure below). The opening price of this week's bar "drops under" the stop-loss that was set under the 50 week MA (see figure below).

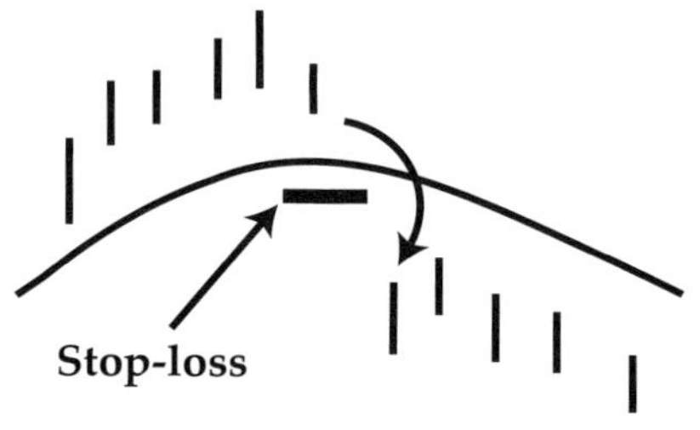

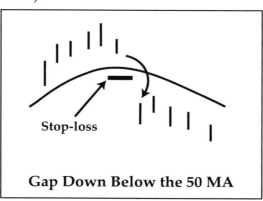

Gap Down Below the 50 MA

In the preparation of this section of the book, I studied the 100 stocks in the NASDAQ-100 index during the two-year period of 2006 through 2007. This study didn't even distinguish between uptrends and downtrends. If you had used the 50-50 Strategy rules during the two-year period, there would not have been a single stock that gapped down below the weekly 50 MA. Gaps are not a big concern on weekly charts. Even when a stock gaps down under your stop-loss, you will still be stopped out; it will just be at a lower price.

Stop-loss Method #2

Previously, I said that a principle of 50-50 Strategy trade management is to always take an equal amount of initial risk on every trade. When price is very high above the 50 MA, you can simply reduce by half the number of shares you can afford. Another way is to calculate the exact number of shares you can afford to account for the **stop-loss dollar amount**. Here's the formula (it will be on your checklist):

Maximum Shares Based on Stop Risk

= **Stop-Loss $Amount / Stop Risk**

= ________________ **Shares**

To compensate for stocks that are bought high off the 50 MA, the number of shares you can buy is adjusted for the amount of the initial stop-loss, or the distance from your expected entry price (you do this before you actually buy the stock) down to $0.25 cents under the 50 MA. Take this number and divide it into your total stop-loss dollar amount (amount of total dollars you'll risk per trade). This tells you how many shares you can afford to buy in order to keep your loss to a fixed amount of 15% of the lot amount. This calculates the number of shares, so that trades bought near the 50 MA will lose (at a maximum) the same amount of money as those bought high off the 50 MA.

Example

Total Capital for Stocks = $50,000
Lot Amount = 10% of Capital
Total Stop-loss Amount = 15% of Lot Amount = $750
Stock Price = $39.40
Initial Stop-loss Risk = $9.45 per share

$$\textbf{Number of Shares} = \frac{\$\ \text{Total Stop-loss Amount}}{\text{Initial Stop-loss Amount}}$$

= $750/$9.45 = **79** shares for the trade

GLOSSARY *BY CANDY SCHAAP*

12(b)-1 fee: An annual fee charged my mutual funds to pay for marketing and distribution costs.

50 MA High: A high formed by the 50 MA as it curves down.

50 MA Low: A low formed by the 50 MA as it turns up.

50 MA: (*See* 50-week MA)

50-50 High Riser: (*See* High Riser)

50-50 Low Riser: (*See* Low Riser)

50-50 Strategy: A trading strategy created by Dr. Charles B. Schaap that consists of buying stocks when price is above the 50-week exponential moving average and RSI 20 is above the 50 level.

50-Week MA: The 50-week moving average used in the 50-50 Strategy; it represents the long-term trend of price.

Accumulation: A stage of the stock cycles where price moves sideways within a relatively narrow range, forming a **base**, as the **BIGs** accumulate shares.

Active Management: A money-management style where investors take an active role in choosing investments based on independent judgment, with the goal of outperforming the market. The opposite style is passive management. *See* **also Indexing.**

Administrative Fees: A fee charged by mutual funds to the cost of buying and selling stocks in the fund.

American Stock Exchange (Amex): An exchange that lists smaller or newer companies and features **exchange traded funds** (**ETFs**).

Ask: The lowest sell price for a security.

Asset Allocation: Dividing investment capital into major asset classes. The most common asset classes are stocks and bonds; others include foreign securities, cash equivalents (money markets, CDs, Treasury Bills), precious metals (gold, silver), and real estate.

Asset(s): An item of economic value which can be converted to cash.

Back-end Load: A commission paid when you sell a mutual fund; it is a deferred sales charge, also called a redemption fee.

Base: A base is a chart pattern where price is neither trending up nor down, but moves sideways for an extended period of time.

Basket Case Screen: A method of screening for stocks in top industries in the market.

Bear: Refers to someone who has a negative market bias and trades from the short side.

Bear Market: A market decline of 20% or more indicative of an economic recession., Bear markets last about 1-2 years.

Behemoths: Big (large-cap), well-known (Ex: Wal-mart) companies that account for about 75% of the total value of the U.S. stock market.

Bid: The highest price any buyer is willing to pay for a security.

BIGs: (Big Institutional Guns) A general term meaning institutional investors.

BOB: Dr. Schaap's acronym for "Breakeven Or Better." BOB is a trade management method to reduce risk by waiting until a stock is at breakeven or better before adding another stock position with risk.

Bonds: Ownership of a debt obligation for a period of more than one year.

Breakeven (risk): A stop loss placed at the entry price. The risk is now at break even.

Brokerage account: An account that allows you to buy stocks, bonds, and mutual funds. *See* also **Trading Platform**.

Bull Market: A long-term uptrend in the stock market associated with a period of economic expansion.

Bull: Refers to someone who has a positive market bias and trades from the long side.

Business Cycle: The muli-year cycle of economic expansion (business activity) and contraction in the U.S. economy.

Buy and Hold: Buying a stock and holding it indefinitely.

Capital Gain: The amount of money received from selling the stock, less the initial investment, is the capital gain (or loss).

Cash Account: A brokerage account that requires all purchases with cash. See also **Margin Account.**

Cash Flow: Money a company has left over after meeting financial obligations.

Certificates of Deposit (CD): Short- or medium-term, interest-bearing, FDIC-insured debt instrument offered by banks. CDs are low risk, low return investments, also known as "time deposits", because the account holder has agreed to keep the money in the account for a specified amount of time, anywhere from three months to six years.

Chart: A graph of the price movement of a security over a given time period.

Chat Room(s): An online forum where you can to talk or type in conversation with other members in real time.

Checklist: The short outline (example: the 50-50 Strategy criteria) of things to check in stock analysis. It often has guidelines for capital allocation and trade management. See also **TOP SCORE.**

Chief Financial Officer (CFO): The executive who is responsible for managing company finances. The "family" CFO assures preservation of investment capital. To invest for success, that person is you.

Closing Price: The last price recorded at the end of the day.

Common Stock: The most widely held type of stock; it represents part ownership in a company. Shareholders have voting rights and a residual claim on assets of the company should the company file for bankruptcy.

Company Risk: The risk of how a company event (accounting fraud, etc) will effect the economic performance (and stock price) of a company. The collapse of Enron is an extreme example of company risk.

Compounding Interest: Interest earned on the deposit amount plus any interest gained on the deposit each year.

Contraction Phase: A period in the economy when **GDP** declines. Businesses generally experience decreasing demand for their products and services.

Correlation: How two assets move (directionally) in relation to one another at any given time.

Covering: A short trade is closed out, or covered, by buying back the stock shares and returning them to the broker.

Criteria: Fundamental or technical conditions necessary for a strategy or screening process. For the **50-50 Trading Strategy**, two minimum criteria must be present before risking capital: Price above the 50-week moving average and the RSI 20 rising above the 50 level. There are also minimum criteria for a stock to be on your watch list. See also **TOP.**

Cyclical Stocks: The stock of a company which is sensitive to business cycles and whose performance is strongly tied to the overall economy.

Daily Chart: A stock graph composed of daily price bars, where each bar represents one day's price action. Daily is a time frame in technical analysis. *See* also **Price Bar.**

Day traders: Day traders enter and exit trades on the same day.

Default: The standard indicator settings pre-set in charting software.

Defensive Stocks: Stocks of companies that have products which are always in demand, such as food, drugs, and utilities.

Demand: The desire to purchase an asset (Ex: stock). If no one is willing to buy at a certain price, there is no demand at that price level. Along with supply, demand is one of the two key determinants of the market price. Supply is created by investors or traders willing to sell stock.

Desk Job Strategy: A method to screen stocks using the 50-50 Strategy formula (used in TDAmeritrade's StrategyDesk™.

Discipline: The ability to follow an investment plan.

Discount Brokerage: A brokerage which offers low commissions, and also provides fewer services to clients. *See* also **Full-service Brokerage.**

Distribution Stage: A stage in the stock cycle that begins when the **markup stage** ends. During this stage, shares are unloaded (distributed) before the price enters a downtrend.

Diversification: A portfolio strategy desiring to reduce exposure to risk by combining a variety of investment assets.

Dividend: A cash distribution of a portion of a company's earnings. *See* also **Income Stock.** A **Dividend Stock** refers to stocks that pay a dividend.

Dow Jones Industrial Average (DJIA): The Dow Jones Industrial average is by far the most famous of all the stock indices. The index is composed of 30 widely traded blue chip stocks. The 30 stocks are chosen by the editors of the Wall Street Journal, which is published by Dow Jones & Company.

Downtrend A stock price is in a downtrend when price is below a falling 50-week moving average. It is the opposite of an uptrend.

Drawdown: Reduction in account equity as compared to a starting amount.

Drawdown Limit: A limit set on the amount of investment losses. Once the limit it reached, trading stops until the plan is reviewed and trading errors are analyzed.

Earnings Growth: Increased net income from one period to the next. Net income is earnings after expenses. **Revenue growth** is gross income.

Earnings: Company profits after expenses are paid.

EarningsGrowth: An increase in earnings from one period (quarter or year) to the next.

Emotional Cycle Stages of investor emotion during the stock cycle (Figure 11.7).

ESP: Acronym for the three concerns when you enter a stock position. **E** is for Entry price, **S** is for Stop-loss price, and **P** is for Position size.

Exchange Traded Funds (ETFs): A collection of stocks (based on an index) which can be bought in single shares; it can be traded like a stock.

Expansion Phase: An period of economic growth when the market is in a long-term uptrend.

Expense Ratio: The operating costs of a mutual fund, including management fees, expressed as a percentage of total assets. The expense ratio does not include brokerage costs and various other transaction costs that contribute to a fund's total expenses.

Exponential Moving Average: An average of closing prices that weighs recent values more heavily than older values. *See* also **Simple Moving Average.**

50 MA High: A high formed by the 50 MA as it curves down.

50 MA Low: A low formed by the 50 MA as it turns up.

50 MA: (*See* 50-week MA)

50-50 High Riser: (*See* High Riser)

50-50 Low Riser: (*See* Low Riser)

50-50 Strategy: A trading strategy created by Dr. Charles B. Schaap that consists of buying stocks when price is above the 50-week exponential moving average and RSI 20 is above the 50 level.

50-Week MA: The 50-week moving average used in the 50-50 Strategy; it represents the long-term trend of price.

Free Market: When the prices of goods and services are determined completely by the mutual consent of sellers and buyers. Prices in a free market are described by the natural law of supply and demand.

Front-end Load: A mutual fund sales charge (purchase fee) which is paid up front, or as soon as you buy a fund.

Full-service Brokerage A company with a physical office location where a stock broker sits at his desk and works all day to handle customer accounts.

Fundamental Analysis: A method of security valuation which involves examining the company's financials and operations, especially sales, earnings, growth potential, assets, debt, management, products, and competition.

Gap Down: Where price opens lower than the close of the previous bar. A weekly gap down is a situation where the entire range of prices for the week is below the range of prices for the previous week, leaving a gap between the price bars. Price can also gap up.

Good-Till-Cancelled (GTC): An order to buy or sell which remains in effect until it is either executed or canceled (although brokers usually set a limit of 30 days). Also called open order. *See* also **Stop Loss.**

Gross Domestic Product (GDP): The broadest measure of economic performance; it represents the total dollar value of all goods and services produced in the United States.

Growth: An investment style that looks for stocks with strong earnings and/or revenue growth. Growth stocks outperform the majority of stocks in the market. *See* also **Growth Stocks.**

Growth and Income:. An investment strategy which seeks to generate income and also grow wealth through capital appreciation.

Growth Stock: The stock of a company which is growing earnings and/or revenue faster than its industry or the overall market. Such companies usually pay little or no dividends, preferring to use the income instead to finance further expansion.

High Riser: An uptrend where the price of a stock is above a rising 50-week moving average. *See* also **Low Riser.**

High: The highest price of the trading session (day or week).

Income: For individuals, money earned through employment and investments.

Income Stock: A stock with a history of paying consistently high dividends.

Income Strategy: An investment strategy to generating a stream of income for living expenses, i.e., through interest-paying bonds and stocks with a high dividend. Choosing dividend-stocks in an uptrend can add to the overall return through capital appreciation.

Index (Indexes or Indices, pl.): A collection of related stocks. The index can include the entire collection of stocks or it can be composed of a representative sample of the collection. For example, the NYSE Composite is an index of all of the stocks that trade on the **New York Stock Exchange (NYSE).**

Indexing: A passive investment approach that uses market index funds to mirror, or match, the performance of a market index (S&P 500, DJIA, NASDAQ, etc.).

Indicator: A mathematical calculation based on price (or volume) which is used on a chart to help analyze price.

Individual Retirement Account: (*See* IRA).

Industry: A basic category of business activity. The term industry is sometimes used to describe a very precise business activity (e.g. semiconductors).

Initial Public Offering (IPO): The first sale of stock to the public. It is often a company without a long history of earnings and its lacks strong institutional support.

Initial Risk: The amount of capital placed at risk when a trade is entered, or the amount that can be lost per share from the entry price to the stop-loss price.

Initial Stop: The stop-loss placed at entry. *See* also **Initial Risk.**

Institutional Ownership: This term refers to the shares of stock owned by institutions, or the **BIGs.** Institutions generally purchase large blocks of a company's outstanding shares and can exert considerable influence. *See* also **BIGs.**

Institutional: Refers to large banks, insurance companies, pension funds, mutual funds, endowment funds, and investment companies. *See* also **BIGs.**

Investing Online: Buying and selling securities over the internet through an online broker. This method gives you direct access to making and monitoring your investments.

Investment: The use money to make more money.

Investment Advisor (IA): Someone in the business of giving investment advice and security recommendations for a fee or commission.

Investment Clubs: Investment clubs are formed as a partnership by a group of amateur investors who pool their money and make investments by a majority vote of the members.

Investment Groups: Informal gathering of novice investors who want contact with other investors and hope to share ideas. There is no pooling of funds.

Investment Income: Earnings from a portfolio of invested assets, or the way money makes money.

Investment Vehicle: A specific asset type intended to accomplish certain goals. Stocks and bonds are examples of investment vehicles.

IRA (Individual Retirement Account): A tax-deferred retirement account for an individual that allows money to be set aside each year, with earnings tax-deferred until withdrawals begin at age 59 1/2 or later.

Large-cap: A company with over $5 billion in market capitalization. These are the big companies that everyone has heard of, such as Wal-Mart (WMT), Microsoft (MSFT) and General Motors (GM).

Leading Economic Indicator: A statistic or indicator that will begin an uptrend before an economic recovery and begin to decline before an economic recession.

Limit Order: An order to buy or sell at a specific price, also called the limit price. This is one of the two most common types of orders, the other being a market order. *See* also **Stop-Limit Order**.

Load: A sales charge added to the purchase and/or sale price of some mutual funds.

Long: A position that is opened by buying a stock. The position profits if the stock price goes higher.

Long-term Investors: This term refers to people with a time horizon of more than 5 years. Long-term investments are based on the long-term trend of the stock price which is best seen on a weekly chart; long-term trends last from a few months to a few years.

Lot: An eqully divided portion of investment capital; it allows an equal amount of money (one lot) to be invested in each stock position.

Low: The lowest price of the trading session (day or week).

Low Riser: An uptrend where the price of a stock is above or below a falling or sideways 50-week MA, where the last 50-week MA high is the highest on the chart. *See* also **High Riser.**

Management Fee: A fee paid to financial managers for their services.

Margin Account: A trading account to buy or sell stocks by borrowing part of the money from the broker (they charge an interest fee).

Markdown Stage (Distribution): A stage of the stock cycle where price is in a downtrend. You will know the markdown stage has begun when price drops below the 50-week MA and does not rise back above it again.

Market Capitalization: The total dollar market value of all of a company's outstanding shares. Market capitalization is calculated by multiplying a company's shares outstanding by the current market

price of one share. The investment community uses this figure in determining a company's size; it is frequently referred to as "market cap."

Market Correction: If the market falls 10-20%, it is a called a **market correction**. Market corrections are larger profit-taking periods in the stock market and can be spurred by economic and geopolitical events.

Market Index: Indexes are a representative sample of stocks in the U.S. market. The three main market indices are the **Standard & Poor's 500 (S&P 500), Dow Jones Industrial Average**, and the **NASDAQ Composite**.

Market Myths: Perceptions about the stock market that have no real basis in fact. Myths represent a collective belief that is pervasive among the crowd. Myths are dangerous when used to explain and justify bad investment decisions.

Market Order: A buy or sell order executed at the best price currently available.

Market Price: A security's last reported bid (sell) or ask (buy) prices.

Market Risk: The risk that the value of investments may decline due to an overall decline in the market.

Market System: A market is a place where buyers and sellers of a particular product or service come together to do business. Your local farmer's market is a perfect example. *See* also **Free Market**

Market Timing: Market timing is making investment decisions based on the market conditions to take advantage of economic expansion (uptrends). The market has major implications for **market timing.** *See* **Leading Economic Indicator.**

Markup Stage: The second stage of the stock cycle when a stock is in an uptrend. The markup stage is the best time for making profits.

MASTER Plan: The *Invest with Success* wealth plan explained in Chapter 19. MASTER stands for **M**arkets, **A**llocation, **S**trategy, **T**rade Management, **E**xpectations, and **R**eassessment.

Mid-cap: Stocks with $1-5 billion in market capitalization.

Money Management: Having a strategy of preserving capital and limiting risk. *See* also **Risk Management.**

Money Market: A fund that invests in debt securities that mature in less than one year.

Money Market Fund: An open-end mutual fund which invests only in money markets.

Moving Average: The average price of a security over a specified time period. The 50-week moving average is based on the average of 50 weeks of closing prices. This line gives a visual representation of price direction, or trend.

Mutual Funds: Financial companies that pool money from a large number of investors, and then invest the money in a variety of assets. Mutual funds are professionally-managed funds. Small investors can buy shares of a mutual fund rather than investing in individual stocks.

NASDAQ: A computerized market exchange which lists a large number technology stocks. The term NASDAQ stands for "National Association of Securities Dealers Automated Quotation System."

NASDAQ Composite: An index of all common stocks listed on NASDAQ, used mainly to track technology stocks.

National Association of Securities Dealers Automated Quotation System (NASDAQ) *See* **NASDAQ.**

Net Asset Value (NAV): The share price of a mutual fund which is calculated at the end of the trading day. It represents the total value of the fund divided by the number of shares owned.

New York Stock Exchange (NYSE): The largest stock exchange in the U.S. is located on Wall Street in New York City. The NYSE is responsible for setting policy, supervising member activities, and listing securities.

No-load Funds: Commission free mutual funds.

Objective: A term used to describe information which is without bias or prejudice.

Objective Criteria: This means that the information you use to make a decision must be undistorted by emotion or personal bias. Everyone can see the same thing because it is a fact. **Subjective** is a term used to describe information that reflects what is taking place within the mind and prejudiced by individual bias.

One Week (Market Week): Five trading days. On a weekly chart, each bar represents all the price movement of five trading days (business days).

Online Broker: A brokerage company which provides trading services to its clients over the internet.

Opening Price: First price of the day.

Option Account: A brokerage account that allows options trading.

Overhead Supply: A quantitative measure of the supply that exists above the current price of a stock; it represents shares of stock which were bought at a higher price than its current price and are likely to be sold if price returns to the higher level, so investors can avoid a loss.

Overvalued: When a stock's price is higher than its fair value.

Paper Trading: Practice buying and selling of stocks without actually entering into any monetary transactions. It is like doing homework exercises.

Passive Management: A strategy that seeks to match the return of the 'market' or an index. Investors do not attempt to choose stocks to outperform the market. *See* also **Indexing.**

Percent Return: Measures the return as a percentage of the asset's price. It is the use of capital to generate profit. *See* also **Return On Investment.**

Plan: A specific method or process to achieve stated and specific goals. When you take control of your finances, your plan is a call to action, not reaction. A plan is a **P**reset **L**ist of **A**ctions **N**ecessary to be taken.

Portfolio: The total collection of an investor's assets. Stock investments are only one part of a portfolio.

Position: The number of shares you own at a given price is called your stock position.

Preferred Stock: A type of stock share which pays a fixed dividend, meaning the payments don't vary based on economic conditions of the company. Preferred stockholders have higher rights for a claim on corporate assets than common stockholders. *See* **Common Stock.**

Preservation of Capital: A conservative investment strategy that seeks to avoid risk to capital. *See* also **Risk Free.**

Price Bar: A line on a stock chart representing price movement. On a weekly chart one bar represents the price fluctuations of the entire week. On a daily chart, each line represents the price fluctuations of one day. A price bar shows the open, high, low, and closing prices.

Professional Management: Means investment decisions are made by an investment professional who is paid a fee. A mutual fund is managed by professionals who do the stock selections, decide what to buy, when to buy, and when to sell.

Profit: The difference between the purchase price and the sell price of an asset, minus commissions.

Profit Investor: A term coined by Dr. Schaap which refers to an investor who only risks money with the expectation of a profitable return. If anyone asks, simply say you are a "**profit investor**."

Prospectus: A formal legal document, filed with the Securities and Exchange Commission that provides details about an investment offering for sale to the public; also known as an "offer document".

Pullback: Periods in an uptrend where price declines back toward a moving average. Most often in a long-term uptrend, price remains above the 50-week Moving Average.

Pullback Risk: It represents the amount of risk per share from the current price to the stop-loss price. It is also the part of a gain at risk during an uptrend

Recession: A period of decline in GDP that lasts at least two consecutive quarters.

Recovery: When business activity steadily expands following an economic contraction. There is a rise in GDP. It is the early part of the expansion phase where **cyclical stocks** outperform.

Relative Strength Index (RSI): An indicator which measures the strength of buying versus selling. The value can range from 0 to 100. For the 50-50 Trading Strategy you will look for RSI rising above the 50 level.

Resistance: A price level at which the stock price goes no higher. This forms a price **peak,** or **high.**

Return The profit you make is your return or reward for having taken the risk.

Return On Investment (R.O.I.): A measure of profitability. ROI measures how effectively capital is used to generate profit; the higher the ROI, the better. *See* also **Yield**.

Revenue Growth: Growth in the gross income from one period (quarter or year) to the next.

Revenue: Proceeds the company receives from the sale of goods or services; it does not include expenses.

Risk It is the chance of something happening which is different from what you expect to happen, or the quantifiable likelihood of less-than-expected returns. Exposure to the consequences of uncertainty constitutes a risk.

Risk Free: No risk of loss. A bank account is considered risk free since you will never get back less than you put in;

Risk Management: A strategy to limit risk. A **stop-loss** is a risk management tool. See also **Money Management.**

Risk Tolerance: An investor's ability to handle potential declines in the value of the portfolio.

RSI: (*See* Relative Strength Index).

Scaling: Buying or selling stock shares in sequential amounts, or not all at once. Scaling allows the investors to gradually enter a stock position based on the stock's performance.

SCORE: Dr. Schaap's acronym for **S**hares outstanding, **C**ash flow, **O**wnership by institutions, **R**evenue growth, and **E**arnings growth. It is a method of rapid fundamental analysis and will give you five key numbers to review which tell you the majority of information.

Screen (noun): A preliminary assessment of investment opportunities based on specific criteria. The criteria are used to choose potential investment candidates.

Screening To Screen, Scanning (verb): The process where the investor chooses specific criteria for an investment and the computer sorts through the hundreds or thousands of possibilities and tells you exactly which investments meet your criteria.

Sector(s): A broad group of securities in the same business activity.

Sector Rotation: The movement of money from one or more sectors into one or more other sectors. During the business cycle, different types of assets are in and out of favor as the economic cycle progresses.

Securities and Exchange Commission (SEC): The primary federal regulatory agency for the securities industry.

Security (Securities): Type of asset. Securities are investment vehicles that represent ownership or debt (i.e., stocks, bonds).

Select Sector SPDRs (S&P Depository Receipts): **ETFs** that divide the S&P 500 into nine sector funds.

Sentiment: The collective attitude of the majority of investors toward market conditions.

Settings: Parameters used to program an indicator. Settings are part of most charting software.

Shares: Issued by companies in order to raise business capital; each stock share represents one unit of ownership.

Shares Outstanding: The overall supply of stock available to be bought and sold in the market.

Short: A position that is opened by selling a stock not owned (they are borrowed from the broker). The position profits if the stock price goes lower.

Sideways Trend: When the price of the stock is trending neither up nor down.

Signal: An objective technical event. The classic signal of the 50-50 Strategy is when 1) price crosses above the 50 MA, and 2) RSI crosses above the 50 level.

SILK Screen: (**S**tock **I**ndustry **L**eaders to **K**eep). Dr. Schaap's method to select stocks which focuses on stocks in top performing industries using a top down approach.

Simple Moving Average: A moving average calculated as a mean value over a rolling previous period of fixed length. *See* also **Exponential Moving Averages**

Small-cap (capitalization): Companies with less than $1 billion in market capitalization. Growth companies are often small-caps.

Speculation: Taking higher risks for higher potential returns.

SPY (SPDR S&P 500 ETF): An ETF which owns the 500 stocks from Standard & Poor's 500 index. It represents the overall stock market.

Stage: One of the four periods in the stock cycle (Accumulation, Mark-up, Distribution and Mark Down).

Stock: A type of security that signifies ownership in a corporation and represents a claim on part of the corporation's assets and earnings.

Stock Broker: A stock salesman; either an individual or firm (brokerage) that collects a commission to act as an intermediary between a buyer and seller.

Stock Cycle: The evolution of a stock's price, from a base to an uptrend, to a price high, and eventually to a downtrend.

Stock Exchanges: General term for the organized buying and selling of stocks through an organized market process.

Stock Market: Where investors go to buy and sell stock of a company.

Stock Symbol: The letters (ticker symbol) representing a company's stock, i.e., GM for General Motors. *See* also **Ticker.**

Stop Limit Order: The order to buy or sell at a specified price or better, but only after the specified price has been reached. A stop-limit order is essentially a combination of a stop order and a limit order. *See* also **Limit Order.**

Stop-loss (Stop-loss Order): A standing order to sell a stock at a predetermined price in order to limit risk to capital.

Stop-Loss Dollar Amount: The total amount of money (for all shares) you may lose if you get stopped out. It is determined by multiplying the number of shares times the initial risk per share.

Stop-loss Rule: Dr. Schaap's rule that governs how much money are you willing to lose (initial risk) in order to see if the stock price will go higher.

Stopped Out: Your position is exited by a sell order when the stop-loss price reached.

Strategy: An investor's plan to guide his investment decisions based on individual goals, risk tolerance, and future needs for capital. It is the part the investment plan which tells you when to buy and sell.

Subjective: A term used to describe information that reflects what is taking place within the mind and prejudiced by individual bias. **Objective Criteria** means that the information you use to make a decision must be undistorted by emotion or personal bias.

Supply: Shares of the stock available for sale. **Demand** is created by those buying stock.

Support: A price at which a stock quits falling; it occurs when demand overcomes supply. The lowest price point reached is called support, or a low.

Swing traders: Swing traders hold trades for a few days to a few weeks.

Technical Analysis: A method of evaluating securities by analyzing the past behavior of price. It may also use chart indicators. Technical analysis is visual, relying on what can be seen on the chart.

Ticker Symbol (Stock Symbol) Letters that are the ticker symbol representing a company's stock, i.e. GM for General Motors.

Ticker: A list of information about stocks and other investment vehicles traded on the stock exchanges. It often includes the number of shares being traded, the current price quote, and the percent change in price (compared to yesterday's price). *See* also **Stock Symbol.**

Time Horizon: The length of time a sum of money is expected to be invested, meaning the time until retirement.

TOP: Dr. Schaap's method of rapid technical analysis. **TOP** stands for **T**rend, **O**verhead supply, and **P**rice.

Top Down: An investing strategy which begins with a look at the overall economic picture (stock market) and then narrows it down to sectors, industries and companies that are expected to perform well. Analysis of the fundamentals of a given security is the final step.

TOP SCORE: An acronym for two parts of rapid stock analysis using the 50-50 Strategy. It checks technicals (TOP) and fundamentals (SCORE).

Trade: To buy or sell an item (a stock). Every investment begins and ends with a trade.

Trade Management: Controlling the entry and exit of any stock investment by procedures you follow to buy a stock, control risk, and take profit.

Trading Platform: A computer software program for placing buy and sell orders.

Trailing Stop: A stop-loss order that is progressively raised to protect open profits. *See* also **Stop-loss.**

Treasury Bill: A negotiable debt obligation issued by the U.S. government having a maturity of one year or less. Exempt from state and local taxes, also called a Bill or T-Bill or U.S. Treasury Bill.

Trend: The prevailing direction of price.

Trough: The stage of the business cycle that marks the end of a period of declining business activity and the transition to expansion.

12(b)-1 fee: An annual fee charged my mutual funds to pay for marketing and distribution costs.

Undervalued: When a stock's price is lower than its fair value.

Uptrend: A rising 50-week moving average. The classic definition of an uptrend is a series of higher highs and higher lows. If price rises from left to right on a chart, it is called an **uptren**d. If price falls from left to right, it is a **downtrend.**

Vehicles: Assets. It is common to hear an asset referred to as investment vehicle. *See* also **Investment Vehicle.**

Watchlist A list of stocks that meet the TOP SCORE criteria but do not yet meet the 50-50 Strategy criteria to buy.

Web Page: An HTML document on the world wide web (www), usually one of many together that make up a **Website**.

Webinar(s): The term refers to "web seminars," or internet conferencing used to conduct live meetings or presentations. In a web conference, each participant sits at his or her own computer and is connected to other participants via the internet. This can be either a downloaded application on each of the attendees' computers or a web-based application where the attendees will simply enter a URL (website address) to enter the conference.

Website: (also web-site) A collection of files that are arranged on the World Wide Web under a common address; an information resource

INDEX